ROLAND BARTHES
THE FIGURES OF WRITING

ROLAND BARTHES

THE FIGURES
OF WRITING

ANDREW BROWN

CLARENDON PRESS · OXFORD
1992

Oxford University Press, Walton Street, Oxford OX2 6DP

Oxford New York Toronto
Delhi Bombay Calcutta Madras Karachi
Petaling Jaya Singapore Hong Kong Tokyo
Nairobi Dar es Salaam Cape Town
Melbourne Auckland
and associated companies in
Berlin Ibadan

Oxford is a trade mark of Oxford University Press

Published in the United States
by Oxford University Press, New York

British Library Cataloguing in Publication Data
Data available

Library of Congress Cataloging in Publication Data
Brown, Andrew, Dr.
The figures of writing in Roland Barthes / Andrew Brown.
Includes bibliographical references and index.
1. Barthes, Roland.   2. Literature—Aesthetics.   3. Rhetoric.
4. Metaphor.   I. Title.
PN45.B75   1992
808'.0014—dc20   91–46422
ISBN 0–19–815171–3

Typeset by Cambridge Composing (UK) Ltd
Printed and bound in
Great Britain by Bookcraft Ltd
Midsomer Norton, Bath

For Jenny
and
Adam

Quel malheur que — alors que j'étais seulement préoccupé de retrouver Gilberte ou Albertine — je n'aie pas fait plus attention à ce monsieur. Je l'avais pris pour un raseur du monde, pour un simple figurant, c'était une *Figure*!

Proust, Le Temps retrouvé

ACKNOWLEDGEMENTS

THIS is the slightly revised version of a Cambridge Ph.D. thesis, and I would like to thank my supervisor Peter Collier for his unstinting help and encouragement, and my examiners Annette Lavers and Michael Moriarty for their generous and acute comments during my viva. I am also grateful to Patrick O'Donovan, Takeshi Matsumura, and Hiroyuki Akama for their perceptive remarks and advice on the original thesis.

CONTENTS

LIST OF ABBREVIATIONS

I USE the following abbreviations. Where possible, they are the same as those adopted by Philippe Roger in his book *Roland Barthes, roman*; and as he points out, his own abbreviations follow those of Barthes himself, which are to be found in *Barthes par lui-même* (Seuil, 'Écrivains de toujours', 1975), 189.

AS	*L'Aventure sémiologique* (Seuil, 1985)
BL	*Le Bruissement de la langue* (Seuil, 1984)
C	Antoine Compagnon (ed.), *Prétexte: Roland Barthes*, Acts du Colloque de Cerisy, 22–9 June 1977 (1978)
CC	*La Chambre claire: note sur la photographie* (Gallimard, 'Les Cahiers du cinéma', 1980)
CV	*Critique et Vérité* (Seuil, 'Tel Quel', 1966)
DZ	*Le Degré zéro de l'écriture* (Seuil, 'Points', 1972)
EC	*Essais critiques* (Seuil, 'Points', 1981)
EpS	*L'Empire des signes* (Flammarion, 'Champs', 1980)
FDA	*Fragments d'un discours amoureux* (Seuil, 'Tel Quel', 1977)
GV	*Le Grain de la voix: entretiens 1962–1980* (Seuil, 1981)
I	*Incidents* (Seuil, 1987)
L	*Leçon inaugurale de la chaire de sémiologie littéraire du Collège de France, prononcée le 7 janvier 1977* (Seuil, 1978)
Mi	*Michelet par lui-même* (Seuil, 'Écrivains de toujours', 1954)
My	*Mythologies* (Seuil, 'Points', 1970)
NEC	*Nouveaux essais critiques* (Seuil, 'Points', 1972)
OO	*L'Obvie et l'obtus* (Seuil, 'Tel Quel', 1982)
PlT	*Le Plaisir du texte* (Seuil, 'Points', 1982)
RB	*Barthes par lui-même* (Seuil, 'Écrivains de toujours', 1975)
SE	*Sollers écrivain* (Seuil, 'Tel Quel', 1979)
SFL	*Sade, Fourier, Loyola* (Seuil, 'Points', 1980)
SM	*Système de la mode* (Seuil, 'Points', 1983)
SR	*Sur Racine* (Seuil, 'Points', 1979)
S/Z	*S/Z* (Seuil, 'Points', 1976)

NOTE

PLACE of publication for all references is Paris unless otherwise stated.

INTRODUCTION

THE pages that follow chart some of the difficulties inherent in reading Barthes. They arise from my feeling that those difficulties have not always been recognized, and that a tendency to try to fit Barthes into the various models of literary theory currently available leads to disappointment. It is true that Barthes himself contributed to so many of these models: Marxism, semiology, ideology critique, reader-response theory, structuralist narratology, psychoanalysis, deconstruction, and, to some extent, feminism. Yet his work seems to offer more than a mere contribution to these disciplines. The question lies in detecting the nature of this 'more'. It is a question to which Barthes himself was extremely sensitive: hence the somewhat intro-verted and anxiously self-questioning nature of his writing. And his answers to this question were always given with an air of provisionality, as if it would not be long before he had found a better way of describing what it was he wanted to do. This theoretical insecurity coexisted with a tendency to keep moving. The first tendency is reflected in his moments of doubt about the value of his endeavour, his frequent sense of having reached an impasse, a theoretical aporia, or a moment of stagnation and repetition. The second tendency takes the form of a capacity for self-renewal, for discovering a new theoretical matrix which would enable him to tackle again, in a slightly different way, the questions that obsessed him throughout his career: how do human beings make meaning? How is this reflected in their social practices? And above all, perhaps: what is the function and status of literature among these practices?

Here is an example of one way Barthes frustrates one kind of reader. It is disconcerting to see him produce a work—*Système de la mode*—that is in some ways the crown of his semiological endeavours, bristling with terminological stringencies, fully armed, rigorously argued, and exhaustively documented, only for him to accompany it with an almost shamefaced apologia of a preface, admitting that semiology has been moving so fast that his labours can be presented to the public only as a *history* of semiology, a language that itself has, he ruefully but lucidly insists, only a limited shelf-life. This typically Barthesian manœuvre is both fascinating and irritating. It is fascinating because it shows us that Barthes is already, as it were, wriggling out of the cocoon of the work he is publishing, refusing to be imprisoned by it, and prepared to stretch his wings elsewhere. And it is irritating because it leaves us at a loss as to what to do with *Système de la mode*.

What we have here is a boundary dispute. *Système de la mode* can be discussed, as it were, in at least two ways: either as belonging to a territory called 'semiology' or as a province of the country called 'Barthes'. In the first case, it can be discussed quite objectively, its influential insights noted, and its weak points corrected. This is one of the ways Barthes's work has swarmed most effectively. Discussions in all the areas of literary theory I mentioned above will find room to incorporate Barthes's insights. His way of clarifying abstruse theoretical concerns by the use of vivid and delicate metaphors make him one of the most quoted of theorists, and it sometimes seems as if his chief role in life was to provide theorists with such quotable insights—as if he were, so to speak, the epigraph-writer-in-chief to contemporary theory. There is nothing wrong with such an approach. Barthes himself was lucid about the fact that, as a theorist, he should expect his works to be judged by the correctness, as well as the creativity, of his ideas. If narratology has gone beyond the rather rudimentary discussions in his essay 'Introduction à l'analyse structurale des récits', that essay is still useful, its insights still necessary. And the complex and highly formalized meditations on the act of reading now found in reader-response theory can incorporate the innovative remarks of *Le Plaisir du texte* even when Barthes's own positions clearly need to be developed and qualified. In other words, Barthes is part of theory and needs discussion as such: in what ways did he get it right, and in what ways is he vulnerable?

Many of the general books about Barthes concentrate on this aspect of his work. One that is distinguished by its rigour of argument, its grasp of Barthes as part of a highly complex set of intellectual movements in post-war France, and above all the clarity and detail of its exposition of Barthes's contributions to semiology, linguistics, and their related disciplines, is Annette Lavers's *Roland Barthes: Structuralism and After*. A more recent work, which looks in rather more detail at Barthes's last decade of production (the 1970s), and raises a number of pertinent questions about Barthes's thoughts on politics, ideology, and culture, is the witty and incisive study *Roland Barthes*, by Michael Moriarty. These two books are probably the best attempts in English to grasp the complexities of Barthes's ideas, rethink and qualify them, and set them out in ways that make sense to the contemporary reader interested in deciding where Barthes stands within a certain tradition of literary theory and semiology.

The Barthes I have chosen to concentrate on is somewhat different. My work examines, as it were, the country 'Barthes' of which semiology, psychoanalysis, political critique, narratology, and allied disciplines are provinces. I am interested, that is, in Barthes as a writer, and I have therefore tried to locate ways in which he seems to be a theorist with a difference. Since theorists frequently tend to see themselves as writers, Barthes's difference may not be so very different after all. In that case, I will at least have shown the ways that theory has drawn close to writing—by turning in on itself, seeing itself as language, a medium as well as a message. But my own feeling is that Barthes's difference is more challenging than that. My evidence for this feeling is partly the decline of interest in Barthes's work that has followed his death. This is not just a posthumous slump: it does not seem to have affected Lacan or Foucault, for instance, to anything like the same degree. In Barthes's case, a general unease about the status and usefulness of his works seems to have played a major role. Part of the problem is that in his last decade, Barthes began to insist on the singularity of his work. Sometimes this comes over as a certain claim, as if Barthes were saying 'I'm not just a theorist—I'm a writer, too!' And sometimes, inseparably, it comes over as an act of self-criticism: 'I'm not a theorist, so don't take me too seriously. But I may not be a writer either. Who am I?' It is the mixture of the claim and its comic, or tragic, qualification that makes it difficult to see what to do with Barthes.

In my treatment, I have not ignored the problems Barthes's work poses: I have constantly registered drawbacks and objections when I thought these needed to be mentioned. In other words, I have taken into account the fact that he says things that are at least partly true: I have made allowance for the signified of his discourse. But my main focus has been on the signifier: not so much what he says, but how he says it, and how the way he says it constantly forces us to qualify our perceptions of what he says. In this preoccupation with the stylistic manœuvres that dominate Barthes's work, my study attempts to build on the insights of Stephen Heath (*Vertige du déplacement: lecture de Barthes*), Steven Ungar (*Roland Barthes: The Professor of Desire*), and Philippe Roger (*Roland Barthes, roman*).

Hence my title: *Figures of Writing*. Figures of speech are the realm of rhetoric, and have been analysed and codified for two and a half millenia. But, for reasons that should become apparent in the course of my discussion, I feel that Barthes is not really concerned to produce figures of speech, despite his own very fertile interest in rhetoric, and the way he sometimes analyses figures of speech in other writers

(Chateaubriand, Balzac, Flaubert) and in himself. Rather, just as a figure of speech is something which adds a certain surplus to the signified, Barthes shows a constant attention to the figures of writing as the ways in which writing itself seems to be in surplus of what it is saying. The figures of writing I have detected at work in Barthes are all factors of complication: they make it difficult to extract 'what Barthes said' (Barthes as theorist) from 'the way he *wrote* it'. A figure of writing is a tactic which runs through Barthes's work, structuring it in various ways that are not always perceptible if one attempts to get straight to the signified. This is why I have, as a first move, sometimes kept the signified at a considerable distance. For instance, my discussion of *Mythologies* brackets the political force of that work to concentrate on a particular set of ambiguities on the level of the signifier—turns of phrase, repeated metaphors, and ambiguities in Barthes's way of phrasing the ideological semes he has detected at work in social language. But the signified should always return, albeit in another place, and I have also tried to show that fixing attention on a figure of writing may help to give a more nuanced view of what, in *Mythologies*, Barthes is saying.

Since the figures of writing I deal with structure Barthes's discourse from beginning to end of his career, I have adopted an approach which is definitely different from most general studies of Barthes: I have not traced his evolution from the early political, sociological, and semiological works, via structuralist narratology, to the psychoanalytically inspired 'turn to the subject' of his last works. This is partly because other works, especially those I have already mentioned, do this extremely well, and I have nothing to add to their analyses. At the same time, I feel that the figures of writing I concentrate on operate with a certain independence of chronology. For instance, early Barthes shows an interest (in *Le Degré zéro de l'écriture*) in something traumatic, an enigmatic 'other' which prevents a writer's language from being entirely public and consciously committed—an 'other' which Barthes locates in the writer's unconscious or bodily determinants, and calls 'style'. And late Barthes is still, in *La Chambre claire*, concerned to isolate something in his own analysis of photographs which resists the terms of his own public and scientific language, something which is equally traumatic. From early to late Barthes, the trauma is thus a figure of writing, cropping up in unexpected places and determining the way Barthes gives shape to his obsessions.

Despite taking examples from all periods of Barthes's career, however, I have tended to concentrate on the works he wrote in the last decade of his life, 1970–80. (This will be what I mean when I refer to 'late' Barthes.) This is for two reasons. First, this decade has not always received its fair share of attention in Barthes criticism. One senses that some commentators, having followed Barthes's structuralist phase with sympathy and excitement, are then perplexed that he seems as it were to abandon the fine methodological distinctions he had devoted so much energy to establishing. It is as if Barthes dedicated one decade, the 1960s, to putting a lot of hard work and political passion into a scientific and combative science of semiology, then spent another decade, the 1970s, throwing it all away, to concentrate instead on telling us how difficult it is to find a decent pen, how he suffers from mild headaches, and how different his body feels when he's on holiday in the countryside rather than having to cope with the stresses and strains of life in Paris. My own view is that for all the discontinuities in Barthes's work, there is one constant: the attempt to make sense of the world in language, and then to ask how much that sense leaves out. A figure of writing will often be particularly active in negotiating the two sides of that question: it helps Barthes articulate meaning, and then points to how that meaning must be provisional, since it cannot be total.

Secondly, it is in the last decade that Barthes's writing starts to turn around and look at itself and its presuppositions. I have taken at least three of my figures (drift, frames, and names) from Barthes's own identification of these operators of discourse in his own work. And it is in the 1970s that this turn leads Barthes closer and closer to assume himself as a new kind of writer: it is in this decade that his finest writing is produced, just as it is in this decade that it becomes more and more difficult to say what kind of writer is producing it.

The figures of writing are 'figures' of 'writing'. They are 'figures' in that they show a close attention to the fine detail of the signifier, to the surface of writing. Like figures of speech, they are often modes of indirection—of saying something in ways that cannot easily be paraphrased. And they are figures of 'writing' in that Barthes's interest in writing remains constant from first to last. First, écriture is the writer's consciously chosen and explicitly signalled commitment to a set of social and political values (Le Degré zéro de l'écriture). Then, writing becomes a set of practices subject to the constraints of an alienated society, as an attempt, in the works of the avant-garde, to find a way of weakening the grip of those constraints, and as a potentially revolutionary practice (Essais critiques, 'La Mort de l'auteur', and S/Z, for instance). Finally, there is the writing of a new type of fiction that

Barthes postulated as his own (unfulfilled) task in *La Chambre claire*. And the figures I deal with seem to me to be essential to Barthes's endeavour to keep a place open for writing—a writing that will never be *quite* the same as theory because it will never be entirely translatable into the speech that Barthes comes increasingly to identify as the mode of theory. Theory, that is, has to 'say' something, to make things explicit: Barthes's figures of writing are meant to add a tuck to theoretical discourse, to say things and write within that saying, to point to an *implicit* level of infolding and complication.

My first two chapters look at the variety of effects Barthes associates with 'drift'. In Chapter 1, 'The Drifter: Losing Ground', I show how one effect of drift is to alert us to the ways in which Barthes's writing functions as a signifying excess to the things he seems to be saying (his 'ground'). This means that Barthes's discourse is many-levelled even when it seems to be transmitting clear signifieds, and that it has an aesthetic complication to it even when it is at its most political. I suggest that Barthes's habit of thinking in terms of one particular metaphor—in which the signifier 'floats over' and 'drifts above' the signified—seems to determine many of his analyses of texts and practices. This chapter introduces a major theme that will run through the others: Barthes's questioning of violence. His own model of meaning as based on binary oppositions comes to seem 'violent' to him: the either/or model of semiology forces the subject into one position or the other if that subject is to fit into a society, to be able to receive and emit intelligible messages, and this stark choice is one that Barthes is increasingly concerned to question. One of the ways he does this is by taking a binary opposition, as a necessary first step in the process of showing how people make sense, and then 'drifting' away from it, in an attempt to demonstrate how the opposition has hierarchized and excluded: it has hierarchized its own terms (so that in the binary pair '*a* versus *b*', precedence is given to *a* over *b*), and it has excluded everything that does not fit (there is no room for anything that is not either *a* or *b*). Drift is thus a critique of the binary model that had proved so powerful for Barthes as a structuralist. (And since Derrida shares this critique of 'binarism', there is a sense in which Barthes here is sharing some of the post-structuralist concerns and techniques of Derrida.) This poses political problems for Barthes: politics is much clearer and more persuasive an activity when it can offer us neat evaluative schemata (proletariat versus bourgeoisie, communism versus capitalism, feminist versus masculinist). Barthes's suspicion of this Manichaeism is one of his *traits d'époque* (but one in which he anticipates a mood that has been more widespread since his death). In drift, he attempts to stay political while creating a slightly different and less binary model of how political evaluation might be carried out. His own suggestions are always very tentative and some are more convincing than others: but one of his points is that the apparently dynamic and militant language of revolutionary change had tended to get stuck in a rut, had not 'changed the world', and that in the circumstances a different set of discursive operations, more flexible and perhaps less confident and self-assured, might loosen the terrain. He shares this interest in political versions of drift with Lyotard, on whom I have drawn for a number of parallels. As to whether either of them succeed in creating new models for political discourse, I think it is a little early to say, although my own feeling is that Barthes's 'drift' is expressed in terms that are too general and abstract to be more than suggestive metaphors for the political field. It is more persuasive as a way of registering a feeling that we do not live in a time of radical innovation, either conceptual, political, or discursive: to drift may be a late option, a *fin de siècle* way of trying to 'keep writing' (in both senses of the phrase) in the face of a scepticism about the possibility (or the value) of writing anything really new. And I end the chapter by showing how Barthes's equivocations about drift make it difficult to read what he has to say about it, since when he writes about drift his own writing starts to drift, to become implicit and complicated rather than clear and distinct.

My second chapter, 'The Drifter: Narratives of Emergence' turns to Barthes's own practice of stating a position and then drifting from it. When he comes to analyse his own writing practices, he decides that one of his idiosyncrasies is a concentration on individual words: he uses old words in unpredictable ways, or he invents new words; sometimes this process is scientific (he is inventing concepts we can all use), sometimes it is anti-scientific (he takes words from the sciences and then uses them in odd, private ways). In both cases he is 'drifting', and in the second kind of move he is using drift as a figure of writing to get him from science and its signifieds to a more aesthetic concentration on signifiers. Sometimes this drift is embodied in nothing more than Barthes's habit of writing ordinary words with a capital letter. The effects of this are both far-reaching and difficult to describe. Likewise, the critic's typical need to quote evidence is subjected to a quizzical gaze in his own writing, which quotes but in very uncritical (or self-reflexive) ways, trying to alert us to the problems and paradoxes of quoting. Finally, all these narratives of emergence

(Barthes's idiolect emerging from a common vocabulary, aesthetic effects from science, his own inflections from a quotable tradition of authorities) are seen from the perspective of psychoanalysis, which has its own story to tell—of how desire emerges from need.

Chapter 3 looks at 'Frames and Names', two closely related figures of writing in that both begin as ways of isolating material and identifying it, whether that material is an object represented in a painting, on the cinema screen, or on the theatre stage, or whether it is an ideological seme in a novel. And both frames and names, in Barthes's treatment, then draw attention to themselves: what have they excluded? Can the effect of framing itself be seen from outside a frame? Can the effect of naming be named? This self-reflexive moment remains abstract and general until the ways it operates in Barthes's texts are shown: here again, the fine detail of some of Barthes's works betrays both a love of framing and naming, and an anxiety about the limits of those operations, as well as a desire on Barthes's part to find ways of writing that will be less dependent on them. For here again, he comes to suspect the violence implicit in certain types of framing and naming, and he is concerned to mute that violence, above all, to develop a model of highly mobile, split, and anonymous subjectivity in which they would lose some of their capacity to control and define.

In Chapter 4, 'The Scribbler', I look at another figure of writing. By scribble, I mean Barthes's fascination for writing itself—writing, as it were, rather than what the writing says. This fascination is staged in a variety of ways. To begin with, I show how Barthes is reacting against the image of interpretation as a cutting away of surfaces to reach depths, or as a digging down to a bedrock of truth. He finds these images violent, and locates them at work in unlikely places. Much of his interest in the visual arts stems from an anti-interpretative stance: confronted with avant-garde canvases especially, he responds not by asking what they are trying to do, but by prolonging their obsessions into his own writing. Here, as elsewhere, I draw loosely on the distinction between 'saying' and 'showing': Barthes becomes increasingly interested not in saying (metalinguistically or theoretically) what (or how) these painters have painted, but in showing it—by mimicking it in his own discourse. In other words, Barthes is revising our image of the critic as someone who interprets an artefact in terms of an external metalanguage: Barthes wants to do, in language, something similar to what the painters have done with paints and canvases. This leads him to ask a number of questions about the boundary between writing and painting, a boundary he finds to be very unstable, both in literary works (*Sarrasine*, by Balzac, a *story* about an *artist*) and in works by various visual artists (Réquichot, Erté, and Twombly in particular) who often draw on the resources of writing to produce, as it were, a new medium, one that is midway between writing-as-signifed (as 'saying things') and writing-as-signifier (as 'not saying anything', as not easily paraphrasable). Here I make use of Lyotard's work on the *figure*. My own use of the word, throughout the book, is looser than his, but in this chapter I show how his *figure* (which is something to be seen and not just understood) acts as a mode of resistance to semiology (for which everything can be 'read', made to articulate meaning). Barthes too is interested in locating this resistance to semiology in painting and other art-forms, such as the images he encounters in Japan, including even the Japanese language as written (as calligraphic and not just communicational); and he is interested in the ways that the *figure* forces us to soften some of the aggression that seems to go with projects of interpretation (as tying down an identity, going straight for the signified 'behind' the haze of signifiers). For Barthes, the canvases of Cy Twombly, with their lazy scribbles and illegible scrawls, are a challenge: in these works, Barthes notes an absence of aggression, an artistic happiness, and an almost maternal tenderness, that he attempts to mimic in his own writing. It is in scribbling, as it were, that Barthes changes over from being a 'critic' (one who interprets, excavates guilty ideological secrets, criticizes) to being an 'artist' (one who produces, adds, and affirms).

I then devote an excursus (Chapter 5) to setting out in some detail the ways in which Barthes negotiates one particular binary opposition, that of speech versus writing. Throughout his work there runs a desire to analyse the discomfitures of speech: it is the place in which personal and social alienations come malevolently alive for him, and his hostility to speech leads him to make a number of choices. For instance, where psychoanalysis has itself dwelt on the *parole vide* of the analysand, on spoken utterances as being forms of miscognition in which the analysand conceals as well as revealing the truth of desire, Barthes takes the critique even further, refusing to believe, with psychoanalysis, that the servitudes of speech can be worked through in the interests of a more subjectively anchored and less neurotically image-fixated *parole pleine*. For Barthes, there is no such thing—or if there is, it is not to be found in speech as such, but in the practice he consistently prefers to call writing. He sees in speech alienation, power, and the signified, and almost no way of overcoming those *archons* of this world: only in writing can their mortifying effects be partly mitigated. One far-reaching ideological result of this is that Barthes does not fit easily into some of the current models of 'enlightenment' practice: he does not believe in dialogue, in an authentic speech act, or in free and open discussion as models of what human praxis should be based on. Or rather, he does ('of course') accept the necessity for all this, but with a considerable lack of enthusiasm and with a baleful eye for the difficulties of achieving it. His real passion is writing, a practice he identifies with a certain discursive silence. This writing is something of a zigzag crack running through the enlightened model of authentic speech as the mode *par excellence* of emancipation. I have called this chapter an excursus because it does not, in itself, deal with a figure of writing: rather it summarizes and makes explicit some of the ways Barthes constantly goes for writing rather than speech, revising—but by no means dissolving—the opposition between them, always in the interests of writing.

That writing can be something of a blind spot is therefore the focus of my final chapter, 'The Trauma'. Beginning with the ways that a sexual trauma or threatening incident in the life of the subject became a linchpin for psychoanalysis, I go on to suggest that such incidents assume increasing importance for Barthes: they are key elements in organizing meaning, and yet they themselves seem devoid of any determinate meaning; and as events, they seem to invite and yet resist incorporation into large-scale narratives, subjective and historical. I examine traumatic phenomena that interested Barthes: the Japanese haiku as a 'writing event' as well as a way to 'write events' while withholding or keeping in suspense any meaning they may have; the problem of denotation in photography; and the question of the referent in fictional writing. The trauma is a figure of writing in that it refuses abreaction (it cannot be therapeutically analysed away or theoretically managed, since it is so singularly subjective), and it becomes a focus of Barthes's last work, *La Chambre claire*, his attempt to write, however indirectly, one particular traumatic event, the death of his own mother.

It has been suggested that one of the reasons for the comparative neglect of Barthes in current theoretical writing is his own failure to address the problem of gender. This reproach is both unjust and just. Unjust in that Barthes was extremely sensitive to gender, both in his early awareness of the particular servility of images of women gener-ated by the media in the France of the 1950s, as registered in *Mythologies*, and in his later capacity to make us realize how powerful a part gender and sexuality play in structuring the ways we read the world and its texts. But there is some justice in the observation, too. Barthes rarely concentrates on women artists or writers, however eclectic and inventive his own canon may in other ways be. And one of the problems in seeing the world as a text is that sexuality itself becomes textualized, so that specific mechanisms of exploitation or domination, in the field of gender, are not analysed. I have occasionally drawn attention to Barthesian metaphors or discursive operations which seem to elide or evade the question of gender. But this is very difficult terrain to negotiate. I will give one example: Barthes's fondness for the metaphor of 'dissemination'. Is this a particularly masculine figure of writing? On one reading, yes: writing as the scattering of seed, its productivity residing in these seeds encountering, not a feminine gamete to produce an insight that can be nurtured and gestated, but another seed. On another reading, less so: a *dis*semination is a scattering, the *Fort!* (or 'gone away!') of narcissistic identity. Indeed, it seems to be this latter emphasis on which Barthes concentrates: writing as depropriation. And in any case, it is hardly enough just to label 'masculinist' or 'feminist' metaphors at work in Barthes. The idea of the *logos spermatikos* has an ancient history: it overlaps with the question of a specifically homosexual eros in Plato (a major, if questioned, theme in Barthes). One result of this is that any such metaphor becomes many-faceted. Dissemination overlooks the need for a recipient, as well as for another kind of seed: but to emphasize this latter need may, for instance, place too much burden on the image of the woman as a mother figure, as well as overlooking the specifically homoerotic component, if such it is, of Barthes's own figures of writing. The ways in which Barthes's writing has been received by women, gay, and lesbian writers would require a book-length study of its own. My own feeling is that Barthes raises more questions about writing and gender than he answers; that the problem here is one of the *relative* indifference his later work shows to real historical factors (compounded by a tendency to discuss 'the text' as if it transcended gender—though maybe there are senses in which it does); and that one salutary effect of his own writing is to create a radical sense of insecurity about the value of certain gender stereotypes, as when Barthes seems challengingly able to use the vocabulary of psychoanalysis without implying, for example, that all fetishistic readers are men and all hysterics women.

This leads to one last question: Barthes has inspired many people because of the *political* and *ethical* dimension of his work. My own book spends a lot of time wondering why, for instance, he writes certain words with a capital letter. It seems difficult to see the link between them, and rather than trying to forge a link, asking whether writing Democracy with a capital D is more or less politically progressive than leaving it with a small d, I have oscillated—between the signifier and the signified. For it seems to me that these wild and unpredictable swerves, from somewhat grandiose questions about 'the writer's responsibility', to a fascination with all that is apparently, from such perspectives, trivial, futile, precious, and evanescent about the act of writing, are what give Barthes's work its power to generate, simultaneously, enlightenment and malaise.

THE DRIFTER
LOSING GROUND

The essence of philosophy provides no ground (*bodenlos*) precisely for peculiarities, and in order to attain philosophy, it is necessary, if its body expresses the sum of its peculiarities, that it cast itself into the abyss *à corps perdu (sich à corps perdu hineinzustürzen)*.

Hegel, *The Difference between the Fichtean and Schellingean Systems of Philosophy*

C'est une pensée qui a glissé, et elle va continuer à glisser ainsi, de métaphore en métaphore. Si bien que, en une seule page, on aura, non pas pris pied, mais perdu pied.

Alain Robbe-Grillet, at the Colloque de Cerisy

Fluidité du 'glissement'.
Français: N'hésite pas à partir.

Michel-Antoine Burnier and Patrick Rambaud,
Le Roland-Barthes sans peine

THE FLOATING SIGNIFIER

Drift is a major theme in Barthes. But it is a paradoxical and self-referential theme, which questions the very possibility of extracting themes from Barthes's work or of defining key notions in it. In following this word 'drift' across some of Barthes's texts, my aim in these first two chapters will be to suggest the variety of ways drift intervenes in his writing, opening up a broad spectrum of meanings, and touching on a number of issues literary theory has been examining in recent years: politics, history, semantics, modernity, the status of science, and the value of the aesthetic. At the same time, I will show how drift refuses to be tied down and stabilized, baffling any desire to arrest the meanings it produces. A theme, etymologically, is something laid down: drift, however, floats.[1]

---

[1] 'Theme', from Greek *tithenai*, 'to lay down'.

La dérive is a concept that occurs especially in Barthes's later texts from 1970 onwards. But is it a concept? It is nowhere defined by Barthes: he uses it as a floating signifier. Indeed, since he follows Lacan in taking the Saussurean formula for the sign (signified over signifier) and rewriting it as Signifier (large S) over signified (small s, sometimes italicized to emphasize further its problematic status), he can go on to picture the signifier as that which floats over and above its signified: the sign, for both Lacan and Barthes, is top-heavy, in that the signifier is separated from its signified by what Lacan calls 'the bar of meaning'. Furthermore, the signified is constructed from the differential play of signifiers between themselves rather than being determined on a one-to-one basis by its signifier. The sign, in the eyes of Lacan and Barthes, is far more unstable than in Saussure, who prefers to picture the signifier and the signified as an indissoluble unit, the first cut, as it were, into the obverse side of a sheet of paper, the second simultaneously being cut into its reverse side. But the ideogram

$$\frac{S}{s}$$

for

$$\frac{Signifier}{signified}$$

allows Barthes, following Lacan's lead but developing his metaphor in somewhat fluid ways, to construe signifiers as being able to *free* themselves from their signifieds: to float away from one meaning, to remain in a state of suspense—and then, perhaps inevitably, to be attracted down again to form an equally unstable liaison with a new signified. When Barthes looks forward (on the back jacket of *S/Z*) to 'une théorie libératoire du Signifiant', he is not claiming that such a theory would celebrate the liberation of the Signifier: he is rather more guardedly suggesting that a certain theory of the Signifier might be liberating. But the Lacanian ideogram does enable Barthes to take up a basic stance on behalf of the signifier, which in his later work is more and more privileged. For while Barthes's career begins with the attempt to decipher (read meanings from) the phenomena of his culture, he later shifts his attention to the more marginal practices in which such meaning is either not vouchsafed, or else is held in suspense. The overall trend in Barthes's work is thus a distancing of the signified. This affects his aesthetics: his ideal can be expressed as the desire for a signifier that should drift over and above the signifieds that it, in differential interaction with other signifiers, and always lightly and tentatively, generates. And conversely, he tends to imagine that anything which *floats* is in the position of the signifier and is therefore to be privileged.

Here is an example, taken from one of Barthes's most important essays on the political position of intellectuals and writers: 'Écrivains, intellectuels, professeurs', published in 1971.[2] Barthes emphasizes the *difficulty* of any such position: all three types of practice mentioned in his title are subject to constraints, neuroses, and frustrations, especially since their radical aspirations for change and experiment are easily absorbed and disarmed by an oppressively liberal society. However, after his extremely negative appraisal of the current situation, Barthes's conclusion is that the teaching relation, in which questions of power and authority are particularly thorny, can to some extent be liberated by allowing it to float—away from what is said (the signified) to the practice and form of its saying. This floating is not a revolutionary dismantling of the teaching relation as such (something demanded by many French students in May 1968): rather, it takes the institutional space of knowledge and its transmission and gently unhooks it from its moorings.

En somme, dans les limites mêmes de l'espace enseignant, tel qu'il est donné, il s'agirait de travailler à tracer patiemment une forme pure, celle du *flottement* (qui est la forme même du signifiant); ce flottement ne détruirait rien; il se contenterait de désorienter la Loi: les nécessités de la promotion, les obligations du métier (que rien n'interdit dès lors d'honorer avec scrupule), les impératifs du savoir, le prestige de la méthode, la critique idéologique, tout est là, *mais qui flotte*.[3]

Floating, then, is 'la forme même du signifiant'. In a similar way, in his 1974 essay 'Au séminaire', Barthes imagines the ideal seminar as a 'lieu suspendu . . . porté par le monde qui l'entoure, mais y résistant aussi'.[4] This bring us back to drift.

THE DERIVATION OF *LA DÉRIVE*

So far, I have translated *dérive* as 'drift', and 'drift' (or verbal forms such as 'drifting') is the translation which standard English versions,

---

[2] *BL*, 345–68. [3] Ibid. 368. [4] Ibid. 369–79 (379).

such as those by Richard Howard (for instance in his version of *The Pleasure of the Text*) and Stephen Heath (in *Image—Music—Text*) adopt. But is this translation adequate? There is an immediate phonetic similarity between the words *dérive* and 'drift': is it significant? And what is the derivation of *dérive*?

In asking this question, I am already mimicking a Barthesian tactic: that of appealing to etymology. But in Barthes's case, the etymology of a word does not give us access to its deeper or more authentic meaning. (He does not share the view, sometimes suggested by Heidegger, that the earlier meanings of, for instance, philosophical concepts are closer to the truth.) He himself frequently uses etymology, but only, he says, as a way of playing the word's past off against its present, rather than claiming that the etymon gives us any firm ground. (The etymology of the word 'etymology' suggests that at some stage, tracing the history of a word back as far as possible *was* seen as a way of restoring lost and more authentic nuances of meaning: an 'etymon' in Greek was, according to Longmans, the 'literal meaning of a word according to its origin', from *etmos*, true.) The fragment 'Étymologies' in *Barthes par lui-même* notes that 'dans l'étymologie, ce n'est pas la vérité ou l'origine du mot qui lui plaît, c'est plutôt l'*effet de surimpression* qu'elle autorise: le mot est vu comme un palimpseste'— and this way of having ideas in language itself, he adds, can be identified with the very practice called writing.[5]

Despite Barthes's scepticism, however, looking at the etymology of *dérive* can be instructive. For apart from emphasizing the aquatic nature of *dérive*, the dictionary suggests that the word is caught up in a certain significant complex of etymological influences ('influence' itself being, of course, another metaphor of flowing), and that the diachronic development of this French word is intersected by a strong cross-current from the English language. The French dictionary *Robert* notes the etymology of *dériver* as a transitive verb: 'lat. *derivare* "détourner un cours d'eau, dériver", de *de-* et *rivus* "petit cours d'eau".' As an intransitive verb, which is how Barthes uses it most often, it is a cross-formation between French *dériver*, meaning 'écarter (du bois flottant) des rives d'un cours d'eau' and the English 'to drive'. This in turn shares its Old High German root, *trīban*, with modern German *Trieb*, whose vicissitudes (as Freud's problematic psychic 'instinct' or 'drive') I shall be returning to. English 'drift', however, whether verbal or substantival, does not seem to have any pertinent etymological connection with *dérive*. None the less, the link between *dérive* and *trĭban* suggests that an interesting, if paradoxical, translation of Barthes's *dérive* might be, not 'drift', but 'drive'. The derivation of the word *dérive* seems to express a fundamental semantic wobble between connotations of activity and passivity, tension and relaxation, that is an important factor in Barthes's *dérive*, veering as it does from 'drift' to 'drive'. Indeed, *dérive* may be taken as emblematic of the later Barthes's attitude to politics in general, and his fraught navigation between two standard images: the Scylla of political activity on the one hand (the writer's 'drive' to act as a committed member of the *polis*, to voice positions, adopt stances, participate in struggle) and the Charybdis of political distance on the other (the writer as 'drifter', dandy, as critical but detached, witness rather than activist). *Dérive* is in general closer to the latter, even if it attempts to question the opposition between activity and passivity. Since 'drift' covers a significant number of the meanings associated with *dérive*, I will be keeping the translation 'drift'. But this is already an ideological decision on my part as translator, and behind 'drift' there should be heard the voice of a repressed 'drive', an avid, combative, committed stance, mediated and deviated (another sense of *dériver*) by the complex multiplicity of factors at work in Barthes's relationships to his own historical situation. This repressed constantly strives to return.

Having shown the problem of origin at work in drift, we can ask another question. In the extract from 'Écrivains, professeurs, intellectuels' just cited, Barthes notes that to make the teaching relation 'float', one has to *work*: 'il s'agirait de travailler à tracer patiemment une forme pure, celle du *flottement*'. What kind of work does drift itself do in Barthes's texts? How does it change things? For if we return to one of Barthes's earliest and most influential writings, *Mythologies*, in which the analysis of petty-bourgeois ideology is inseparable from the critical and transformative powers of the science of semiology, drift would not at first sight seem to play a very important role at all.

THE SEMIOLOGIST ENTERS THE RING

Mythologies examines the ways the petty bourgeoisie in twentieth-century France naturalizes and universalizes its own values via specific material mechanisms, some of them similar to what Althusser was to call the 'ideological state apparatuses': Barthes examines the way apparently unpolitical activities—all-in wrestling, the Tour de France, strip-tease, drinking wine or milk, spreading Astra margarine on your bread, washing your Clothes in Omo or Persil—are all bearers of certain ideological attitudes.[6] The tone of these essays is generally satirical: behind the care with which Barthes dismantles the sign-systems of his society lurks the *saeva indignatio* of the *marxisant* semiologist. Where French culture pretends to be entirely natural, Barthes shows its deeply historical and political character. There is thus a sense in which history is indeed the signified of the *Mythologies*, as has been claimed.[7] Nature ('the way things are'—according to one particular social class, the bourgeoisie, which secretly hopes that things had better stay that way if its own power is to be maintained) plays the part of a false totality: in the *Mythologies*, Barthes sees history as the opposite of nature—as the realm of freedom, as, potentially, a true universality.

But whatever the status of history in *Mythologies*, Barthes does not see it as providing a firm ground on which to stand. For one thing, his own historically minded semiology is never entirely exterior to the myths it describes. Barthes's postface to *Mythologies*, 'Le Mythe, aujourd'hui', was written after the individual essays had appeared (mainly in the left-wing paper *Lettres nouvelles*): it provides his disparate *mythologies* with a rather more unified scientific basis, elaborated a posteriori. But in the closing pages of that influential postface, as indeed in the preface, he is aware of the problems of claiming to be the detached intellectual, mocking the myths of everyday life from a safe distance. Speaking in the name of history, he says, partly excludes the semiologist from that very history: 'en un sens, le mythologue est exclu de l'histoire au nom même de qui il prétend agir'.[8] One might hesitate to endorse Barthes here: intellectuals (as he also says) are still part of history even if their discourse is separated from the historical forces (for Barthes, the proletariat) in whose name they claim to speak. But for Barthes, this separation is the cause of considerable anguish. On the one hand, he cites the French revolutionary Saint-Just ('Ce qui constitue la République,

---

[6] On ideological state apparatuses, see Louis Althusser, *Lenin and Philosophy and Other Essays*, trans. Ben Brewster (London, 1971), 158. On the materiality of ideology, see id., *Positions* (1976), 'L'idéologie a une existence matérielle' (105): even the handshake is one such ideological apparatus (110).

[7] Bennington and Young's introd. to Derek Attridge, Geoff Bennington, and Robert Young (eds.), *Post-Structuralism and the Question of History* (Cambridge, 1987) talks of Barthes's 'constant invocation of history as the repressed of naturalizing mythical discourse' (3).

[8] *My*, 245.

c'est la destruction totale de ce qui lui est opposé'), and suggests that our times are so dark that the *mythologue* is condemned to be the pure negation of the present: 'il y a pour tel homme une nuit subjective de l'histoire, où l'avenir se fait essence, destruction essentielle du passé'.[9] This night of history adds a sombre edge to Barthes's reflections, whatever the confident sweep with which he has just elaborated his semiological critique of ideology. And on the other hand, he extends his feelings about the alienation of the intellectual, showing considerable sensitivity about the fact that as an analyst of myth, he has had to separate himself out from those who consume myth. To liberate myth, he claims, in a society so stiflingly homogeneous as his own, means to separate oneself from the entire community—'et ce n'est pas rien'.[10] This leads him to a somewhat troubled afterthought about one of his *mythologies*, namely 'La Littérature selon Minou Drouet'. Minou Drouet, the girl-prodigy whose productions are dismissed by Barthes as 'une poésie sage, sucrée, toute fondée sur la croyance que la poésie, c'est une affaire de métaphore', is seen by him as having been co-opted into a petty-bourgeois notion of poetry as a 'préciosité popote'.[11] But in 'Le Mythe, aujourd'hui', he softens his critique somewhat, noting that by seeing her as the mere agent of a pernicious myth, he has had to bracket out the possibility that there may be more to Drouet than that: 'j'ai dû ignorer en elle, sous le mythe énorme dont on l'embarrasse, comme une possibilité tendre, ouverte'.[12] The belated gentleness of his language here is not merely a question of giving a child the benefit of the doubt, or distinguishing between Minou Drouet herself and those who have been exploiting her: it is characteristic of his last thoughts on the position of the *mythologue* in general: condemned to a cerebral metalanguage (semiology), the *mythologue* may fail to register the affective or practical side of the objects being submitted to ideological analysis. The Citroën D.S. 19 may be a mid-twentieth-century version of the great medieval cathedrals, as he imaginatively suggests in 'La Nouvelle Citroën'. But it is also a car, with a certain speed and certain aerodynamic advantages.[13] Wine may be one of the many signs of Frenchness, or what Barthes neologistically baptizes *la francité*, but that is not enough to make him turn teetotal. Barthes sums up the dilemma thus: 'le vin est objectivement bon, et *en même temps*, la bonté du vin est un mythe: voilà l'aporie'.[14]

[9] *My*, 246. [10] Ibid. 245.
[11] Ibid. 156. [12] Ibid. 245 n. 29.
[13] Ibid. 150, and 246. [14] Ibid. 246.

Furthermore, the *mythologue* is stuck in the role of denouncing the abstraction of the sign-systems of bourgeois ideology in an equally abstract language. Barthes suggests that he has found this restriction difficult to sustain and has indulged in a 'thickening' of the mythical objects he is analysing: 'souffrant de travailler sans cesse sur l'évaporation du réel, je me suis mis à l'épaissir excessivement, à lui trouver une compacité surprenante, savoureuse à moi-même'.[15]

None of this suggests that the polemical force of Barthes's analyses need be disarmed: his methodological scruples are acute but not paralysing, and he analyses his own position with considerable lucidity, aware as he is that the limits of his project are dictated by his own social and historical position. None the less, there is a sense in which the *Mythologies* are indeed ambiguous in status: sociological in ethos, semiological in method, and acutely political in import, they are also autobiographical (we see Barthes's own sensibility registering impressions received at the music-hall, at a wrestling-match, at the barber's, at the cinema, at the theatre); and above all, perhaps, they are stylistic *tours de force*: prose poems that bear comparison with Baudelaire's *Le Spleen de Paris* as much as with any sociological article.

In fact, it is Baudelaire who is cited as an epigraph to the first myth to be analysed, in 'Le Monde où l'on catche': the epigraph talks of 'la vérité emphatique du geste dans les grandes circonstances de la vie', a quotation of which Barthes is extremely fond, repeating it frequently throughout his work: here he uses it to emphasize the artificial theatricality of *le catch*, as the French call all-in wrestling. But wrestling turns out to be a rather atypical myth for Barthes to start with, since the practice behind the myth is one that he too enjoys. And the essay suggests that despite its capacity to inspire various mythical images (the myth suggests that the object of the match is to win, though everyone seems to know, subconsciously, that its truth lies elsewhere), wrestling is an activity that is laudably open and frank about its own mythicality: it seems to be an activity that parodies myth at the same time that it exploits it. The excessive clarity of the signs deployed in wrestling, its *explicitly* theatrical and agonistic aspects, are positive values for Barthes, whatever his suspicion of the false euphoria induced by mythical clarity when such clarity disguises complexity and diversity. Wrestling lays bare the system of its signs in such a way that their very paroxystic exaggeration should debar the spectator from seeing them as natural.

---

[15] *My*, 247.

But the degree of clarity with which signs emphasize their status as signs is, as later works by Barthes show, an important part of his aesthetic and political judgement—his 'taste'. The essays on music demonstrate this with great power.[16] In singing, excessive clarity of diction is made to serve not the *act* of meaning (semiosis) but the *fact* of feeling (emotional expressiveness). Generalizing from Barthes's reflections on singing to the rest of his work, it is possible to conclude that Barthes's taste considers excessive clarity vulgar, but only if it is a clarity in the service of expression, in other words as something 'natural' and culturally unmediated. On the other hand, he considers such clarity as distinguished if it is made to serve the ends either of intellectual demonstration (as in Brecht's epic theatre) or of strong but empty signs (whose spectacular artifice voids them of a signified, as is the case with the 'Japan' depicted in *L'Empire des signes*). In either case, what he most fervently condemns is the notion that decrees that Racine can only be played straight, the 'natural' way, because, as ideology tautologically expresses it, 'Racine est Racine'.[17] Even the simplistic morality that all-in wrestling promotes is preferable to this 'sécurité admirable du néant'.[18] So it is wrong to imagine that Barthes condemns all clarity, despite some of his comments in 'Le Mythe, aujourd'hui'.[19] Barthes's hostility towards myth is not an attack on its clarity, but on the fact that its clarity is in fact based on obscurantism (the myth conceals social contradictions).

So 'Le Monde où l'on catche' is an especially interesting essay because of Barthes's double-edged appraisal of its potential. On the one hand, it seems *too* clear: with its Manichaean separation of heroes from villains, it creates the illusion that it can clarify the complexity of the world.

Sur le Ring et au fond même de leur ignominie volontaire, les catcheurs restent des dieux, parce qu'ils sont, pour quelques instants, la clef qui ouvre la Nature, le geste pur qui sépare le Bien du Mal et dévoile la figure d'une Justice enfin intelligible.[20]

---

[16] See 'L'Art vocal bourgeois' (ibid. 168–70) and the essays collected in the final section of *OO*, esp. the piece on Panzéra and Fischer-Dieskau entitled 'Le Grain de la voix' (236–45).

[17] *My*, 96–8.

[18] Ibid. 98.

[19] See esp. ibid. 231: 'le mythe ... fonde une clarté heureuse: les choses ont l'air de signifier toutes seules'.

[20] Ibid. 24.

But any sense of justice generated by the spectacle is surely simplistic: all transgression is automatically punished, *œil pour œil, dent pour dent,* one kick up the behind provoking another in return.[21] But even if its attempts to show justice in action are simplistic, wrestling does clarify one activity superlatively well: wrestling itself. The great hulks of flesh grappling with each other in the ring are in fact acting in the service of a convention which shows its own conventionality and points to its signs *as signs.* Barthes is indulgent about the *beauté morale* of wrestling since the harsh *lex talionis* it stages is at least preferable to the evasions and half-truths of bourgeois ideology: it is a step in the direction of converting blind nature into immanent human justice. And wrestling is entirely open about its signs: it exposes its mechanisms and leaves nothing concealed. Its very excess—its camp theatricality—is progressive.

And what wrestling accomplishes in theatrical terms, the semiologist must do in formal terms: lay bare, even at the cost of a certain simplication, the devices of a society that constantly naturalizes its meanings; and lay bare too the devices of semiology itself. Indeed, in so far as wrestling is a system of strong signs that foregrounds its own conventions, it is the equivalent of a *literary* form that has already demystified itself. In wrestling we have an example of a *popular* cultural practice that is not merely mythical but enlightening as well: it thus parallels Chaplin's films. Whereas wrestling demystifies itself by laying bare its devices, Chaplin demystifies the audience by showing the blindness of his protagonists to their subjection.[22] Barthes's affirmative reading of such popular art forms is thus an alternative to their dismissal in other Marxist critiques. Adorno, for instance, was equally suspicious of both Brecht and Chaplin.[23]

Barthes thus sees wrestling as a cultural mode that, as much as the

[21] *My,* 20. Umberto Eco and Isabella Pezzini, in 'La Sémiologie des *Mythologies*', *Communications,* 36 (Oct. 1982), 19–42, note the ambiguity of 'catch' as analysed by Barthes, but finally decide that it is less than the heroic spectacle it purports to be: we do not in fact see (as Barthes suggests we do) the clash of Good and Evil, but 'quelque chose comme l'affirmation d'une justice de petit cabotage, où c'est le plus malin qui gagne' (27). I am not sure this is correct: Barthes shows how fluctuating and contradictory the spectators' demands and reactions can be, whatever the clarity of the myth: and he himself sees positive aspects in the *form* of wrestling (its self-interruptions).

[22] Barthes discusses Chaplin in 'Le Pauvre et le prolétaire' (*My,* 40–2). Chaplin's procedure is here seen as Brechtean: the audience is silently (non-discursively) *shown* the reasons for the protagonists' alienation (41).

[23] See *Aesthetics and Politics: Debates between Bloch, Lukács, Brecht, Benjamin, Adorno* (London, 1977), 106–7, for a summary of Adorno's quarrel with Benjamin on this issue.

most vigilant and self-reflexive products of high art, demystifies itself. It is at least as lucid about its own procedures as the novel, which theatrically stages its own conventions, as Barthes claims elsewhere: 'l'écriture romanesque . . . a pour charge de placer le masque et en même temps de le désigner'.[24] Both wrestling and the novel, Barthes is claiming, have an aesthetic force which should qualify their capacity to be the mere transmitters of pernicious ideological attitudes.

This parallels the observation made by Paul de Man that the difference between myth and fiction lies in the fact that 'the fiction is not myth, for it knows and names itself as fiction. It is not a demystification, it is demystified from the start.'[25] (This parallel is pertinent even though de Man's sense of 'myth' is somewhat closer to ordinary usage than Barthes's. For Barthes, 'myth' has the more political charge associated in other kinds of critique with the word 'ideology'.) De Man's suggestion in turn raises three questions. First, if cultural activities can be said to have demystified themselves already, do we need a critic to tell us so? The statement that fiction names itself as fiction (that it has suspended all truth claims) is not a fiction, but the truth: paradoxically, we still need a voice from outside the fiction to tell us that the fiction has named itself as fictional, just as, in Barthes's metaphor, we need an unmasker to show us that the novel is pointing to its own status as a complex semiotic construction.[26]

Secondly, where de Man tends to imagine that only 'high' literary products can demystify themselves, Barthes points out with considerable acumen that the forms of popular culture are equally capable of such self-reflexive vigilance. His later work frequently loses sight of this, since he increasingly assumes that all culture except that of the avant-garde is petty bourgeois, in other words a degraded and clumsy mimicking of high bourgeois cultural forms, so that there can be little question of 'low' culture being anything other than farcically repetitive.[27] None the less, here in Mythologies, vengeful and persuasive denunciations of the myths of everyday life coexist with, and sometimes mutate into, more positive attitudes. 'Le Monde où l'on catche' (on wrestling), 'Le Pauvre et le prolétaire' (on Chaplin), 'Le Visage de Garbo' (comparing the screen presences of Garbo and Hepburn),

---

[24] DZ, 28.
[25] 'Criticism and Crisis', in Blindness and Insight: Essays in the Rhetoric of Contemporary Criticism (2nd edn., London, 1983), 3–19 (18).
[26] I will be examining this paradox in more detail later (Ch. 3, below).
[27] This criticism is made very effectively by Michael Moriarty in Roland Barthes (Cambridge, 1991), 159–67.

'Puissance et désinvolture' (on gangster movies), 'Le Bifteck et les frites', 'Nautilus et bateau ivre', 'Le Tour de France comme épopée', 'La Nouvelle Citroën', and the extremely beautiful celebration of the *féerie profonde* created by jugglers and comic turns in 'Au music-hall', all, as well as containing analyses of the ways myths come into being and are sustained by various cultural forms, have a positive element: this is largely because in most of them, Barthes can show considerable sympathy with their popularity. And there is no reason why this affirmative moment should not coexist with the denunciatory stance of the *marxisant* satirist.

Thirdly, Barthes is aware that his role as the analyst unmasking myths is a vulnerable one. He shows, in 'Le Mythe, aujourd'hui', that the myth does not mask anything: it abolishes the distinction commonly made in ideological analysis between the latent and the patent, because it can always claim that it is presenting the world just as it is, without any ideological input: 'Le mythe ne cache rien et il n'affiche rien: il déforme', so that instead of being forced to give away its concepts—its ideological meanings—the myth naturalizes them.[28] Furthermore, myth may be demystified, or may demystify itself, and still survive as myth. This has become even clearer since the 1950s: myths can now be far more open, adverts may be self-reflexive to the *n*th degree, relying on self-caricature and a complacently *outré* excessiveness—and they still sell their products. This casts doubt on the enlightenment notion that to *know* (to identify the meaning and mechanism of the myth) will automatically abolish the myth. And in any case, in the society avid for images which Barthes is analysing, the *mythologue* all too rapidly becomes a mythical figure, the critic recuperated, the external stance internalized and tamed. The unmasker too is forced to wear a mask. (This is a point made most succinctly, perhaps, by the cover of Louis-Jean Calvet's interesting early study *Roland Barthes: un regard politique sur le signe*: it bears a sketch of Barthes holding a mask of his own face in front of him: it is the *mask* that is sardonically sticking its tongue out.)

In actual practice, Barthes shows that the best way of demystifying myth may be not by analysing it but by mimicking it. So as well as saying myth (analysing it from a metalinguistic standpoint), he shows it. To show rather than to say how ideology works is a practice he admired in Brecht.[29] And after all, the terms of analysis set out in 'Le

---

[28] *My*, 215.
[29] This distinction between 'showing' and 'saying' is, of course, crucial to the philosophy of Wittgenstein.

Mythe, aujourd'hui' are belated: Barthes does not analyse any of his *mythologies* in such technical ways, but depends on a more varied approach.

One way of 'saying' the myth, for example, is by ending an essay with a *clausule*, a biting sentence that points out the material interests that are really at stake. For instance, having dwelt on the different ways that Persil and Omo are marketed, the various kinds of cleansing activities that their soap-suds can accomplish, he notes that behind the apparent choice offered by the free market lies the monolithic power of Unilever.[30] And at the end of the analysis of a particularly rosy-tinted and patronizing film (called *Continent perdu*) about the Malay Archipelago, Barthes notes how such orientalist fantasies ignore current political realities and refers to the 1955 Bandung Conference of non-aligned nations: 'On voit donc que les "belles images" de *Continent perdu* ne peuvent être innocentes: il ne peut être innocent de *perdre* le continent qui s'est retrouvé à Bandoeng.'[31]

At other times, rather than 'saying' the myth, spelling out its meaning, he prefers to concentrate on 'showing' it. This is particularly true of the way he will weave his own imaginative webs around some of the myths he detects, dwelling on their concrete embodiment in various kinds of substance, from soap-suds to milk, from Garbo's face to the shiny metal of the new Citroën. These two approaches can coexist in one and the same essay—the 'showing' involved in a *psychanalyse substantielle* of the myths of substance (whose bearers are such things as food, drink, and detergents) sometimes giving way to a 'saying', as when the pleasures of drinking wine are dwelt on, but it is also pointed out that Algerian wine—produced in a Muslim country where alcohol consumption is prohibited—is the result of French imperialism.[32] And there is another way of describing the difference between them. The distanced, metalinguistic stance of saying is also a technique for *interrupting* the myth, stopping it in its tracks, and holding it up for our inspection. The more mimetic impulse to derive a complex material image from the myth, to show its textured materiality (as well as say its abstract meaning) is a way of *prolonging* the myth to an excessive degree and making it explicit in this more ironic way.

Thus one of the reasons Barthes is indulgent towards wrestling is that it interrupts itself, foregrounds its own meanings, explicitly shows what it is about. Barthes even goes so far as to identify it with Greek

[30] *My*, 40.   [31] Ibid. 165.   [32] Ibid. 77.

theatre, which is similarly frank about its civic aims—unlike bourgeois theatre, which is far more dishonest. The contrast between, on the one hand, the floodlit splendour of wrestling and the sunlit open-air theatres of ancient Greece, and, on the other hand, the dark and secretive indoor theatres of the bourgeoisie, is emblematic of this difference.[33] But above all, wrestling as an art of interruption and self-analysis reponds to a semiological instinct in Barthes himself, one that he later dwells on in 'Le cercle des fragments', an item in *Barthes par lui-même*. Here, he notes how he intuitively saw in wrestling not a suffocatingly coherent myth, but a far more open-ended series of rhetorical performances (or *figures*).

Le catch, il le voyait déjà comme une suite de fragments, une somme de spectacles, car 'au catch, c'est chaque moment qui est intelligible, non la durée'. . .; il regardait avec étonnement et prédilection cet artifice sportif, soumis dans sa structure même à l'asyndète et à l'anacoluthe, figures de l'interruption et du court-circuit.[34]

Mythologies overall similarly constitutes *une somme de spectacles*: hence Barthes's description of them, in the same fragment, as *tableautins*. They are like the *Gestus* of Brecht's theatre, an interruption in the action of the piece that enables its significance to be made clear.[35] So in the *Mythologies*, Barthes is frequently the all-in wrestler, holding in a semiological half-nelson his enemy, Petty-Bourgeois Ideology, a voluble and evasive awkward customer, 'fabulant intarissablement autour de son mécontentement'.[36] In this way, Barthes interrupts the murmur of myth and forces it to say its real meaning.

But in another tactic, Barthes will prolong and show the myth. Instead of flooring the myth, he drifts in and away from it. A good example of that, to which I will now turn, is 'Paris n'a pas été inondé'.

THE SEMIOLOGIST AND THE FLOODS

The main paradox of 'Paris n'a pas été inondé' lies in Barthes's observation that the floods that occurred in France in January 1955

---

[33] On Greek theatre, see the article 'Le Théâtre grec' in *OO*, 63–85, and 'Pouvoirs de la tragédie antique', *Théâtre populaire*, 2 (Sept. 1953), 12–22. On bourgeois theatre as a secretive theatre, see *EpS*, 80.

[34] *RB*, 97.

[35] On Brecht's *Gestus* as interruption, see Walter Benjamin, 'What is Epic Theatre? [Second Version]', in *Understanding Brecht*, trans. Anna Bostock (London, 1973), 15–22 (18–20).

[36] *My*, 16.

were less a catastrophe than an occasion for festival. The essay's critical thrust lies in its exposure of the way a real disaster causing real problems was enjoyed by those who were not themselves severely affected: and Barthes berates the media who turned the floods into an aesthetic object, a series of images to be consumed. Yet, although these points are clearly made by Barthes, the essay is more ambiguous than this reduction suggests. The floods renewed the way people perceived their environment: they thus acted, one might say, as a form of defamiliarization, altering perceptions without appearing unmanageably threatening.[37] The freshness of this new vision of a flooded world was based, Barthes says, on a severing of links with the real world: objects floated on the waters or rose majestically above the floods, separated from their roots, 'privés de la substance raisonnable par excellence, la Terre'.[38] This notation is curious—why is the Earth (here capitalized to give it extra weight) a *reasonable* substance?

The answer is that Barthes is elaborating his own myth as much as analysing an ideology. Here, 'myth' is close to its meaning in the work of the epistemologist and critic Gaston Bachelard, who divided the myths of substance that he discovered in the obsessions of poets and philosophers, according to the dominance in them of one of the four medieval elements, earth, air, fire, and water. Bachelard suggests a general equation between *water* and *reverie*, both of which involve a loss of ground: 'L'eau est vraiment l'élément transitoire . . . L'être voué à l'eau est un être en vertige.'[39] The earth, on the other hand, is associated either with the will (the will as heroic transformer of raw materials, for instance) or with repose (as in the back-to-the-womb temptation offered by caverns and grottoes).[40] Barthes is basing his own evaluation of the earth as reasonable (as opposed to the more irrational water) on similarly mythical considerations.

The rest of the essay adds further twists to the argument. To be freed from the earth may be euphoric, but it is dangerous, thinks Barthes: it stops people thinking about the causes of the disaster, and for the *marxisant* semiologist, committed to the belief that the human

---

[37] *My*, 61.
[38] Ibid.
[39] *L'Eau et les rêves: essai sur l'imagination de la matière* (1942), 8.
[40] See *La Terre et les rêveries de la volonté: essai sur l'imagination des forces* (1948), and *La Terre et les rêveries de repos: essai sur les images de l'intimité* (1948), respectively. Bachelard is an early and important influence on Barthes, who cites his mythical contrast between wine and water, albeit to correct it on historico–sociological grounds to a more pertinent opposition between wine and milk. See Bachelard, *La Terre et les rêveries de repos*, 323–32, and Barthes, 'Le Vin et le lait', in *My*, 74–7.

environment is not subject to blind nature but manipulable by praxis, such an attitude is irresponsible. The floating world created by the newspaper images obliterated the solid ground of action while not being enough of a disaster to force people to rethink ways of preventing any future floods.

Cette rupture a eu le mérite de rester curieuse, sans être magiquement menaçante: la nappe d'eau a agi comme un truquage réussi mais connu, les hommes ont eu le plaisir de voir des formes modifiées, mais somme toute 'naturelles', leur esprit a pu rester fixé sur l'effet sans régresser dans l'angoisse vers l'obscurité des causes. La crue a bouleversé l'optique quotidienne, sans pourtant la *dériver* vers le fantastique; les objets ont été partiellement oblitérés, non déformés: le spectacle a été singulier mais raisonnable.[41]

The floods have not sent their victims drifting helplessly away: they have not achieved the awesome status associated with major natural disasters. The perceiving subject can observe the floods without feeling threatened. In Kant's term, they do not arouse the idea of the 'sublime'.[42] The earth is reason: the floods, with the improvised boats that people hastily assemble in order to do such ordinary things as the shopping, lead to an attempt to reconcile, on the level of myth, the activities associated with the earth (walking) and those linked to the water (floating as escape and reverie), so that to float is in effect a way of walking on the water.[43] *Mythos*, so to speak, floats above *logos*.

Barthes's view of the floods as an aesthetic image smoothing over the contradictions and hard edges of reality needs to be counter-pointed with his later valorization of literature, which is often couched in similar 'mythical' terms ('myth', here again, being closer to Bachelard's sense). For instance: 'l'écriture . . . donne du souffle au monde'; and 'la littérature ne permet pas de marcher, mais elle permet de respirer'.[44] It is common to see ideology as working in similarly mythical ways, reconciling in the imaginary what cannot be reconciled in reality. Barthes is saying that literature enables us not to walk (to change the world at ground level, as it were) but only to breathe (to understand the world symbolically). Of course, literature may also

[41] *My*, 61, my emphasis.

[42] 'It is rather in its chaos, or in its wildest and most irregular disorder and desolation, provided it gives signs of magnitude and power, that nature chiefly excites the ideas of the sublime' (*The Critique of Judgement*, trans. James Creed Meredith (Oxford, 1952), bk II, 'Analytic of the Sublime', sect. 23, p. 92).

[43] *My*, 62–3.

[44] 'Littérature et signification', in *EC*, 258–76 (264). For Bachelard, the air—another element which favours drift—is associated with the mobility of e.g. day-dreams: see *L'Air et les songes: essai sur l'imagination du mouvement* (1943).

interrupt that flow, be more riven with contradiction, and thus illuminate real contradictions too.[45] But his image of the floods here, and the metaphors he uses to describe them, suggest that there is something 'literary' about them: and he continues this literariness by dwelling on the (rather pleasant) sensations of floating, gliding, and drifting that the floods create. The newspaper photos of the floods invite imaginative collaboration: 'A cet apaisement de la vue . . . correspond évidemment tout un mythe heureux du glissement: devant les photos d'inondation, chaque lecteur se sent glisser par procuration.'[46] Barthes responds by depicting the scene with the care of a Dutch landscape-painter. This mimicry enables us to enjoy the floods as an aesthetic object as well as to understand them as an example of how myth works. This duplicity of response, that I have already suggested is fundamental to the success of the *Mythologies*, enables us to participate imaginatively as well as recognize and understand.

Indeed, this is a myth with a strong affirmative momentum to it. For instance, if the earth is the real place of political struggle, it is also the locus of property, and Barthes points out how the dividing lines of property are abolished by the gentle anarchy of the rising waters: the flood expropriates:

les lignes habituelles du cadastre, les rideaux d'arbres, les rangées de maisons, les routes, le lit même du fleuve, cette stabilité angulaire qui prépare si bien les formes de la propriété, tout cela a été gommé, étendu de l'angle au plan: plus de voies, *plus de rives*, plus de directions; une substance plane qui ne va nulle part, et qui suspend ainsi le devenir de l'homme, le détache d'une raison, d'une ustensilité des lieux.[47]

'Plus de rives': a *dérive*. And while the essay hovers between positive and negative evaluations of the myths identified, the final myth (that of Noah's ark, of which Barthes is reminded by the flotilla of vessels that became a common sight during the floods) is a happy one:

Car l'Arche est un mythe heureux: l'humanité y prend ses distances à l'égard des éléments, elle s'y concentre et y élabore la conscience nécessaire de ses

---

[45] For a comparison of the different ways in which myth (in Lévi-Strauss's sense) and ideology reconcile opposed factors, see Jorge Larrain, *The Concept of Ideology* (London, 1979), 145. The notion of social contradictions being smoothed over in ideology is central to Althusser, though the Althusserian Pierre Macherey suggests, in *Pour une théorie de la production littéraire* (1966), that the contradictions of an apparently ideologically saturated medium such as literature can in fact be liberating indices of social contradictions.

[46] *My*, 62.

[47] Ibid. 61–2, my emphasis.

pouvoirs, faisant sortir du malheur même l'évidence que le monde est maniable.[48]

In other words the apparently self-indulgent drift made possible by the floods is a critical distance that makes new forms of praxis possible: what seemed passive is made active, a drift becomes a potential drive. 'Paris n'a pas été inondé' is thus partly grounded on the reasonable earth of enlightened semiology, with its overt stance of critique, and its political values of praxis, rationality, and purpose (the solidarity experienced during the flood must not, after all, conceal the fact that most of the time it is replaced by social conflict and division). But Barthes's essay is also prepared to participate in the drift it depicts, in ways that are ultimately as 'en-lightening' as a heavier and more earthbound analysis. While it would be exaggerated to suggest that, at the end of the essay, the reader has lost all bearings ('plus de voies, plus de rives'), it is none the less true that the *rives* of semiology are constantly being overflowed by the *dérive* of writing.

On other occasions, it is clear that Barthes's own values are coming into play. The techniques of 'Le Mythe, aujourd'hui', handled by any other semiologist, would not necessarily produce the result of the individual *Mythologies* even if that method were applied to the same corpus of material selected by Barthes. Or rather, even if it did show, objectively, how each myth works (the connotations it naturalizes), the values embodied in the practices of myth can still be responded to in different ways. Some of the myths show an evaluative swerve on Barthes's part. 'Jouets', for instance, perspicaciously points out how toys condition children to adopt certain gender roles, which is a relatively objective point, but it also praises wooden toys at the expense of plastic toys. The reasons for this are cogent enough (wooden toys do not break so easily and encourage the child to be more creative), but it would be equally pertinent to suggest that wooden toys are a sign of middle-class nostalgia for an almost vanished *temps d'artisanat.* Since Barthes is so hostile to the myth of nature as 'the way things are', his essay celebrates the naturalness of wood: 'Les jouets cour- ants', he comments on the new plastic toys already flooding the markets in the 1950s, 'sont d'une matière ingrate, produits d'une chimie, non d'une nature', and 'Le bois fait des objets essentiels, des objets de toujours.'[49] Barthes *likes* wood (he sees it as a maternal substance, referring to the way it unites *fermeté* with *tendreur*) and this leads to a drift—a swerve of desire—in his analysis. Likewise, Philippe Roger has pointed out how Barthes's dislike of images in general (especially media or advertising images) distorts his perceptions of the cultural objects he is discussing: Barthes describes the Harcourt studio photos as frequently depicting actors and actresses from below, and thus from an *angle aberrant de la vue*, an angle which encourages the spectator to envisage these theatre stars as endowed with a superterrestrial nobility. As Roger notes, few if any Harcourt shots are taken from this *angle aberrant*.[50] He suggests that Barthes's mistaken generalization arises both from his (in some ways justifiable) dislike of these photos and the fact that they do tend to be suspended, like Olympian deities, at some height above the staircase in Parisian theatres (so that it is the spectator who is forced to look respectfully up, rather than the actors and actresses who are pensively gazing skyward).

Drift as moving over (or through) water appears as a theme on at least one other occasion in *Mythologies*, this time in a less detached and comfortable form. In 'Nautilus et bateau ivre', Barthes suggests that Jules Verne is the narrator not so much of adventure stories of daring exploration as of an imperturbable appropriation of nature. Verne's novel *L'Île mystérieuse* shows how an island can become the perfect bourgeois world of self-contained home comforts: and the submarine *Nautilus*, from *Vingt mille lieues sous la mer*, is a cosy microcosm. The real image of a vessel open to the strangeness and violence of nature, for Barthes, is Rimbaud's rudderless *bateau ivre*, at the mercy of the elements, drifting, out of control. This loss of direction is seen by Barthes as something positive, since the homely technocracies of Verne are no match for the drunken boat when it comes to ejecting human beings out of their narcissistic caves into 'une poétique véritable de l'exploration'.[51]

Drift is thus a theme in Barthes, something to which his body responds. But it is a paradoxical theme in that it floats—that is, it moves across Barthes's work as a whole, appearing in various places with rather different values each time. And as well as being an

---

[50] Ibid. 25. Philippe Roger's paper 'Image, imago, imaginaire chez Roland Barthes' was given at the University of Cambridge on 6 Feb. 1991.

[51] *My*, 82. This total, unprotected drift is much closer to Kant's 'sublime'. I mention this because there seem to be two kinds of thematic drift at work in Barthes: one close to Kant's sense of 'beautiful', the other to the 'sublime'. In the first, the mind is in control of its experience: in the second, such control is threatened or abdicated. In *PlT*, Barthes's *plaisir* is close to Kant's 'beautiful', Barthes's *jouissance* to Kant's 'sublime'.

unpredictable theme, it is a tactic in Barthes's own writing: it is his way of distancing himself from any phenomenon he is examining while at the same time continuing that phenomenon, prolonging its salient characteristics, drawing it out. This increasingly becomes his main method of exposing the objects of his study. Instead of occupying the oppositional stance of critique, he adopts a more oblique approach, one which involves what might be called a 'subversive complicity' with the material he is discussing. I now want to turn to a particular example of this tactic of drifting as it affects Barthes's ambiguity of response, an ambiguity that is, as always, combined with political sensitivity.

DRIFTING EASTWARDS

My example is a Barthes text published in 1971: the preface to Pierre Loti's *Aziyadé*.[52] This novel tells the story of two lovers forced to separate: it takes place in Turkey, during the Turkish-Russian War, but, as Barthes hastens to add, the plot is of less importance than the *incidents* that punctuate it. In this essay, Barthes's writing has taken on some of the features associated with his later works (approximately post-1970): it is a series of numbered and enigmatically titled sections, each of which examines one feature of Loti's novel. And, of most interest to us at this juncture, one of the sections of Barthes's essay is called 'La Dérive'. According to Barthes, Loti depicts in his novel the character of a 'hippy dandy', a man who prefers the backwater of Istanbul to the dynamic imperialist expansionism of his own country, Britain. (In the novel, the male hero is British, but he is given the name Loti—which was the pseudonym of the novel's author, Julien Viaud.) Barthes comments: 'Cette forme de refus ou de soustraction hors de l'Occident n'est ni violente, ni ascétique, ni politique: c'est très exactement une *dérive: Aziyadé* est le roman de la Dérive.'[53] It is important to note what Barthes is here excluding from drift: violence, ascesis, and politics. (These three are thus tacitly associated with each other.) It is important too to see how *dérive*, an ordinary noun (even if its precise significance in Barthes's text is enigmatic), is capitalized into *Dérive*—thus transforming it in ways I shall examine in my next chapter.

The drifting that Loti enjoys is not merely aquatic, despite his

---

[52] 'Pierre Loti: *Aziyadé*', *NEC*, 170–87.   [53] Ibid. 184.

romantic boat-rides with Aziyadé in Salonika. His whole existence as an expatriate Briton in Istanbul is that of a drifter, and his refusal of the West is not a violent rejection but something cooler; what Barthes, still identifying Loti as a proto-hippy, calls 'une contestation très paresseuse'.[54] This is in contrast with a far more critical Barthes article of 1969, in which he had dismissed the hippies' rejection of technocracy as merely an automatic inversion of values rather than a new and creative practice, and suggested that there was something still rather violent about their attitude to society.[55]

This accusation cannot be made about Loti, who is not rejecting so much as drifting away from his own culture.

Il existe des villes de Dérive . . . tel sans doute le Stamboul de Loti. La ville est alors une sorte d'eau qui à la fois porte et emporte loin de la rive du réel: on s'y trouve immobile (soustrait à toute compétition) et déporté (soustrait à tout ordre conservateur). Curieusement, Loti parle lui-même de la dérive (rare moment vraiment symbolique de ce discours sans secret): dans les eaux de Salonique, la barque où Aziyadé et lui font leurs promenades amoureuses est 'un lit qui flotte', 'un lit qui dérive' . . . Y a-t-il image plus voluptueuse que celle de ce lit en dérive? Image profonde, car elle réunit trois idées: celle de l'amour, celle du flottement et la pensée que le désir est une force en dérive—ce pour quoi on a proposé comme la meilleure approche, sinon comme la meilleure traduction, de la pulsion freudienne (concept qui a provoqué bien des discussions) le mot même de *dérive*.[56]

Barthes here goes out of his way to defend Loti (the author—and also the character) from the charge of irresponsible escapism. And he also questions the rather obvious conclusion that Loti is indulging in orientalism, that set of attitudes and prejudices developed by Europe in its discourse on 'the East'. In orientalism, the West constructs the East as an inverted mirror image of its own values. Orientalism is thus narcissistic in its failure to open itself to the otherness of the East: even its ploy of praising the East (for its mysterious wisdom or its tranquil, lotus-eating *art de vivre*) is a way of keeping the Orient in its place, paralysing its history and homogenizing its heterogeneity (thus refusing to accept that the East is as varied and divided as the West). West/East is a paradigm created and controlled by the West.[57]

[54] *NEC*, 184.
[55] 'Un cas de critique culturelle', *Communications*, 14 (Nov. 1969), 97–9. The hippy's lifestyle is that of 'un bourgeois *retourné*' (99).
[56] *NEC*, 60.
[57] For a general examination of what is at stake in this miscognition of 'the East' by 'the West', see Edward W. Said, *Orientalism* (London, 1978).

There is clearly a certain degree of orientalism at work in Barthes, as well as Loti. But Barthes follows Loti in *not* jumping across the binary division from the West to the East but in *drifting* eastwards. And in this process it ceases to be clear where the East really is. As Barthes asks, in the heading to one of the sections of his essay, 'Mais où est l'Orient?' Loti's East is distanced not only from the West but from the East of his own time: it is a fantasmatic, archaic, and imaginarily reconstructed Turkey to which he travels. In drift, as the extract above suggests, you do not move (you are *immobile*) and yet you do not stay in the same place either (you are *déporté*—both 'deported' and 'carried off course'): drift complicates the very notion of place, and thus of the places from which one pronounces value-judgements. In drifting, Loti is partly complicitous with orientalist modes of thought, but is also detaching himself from them by questioning, implicitly, the binary oppositions West/East, self/other, home/abroad, responsibility/escape. To take a parallel from another perpetual tourist cited with admiration in Barthes's last piece of writing (Stendhal, discussed in 'On échoue toujours à parler de ce qu'on aime'), drift is a way of reacting to the otherness within you, the foreignness of home (and the feeling of being at home that one may encounter abroad). 'Stendhal a cette passion rare, la passion de l'autre—ou pour le dire plus subtilement: la passion de cet autre qui est en lui-même.'[58] Loti is both in the West (which he does not reject) and in the East (to which he silently assents, in which he acquiesces). It is the drift of writing which creates this straddling effect. Just as Barthes is both inside and outside the myth of the floods, enjoying it only to detach himself critically from it, Loti is both inside and outside the myth of the mystic and languorous East. And finally, Barthes sees the 'old-fashioned' book *Aziyadé* as having something modern about it in that 'l'écriture . . . désitue le sujet qui écrit, le déroute'. Above all, the story exists less to be told than to act as the signifier of drift: 'le mouvement du discours est dans la métaphore renouvelée qui dit toujours le *rien* de la Dérive'.[59] Loti's stay in Turkey is ultimately without reason: it 'n'appartient à aucune détermination, à aucune téléologie: quelque chose qui est très souvent du pur signifiant a été énoncé—et le signifiant n'est jamais démodé'.[60] The signifier, which has no purpose, like the rose of the mystic Angelus Silesius, is here seen as inseparable from the detached movement-in-stasis of drift: 'Die Rose ist ohne warum, | Sie blühet, weil sie blühet' ('The rose is

---

[58] *BL*, 333–42 (335).   [59] *NEC*, 186.   [60] Ibid. 187.

without a "why" | It blossoms because it blossoms'): 'le voyage—le séjour turc de Loti—est sans mobile et sans fin, il n'a ni *pourquoi* ni *pour quoi*'.[61] From material which is unpromising from the point of the view of a defender of the avant-garde, and ideologically extremely dubious, Barthes manages to rescue the signifier—as flotsam.

THE VIOLENCE OF MEANING

Barthes praises *Aziyadé* for its floating of the signifier, its refusal to occupy pre-existing places on one side or another of the binary schemata that govern meaning. And this floating is inseparable from Barthes's increasing sensitivity to a violence that he considers is inseparable from the way meaning is generated in Western languages.

Barthes's critique of violence frequently leads him to face up to contradictions in his own work. Here is one fragment from *Barthes par lui-même*, called 'Hétérologie et violence':

> Il ne parvient pas à s'expliquer comment il peut d'un côté soutenir (avec d'autres) une théorie textuelle de l'hétérologie (donc de la rupture) et de l'autre amorcer sans cesse une critique de la violence (sans jamais, il est vrai, la développer et l'assumer jusqu'au bout). Comment faire route avec l'avant-garde et ses parrains, lorsqu'on a *le goût irénique de la dérive?* [my emphasis]— A moins que précisément il ne vaille la peine, fût-ce au prix d'un certain retrait, de faire comme si l'on entrevoyait un *autre style* de schize.[62]

The avant-garde—or rather, Barthes's avant-garde, as theorized in the writings of the cultural journal *Tel Quel*—sees history as rupture, not flow. This is ultimately a model of violence rather than drift. In so far as Barthes shares the values of this avant-garde, he is worried by the apparent necessity of accepting the violence that goes with it. His response is to try and find a third way between avant-garde *rupture* on one hand and too smooth and evolutionary (or reformist) a view of history on the other. He labels this 'un *autre style* de schize'. *Schize* is a reference to a psychoanalytic topic, that of the 'split self', especially in schizoid mechanisms such as the splitting-off of part of the ego. The result of such a *schize* is not neurosis (in which repressed material strives to return from the unconscious) but psychosis (in which the unpalatable material is not repressed but foreclosed in another part of the ego). *Schize* is thus a form of dissociation. As an alternative to the

---

[61] *NEC*, 187.   [62] *RB*, 106.

neurotic defences produced as a response to the Oedipal pressures brought to bear on the subject in the process of socialization, Gilles Deleuze and Félix Guattari, in *Capitalisme et schizophrénie: l'Anti-Œdipe*, celebrate the far more radical escape routes adopted by the schizophrenic. They tend to see the psychotic mechanisms visible in the work of artists such as Van Gogh or Artaud as a far more violently original response to the stagnation of a neurotic society than an institutionalized and conformist psychoanalysis whose only aim is to 'cure' psychic discontent and illness by forcing analysands into social moulds. What Barthes is suggesting is that his *dérive* may be as effective a rebellion against social structures as the *schize* advocated by Deleuze and Guattari: but his *schize* is not violent. Indeed, he is quite close to one trend in the 'schizo-politics' they are concerned to elaborate. For one of the themes Barthesian drift encounters is transgression. The avant-garde (again, especially, *Tel Quel*) celebrated transgression (as theorized above all in the work of Georges Bataille). But for Barthes, transgression can lead to paradoxes. For one might decide to transgress transgression itself. And this leads to two possibilities.

First, since any transgression leads to the establishment of new norms, one can transgress those norms in turn. In *Barthes par lui-même* he notes that transgression of the earlier bourgeois norms has produced new freedoms in sexual practice and discourse: but one could transgress the *new* norm in turn, by celebrating something that has become a new taboo, namely the affective side of sexuality, what Barthes provocatively calls 'sentimentality'; and he therefore suggests: 'ne serait-ce pas *la dernière* des transgressions? la transgression de la transgression?'[63] This would be a transgression against the latest law, the latest discursive fashion.

Secondly, to transgress the formal demand of transgression might lead to dropping a preoccupation with transgression altogether, refusing to see one's solutions to social pressures in the light of the rhetoric of transgression. This would lead to a position indeterminate from the point of view of transgression itself (neither conformist nor transgressive), though still potentially creative and innovative. It is Deleuze and Guattari who suggest that the modernist preoccupation with transgression may be at base a fascination with the very law it aims to transgress, and thus a form of mere *religiosité*.[64] In other words, they transgress

---

[63] *RB*, 70.
[64] *Capitalisme et schizophrénie*, i. *L'Anti-Œdipe* (1972), 132.

the modernist demand for transgression by suspending it. There is thus a sense in which their 'schizo-politics' is a dissociative rather than a contestatory model. Like Barthes, they want solutions that do not fall back on a mere inversion of binary paradigms, something which they consider is symptomatic of neurosis. Barthes considers that there is something violent about such paradigms: the very formula of such a paradigm is '*a* versus *b*'. Although Barthes as a semiologist is concerned to pinpoint the way such paradigms underlie the most apparently 'natural' cultural meanings, that is only a first step. Having identified such binarism as violent (even where it seems not to be), Barthes argues that binarism as such tends to reside in an opposition in which one term is marked as good and the other bad: furthermore, any binary opposition claims to exhaust the possibilities (everything must be either *a* or *b*). His response to this violence (which is neurotic in so far as the 'bad' term constantly haunts the 'good' term and strives to return, to overthrow the latter's predominance) is close to the dissociation of Deleuze and Guattari, it is indeed 'un *autre style* de schize', even less violent than theirs. It is what he calls *dérive*. But this drift raises further questions about the relationship between avant-garde art and avant-garde politics.

THE POLITICS OF DRIFT

The fragment 'Décomposer/détruire' in *Barthes par lui-même* proposes an explicitly political rationale for drift's necessity.[65] The negation of bourgeois consciousness (which the postface to *Mythologies* had seemed to demand) cannot take place from outside, since, in the West at least, no such external site is available: bourgeois ideology has no outside. This notion acts as a ground bass to Barthes's political reflections, audible, for instance, as a lucidly pessimistic programme for a certain avant-garde in the 1971 preface to *Sade, Fourier, Loyola*. Barthes here suggests that not only can no 'innocent' discourse be sustained against ideology (something with which it is possible to agree): he also claims that ideology is everywhere and that there is no 'place of language' outside it:

En fait, il n'y a aujourd'hui aucun lieu de langage extérieur à l'idéologie bourgeoise: notre langage vient d'elle, y retourne, y reste enfermé. La seule riposte possible n'est ni l'affrontement ni la destruction, mais seulement le

---

[65] *RB*, 67.

vol: fragmenter le texte ancien de la culture, de la science, de la littérature, et en disséminer les traits selon des formules méconnaissables, de la même façon que l'on maquille une marchandise volée.[66]

This sweeping assertion turns bourgeois ideology into a suffocating smog that we are forced to breathe every time we open our mouths. And it is a suggestive point. For it unites two common feelings: that the late twentieth century is a time of exhaustion and repetition; and that revolutionary change, either aesthetic or political, is for the time being impossible.[67]

Furthermore, his use of the word *disséminer* to identify a potential escape route alerts us to a parallel with Jacques Derrida.[68] Derrida considers that from the time of Plato, philosophy in the West (and perhaps philosophy as a peculiarly 'Western' product, in that he is unsure whether there is such a thing as philosophy outside the 'closure' of the West) has been metaphysical. Metaphysics is preoccupied with 'beings' rather than 'Being' (Heidegger's point): it is definitional and essentialist, and operates with pairs of binary opposites, one of which is (and this is what Derrida shows to be a questionable manœuvre) prioritized over the other. Thus presence is seen as prior to, and greater than, absence: as a corollary, speech is seen as prior to and greater than writing, because speech implies the presence of a speaker whereas writing can function (if only, according to Plato, as a permanently possible *mal*function) in the absence of any such speaker. Derrida is concerned to question the stability of such binary oppositions. As a first move he shows how they cannot be separated from each other (it is impossible to think of presence without thinking, if only implicitly, of its opposite, absence, so that the positively evaluated term is never pure but shadowed by its negative). As a second move he asks what happens if we invert the traditional evaluation, seeing absence as paradoxically more powerful than presence, writing as in some sense prior to speech (in that both speech and writing are modes of articulation: they divide signs one from another, and the dividing lines between signs can be seen as a primordial form of writing or *archi-écriture*). And as a third move he shows how this reversal forces us to re-evaluate the terms of the

---

[66] *SFL*, 15.

[67] Both these attitudes give a certain pathos to the notion of 'post-modernism'. Although Barthes hardly if ever uses this word, his formulations of 'modernism', 'modernity', or 'the avant-garde' frequently overlap with aspects of the 'post-modern' set out, in their different ways, by Jean-François Lyotard and Fredric Jameson.

[68] See the title of the collection of essays by Derrida: *La Dissémination*.

opposition with which we started (so that we need to try and think beyond the binary opposites presence/absence, speech/writing, and so on). But Derrida is convinced that it is difficult to move beyond metaphysics: although he himself sets out his programme in schematic terms similar to those I have just used (in, for instance, his interviews with *Tel Quel* writers collected as *Positions*), his practice is far more complex, demonstrating that outplaying the grip of metaphysics is a matter of the greatest subtlety. It is a question less of escaping from metaphysics than identifying the moments when, within the metaphysical tradition itself, there are slippages and paradoxes: when the monument of metaphysics reveals its scars, cracks, and fissures: when, to use another metaphor (Derrida uses many), metaphysical language starts to *disséminer* in unpredictable and potentially liberating ways. Which brings us back to Barthes: for where Derrida talks of metaphysics, Barthes tends to focus on one particular product of metaphysics, namely what he calls 'bourgeois ideology', which shares all the features of metaphysics outlined above (basically, essentialism and, in linguistic and conceptual terms, binarism). At other times, Barthes will broaden his horizons, talking for instance (on the back cover of *L'Empire des signes*) of *la sémiocratie occidentale* (Derrida's logocentrism here being reformulated: Barthes focuses on the rule, not of the *logos*, but of the *sēmeion*, the sign). It is this regime, Barthes suggests, that has dominated Western systems of meaning 'from Plato to *France-Dimanche*', though it now may be crumbling, enabling us to see the emergence of something else.[69] For Derrida, it is impossible to combat metaphysics directly, since the very concepts one will use are derived from that tradition: for Barthes, it is impossible to combat bourgeois ideology directly, since 'notre langage vient d'elle'. And stated thus, his claim becomes more dubious: moving from a large-scale philosophical meditation on the reign of metaphysics to a geographically and historically local set of circumstances (for the preface to *Sade, Fourier, Loyola* is as much as anything else an intervention in the *Tel Quel* debate on the destiny of avant-garde art and politics in the France of the 1970s) needs a lot of relays and mediations that Barthes himself increasingly takes for granted. (He tends to rely, at this stage in his writing, on his colleagues at *Tel Quel*, especially Julia Kristeva, whose work—especially *La Révolution du langage poétique*—does concentrate in considerable detail on the political problems posed, at a specific historical juncture, by metaphysical modes of thinking.)

[69] 'La Mythologie aujourd'hui', in *BL*, 79–82 (81).

It certainly cannot be taken for granted, as Barthes tries to assert, that there is no site of language outside the domain of bourgeois ideology: he exaggerates the unity of that ideology and fails to address the question of how individuals (not just avant-garde artists) receive it. After all, bourgeois ideology can thrive on fragmentation and dissemination: these may indeed be actively promoted by it. Hence the ambiguity of post-modernism, which is both parodic and conformist in its mimicry of and dependence on a circulation of signs and stories that may seem uncontrolled, though in fact that circulation is tied to the current mechanisms of capitalism. Where Barthes celebrates such a circulation, he shares that ambiguity.

In any case, even the more monolithic manifestations of ideology are always subject to fragmentation and dissemination by its 'non-artistic' recipients, who, at least sometimes, are capable of distorting, parodying, and travestying ideological contents with considerable zest: there may be, to parody Du Marsais, at least as many counter-ideological moves to be overheard in the streets as are to be found in the pages of *Tel Quel*. In other words, this, together with my previous point, suggests that fragmentation in itself is an ideologically neutral operation.

Despite these reservations, it is at least clear that, given his own historical circumstances, Barthes thought that the only escape from ideology was subversion from within. Destruction from without is impossible: as he says in the 'Décomposer/détruire' fragment, 'pour *détruire* la conscience bourgeoise, il faut s'en absenter, et cette exteriorité n'est possible que dans une situation révolutionnaire'—as in Mao's China.[70] For in the West, revolution itself can never be a pure 'other', a political correction from the outside. Revolution *can* occur in China because China has a different sign-system to that of Western semiosis. In *Le Degré zéro de l'écriture*, Barthes claims that in the West, the painting of a nut *signifies* 'a nut' and naturalizes its process of signification: in the East, the painting of the nut does not signal its own status as representation.[71] This generalization is somewhat dubious, since if taken literally it implies that all Chinese painting is in some bizarre way hyper-realist. But it is considerations of this kind that determine Barthes's comments on the revolutionary potential of the East where, presumably, a revolution can be a revolution without having to generate the signs of revolutionariness. But in the West, the idea of revolution has not been able to resist the formidable recuperative powers of bourgeois consciousness: our very notion of

[70] *RB*, 67.   [71] *DZ*, 28.

revolution, whether it is an event feared or longed for, is infected by the generalized semiosis of the West: 'revolution' too will be converted into a sign.

Barthes's argument abstains from asking what is really happening in China. It has to do with signs and images: to a Western observer it *appears* that, in the East, the revolution is not a myth: it is the absolutely 'other', the thing itself. But as such, it cannot, from the West, be *written*. Barthes's analysis thus slips from a historical point (China's revolutionary potential versus the stagnation and decadence of Europe) to a semiological point (images of that revolution as generated by Western intellectuals—especially, again, *Tel Quel*), and from semiology to the question of language.

For Barthes, a decision in favour of China (for the Cultural Revolution, or an equivalent upheaval in France) is something that is, if not exactly extra-linguistic, at least a 'leap of faith' made in a kind of discursive silence. On the one hand, the militant may be defined as the person who abdicates subjective speech in favour of political stereotypes: the militant agrees to act as a mouthpiece for a generalized militant discourse, agrees *to be spoken*, to produce what Barthes calls 'un discours ressassant, tautologique, militant'.[72] On the other hand, the militant may concentrate on political praxis, ignoring—as far as possible—the problem of language: Barthes imagines the militant as attempting to occupy 'l'espace du non-discours ("ne parlons pas, n'écrivons pas: militons")'.[73] For Barthes, in other words, bourgeois ideology is a murmur, a babble, a kind of speech, and the opponent of ideology is forced either into a counter-babble or into silence. Barthes himself wishes to occupy neither of these positions, and his response is to emphasize *writing* as a mixed term between the noisy speech of ideology and the counter-speech or silent action of the revolutionary. This explains why drift is a figure of writing, for writing shares both the subjective silence of the militant (the decision to work against bourgeois society and for its 'other') and the complicitous speech of a particular culture (which pulls us back into a recognition of the subject's collusion with the language of ideology— 'notre langage vient d'elle'). This is ultimately why drift prevails over the celebration of absolute 'otherness', which can be asserted (and is asserted many times over in Barthes's Utopian moments) but cannot be represented. Drift, a paradoxical mixture of stasis and movement, of collusion and distance, is one way Barthes figures writing as a

---

[72] *RB*, 108.   [73] *SFL*, 15.

solution to (or dissolution of) the antinomies of his culture. It can include fragmentation and dissemination among its tactics, since drift is a complication of, rather than an escape from, the binary opposites of ideology: it consists in finding pockets of resistance within that ideology rather than attempting to leap outside it.

One such pocket of resistance, for instance, may consist of some of the pleasures of bourgeois society. 'Son rêve (avouable?) serait de transporter dans une société socialiste certains des *charmes* (je ne dis pas: des valeurs) de l'art de vivre bourgeois (il y en a—il y en avait quelques-uns): c'est ce qu'il appelle le *contretemps*.'[74] Presumably one of these charms is identified on page 24 of the same work: 'De génération en génération, le thé: indice bourgeois et charme certain.' Barthes's representations of a post-revolutionary society as socialism plus high tea is, however, as he makes clear, the vision of a *writer*, someone who can prefigure the release of a signifying practice (such as drinking tea—rather more bourgeois in France than Britain) from its ideological magma: Barthes talks, in connection with *le contretemps*, of an *échappée du Signifiant*. In this way, just as Loti drifting around the Orient is both inside and outside the East, Barthes attempts to inscribe 'the other', the East, into his own writing—and for Barthes, the East is partly the languorous Levant of Loti, partly (and less enthusiastically) the China of the Cultural Revolution, but above all the Japan whose heady mixture of feudalism and modernism, full signs and empty meanings, is celebrated in *L'Empire des signes*.

But this inscription is also an attempt to overcome the orientalist paradigm (West/East): already it is clear that an East that contains Loti, Mao Zedong, and the Japan of Bunraku theatre, Zen gardens, and Sumo wrestling is difficult to essentialize: in his responses to *this* East, Barthes is responding to something within himself, and he acts as one of the sites in which the coherence and homogeneity of the West can begin to release their potential for dissemination and renewal—their drift towards Utopia or the even more enigmatic loss of place Barthes calls 'atopia'.

FROM UTOPIA TO ATOPIA

Barthes par lui-même oscillates between claiming that the writer needs to prepare the way for radically new social forms by presenting images

[74] *RB*, 64.

of Utopia, and deciding that *l'atopie*—an undecidable mixture of old and new—is better than the absolute newness of *l'utopie*. The former argument, in praise of the idea of Utopia, is presented in the fragment 'A quoi sert l'utopie'. Barthes reflects that Utopia enables the writer to begin writing: the image of Utopia (as the 'good place', the place where 'all would be well', the *eu-topia*, rather than just the place that at present does not exist, is nowhere, *ou-topia*) shows up the present world in its dereliction, allows its disgrace to be seen. Utopia thus creates meaning.

> A quoi sert l'utopie? A faire du sens. Face au présent, à mon présent, l'utopie est un terme second qui permet de faire jouer le déclic du signe: le discours sur le réel devient possible, je sors de l'aphasie où me plonge l'affolement de tout ce qui ne va pas en moi, dans ce monde qui est le mien.[75]

Barthes here seems quite prepared to think of *utopie* as in some sense the negation of and alternative to the present, without asking from where this image of otherness derives its authority. And in this fragment he also revises some other earlier statements. Whereas the political theory developed in *les écrits révolutionnaires* has to keep the question of human freedom open, without prejudging the answer, the writer—contrary to Barthes's many indications in other texts—dares to answer the question with a vision of futurity. 'L'utopie serait alors le tabou de la Révolution, et l'écrivain aurait à charge de le transgresser.'[76] This is an interesting manœuvre: to claim that the writer—even the left-wing writer—can give us images of Utopia, be affirmative as well as negative, sets Barthes apart from the suspicion directed towards Utopianism in much Marxist thought. (Marx's own theories were partly formed in reaction against the Utopian imaginings of Proudhon, Saint-Simon, and Barthes's own much-admired Fourier: this century the work of the Frankfurt School has tended to concentrate on the critique of the present—Adorno's 'negative dialectics'—rather than dwelling on any future reconciliation: it is far rarer to find a political theorist such as Ernst Bloch actively seeking out and developing the positive images in which people have constantly embodied their hopes for the future, as in *The Principle of Hope*.) For Barthes, the writer (whose function is here implicitly distinguished from that of the

---

[75] *RB*, 80.
[76] Ibid. 81. An earlier essay, 'La Réponse de Kafka' (1960) (*EC*, 138–42), had suggested that the writer's answer must be a way of keeping the question open: in *RB*, Barthes is prepared to allow the writer to fill the empty form of Utopia with some determinate content.

political theoretician or the activist) acknowledges the taboo on representations of the positive—but also breaks it.

So although Barthes begins with a binary opposition (present time/ Utopian future) which he seems to respect, by the end of the fragment he has suggested that the writer overcomes that opposition by seeing the present in the light of an imagined future. Utopia is the binary opposite of the present (so that there is a danger that images of the future will be mere negations of that present, automatic and resentful 'reactions' against it in the Nietzschean sense). But one can also say, vice versa, that the present is the binary opposite of the future (so that the miseries of the present are illuminated by the idea that they could be changed): in this case, Utopia is the active and radiant image that shows up the morose negativities of the present. Barthes's sense of the interplay between present time and Utopian future is acute, and he shows that the 'otherness' of the second term (Utopian future) cannot be absolute. It also brings him closer to Adorno than one would expect, since Adorno, in an untypical (but powerful) moment, the last fragment ('Finale') of *Minima Moralia*, equally demonstrates how inseparable Utopia is from any attempt to evaluate a present that has always fallen both from its past and, even more, from its future:

The only philosophy which can be responsibly practised in face of despair is the attempt to contemplate all things as they would present themselves from the standpoint of redemption. Knowledge has no light but that shed on the world by redemption: all else is reconstruction, mere technique. Perspectives must be fashioned that displace and estrange the world, reveal it to be, with its rifts and crevices, as indigent and distorted as it will appear one day in the messianic light.[77]

The rest of Adorno's fragment is full of complexities that I can go into only briefly here. He suggests that such perspectives should be gained 'without velleity or violence'; that this is both very simple and also absolutely impossible, since it requires 'a standpoint removed, even though by a hair's breadth, from the scope of existence' (in other words it must move outside the given); and that all knowledge (and, presumably, all images of Utopia which are among the very determinants of such knowledge of the present) is tainted 'by the same distortion and indigence which it seeks to escape'. All these points correspond to notions I have been excerpting from Barthes. Perhaps this can best be seen by citing the 'finale' of one of *his* works. At the

---

[77] Theodor Adorno, *Minima Moralia: Reflections from Damaged Life*, trans. E. F. N. Jephcott (London, 1974), 247.

end of *Le Degré zéro de l'écriture* Barthes reflects on the indictment of literature that he has drawn up: separated out from social languages which it strives in vain to rejoin, and frozen into a reified cultural form, literature bears the stigmata of alienation imprinted on it by the failure of history to realize its dream of emancipation. *And yet* it is still, ambiguously, the place in which Utopian longings can be sheltered.

Il y a donc dans toute écriture présente une double postulation: il y a le mouvement d'une rupture et celui d'un avènement, il y a le dessin même de toute situation révolutionnaire, dont l'ambiguïté fondamentale est qu'il faut bien que la Révolution puise dans ce qu'elle veut détruire l'image même de ce qu'elle veut posséder.[78]

Dreaming forward, avidly if guiltily, to a time when it will no longer be alienated, 'la Littérature devient l'Utopie du langage'. Both Barthes and Adorno, in other words, suggest that properly Utopian thinking involves treating binary oppositions (present time/Utopian future, for instance) with a dialectical subtlety that is closer to Barthes's drift than to any more directly oppositional stance.

Whatever the drift of Barthes's musings on utopia, he is sometimes concerned to emphasize the pathos of the choice facing the avantgarde writer, and ties this choice down to an either/or. Convinced (for reasons that I have already suggested need to be questioned) that neither *la signifiance*, that mode of meaning in which the violence of Western semiosis will have been defused, nor *jouissance*, the challenging sense of lost bearings, lost identities, and lost essences, can be produced by mass culture, Barthes surmises that such a writer is faced to seek *signifiance* and *jouissance* where they have taken refuge, in

une alternative excessive: ou bien dans une pratique mandarinale (issue d'une *exténuation* de la culture bourgeoise), ou bien dans une idée utopique (celle d'une culture à venir, surgie d'une révolution *radicale, inouïe, imprévisible*, dont celui qui écrit aujourd'hui ne sait qu'une chose: c'est que, tel Moïse, il n'y entrera pas).[79]

Either, to echo the terms of the preface to *Sade, Fourier, Loyola*, the fragmentation and dissemination of bourgeois culture (which is, for Barthes, *all* culture): or Utopia—but a Utopia which the writer will never enter. The 'either' seems close to drift as I have been describing it: the 'or' is the leap into the radically 'other'.

But this 'or' is more complex than it seems. On the one hand,

---

[78] *DZ*, 64.   [79] *PlT*, 63.

Moses was indeed the destroyer of images, thundering against the Israelites who wanted Utopia now and worshipped an idol (the Golden Calf). This prophetic Moses is echoed by those (Adorno again) who refuse to indulge in Utopian images. But there is another negation to Moses: he did not enter Palestine. And this affects Barthes's simile (the writer is like Moses) in another way. Either today's writer will not reach Utopia because Utopia will take more than a lifetime to achieve, or, on a deeper level, the Utopia figured in the writer's works may be of a kind that is impossible to realize as such: it may reside only in writing (which is not to deny that its force may help to bring about a *different* Utopia). Indeed, Barthes's equation of the avant-garde writer with Moses is even more complex, since the 'pure writing' he advocates (writing as a practice, as a text released from the alienated meanings inscribed into present-day literary production) is itself a Utopian image, a 'not yet'. The literary text itself (and not just the reality it prefigures) is still to come, as the title of Blanchot's *Le Livre à venir*, which explores this notion, suggests. The writer today is pointing both towards Utopia (the Promised Land) and towards a yet-to-be-achieved writing which would be fully *adequate* to that Utopia. All of which suggests that Barthes's drift is less casual than it may appear: it shares some of the pathos attached to the image, frequently encountered today, of writing as wandering (as Moses and the Israelites wandered): writing is drift as nomadic and homeless, lost in the desert of the present. Derrida, Levinas, and Deleuze and Guattari have all (in very different ways) explored such an image. There is for instance a sense in which *la dérive* shares some of the features of Derrida's *différance*. It acknowledges the past (for the text is always already written, the revolution's values necessarily taken from today's reality), but it also plunges forward, both in its refusal to rest in any definitive signified, and in a movement which Derrida 'shockingly' locates in Heidegger, and calls hope.[80] Taking the Cultural Revolution as the absolutely new, as did *Tel Quel* ('Vive la pensée-maotsétoung!') certainly injected a novel theoretical discourse into the world of Gaullist France, but it was idolatrous and premature in reifying the Cultural Revolution as something absolutely 'other' (as the 'révolution *radicale, inouïe, imprévisible*' to which Barthes looks forward—but for which his models are tentative, and almost entirely literary or textual).[81]

---

[80] This occurs in the discussion of Heidegger with which 'La Différance' ends, in *Marges—de la philosophie*, 1–29 (29).

[81] Barthes shows a less absolute and more sociological awareness of the problems of

Barthes's obliquities and hesitations, his complications of the binary oppositions West/East, self/other, old/new, present time/Utopian future, can thus lead to rather delicate balancing acts. His visit to China, in company with other *Tel Quel* writers—all of whom were far more enthusiastic about the Cultural Revolution—produced a curious text, first published in *Le Monde*, and later separately as *Alors la Chine?* Its difficulty lies above all in its attempt not to say what he thinks about the revolutionary republic, but to write it, to produce a text in which his affirmations and hesitations would be at work in the language itself rather than being instantaneously converted into revolutionary fervour (or reactionary rejection). In one sense, the strategy did not work, since Barthes's silence was converted into a sign (of something considerably less than enthusiasm). He later acknowledged this in *Barthes par lui-même*: he originally wanted, he claims, to tell his readers that 'il *acquiesçait* dans le silence'.[82] How had his original article written that silence? Partly by concluding with a plea for a special kind of discourse, 'celui d'*une dérive légère*, ou encore d'une envie de silence'.[83] He reacted to China and the yes/no it seemed to demand by evading the choice, going for a drifting, musing response. Writing, for him, was thus a way of deferring speech, perhaps for ever: what he wants to say is a sympathetic 'No comment', and he has signified this by his tenuous ellipses and his brief visions of what for him was important about China. (He rather beautifully evokes a China whose main characteristic is a strangely attractive *fadeur*, a certain insipidity or blandness: this is certainly preferable to celebrating the violence of the Cultural Revolution, but it is deliberately elusive.) But the fact that the readers of *Le Monde* felt obliged to turn this ambivalent writing into an either/or, a statement *pro* or *contra* China, meant that Barthes was caught in a trap already described by Bacon. 'They will so beset a man with questions, and draw him on, and pick it out of him, that, without an absurd silence, he must show an inclination one

---

avant-garde art and progressive politics in some of his interviews. In one given to *Le Figaro* in 1974, he discriminates between politics (in which the revolution may occur violently and abruptly) and culture (in which 'aucune révolution ne peut faire l'économie d'une longue période de contradictions': the objection that avant-garde writers are politically ineffectual usually comes, he notes, from 'milieux bourgeois, qui ont de la révolution une idée paradoxalement plus souveraine que les révolutionnaires eux-mêmes' ('Roland Barthes contre les idées reçues', in *GV*, 179–85 (180–1)).

[82] *RB*, 52.
[83] *Alors la Chine?* (1975), 14, my emphasis.

way; or if he do not, they will gather as much by his silence as by his speech.'[84]

I refer to Bacon because, in another attempt to alert us to the masks forced upon the writer (the social roles writers are forced to adopt, as well as those they frequently assume as a deliberate disguise), Barthes takes Bacon's 'simulator in the affirmative' ('when a man industriously and expressly feigns and pretends to be that he is not') as an emblematic figure of the pleasure of the text, and by extension, of subversion from within.[85] In *Alors la Chine?* his *hallucination négative* of China is a tactical response to 'la façon dont beaucoup d'Occidentaux hallucinent de leur côté la Chine populaire: selon un mode dogmatique, violemment affirmatif/négatif ou faussement libéral'.[86]

I would draw three points from this episode. The first is that Barthes found himself struggling against the entrenched image of the battling and voluble French intellectual, not only active and committed, but prepared to convey this *prise de position* in speech. The heroic icons of this commitment, in recent times, are Sartre, Beauvoir, and Foucault; Voltaire and Zola (the author of 'J'accuse') are their forebears. Barthes, part of a slow mutation in the status of the intellectual, suffered greatly by comparison with figures such as these, or even with his colleagues at *Tel Quel*: 'ce que réclame le public intellectuel, c'est un *choix*: il fallait sortir de la Chine comme un taureau qui jaillit du toril dans l'arène comble: furieux ou triomphant'.[87] Alain Robbe-Grillet suggests, in his 'autobiographical' *Le Miroir qui revient*, that Barthes was to continue, unavailingly, to struggle against the *idée fixe* that he was a thinker, one who represents universal claims to a heterogeneous public.[88]

Secondly, and on a less ethological level (aware of the demands made on the intellectual caste in France, Barthes frequently envisaged an *Éthologie des intellectuels*), he was also expressing a desire for a form

[84] 'Of Simulation and Dissimulation', *The Essays*, ed. John Pitcher (Hamondsworth, 1985), 76–8 (77–8).

[85] Ibid. 77. See *P/T*, 9: 'Le plaisir du texte: tel le simulateur de Bacon, il peut dire: *ne jamais s'excuser, ne jamais s'expliquer.*'

[86] *Alors la Chine?*, 14.

[87] *RB*, 52.

[88] *Le Miroir qui revient* (1984), 63–4. The change in the notion of what constitutes intellectual commitment in France has been charted by Jean-François Lyotard, in *Tombeau de l'intellectuel et autres papiers* (1984). Françoise Gaillard makes Barthes part of this mutation: 'Avec Roland Barthes, c'est une autre figure de l'intellectuel qui s'esquisse, celle de l'intellectuel dissolvant et non opposant' ('Barthes juge de Roland', *Communications*, 36 (Oct. 1982), 75–83 (79)).

of political engagement that might be written, rather than spoken: this was part of a far-reaching endeavour to understand the ways in which writing was becoming a model of practice in general, and hence what forms a written politics might take.[89]

Il veut bien être *sujet*, mais non *parleur* politique (le *parleur*: celui qui débite son discours, le raconte, et en même temps le notifie, le signe). Et c'est parce qu'il ne parvient pas à décoller le réel politique de son discours général, *répété*, que le politique lui est forclos . . . c'est comme s'il était le témoin historique d'une contradiction: celle d'un sujet politique *sensible, avide et silencieux* (il ne faut pas séparer ces mots).[90]

This hostility to political 'speech' (and speechifying) and the counter-vailing quest for a political 'writing' is a leitmotif that runs through Barthes's work, and I will be examining it in more detail later.

The third point is that Barthes's resistance to Utopia derives partly from his feeling that any candidate for Utopian status in the real world of politics and history is going, eventually, to disappoint. (Twentieth-century history provides considerable support for his view, not least in the case of China.) His notion of drift is a response to this: although the casualness of drift seems to imply considerable collusion with the *status quo* (as the character Loti in *Aziyadé* never really *rejects* the imperialist expansionism of the British Empire whose subject he is), its potentially, if implicitly, critical detachment must not be forgotten. Even the discourse of Utopia (celebrating it when it is located—in Maoist China for instance) always risks being too brutal: above all, to return to his considerations in 'A quoi sert l'utopie', Utopia is a mechanism of meaning, and it shares the violent divisiveness of binary oppositions that underlie all meaning. So, in a different fragment from *Barthes par lui-même*, called 'L'Atopie', he contrasts Utopian discourse with its atopian derivative.

Fiché: je suis fiché, assigné à un lieu (intellectuel), à une résidence de caste (sinon de classe). Contre quoi une seule doctrine intérieure: celle de l'*atopie* (de l'habitacle en dérive). L'atopie est supérieure à l'utopie (l'utopie est réactive, tactique, littéraire, elle procède du sens et le fait marcher).[91]

Barthes takes refuge in his floating boat, his *habitacle en dérive*, from the world of public images. This is a *doctrine intérieure* and in some ways a retreat. But what is internalized in drift is not just the high-flying dream: it is also meaning as the place of identities and imagos.

---

[89] For the projected *Éthologie des intellectuels*, see *RB*, 153.
[90] Ibid. 57. [91] Ibid. 53.

If the binary oppositions still operative in Utopian thinking are internalized, they are thereby complicated: the lines of division need no longer run between self and other but between self and self. So atopia is one way in which Barthes refuses to occupy any of the positions offered him by public discourse, since he refuses to accept either that they are the only positions available ('Alors la Chine?'— 'J'aime/Je n'aime pas') or that he, as subject, can overcome the contradictions within himself by smoothly adopting a fixed persona.[92] So although Barthes sometimes accepts the need for the writer (especially, perhaps, the 'imaginative' writer or, in more Barthesian language, the creator of Fictions) to develop images of Utopia, he at other times responds to the intellectual's need to demonstrate choice and commitment (in the name of tacit Utopian values such as emancipation and enlightenment) by refusing to voice such commitment in any but indirect ways, in case one falls prey to the temptation of identifying—idolatrously and prematurely—any present reality with Utopia. Atopia, so to speak, is the mental (or written—but not spoken) reservation that leads Barthes to abstain from giving any definitive assent to images of Utopia that might be generated by current political developments.

Barthes's argument—his drift from Utopia to atopia, from any topos (any geographical or rhetorical place) that is affirmed as *eu-topos* (a good place), to a loss of all topoi (and thus the loss of such identities and meanings)—may seem peculiarly tortured (at least as I have tried to summarize it), but it is one way in which he responds to the problem he inherited from Sartre: that of *engagement*. Barthes's hesitations may seem far less inspiring than Sartre's commitment to commitment, but he is honest in facing up to the complexities and traps that await anyone who wants to register a belief in certain values while refusing to treat language as merely a tool for the expression of such values. This in turn suggests that Barthes is, in his post-1970 works especially, constantly drifting between the role of intellectual (expected, at least in France, to voice opinions on current affairs) and that of writer (in the more problematic and frequently discredited sense of one whose first commitment is always to language). This suggests in turn that it may be where Barthes does not seem to be conveying explicitly political opinions that his politics may be most

---

[92] Barthes sets out his likes and dislikes in a deliberately pell-mell form, emphasizing the chaos of tastes and revulsions that arranges itself around a binary opposition, in the fragment 'J'aime/je n'aime pas', *RB*, 120–1.

insistent—silently written and difficult to read: perhaps even 'unreadable', and thus 'writable', in other words offered to the reader as the pretext of a whole set of new practices. This distinction between readable and writable texts is found in *S/Z*, where Barthes distinguishes between readable, classical texts (such as nineteenth-century realist novels), whose reading may terminate in commentary, judgement, and opinion, and radical avant-garde texts, which are unreadable but writable. The latter, in other words, cannot be interpreted or evaluated by current criteria, and they therefore lead us to rewrite those criteria: such texts cannot be judged realistic or unrealistic, for instance, because they seem to suspend the pertinence of that opposition, forcing us to ask again what we mean by realism (and therefore what we mean by reality). Barthes's atopia, his *inner* doctrine of drift, is in this sense a *recul pour mieux sauter*—or, as it were, a *dérive pour mieux agir*. For the idea that politics may be a text, and thus writable (a practice of writing), rather than an array of all-too-readable stereotypes, is a possibility that Barthes entertains in a fragment of *Barthes par lui-même* entitled 'Le Texte politique': the political is both *ennui* and *jouissance* (so that the position of the subject in it is never secure, but always exposed—adrift); it is also (again like drift) a complex and communal space, one beyond binary division and the Manichaean tendencies of judgemental positioning—it is 'un espace obstinément polysémique, le lieu privilégié d'une interprétation perpétuelle (si elle est suffisamment systématique, une interprétation n'y sera jamais démentie, à l'infini)'.[93] Barthes suggests on the basis of these observations—in which he is far less hostile to political discourse than usual—that 'le Politique est du *textuel* pur: une forme exorbitante, exaspérée, du Texte, une forme inouïe qui, par ses débordements et ses masques, dépasse peut-être notre entendement actuel du Texte'.[94] Politics (or rather 'the political'— Barthes here silently discriminates between *le politique* and *la politique*) would thus be a text beyond the text, one that we practise without necessarily being able to read (to interpret in any definite way). *Le politique*, as a set of discourses, theories, and practices considered in the abstract, is preferred to *la politique*, it seems, because of Barthes's general lack of interest in the institutions of French political life, especially political parties, that he identifies with *la politique*. (Indeed, for him, *la politique* sometimes seems close to what the French sceptically call *la politique politicienne*—the undignified politicking of

---

[93] *RB*, 150.   [94] Ibid.

politicos. This has been a topos of one particular *doxa* since at least de Gaulle, and it is interesting that Barthes takes so little trouble to distance himself from it—though he is not alone, even among left-wing writers, in sharing this unease about the ways 'politics' is institutionalized.)

At all events, the distinction is Barthes's way of keeping the political—as 'writing', as 'text': as practice and transformation. But he leaves us in no doubt as to the vulnerability of his enterprise. His comments make most sense when seen in two contexts. The first is Barthes's refusal to allow the functions of the writer to be taken over by theory or politics: the latter, he claims, need direct (and transitive) discourse, whereas the writer (the kind of writer he increasingly identifies with) is committed to the *indirections* of language. The second is the European post-war questioning of traditional forms of belief and commitment (in politics and religion). Binary opposites (of the cold-war kind) no longer seem so pertinent: in the 1970s in France, the accelerating turnover of ideological options (Philippe Sollers at *Tel Quel* being a particularly bracing case, moving from fellow-travelling pro-Communist literary experimentalism, via Maoism, to a fascination with the United States and Roman Catholicism, almost in the space of a decade) made it increasingly difficult to identify in what topos Utopian aspirations could be found. Barthes's *doctrine intérieure* of writing as drift, obliquely dissenting from all positions, ironically detached but sensitive and avid even in his silence, was one way of sheltering such dreams from the funereal laws governing the clash of intellectual languages. As such, it was as fragile, and as resistant, as any other movement in which dreams and aspirations are internalized and then released again into circulation— as in the Mallarmé sonnet:

> Quand l'ombre menaça de la fatale loi
> Tel vieux Rêve, désir et mal de mes vertèbres,
> Affligé de périr sous les plafonds funèbres
> Il a ployé son aile indubitable en moi.[95]

Mallarmé interiorizes his dream and externalizes this manœuvre in the public act of writing a poem. What his poem says (the affirmation of a certain move inwards) is complicated by his performance of it *as*

[95] Mallarmé, 'Quand l'ombre menaça de la fatale loi', from 'Plusieurs sonnets', in *Poésies* (1945).

writing.[96] Barthes adopts a *doctrine intérieure* and then discusses it in public, as in *Barthes par lui-même*. In both cases the outer is made inner and the new interiority then extroverted. Drift is such a complication, a folding in discourse ('Il a *ployé* son aile'). Barthes's interiorization (his drift) was a particularly exposed position in the 1970s. But that is what, for him, writing (as the public and communal performance of a singularity) was about.

LYOTARD'S DRIFT

Barthes shares his questioning of the way politics tends to operate on the basis of outmoded evaluative schemes with Jean-François Lyotard, whose collection of essays *Dérive à partir de Marx et Freud* suggests other ways of understanding drift against a political background. (The very notion of drift is of course difficult to imagine without there being some background against which it is read.) The opening piece in the collection of essays is itself entitled 'Dérives': Lyotard worries about the fact that a preface tends to emphasize the unity of a book, whereas he is concerned, on the contrary, to ensure that the thoughts contained within the book's covers are disseminated and dispersed, that any imaginary unity that might envelope them is torn apart. He asks why he has decided to preface essays that should be allowed to speak for themselves, and replies: 'Non pour en donner la clé, l'unité, mais plutôt pour les faire dériver un peu plus fort qu'il n'apparaît.'[97] And Lyotard goes on to make several claims for the kind of writing that he has produced, and for the effects he hopes it will have. Each text, he suggests, has a potential capacity for displacement, *un principe de déplaçabilité*, that he identifies with the energy of *Verschiebbarkeit* Freud detected in the dream-work.[98] This displacement of energy means that the important thing about a text is not the way it seems centred on its meaning (for that meaning is, in any case, striated and contradictory), but rather its power to make things happen—to produce *effects*, whether these take the form of other texts or of

---

[96] See the discussion of this sonnet by Malcolm Bowie, 'Genius at nightfall: Mallarmé's "Quand l'ombre menaça de la fatale loi . . ."', in Christopher Prendergast (ed.), *Nineteenth–Century French Poetry: Introductions to Close Reading*, (Cambridge, 1990), 225–42.

[97] *Dérive à partir de Marx et Freud* (1973), 5.

[98] See e.g. *The Interpretation of Dreams*, in *The Pelican Freud Library*, ed. Angela Richards, (Harmondsworth, 1973–86), iv. 417. Lyotard has shown great interest in Freud's idea of the dream-work (*Traumarbeit*), which 'does not think'.

'peintures, photographies, séquences de film, actions politiques, décisions, inspirations érotiques, refus d'obéir, initiatives écono- miques'.[99] Drift (which, Lyotard points out, has carried him away from any 'positions' he may have occupied at the time of writing these essays) means a breaking down of the barrier between the text and whatever tends to be predicated as the text's 'other' ('the real', 'the world'). This questioning of a restrictive binary paradigm, as well as the disregard for metalinguistic distance, is clearly an element in Barthes's own thinking on drift.

   Lyotard's texts do not attempt to dictate the form taken by the praxis they stimulate. None the less, Lyotard's discussion opens out on to the political scene of France in the 1960s and 1970s more explicitly than most of the texts in which Barthes talks of drift. Lyotard repeats that his attitude to the left-wing currents of thought available during these two decades is not one of critique, but one of drift: those traditions (of revolutionary communism, anarchism, or social democratic reform) tended to insist on a certain effectiveness (they wanted to change things, to exercise some form of power): Lyotard responds by questioning the very need for effectiveness. This reply in itself pre-empts the possible accusation that the leftist groups whose vicissitudes Lyotard is describing were ultimately powerless to change the political situation. This, counters Lyotard, is really no argument at all. For if Lyotard and his comrades on the review *Socialisme ou barbarie* were ineffectual, 'c'était les choses qui déri- vaient et se montraient efficaces'.[100] In the face of the experiments carried out by students and others, political parties and *groupuscules* were impotent: and Lyotard suggests that the very criterion of effectiveness tends to be reactionary, since one judges the effective- ness of an action by whether it changes things by the criteria of a theory or practice *already in operation*.

> Il n'y a pas d'efficacité révolutionnaire, parce que l'efficacité est un concept et une pratique de pouvoir, contre-révolutionnaire en son principe; il y a une perception et une production de mots, pratiques, formes, qui peuvent être révolutionnaires sans garantie si elles sont assez sensibles pour dériver selon les grands courants, les grands *Triebe*, les flux majeurs qui vont venir déplacer tous les dispositifs visibles et changer la notion même d'opérativité.[101]

Drift means that the standards of judgement are themselves affected by practice—which means they are impossible to *apply* in any imme-

---

[99] *Dérive à partir de Marx et Freud*, 6.
[100] Ibid. 12.   [101] Ibid.

diate way. This is perhaps the force of Lyotard's *sans garantie*—there is no guarantee because there is no scientific standpoint that remains impervious to change and history. And it can be seen as a parallel to Barthes's demand for a writable rather than just readable politics.

Lyotard's preface to *Dérive à partir de Marx et Freud* (published as a book at about the same time, 1973, that the notion of drift begins to appear increasingly frequently in Barthes) suggests three things. First, it is a feature of drift itself that it is not part of any author's idiolect: in attempting to discover how the term drift *works* in Barthes, we do not (indeed, cannot) content ourselves with a lexical examination of all the occasions on which Barthes sees fit to bring in this enigmatic term. It is legitimate for us to drift away from Barthes's texts into other textual sites, to see what *they* do with drift, what drift does with them. In the same way, Lyotard detects a certain form of drift in the Freudian notions of *Verschiebbarkeit* and *Trieb*, and Barthes too, as we have seen, alludes in his essay on *Aziyadé* to the way Lacan raised the possibility of translating Freud's word for the drive, *Trieb*, by the French *dérive*.[102]

Secondly, drift itself is less a word, concept, or tactic to be interpreted, than a figure of openness whose effect is merely that it has effects that transcend any effectiveness laid down beforehand. Drift thus becomes a figure of writing as force (as drive, in both the common and the psychoanalytical sense of the word), inscribing certain dispositions in the reader, reactions that themselves cannot be predicted, theoretically exhausted or metalinguistically managed.

Thirdly, drift, in both Barthes and Lyotard, can be seen as a critique of the idea of any large-scale strategy. A strategy cannot respond rapidly enough to historical changes: it needs to be replaced by the idea of a tactic. What is a tactic if not a microstrategy? The difference, which can never be absolute, lies in the way history is imagined: as large-scale narrative (which suggests a need for long-range strategies) or as a complex field of dispersal in which the important thing is a flexible capacity to cope, tactically, with surprises.[103] These surprises may be aesthetic or political—or both. As Barthes puts it, in what he

---

[102] 'Nous relevons ici le gant du défi qu'on nous porte à traduire du nom d'instinct ce que Freud appelle *Trieb*: ce que *drive* traduirait assez bien en anglais, mais qu'on y évite, et ce pour quoi le mot *dérive* serait en français notre recours de désespoir, au cas où nous n'arriverions pas à donner à la bâtardise du mot *pulsion* son point de frappe' (Jacques Lacan, 'Subversion du sujet et dialectique du désir', in *Écrits* (1977), 793–827 (803)).

[103] The opposition between tactic and strategy can be seen at work in the suspicion of grand narratives expressed by Lyotard in *La Condition postmoderne* (1979).

suggests might be an addendum to *Le Plaisir du texte*: 'la jouissance, ce n'est pas ce qui *répond* au désir (le satisfait), mais ce qui le surprend, l'excède, le déroute, le *dérive*'.[104] Since Barthes (like Lyotard) re-evaluates history in the light of modernist narrative experiments, thus questioning the image of history as a traditional grand narrative, his attention to the historicity of his terms leads to their being figured as local, transitory, and singular.[105]

Barthes's fragment 'Tactique/stratégie' expressed this clearly. 'Le mouvement de son œuvre est tactique: il s'agit de se déplacer, de barrer, comme aux barres, mais non de conquérir.'[106] He gives examples of tactical notions that are drifting negativities, refusing to settle into positivity. The idea of literary ambiguity is one such negativity: it has little value in itself: 'ce n'est qu'une petite machine de guerre contre la loi philologique, la tyrannie universitaire du sens droit'. His work is thus '*une tactique sans stratégie*': its war-machines, brought into action in local skirmishes and then dismantled, resemble those celebrated by Deleuze and Guattari. The drifter is, as I have already suggested, a nomad.[107]

WAITING FOR A BREAK

As part of any general investigation of the theme of drift, Derrida's frequent use and eventual suspicion of the term needs to be noted.

J'ai abusé de ce mot, il ne me satisfait guère. *Dérive* désigne un mouvement trop continu: plutôt indifférencié, trop homogène, il paraît éloigner sans saccade d'une origine supposée, d'une rive encore, et d'un bord au trait invisible.[108]

---

[104] *RB*, 116 ('*le dérive*'—my emphasis).

[105] In *Le Différend* Lyotard steers a careful course between the demands of the universal and the respect due to the singular.

[106] *RB*, 175.

[107] Deleuze and Guattari set out the theory of nomads and their war-machines, forever harrying the bloated, sedentary power of the state, in *Capitalisme et schizophrénie*, ii. *Mille plateaux* (1980) (434–527). They discuss the existence of a ' "science mineure", ou "nomade" ', one which works in terms of *devenir* and *hétérogénéité*, and take the Lucretian *clinamen* as an example of how such a science works: 'la fameuse déclinaison de l'atome fournit un tel modèle d'hétérogénéité, et de passage ou de devenir dans l'hétérogène ... Le *clinamen*, c'est le plus petit angle par lequel l'atome s'écarte de la droite. C'est un passage à la limite, un modèle "exhaustif", paradoxal' (447). This 'smallest angle' is that of drift, as Ch. 2, below, will make clearer.

[108] 'Spéculer—sur "Freud" ', in *La Carte postale de Socrate à Freud et au-delà* (1980), 279.

But Derrida also casts suspicion on another intellectual myth: that of the epistemological break, a discursive revolution of the kind brought about by Marx and Freud. The notion of the epistemological break has dominated much twentieth-century French thinking: its avatars can be found in Bachelard, Foucault, and Althusser. For instance, Althusser detected a *coupure épistémologique* in Marx's work, a break which occurred around 1845 and divided the early Marx (Utopian, Hegelian, and humanist) from the mature Marx (scientific and structuralist, seeing productive forces and relations rather than individual human beings as the motor of history).

Barthes sometimes situates his own work within the parameters of the modernism opened up by Marx, Freud, and Nietzsche. He tends to accept, with Foucault, that these three represent a new epistēmē, a new order of knowledge: he does not, as Derrida does (in *Positions*), pick the notion of such a break to pieces.[109] His own contributions to literary theory (his view that the old idea of an *œuvre*, with a closure and a meaning guaranteed by the intentions of an identifiable and unified authorial presence, is mutating into the new epistemological object he calls *texte*, for instance) are located very much as late swerves within this modernist epistēmē: this particular shift from work to text 'participe d'un glissement épistémologique, plus que d'une véritable coupure ... Ce que l'Histoire, notre Histoire, nous permet aujourd'hui, c'est seulement de glisser, de varier, de dépasser, de répudier.'[110] This is Barthes as the writer of lateness and decadence: his modernism is frequently a late and eclectic version of modernism, as well as summing up the achievements of that modernism in a new and invigorating set of theoretical retrospectives. Drift would thus be a 'dandy' tactic *faute de mieux*, for lack, that is, of anything radically new 'dans une situation historique donnée—de pessimisme et de rejet'.[111] It coexists with the *fin de siècle* sense of an ending expressed in *Leçon*, Barthes's inaugural lecture at the Collège de France: we can explore a 'desacralized' literature in the ways we want to: this is a 'moment d'apocalypse douce, moment historique de la plus grande jouissance'.[112]

But the metaphor of writing as *text* (as woven tissue) is, in any case, better able to cope with drift than with the notion of a break. (An alternative view, of course, would be that the dismissal of the notion

---

[109] 'Sémiologie et grammatologie', in *Positions*, 25–50 (35).
[110] 'De l'œuvre au texte', in *BL*, 69–77 (69–70).
[111] *RB*, 110.   [112] *L*, 41.

of the epistemological break is a pernicious result of seeing history in merely textual terms.) This is why even a relatively apocalyptic form of writing, such as that of Derrida (for whom we may be emerging from the closure of metaphysics towards revolutions that as yet have no name) is still extremely cautious about the very notion of apocalypse, far less strident than, for instance, Foucault in issuing obituaries for man. (Derrida's essay *Sur un ton apocalyptique naguère adopté en philosophie* is his most detailed analysis of the apocalyptic mood.) It is significant that when Derrida, who like Barthes frequently employs the metaphor of text as woven, rejects the concept of such a break, he relies on precisely this metaphor: 'je ne crois pas à la rupture décisive, à l'unicité d'une "coupure épistémologique", comme on le dit souvent aujourd'hui. Les coupures se réinscrivent toujours, fatalement, dans un tissu ancien qu'il faut continuer à défaire, interminablement.'[113] This textualization of history questions any premature idea of a break: it is a parallel to the realization that metaphysics can be subverted only from within. And if we are condemned to unpicking the threads of metaphysics, only to involuntarily recompose the warp and the weft of our tradition, Penelope at home in Ithaca, spinning and unspinning, is a better figure of writing than Alexander of Macedon, who, cutting rather than untying the Gordian knot, can stand as a figure of the epistemological break. For Derrida, drift is too continuous an image for the way ideas change with time, and the epistemological break too discontinuous.

But drift in Barthes is not as homogeneous as Derrida, referring to his own texts, imagines it: drift in Barthes attempts to suspend the opposition between continuity and discontinuity, to find the heterogeneous other inside—not outside—the self (and vice versa). Indeed, drift for Barthes is the figure which attempts to move beyond all binary oppositions (all meaning as antithetical), even if those oppositions have to be posed before they can be drifted out of. Sometimes he finds other names for this manœuvre. One is *corps*: the body is never exhausted by the binary opposites of the symbolic order of language, and constantly subverts them. For example, the narrator of Balzac's *Sarrasine* is sitting 'dans l'embrasure d'une fenêtre' and can survey both the warmth and light of the ball taking place inside the house, and the wintry scene in the garden outside: he describes this antithesis—which, as the antithesis between life and death, will run through the story—in absolute and rhetorically charged terms, to

---

[113] *Positions*, 35.

draw the maximum of meaning from it: but his body, lodged between the inside and the outside, is itself disturbingly difficult to locate within the paradigm that it opens up: 'le corps est le lieu de la transgression mise en œuvre par le récit: c'est au niveau du corps que la barre de l'adversion doit sauter, que les deux *inconciliabilia* de l'Antithèse . . . sont appelés à se rejoindre'.[114]

Another name for the locus of drift is *le neutre*: the 'third term', 'neither *a* nor *b*'. The *neutre* is a term taken from linguistics, where *neutralisation* refers to 'la perte du sens dans certaines oppositions pertinentes', so that, continues Barthes, 'le *Neutre*' is for him a 'catégorie éthique . . . nécessaire pour lever la marque intolérable du sens affiché, du sens oppressif'.[115]

And a third locus of drift is praxis: in this case, Barthes takes from Marx the idea that binary oppositions are fundamentally ideological and linguistic, and can be overcome in the real world of social practice (Barthes quotes from the *Economic and Philosophical Manuscripts*: 'C'est seulement dans l'existence sociale que les antinomies telles que subjectivisme et objectivisme, spiritualisme et matérialisme, activité et passivité perdent leur caractère antinomique.')[116]

Thus, as a floating signifier, drift can come to stand for a great number of effects, which may ultimately need to be plottable against some horizon: but within Barthes's texts that horizon—that context—varies. Bourdieu states how easily terms can be reified once taken out of the historical context that gave them dynamic tension and polemical edge.[117] This is correct, but reification befalls over-contextualized terms too: drift, ideally, dissolves this reification. But in so doing, it creates problems for the reader.

READING DRIFT, DRIFTING READING

How are we to read drift? In particular, how are we to read a particularly opaque fragment on drift in *Le Plaisir du texte*? Here is the fragment ('Dérive') in question.

Le plaisir du texte n'est pas forcément de type triomphant, héroïque, musclé. Pas besoin de se cambrer. Mon plaisir peut très bien prendre la forme d'une dérive. La dérive advient chaque fois que *je ne respecte pas le tout*, et qu'à force de paraître emporté ici et là au gré des illusions, séductions, et

---

[114] *S/Z*, 35.   [115] *RB*, 128.   [116] Ibid. 136.
[117] 'Fieldwork in Philosophy', *Choses dites*, 13–46 (27–8).

intimidations de langage, tel un bouchon sur la vague, je reste immobile, pivotant sur la jouissance *intraitable* qui me lie au texte (au monde). Il y a dérive, chaque fois que le langage social, le sociolecte, *me manque* (comme on dit: *le cœur me manque*). Ce pour quoi un autre nom de la dérive, ce serait: *l'Intraitable*—ou peut-être encore: la Bêtise.

Cependant, si l'on y parvenait, dire la dérive serait aujourd'hui un discours suicidaire.[118]

If we were to summarize this fragment's content, where would we begin?

Any paraphrase risks levelling out the text's seductive difficulties and veiled suggestiveness. A rather different, more drifting reading will take the signified into account but, so to speak, only out of the corner of its eye: it will constantly shift its focus back to textual signifiers whose signified keeps flickering uncannily into life, like a star always on the edge of the visual field. A drifting reading will pick out such features of the text as its style—a refusal to define or explain in the terms of what is accepted as theoretical discourse, together with the conversational ellipses ('Pas besoin de se cambrer') which stop the text appearing too intimidatingly terroristic, and the use of triads ('triomphant, héroïque, musclé', 'illusions, séductions, et intimidations de langage') which pull an otherwise wayward fragment back into the codes of French *bien-écrire*. It will note the ambiguous grammar of the opening words, for 'Le plaisir du texte', as well as being the book's title, may reflect the way the text itself is frequently subjectified ('le texte périme les attitudes grammaticales').[119] The pleasure *of* the text is thus a subjective as well as objective genitive. A drifting reading will also note the central development of drift as a *metaphor* (the cork); it will pick out the emphases (the italicization of certain phrases); it will detail the way the text accumulates parallels, uprooting any meaning that its terms might otherwise seem to have (a number of identifications flash out like momentary sparks of sense: text = world: *la dérive* = *l'Intraitable* = *la Bêtise*); it will worry about the empty space separating the text's penultimate sentence from the last sentence, which thus seems to acquire the status of an afterthought, a tentative new direction ('Cependant . . .'); and it will note the grammatically bizarre form of the last sentence (a successful saying of drift would be suicidal—perhaps because drift cannot be said, only written).

Furthermore, in trying to read the fragment, we necessarily stray towards other parts of *Le Plaisir du texte*, thus wondering whether the critique of heroic readings is part of the wider Barthesian critique of intellectual heroics in general. 'Beaucoup trop d'héroïsme encore dans nos langages; dans les meilleurs—je pense à celui de Bataille—, éréthisme de certaines expressions et finalement une sorte d'*héroïsme insidieux.*'[120] We could also ask whether the fact that writing is gratuitous may not throw light on the statement that *dire la dérive* would these days be *un discours suicidaire*, one that negates its own gratuity by bringing drift back into public circulation. We may also want to suggest that there is a link between unsayable drift and unsayable *jouissance.*[121]

While a paraphrase would try to tie the text down (position its themes as signifieds), the drifting reading would allow the text to perform itself as an offer of meaning that is never definitively honoured. But drift itself means that even this statement is too oppositional, polemical, and heroic. It suggests that the 'good' reading floats and drifts, the 'bad' reading defines, limits, grasps at meaning. It is not a question of an opposition, for a drifting reading will encounter meaning-effects as well as pleasure-effects, and they will not always be different. We can read 'Dérive' in *Le Plaisir du texte* driftingly (which uproots any tentative theoretical security we may attain by interpretation), but since to drift is to some extent to ignore metalinguistic instructions, whether overt of covert, of the form 'you must drift', a drifting reading of the fragment on drift may well take the form of an attempt to see what Barthes is saying in paraphrasable, discursive terms. Indeed, if we deliberately decide to drift *in* the text 'Dérive', we are failing to turn back the text's implicit instructions on themselves: even our notion of drift as drift comes from a momentary freezing of that word's meaning (we have to read the text as being 'about' something called 'drift' even though drift operationally questions the notion of a text being 'about' anything).

While drift is a positive term in Barthes, then, it has the paradoxical property of not being in opposition to any one term that can then be designated as negative. Drift is not mobility to the immobility of definition and paraphrase: it might well condemn the text to the stasis of incomprehensibility while attention to the signified enables debate to get under way. Barthes's fragment mimics, but not quite successfully, its referent. (If its mimicry were entirely successful, it would have no referent: it would thus not be mimicking anything at all.) It

---

[120] Ibid. 50.
[121] On gratuity, see ibid. 41, 57; on unsayable *jouissance* see ibid. 36.

also draws the reader into its own forcefield. I discover that the text is partly talking about how it is to be read, and thus about me, the reader. My attempt to control it metalinguistically is already mirrored in the text's own, strangely static, turmoil. Since I wrestle with its potential meanings only to find that something in the fragment forever resists, intractably, I am condemned to stupidity. Not only can I not say drift, I cannot say 'drift', that is, interpret the fragment that is thus called. But I can only fail to interpret the fragment because I want to interpret it, and have always necessarily pre-interpreted it. This resistance (of writing to speech), this excess of signifier over signified, together with the appeal the signifier makes to be named, is one aspect of what Barthes calls *jouissance*. But it is not an easy position: it is a way of setting up new tensions in the reader that are just as binding as the hermeneutic drive that, according to Barthes, has tended to power reading hitherto.[122]

This discussion may seem not to have advanced us very far. Lyotard too suggests that drift is so radical that it displaces the landmarks by which one could judge of movement: it is less a question of reaching any destination than of an *intensity* (and thus a tension) that may be unlocatable in kinetic terms. Since drift is an aquatic metaphor, Lyotard contrasts the *Odyssey* (in which the hero's sea-borne wanderings, like those of the spirit in history, according to Hegel, culminate in a moment of *nostos*, return, and reappropriation) to a later avatar of the Homeric theme, 'l'intense dérive sur place où s'entrechoquent les fragments, dans l'*Ulysse* de Joyce'.[123] The drift that is allegorized in the fragment 'Dérive' of *Le Plaisir du texte* is, despite the relaxation it seems to offer the reader, an intense semantic whirlpool: it is difficult to know what exactly escapes from its vortex.

But, to conclude this chapter, the fact that I want to understand the text so that I can follow what I suspect its instructions may be saying (namely, read for pleasure and suspend the hermeneutic drive: just drift along) shows that drift is characteristic of the problems that face us in trying to read Barthes in general. For it often seems, in Barthes, as if we are being placed in a double bind, instructed not to follow instructions, as if the category of the writable (which cannot be

---

[122] Marian Hobson, 'History traces', in Attridge, Bennington, and Young (eds.), *Post-Structuralism and the Question of History* (101–15) casts considerable light on a rather more complex problem in Derrida, many of whose terms (notably *différance*) threaten, like Barthes's drift, to settle into self-paralysing immobility but in fact stage a certain impetus and follow a certain trajectory.

[123] *Dérive à partir de Marx et Freud*, 9.

understood—like the fragment on drift) meant that we could turn away from the text, either to write our own text, or to participate in that generalized writing that Barthes sees as the form a liberating praxis will take. But to do so means pre-understanding the terms in which this possibility seems to be offered to us. Does this mean that we are left adrift, all ground lost? Far from it: while drift shows the dangers of trying to jump from capitalist Paris to Maoist China, from repressive meaning into terrorist non-meaning, or from history into Utopia, it does not immobilize us entirely. Drift is one of the terms that sets up a complex forcefield in Barthes's writing: debatable when stated as a political programme (as it is, to some extent, in Lyotard and frequently, as subversion from within, in Barthes), it is more significant as a way of showing how difficult it is for writing to perform what it represents, or even to say what it has written.

For drift is ultimately, for Barthes, a praxis specific to writing. Furthermore, as I shall now, in my next chapter, be suggesting, he stages this praxis in a variety of ways, which can themselves be seen as having a narrative tension in them. The complex of ideas Barthes associates with drift includes two major aspects. One is the historicity of discourse (and this affects the relations Barthes entertains with the scientific discourses around him, science being everything that is most contemporary). Another is, of course, narrative form itself, as the attempt to plot a certain emergence: something whose very newness is not the result of any epistemological break (for such a break is visible only retrospectively), but of a difference that we can recognize even if we cannot name it.[124] Barthes thus tells the story of how the aesthetic (especially in its mode as avant-garde) emerges from a certain matrix that can be seen as such only because of the newness to which it gives birth. And, to draw a parallel with how a particular science too has its stories of emergence, I will discuss Freud's theory of the transmutation of need into desire. While drift may lead us to think we have lost all ground, then, there is no need to see it as leaving everything where it already was. Barthes is that paradoxical thing, a committed drifter: and drift itself, the process in which that distanced commitment may at any time return, is writing as difference, *différance*, and drive.

---

[124] Drift as the smallest difference may make all the difference.

2

THE DRIFTER
NARRATIVES OF EMERGENCE

DRIFT: THE IMPURE LEXICON

Barthes's drift is a response to the violence inscribed within meaning: violence and meaning are for him inseparable because of his model of language, in which meaning is generated by binary opposites which function in an apparently value-free way, but which on a deeper level divide up the world in an imperious and surreptitiously evaluative fashion. These were the themes I examined in my last chapter, and I now want to broaden the argument to look at other aspects of drift, notably those that are susceptible to narrativization—how Barthes goes about putting his drift into practice.

To approach this particular theme, it is worth looking more closely at ways in which drift is related to *system*. For another focus for Barthes's obsession with violence can be found in his work on discursive systems. He is particularly fascinated by the way some of the most powerful systems seem capable of absorbing all attempts to attack them. Some such systems even interpret the fact that they are being criticized as evidence of the truths they proclaim. Psychoanalysis is a case in point. For psychoanalysis, resistance to Freud's discoveries is a demonstration of the very power of the unconscious that Freud's theories describe: faced with the unpalatable reality of the unconscious, we will always want to repress it. Another such system is Marxism: to reject Marxism can always be seen, by a Marxist, as stemming not from disinterested intellectual objections, but from the objector's position in the apparatus of production: to refuse Marxism is to identify yourself as blinded by ideology, so that your critique can again be explained (and thus its potential force disarmed) by the Marxist assumption that it stems from your own alienation: in attempting to criticize Marxism, you therefore end up providing further evidence of its truth. These systems (psychoanalysis and Marxism) are part of the modern epistēmē, but Barthes suggests that the systematic incorporation of opposing points of view is much older: he detects it at work in Christianity, citing Pascal ('Tu ne me chercherais pas, si tu ne m'avais déjà trouvé'): a refusal of God can be interpreted as a search for God.[1] Barthes points out that capitalism can do without *this* systematic violence, since it has at its disposal the muted and diffuse violence of nature ('the way things are') as expressed in the *doxa*. But the systems he names have what he calls self-sustaining *figures de système* at their disposal: in psychoanalysis, the *figure de système* lies in pointing out unconscious determinants; that of Marxism in pointing out class interest. The *figure de système* of Christianity is more difficult to determine, but Barthes would presumably suggest that, for Pascal, unbelief is a symptom of the 'misère de l'homme sans Dieu', which in turn is inseparable from the corresponding idea that 'il y a un Réparateur'.[2]

Although Barthes does not look for any other *figures de système*, they are indeed at the basis of any powerful—and thus successful—system of thought. For instance, the 'Cogito' of Descartes turns on a slightly different kind of figure. One can imagine the dialogues between proponents of these systems and those who are outside the system— the sceptics. Psychoanalyst to sceptic: your refusal to believe you have an unconscious is just what psychoanalysis predicts. Descartes to (radical) sceptic: your doubt of the reality of the mind is itself a mental process. *Figures de système* abound: any critic who dislikes literary theory ends up making statements that are of necessity theoretical, at least according to theory itself.

Barthes brackets the truth-claims of such systems: he is interested in them just as totalizing discursive phenomena. He also takes it for granted that faced with such systems, one will want to resist them— as he does, since he objects to the drive toward domination they embody. The only way of responding, suggests Barthes, apart from taking refuge in another system, is to try to suspend the power-effects inscribed within any system. But this is difficult.

Ces figures de système ont une grande force (c'est leur intérêt) et il est très difficile d'y échapper—pour autant qu'on on veuille non pas contredire le système au nom d'un autre système mais seulement 'suspendre', fuir la volonté de domination que de tels langages impliquent. Comment supporter, limiter, éloigner les pouvoirs de langage? Comment fuir les 'fanatismes' (les 'racismes de langage')?

A vieille question, pas de réponse encore nouvelle, me semble-t-il. L'Histoire n'a produit aucun *saut* du Discours: là où la Révolution a eu lieu, elle n'a pu 'changer le langage'. Le refus des intimidations de langage consiste donc, modestement, à *dériver* à l'intérieur de mots connus (sans trop s'inquié-

---

[1] Barthes cites these ex. in 'L'Image' (*BL*, 389–97 (392)), and *PlT*, 48.
[2] Pascal, *Pensées*, no. 6.

ter s'ils sont démodés); par exemple: la Tolérance, la Démocratie, le Contrat.[3]

Barthes's logic implies that if we argue with systems, we lose, at least as far as they are concerned. In 'L'Image', and in general throughout the Colloque de Cerisy devoted to Barthes's work, Barthes feels a similar fascination for—and revulsion from—Socrates, who generally manages to corner his opponents into contradicting themselves, and therefore proving his point that they do not really know what they thought they knew. The mistake of Socrates' opponents was that they stayed to argue. Thrasymachus, who in Book I of *The Republic* puts forward the case that justice is the interest of the stronger (that 'might is right'), is defeated in argument: perhaps the Thrasymachean position would have been better expressed if Thrasymachus had challenged Socrates to a wrestling match: whoever won would have then been proved right.[4] While Barthes would not want to adopt the Thrasymachean position, he shares the latter's sense of frustration, the feeling that the systematic argumentation of Socrates is somehow forcing his interlocutor to caricature his own position. By accepting the terms set implicitly by Socrates (to be driven to contradict yourself is to lose an argument), Thrasymachus fails to do his position justice. He is too Socratic for the good of his own ideology (which is why Glaucon and Adeimantus feel obliged to take up Thrasymachus' argument in more subtle ways than those he himself has been able to use).[5]

Barthes is suggesting that 'strong systems' seem to win because if you try to argue against them, you will be trapped in a *figure de système*. Two responses to strong systems are possible: systematic critique or silence. Neither is acceptable to Barthes, but for a typically Barthesian reason: he wants not to win but he does not want to be defeated either. He wants to be neither invincible (to 'impose on' people, as he repeatedly puts it in 'L'Image': such an imposition is the mark, for him, of an impostor) nor turned into a mere image by another system (for Marxism, a bourgeois individualist; for psychoanalysis, a neurotic). In other words, he does not want to elaborate a system, since that

---

[3] *BL*, 393.

[4] Plato, the creator of these dialogues, seems to have been an excellent wrestler. The Socratic *eristic* as a 'monde où l'on catche', perhaps.

[5] A similar sensitivity to the many different language games one can play, and to the fact that no one language game should be allowed to dictate its rules to others if they are to be respected in their difference, is shown in Jean-François Lyotard, *Le Différend* (1983).

would be to occupy a new position of power, but neither does he want to be labelled by any other system.

Barthes then makes a rather different point: that the chronological wavelengths of history and discourse are unequal. The Revolution did not 'change language'. This takes up an earlier point about the French Revolution in *Le Degré zéro de l'écriture*. *L'écriture bourgeoise* remained practically unchanged in its basic ethos and techniques from Fénelon to Mérimée: this was because the bourgeoisie had already held intellectual power before the Revolution, which merely gave it access to political power as well. Only with the prospect of its losing that power (around 1848) did bourgeois writing begin to disintegrate, and after that date 'les écritures commencent à se multiplier'.[6] Hence his awareness that a political revolution would not necessarily change the epistēmē.

His next move is rather odd. Where he had been talking of *figures de système*, figures which are themselves systematic and guarantee the universal validity and closure of the systems for which they stand, he now shifts his attention to the lexicon of such systems, rather than their structural consistency. His response to the intimidation of systems is to take individual words that have been viewed with some suspicion by strong systems and then use them with a certain modest defiance. This is what he here calls 'drift'. But where does he take such words from? *Tolérance, Démocratie, Contrat* are none of them a distinctive element in any one system, though 'democracy' is clearly a contentious issue in Marxist thought, and 'contract', as Barthes notes, is enveloped by 'tout un dossier sociopolitique, psychanalytique aussi'.[7] What seems to be the case is that Barthes has identified various contemporary problems (for, as he goes on to say, 'tolerance' is a useful word in times when intolerance seems to be spreading), and in this light suggests that the strong systems have at least one weak point: they fail to address the values registered in the words he is using. Instead of attempting to argue systematically with systems—with the modern epistēmē on its own terms, for example— Barthes prefers to identify a problem that is of existential importance to him, that he feels is not addressed by such systems, and which can be summarized in a word that is *not* a major part of what he sometimes calls the 'vulgate' (the codified conceptual and rhetorical apparatus) of psychoanalysis or Marxism.

[6] *DZ*, 43–5.   [7] *BL*, 393.

It is not clear that such a tactic is as disarming as Barthes would like. As he goes on to remind us, a word like 'democracy' has been acutely analysed in Marxist discourse, which has identified the way the word has sometimes been restricted to refer to the practices of Western 'liberal' democracies—which, for Marxism, are only very imperfectly democratic. So Barthes has chosen a word that Marxism at least can accommodate perfectly well, given its own highly developed theories of what a real democracy could be like. As he notes of the word *Démocratie*, it is 'un mot saturé de désillusions, jusqu'au dégoût, parfois jusqu'à la violence; les leurres de la démocratie bourgeoise ont été abondamment démystifiés'.[8] But he protests against the tendency to foreclose the word 'democracy' from discourse altogether. First, he points out that while certain usages of the word 'democracy' no doubt need to be demystified, others still register values to which he would assent. But secondly, and more provocatively, he suggests a new meaning for the word. One could define democracy, he says, 'non comme la réalisation d'une grégarité étouffante, mais comme "ce qui devrait produire des âmes aristocratiques" (dit un commentateur de Spinoza)'.[9] The provocation lies in defining the word 'democracy' by linking it positively to the word 'aristocratic'. Barthes is not suggesting that an aristocratic soul is the soul of an aristocrat, but he *is* re-evaluating both 'democracy' and 'aristocracy' in a way whose trangression resides in the overcoming of a taboo: the ban on the positive use of the word 'aristocratic' in left-wing discourse. Indeed, the word 'aristocratic' recurs with increasing frequency in his late works. In *Le Plaisir du texte*, for instance, he suggests that we should read even avant-garde texts with the leisurely circumspection and enjoyment that used to be devoted to classical texts: we should be 'des lecteurs *aristocratiques*'.[10] The word 'aristocratic' is an odd one to choose given that its etymology (as 'rule of the *aristoi*, the warrior nobility') makes explicit reference to political power. But Barthes's usage seems to want to disempower the word, to align it with what he sees as its Nietzschean sense (the aristocratic is that which is creative and artistic, active rather than reactive: it refuses to fight back, it disdains to defend itself, it does not play the game of power).

Since *grégarité étouffante* is one of the ways Barthes refers to his own society, it reflects his hostility to the pseudo-democratic aspects of

---

[8] *BL*, 393.   [9] Ibid.   [10] *PlT*, 24.

'mass' culture in a capitalist regime, as well as the risk that socialism might not be capable of sustaining its own more pluralist vision against the suffocating effects of such homogenization. But although Barthes's values are indissociable from those of such socialist pluralism (remember his desire to maintain some of the 'charms' of bourgeois culture in a socialist society, as expressed in *Barthes par lui-même*), he does not make his point in discursive terms. Rather, he takes off at a tangent from the (to him, stifling) conformism of such political language. From the strong system of Marxism he extracts a sensitive word, cuts it free of the system of syntagms and discursive stereotypes in which it is enmeshed, coaxes it in the direction of another system, that of Spinoza (but without letting it be absorbed by this new context: Barthes is not a 'Spinozist') and thereby enables himself to perform a provocative semantic and evaluative ellipsis (*democracy* is not the rule of the *demos*, but what produces *aristocratic souls*). This procedure is one of the ways he attempts to escape from the repressive double-bind of the *figure de système*: he calls it drift, and we can now give one potential definition of drift, as a *figure d'anti-système*.

This method is of course vulnerable. To use the word 'tolerance' is to expose oneself to the liberal connotations with which it is saturated, as are the other words Barthes mentions; 'democracy' and 'contract'. Indeed, the three words together can suggest that Barthes' values, in 'L'Image', hang together in a more systematic say, expressive of a certain enlightened liberalism. The way he reuses them is far from liberal, but one has to read him carefully to discover this. Since his essay is an attack on images, it seems that he is showing how prematurely images can be created, in the intellectual and political worlds especially: he is forcing us to go beyond images we may have formed of him, by looking more closely at his writing. Only then will we register the difference between Barthes's *Tolérance* and other kinds.

Barthes's late works swarm with increasing numbers of outmoded, apparently naïve, or politically sensitive words. We have seen him advising us to be aristocrats of reading; he also praises Schumann for his 'nobility', his dissociation from the world. In his last series of lectures at the Collège de France, he spoke of the novel he wanted to write (the novel that he fantasized about) as something he hoped would be *simple, filial*, and *désirable*.[11] In *La Chambre claire* he resorts to the word *pitié*—a sentiment 'au nom bizarrement démodé', he notes: it is strangely out of date, how strange that it should be

---

[11] Lecture given at the Collège de France on 23 Feb. 1980 (personal notes).

considered out of date.[12] There is a theoretical (or metaphorical) reasoning behind this aspect of his lexical drift: like Giambattista Vico, he sees history as moving in a spiral: the history of discourse can therefore operate in the same way, the old words return but at a different level ('the seim anew' says another Viconian, the Joyce of *Finnegans Wake*). Michelet is not read as much as he should be, claims Barthes in a 1972 essay 'Aujourd'hui, Michelet', because his vocabulary is notoriously full of pathos-laden words that we resist (*Action, Éducation, Peuple, Liberté*): but the magic of these words can be restored if we read them not only against Michelet's context but against our own.[13] This is true of the word *liberté*, with the new connotations and hesitations that have accrued to it as it has spiralled from Michelet's discourse into ours; and Barthes, who usually sees *Nature* as something to be rejected (because ideologically, *nature* is made to stand for 'the way things are and always should be'), here remembers that in Michelet the word arouses different echoes, some of which are important for our own ecologically minded age.[14]

That the spiral of history underlies drift is made clear in a fragment of *Barthes par lui-même* called 'Dialectiques'. Binary opposites have left their mark everywhere in his work, notes Barthes, but he also attempts to escape from them. And he does this not by treating them as a thesis and antithesis to be synthesized, as in some degraded versions of the dialectic, but by finding the 'third term' that will unsettle them.

En lui, une autre dialectique se dessine, cherche à s'énoncer: la contradiction des termes cède à ses yeux par la découverte d'un troisième terme, qui n'est pas de synthèse, mais de *déport*: toute chose revient, mais elle revient comme Fiction, c'est-à-dire à un autre tour de la spirale.[15]

The important thing is that this third term can be identified not as anything systematic, but as *one* word—such as *dérive* itself. Since I have already shown how drift is an attempt to escape from the binary prison, it is clear how closely linked it is to the spiral of history. (And the spiral in its turn is a progressive, enlightened view of history, but one which acknowledges that the historical line twists, turns, and returns.) Why does Barthes say here that what returns does so as Fiction? Partly because *déport* involves an aesthetic effect (it is, for

---

[12] *CC*, 179.   [13] *BL*, 225–37.

[14] Ibid. 235.   [15] *RB*, 73.

instance, close to the *transport* that etymologically underlies the word 'metaphor', and metaphors are figures of the indirect and thus, for Barthes, of the aesthetic). To go back to the terms of 'L'Image', Barthes's new uses of *Tolérance*, *Démocratie*, *Contrat* are signalled as new (partly by capitalizing them—I will be returning to this shortly). But also, their fictionality lies in their self-conscious difference: they are different from what they used to be (and they make us travel back along the spiral of history to earlier uses which may have been forgotten but whose force can be reawoken); and they are different from what they are in other contemporary discourses (the political or the psychoanalytical, for instance). It is this difference which for Barthes converts a word into a new signifier (by prising it away, temporarily, for its immediate signified, allowing it to drift), and which is one of the connotations of the word *Fiction*. Fiction is the distance with which Barthes increasingly marks his own operators of discourse. (He thus distances himself from those kinds of theory which do not pay enough attention to the fragility of their terms and the construct- edness and artificiality of their lexicon, just as he questions discourses which use words as simple encodings of simple evaluations, a practice he calls 'Stalinist'.)[16]

Barthes also says (in 'L'Image') that words have layers, some of the layers being good, others bad: 'il faut trier, établir une géologie différentielle'.[17] *Tolérance*, *Démocratie* and *Contrat*, are laden with connotations: some of these semes he wishes to keep, others to reject. Words are tied up with the struggles in which they have played a part, and it is this sense of words as still subject to history, still in process, that Barthes wants to emphasize in the notion of drift. The sociologist Pierre Bourdieu makes a somewhat different point about linguistic struggle in 'Fieldwork in Philosophy'. He notes that words such as 'spontaneism', 'centralism', 'voluntarism' were all originally weapons, 'fighting words', that have been turned into transhistorical, philosoph- ical concepts. These words, often coined as insults, have been eternalized by certain Marxist philosophers.[18] Unlike Barthes, Bour- dieu does not suggest reappropriating them, however: his point is that once they have served, tactically and within a certain context, it is difficult to reinvigorate them. Barthes *does* want the 'old words' back (though probably not those mentioned by Bourdieu). He does not want them as transhistorical concepts, however. And when he does get them back, they become strange and beautiful (revivifying an

---

[16] *DZ*, 21.   [17] *BL*, 393.   [18] *Choses dites*, (1987), 27–8.

intellectual term can have an aesthetic effect—turning it into a Fiction—as great as that created by the sensitive deployment of an archaic word or turn of phrase in poetry: 'we'll git 'em *all* back', as Robert Bridges said to Ezra Pound of words that seemed to have been abandoned by modern poets).

Just to emphasize the fact that Barthes is less idiosyncratic than he seems, it is worth noting that his *géologie différentielle* is close to the way Nietzsche too subjects some of the key concepts of various types of discourse to analysis: for instance, in his examination of ascetic ideals, he notes that the ideals of 'poverty, humility, chastity' are found in the lives of 'all the great, fruitful, inventive spirits'.[19] This does not mean that these creative types share the ideology of asceticism (for they do not have the religious belief on which that ideology reposes): conversely, it *does* mean that a Nietzschean critique of asceticism does not place a ban on either the words 'poverty', 'humility', 'chastity', or even on the practices to which those words refer. Barthes, like Nietzsche, refuses to see words as monoliths, to be accepted or rejected *en bloc*. A more recent parallel would be Derrida, whose deconstructive tactice frequently start from the examination of one particular word—'pharmakon', 'hymēn', 'parergon'—and show how its meaning cannot be defined within the system of whose lexicon it is an important element.[20] These words are not part of common discourse, however, and Derrida is more attentive than Barthes to the systematic nature of their use and reuse.

Barthes, therefore, sometimes focuses on the way his lexical experiments (which do not, he admits, have the radical dignity of the experiments in syntax associated with the French avant-garde since Mallarmé) belong to a specific historical juncture: they place him in the rearguard of the vanguard.

Ne pourrait-il se définir ainsi: le rêve d'une syntaxe pure et le plaisir d'un lexique impur, hétérologique (qui mélange l'origine, la spécialité des mots)? Ce dosage rendrait compte d'une certaine situation historique, mais aussi d'une donnée de consommation: lu un peu plus que la pure avant-garde, mais beaucoup moins qu'un auteur de grande culture.[21]

---

[19] Nietzsche, *On the Genealogy of Morals*, trans. Walter Kaufmann and R. J. Hollingdale (New York, 1967), ch. 3, Sect. 8.

[20] See 'La Pharmacie de Platon' and 'La Double Séance' in *La Dissémination* (1972), 69–198 and 199–318, respectively, and 'Parergon', in *La Vérité en peinture* (1978), 21–168.

[21] *RB*, 120.

Concentrating on his 'impure lexicon'—including his refurbishing of old-fashioned words, what might be called his 'neopalaeonymy'—leads Barthes to underestimate his own very high degree of syntactic originality, which could be summed up in the two words 'parataxis' and 'parenthesis'. Barthes's parataxis is most evident in his tendency to string arguments along with colons and semicolons rather than a high degree of hypotactic subordination: subordination is an effect he wants to avoid, given his sensitivity to the hierarchical connotations of such a word. And parenthesis is an alternative to such subordination in that his discourse is one in which the hesitations, qualifications, digressions, second thoughts, and internal paraphrases or expansions of what has just been said, are as important as the main clause. Barthes both says and shows this in a number of discussions of his own work, most clearly in 'En écharpe', a fragment in *Barthes par lui-même*, where he dismisses, with magnificent exaggeration, his theoretical writings (*on* cinema, language, society, and so on) as insignificant, adding: 'La pertinence, menue, (s'il s'en trouve), ne vient que dans des marges, des incises, des parenthèses, *en écharpe*: c'est la voix *off* du sujet.'[22] Barthes's syntax is of the self-devouring kind, puncturing itself at every semicolon and quizzing its own assertiveness every time it opens a parenthesis. And not to close the parenthesis—or rather, to write in such a way that the *reader* is constantly encouraged to go off at a parenthetical tangent—is, he says, a way of drifting. 'Le rêve serait donc: ni un texte de vanité, ni un texte de lucidité, mais un texte aux guillemets incertains, aux parenthèses flottantes (ne jamais fermer la parenthèse, c'est très exactement: *dériver*). Cela dépend aussi du lecteur, qui produit l'*échelonnement* des lectures.'[23] Despite these syntactic ploys, Barthes dwells more on his impure lexicon.[24]

A number of further points must be made. Drift—the fact that a word *is* being used differently—can only be measured against a certain relatively fixed background. Barthes can '*dériver* à l'intérieur de mots connus', as he puts it in 'L'Image', because he can take for granted a relative semantic stability against which his drift can be charted. Furthermore, although drift may seem to concentrate on plucking

---

[22] *RB*, 77.

[23] Ibid. 110 The parentheses within parentheses within parentheses of Raymond Roussel's *Nouvelles Impressions d'Afrique* (1963) provide a radical example of what Barthes is here suggesting.

[24] In their feeble but occasionally instructive parody of Barthes, Michel-Antoine Burnier and Patrick Rambaud note that Barthes's phrase 'le lexique impur' is itself an impure syntagm—at least by the grey norm of French prose that is their standard (*Le Roland-Barthes sans peine* (1978), 27).

individual items within a systematic lexicon, the new, drifting words may always have a potentially systematic relation among themselves (as I have suggested is the case with *Tolérance*, *Démocratie*, and *Contrat*). And Barthes sometimes drifts more systematically—by taking a system and subjecting it to a relatively coherent sheering. This practice he refers to as 'anamorphosis', a word he uses in connection with the way a critic inspired by structuralism may 'map' Racine into the languages of modernism (as he himself did in *Sur Racine*, and as he makes clear in *Critique et vérité*.)[25]

Furthermore, on this somewhat more systematic level, there is a drift from 'early' Barthes to 'late' Barthes. The former is systematic and discursive: this trend culminates in the scientific formalization of fashion writing (*Système de la mode*). The latter both drifts within and away from positions established in the early work (there are no great repudiations) and adopts a more fragmentary and less dissertative form. This means that one constant horizon for the drift of the late work is, simply, the early work. We are less worried about Barthes being taken in by the liberal connotations of *Démocratie* (in 'L'Image') because he as much as anyone laid bear the mechanisms of an allegedly liberal ideology in *Mythologies*, just as the succinctness of the fragments (in *Barthes par lui-même*, for instance) is a concentrate of over two decades of more systematic thinking in which Barthes spent much of his time drawing subtle methodological distinctions, especially in his contributions to the nascent science of semiology. However much drift may seem to act as a *figure d'anti-système*, then, one that other people may be able to appropriate in order to defuse the aggressivity of intellectual discourses or the coded stereotypes of binary thinking, it is most at home in Barthes's own work, where its force relies on a background of careful and methodical scientific elaboration. There is an implicit narrative here: system first, then drift.

But even when Barthes has prepared us for it, drift is a teasing and troubling tactic. Sometimes, for instance, the late Barthes mimics the technical language of his more scientific treatises, but he does so in the parodic way of coining pseudo-scientific neologisms. In a sense, neologisms do not pose any of the problems of Barthes's drifting words. When we read *Tolérance* in late Barthes, we have to ask what kind of tolerance Barthes is talking about, and construct a new meaning for the word on the basis of what we know of its history in

[25] *CV*, 64.

different discourses as well as the tactical re-evaluations to which Barthes is inviting us. But when Barthes creates a neologism, he generally defines it. (And a neologism is, as it were, signed: we know that Barthes is creating it.)

It is worth remembering that Barthes's first defence and illustration of the neologism occurs, not in the course of any celebration of the free flight of the signifier, but in the combative context of 'Le Mythe, aujourd'hui'. Force to find labels for the signifieds of connotation he uncovers at the heart of the myth, Barthes invents such hybrids as *la francité, la basquité,* and *la bouvard-et-pécuché-ité.* Based on Saussure's notion of partially motivated signs that function by *analogie relative,* these words, whatever stylistic resistances they may raise, have a clear morphology and significance.[26]

The same is true of the sciences Barthes postulates, such as *bathmologie,* the science of the degrees of language, *hyphologie,* the science of spiders' webs (and thus of texts), *anagnosologie,* the science of reading, and *diaphorologie,* the 'science des Moires', a science, that is, that deals with everything that shimmers.[27] Barthes explains what he means in each case, and there is no reason why such sciences could not exist (just as *sémiologie,* postulated by Saussure, has come into existence), even though they are also Barthesian jokes. Words taken from 'learned' (or 'dead') languages, especially Latin and that language of the *logos* (or at least of the -ology) *par excellence,* Greek, are put to idiomatic but still scientific use (*studium* and *punctum* in *La Chambre claire*): but they offer little resistance to the reader's understanding. Indeed, however much Barthes may be parodying scientific discourse, these are true concepts: Barthes can define them for us, and we can accept his definition. The fact that we are not forced to agree about their application (different people will necessarily locate the *punctum,* the emotive centre of a particular photo, in different places) only emphasizes their status as concepts: Barthes may have invented them, but their signified is clear. A word like *punctum* is thus a private invention susceptible of becoming public intellectual property.

[26] Barthes discusses Saussure's 'relative analogy' in 'Éléments de sémiologie' (*AS,* 9–84, esp. 48). The same semiological handbook earlier makes a point about the more general difficulties of definition in the human sciences: Barthes lists the different ways in which 'signal', 'index', 'icon', 'symbol', 'sign', and 'allegory' divide the semantic field between them in Hegel, Wallon, Peirce, and Jung (38).

[27] These ex. are taken, respectively, from 'Le second degré et les autres', in *RB,* 71; *PlT,* 101; 'Sur la lecture', in *BL,* 37–47 (38); and 'Délibération', in *BL,* 399–413 (406).

More difficult are the words that are not neologisms, but which Barthes takes from public discourse so as to give them his own subjective twist: *dérive, texte, écriture, jouissance,* for instance. These are not defined. Any metalinguistic expansion of a conceptual or definitional kind tends to be limited. Metaphorical treatment, on the other hand, is multiplied. Barthes lists several metaphors with which his work approaches *texte,* in the fragment 'En écharpe' of *Barthes par lui-même:*

> Le *Texte* n'est jamais approché que métaphoriquement: c'est le champ de l'aruspice, c'est une banquette, un cube à facettes, un excipient, un ragoût japonais, un charivari de décors, une tresse, une dentelle de Valenciennes, un oued marocain, un écran télévisuel en panne, une pâte fueilletée, un oignon, etc.[28]

It is indeed in approaching *texte* metaphorically that Barthes's 'work' itself approaches the status of the 'text'.

WRITING: FROM DRIFT TO *DRIFT*

> I fear those big words, Stephen said, which make us so unhappy.
>
> James Joyce, *Ulysses.*

> LES CAPITALES. Elles appellent à respecter des mots jusque-là tenus pour ordinaires, et on se doit particulièrement de les placer devant **Voix, Modèle, Je, Moi, Doxa, Valeur, Paradoxe, Sens, Code.**
>
> Michel-Antoine Burnier and Patrick Rambaud, *Le Roland-Barthes sans peine*

In 'La mollesse des grands mots', a fragment of *Barthes par lui-même,* Barthes refers to the two classes of 'big words' found in his work: both sorts are vague (lack clear definition): the first set are resonant words like *Déterminisme, Histoire, Nature:* others, like *écriture* and *style,* are idiolectal, in other words given a Barthesian twist. The intellectual vagueness of these words, he claims, is part of their existential precision. The first set of words is particularly interesting: Barthes's fondness for capitalization has often been noted: capitals add emphasis, but also make these words similar to proper names, and proper names are not concepts. *Histoire* is never defined, even though Barthes clearly

---

[28] *RB*, 78.

uses it in ways rather different from those hallowed by common usage (for him, it is 'une idée morale: elle permet de relativiser le naturel et de croire à un sens du temps'.)[29] Rather than hypostatizing the word, Barthes capitalizes it in order to personify it, turn it into a persona in his text, on whose stage it can act out various roles: *Histoire* is theatricalized. Barthes wants to use this word since its presence in general social discourse is important to him: but he uses it with a certain detachment. Drift here takes the form, simply and paradoxically, of a capital letter which both underlines and undermines the word's solidity: it engages the word in a dialogue with itself and its context.

This taste for personifying abstract notions merely in writing, by 'marking' the word with a capital letter, is one of later Barthes's most striking stylistic features: it leads him to such protracted flights of fancy as that towards the end of his preface to *Tricks* by Renaud Camus, a book which, in Barthes's opinion, invents a new way of talking about the sexual act.

Alors qu'ordinairement ce sont des sortes de Harpies qui président au contrat érotique, laissant chacun dans une solitude glacée, ici, c'est la déesse Eunoia, l'Euménide, la Bienveillante, qui accompagne les deux partenaires . . . Cette déesse a d'ailleurs son cortège: la Politesse, l'Obligeance, l'Humour, l'Élan généreux, tel celui qui saisit le narrateur (au cours d'un *trick* américain) et le fait délirer gentiment sur l'auteur de cette préface.[30]

These delicate personifications capitalize on (and emphasize) the stylistic discretion he detects in Camus's work.

Barthes's capitals are partly a stylistic reminiscence of Michelet, whose capitalizations were more of a *trait d'époque*. ('Elle fut la Haine et la Vengeance sans transaction' says Balzac of La Cousine Bette, for instance.) It is therefore ironic that in the essay on Michelet to which I have already referred, Barthes drops an apologetic footnote claiming that he himself has been writing *Histoire* with a capital letter not to *diviniser* history but to distinguish between *Histoire* (history) and *histoire* (story).[31] Barthes hardly ever writes the French word for history *without* a capital (see for instance the first page of his first book, *Le Degré zéro de l'écriture*).[32]

In an essay on Georges Bataille, Barthes notes other punctuational modes of distinguishing *écriture*, which marks the writer's values, from

---

[29] *RB*, 129
[30] 'Préface à *Tricks* de Renaud Camus', in *BL*, 327–31 (330–1).
[31] Ibid. 233.   [32] *DZ*, 7.

écrivance, in which the traces of the writer's body have been censored: italics and inverted commas around a word turn it from a *mot-savoir* to what he calls a *mot-valeur*, a *vocable*.

Les mots-valeurs (les vocables) mettent le désir dans le texte (dans le tissu de l'énonciation)—et l'en font sortir: le désir n'est pas dans le texte par les mots qui le 'représentent', qui le racontent, mais par des mots suffisamment découpés, suffisamment brillants, triomphants, pour se faire aimer, à la façon de fétiches.[33]

It is in these individual words (rather than in the logical operators of demonstration) that Barthes locates the major nodes of the writer's discourse: in Bataille, the *mots-valeurs* together form a network, an *appareil terminologique*.[34] Barthes's own *vocables* are frequently those words he capitalizes, that can then, as figures, be invoked: in them, too, the voice of the writer can be fantasmatically heard—the voice, that is, rather than what it says. We hear the writer's voice, paradoxically, in and through the written marks of silent punctuation, which seem to tell us with what emphasis or tone the words are to be pronounced. Barthes notes that Nietzsche's writing is markedly punctuational as a way of insisting on his values. But how does one pronounce a capital letter? (Italics at least allow one to *dwell* on, or *emphasize*, a word.) The majuscule is writing *par excellence*.[35] When Barthes in his later works uses intellectually discredited words (*noblesse*, *pitié*, *aristocratique*), when he resurrects the romantic couple of *Amour* and *Mort* in *La Chambre claire*, we have to read them as provocative and poetic at one and the same time. This, at least, is what Walter Benjamin's comments on a similar tactic in Baudelaire would suggest.

For the *coup de main* which Baudelaire calls writing poetry, he takes allegories into his confidence. They are the only ones that have been let in on the secret. Where *la Mort* or *le Souvenir*, *le Repentir* or *le Mal* appear, centres of poetic strategy are located. The flash-like appearance of these figures, recognizable by their majuscule, in a text which does not disdain the most banal word betrays Baudelaire's hand. His technique is the technique of the *putsch*.[36]

---

[33] 'Les Sorties du texte', in *BL*, 271–83 (282–3).

[34] Ibid. 282.

[35] Again, Burnier and Rambaud note Barthes's attention to punctuation, but they oversimplify its effect to mere decorative prettiness ('La Règle de surponctuation', in *Le Roland-Barthes sans peine*, 34–6).

[36] 'The Paris of the Second Empire in Baudelaire', in *Charles Baudelaire: A Lyric Poet in the Era of High Capitalism*, trans. Harry Zohn (London, 1973), 9–106 (100). When Barthes is contrasted with e.g. Derrida, it is sometimes so that Derrida's patient and systematic unravellings of metaphysics may be held up as a better model. Presumably Barthes is too impatient, not mediated enough: too fixated on the lexicon

Barthes's figures, frequently allegorized and thus capitalized banalities, have precisely this whiff of naïve archaism, tinged with a sense for literary tactics and a deliberate revolt against over-systematic discourses. Barthes's drifting words are one aspect of his role as the silent Blanqui of theory, the one who resists theory from within theory.

WRITING: FROM SCIENCE TO THE AESTHETIC

Barthes shows a great interest in the way that Bataille, even when writing academic articles, soon starts to use *different* words to mark his distance from scientific discourse. In 'Les Sorties du texte', Barthes cites the use of the phrase 'la saleté la plus écœurante' in Bataille's 'anthropological' essay on the big toe.[37] Barthes approves of this transgression since he too wants to slip out of the scientific mode of some of his writings. This involves him, increasingly, in turning science into a bugbear: it is the realm of a pseudo-objectivity in which subjectivity has been 'castrated'. Indeed, *science* becomes an increasingly vague and distorted term in late Barthes: it is turned into something repellent and repressive. But this desiccated image is largely of Barthes's own making. Although he does register a valid protest against the abuses of scientific discourse (abuses which for Barthes are largely the result of science sometimes failing to shake off

---

and not enough on the grammar—a reproach he addresses to himself, as we have seen. But it is also true that every self-reproach of his is also a self-affirmation. This should make us pause before accepting at face value such criticisms as those of Ian McLeod who, in a brief and dismissive note on *L*, says that it 'mimics a deconstructive strategy' but 'finally regresses from Derrida's positions'. McLeod portrays Barthes as a 'brilliant assimilator of terminology from disciplines he never really understood' ('Powers Plural: Barthes's "Lecture"', *Oxford Literary Review*, 4: 1 (autumn 1979), 29–30). It is not clear that *L* is mimicking deconstruction, despite Barthes's use of the word. Derrida would be the last to claim any copyright on the word.) If he is, the results of mimicry are, I am suggesting, far more unpredictable than McLeod gives credit for. McLeod's suspicion that Barthes is really out to ensure that 'literature' can survive is more interesting, and I would agree with his claim, though after Barthes it is far more difficult than it was before him to see where the limits of literature may lie. Adorno similarly criticized Benjamin for a lack of dialectical rigour in his approach to Baudelaire: see the correspondence between them in *Aesthetics and Politics: Debates between Bloch, Lukács, Brecht, Benjamin, Adorno* (London, 1977), 100–41. The (unnamed) presenter of this correspondence discusses Adorno's grounds for complaint: see esp. 104. My own feeling is that Benjamin himself *was* being Baudelairean and *putschist* rather than properly dialectical.

[37] *BL*, 281. Georges Bataille's essay 'Le Gros Orteil' is in *Œuvres complètes* (1970–87), 200–4.

its nineteenth-century positivism: science as 'scientism'), it is difficult to know what science means for Barthes.

But the semantic drift of the word *science* in Barthes is partly the result of the fact that it is a less specific word in French than in English. While 'science' in English is associated first and foremost with the physical sciences (Dilthey's *Naturwissenschaften*) and by extension with the soft sciences (or human sciences: Dilthey's *Geisteswissenschaften*), such as sociology or economics, *la science* in French can refer to a wider range of activities—physical sciences, human sciences, or organized knowledge in general. (French *science* has kept closer to its Latin root *scientia*, knowledge: when Gargantua advises his son Pantagruel to become 'un abysme de science', he wants him to learn everything there is to learn.) When Barthes refers to *science*, it is rarely the physical sciences that he has in mind: indeed, in *Le Plaisir du texte*, where the polemic against science is particularly lively, the word applies both to the sciences he himself had helped establish (semiology, narratology, and structuralist linguistics), and also to two intellectual fields whose scientificity was once the object of fierce debate—psychoanalysis and Marxism. (The first has been seen as the science of the subject: the second, at least in Althusser's view, as the science of history.) From this, it appears that what Barthes objects to is the way science—especially when controversial and vulnerable—becomes arrogant, claims a universality and objectivity which it does not merit. So Barthes repeats Nietzsche's claim that we are not yet subtle enough to perceive 'becoming': we 'scientifically' catch the world of phenomena in the net of concepts that immobilize and reify their referents.[38] Barthes is here drifting in the word *science* in a very instructive way, suggesting that it is his own earlier and apparently more 'scientific' works (in narratology or semiology) that are not yet scientific because they are too conceptually rigid. The paradox is that it is partly a discipline he here dismisses as yet another such science (psychoanalysis) that has led Barthes to turn back to the subject, to the investments of desire that govern even the most objective research.[39]

The very term *science*, with its connotations of objectivity, conceptual rigour, and universality, is thus in Barthes's writings subjected to drift

[38] *P/T*, 96, and *S/Z*, 9.
[39] Even the so-called 'hard sciences' such as sub-atomic physics have been undergoing such a questioning of objectivity for at least a century, from relativity to the latest developments in quantum theory: the observed cannot be separated from the observer, even if that observer is hardly a 'subject'.

as semantic vagueness. And if science (our old image of science) demands a certain accuracy in definition, Barthes subverts such a demand by submitting particular concepts to a semantic glissando: the system (the scientific matrix) from which the word is taken is never merely rejected, but held in suspense—as a potential source of metaphors: 'je crois de plus en plus à la valeur métaphorique de la science'.[40] Such an operation, as Barthes points out, is provocative: the taboos of science are essentially linguistic. In a sense, his appropriation of scientific terms is more a suspension of the scientific value of his own work than a critique of science as such: he wants to be recognized less as a *savant* than as an *écrivain*, less as one who knows than as one who writes. This new status is one of the reasons why commenting on Barthes's work can be difficult. For while, in the case of scientific writing, we can debate the correctness or otherwise of the propositions being put forward, since such writing is explicitly predicated on truth-values, Barthes repeatedly asserts that his writing is not out to speak the truth. But neither is it out to invent. It forces us to read it as neither fact nor fiction. Or rather, it is fact that swerves into fiction, just as it insists that the truth can sometimes be reached only through subjective obliquity and aesthetic indirection. Barthes's lifelong habit of using words that are taken from highly complex and controversial sciences, rather than saying something personal in relatively ordinary language, as an essayist traditionally does, places us in a peculiarly uncomfortable position: we cannot treat Barthes's texts as mere personal statements, since their writing has the theoretical self-reflexivity we associate with the intellectual languages current in the public sphere, as well as deploying the communal lexicon of science; nor are they scientific, since he inflects them by his own avowed appropriative deformation—and indeed, at another turn in the argument, his subjective reuse of them is itself subtly scientific, since he has alerted us to the fact that his own view of science involves taking seriously the investments of the subject.[41]

In 'L'Image', for instance, Barthes uses the word *corruption* to refer to his appropriation of languages and vocabularies for his own ends.

[40] 'Digressions', in *BL*, 83–96 (85).
[41] See e.g. Barthes's remarks in a late lecture '"Longtemps, je me suis couché de bonne heure"', in *BL*, 313–25, esp. 325: 'Peut-être est-ce finalement au cœur de cette subjectivité, de cette intimité même dont je vous ai entretenus, peut-être est-ce à la "cime de mon particulier" que je suis scientifique sans le savoir, tourné confusément vers cette *Scienza Nuova* dont parlait Vico: ne devra-t-elle pas exprimer à la fois la brillance et la souffrance du monde, ce qui, en lui, me séduit et m'indigne?'

Corruption can help 'déjouer l'Image', that image which freezes the subject into a particular posture. The image that Barthes seems particularly concerned to undo here is that of himself as a theoretician.

Un moyen de déjouer l'Image, c'est peut-être de corrompre les langages, les vocabulaires; la preuve qu'on y parvient, c'est de susciter l'indignation, la réprobation des puristes, des spécialistes. Je cite les autres, en acceptant de les déformer: je fais glisser le sens des mots (je renvoie ici au *Montaigne* d'Antoine Compagnon). Ainsi pour la Sémiologie, que j'avais aidé à constituer, j'ai été mon propre corrupteur, je suis passé du côté des Corrupteurs. On pourrait dire que le champ de cette Corruption est l'esthétique, la littérature: 'catastrophe' est un mot technique en mathématiques, chez R. Thom; je puis mal employer 'Catastrophe', qui devient alors quelque chose de 'beau'. Il n'y a d'Histoire que parce que les mots se corrompent.[42]

One thing to note immediately in this dense paragraph is the way Barthes both appropriates a notion by capitalizing it (baptizing it with his mark) and at the same time expropriates the very same notion by unfixing its meaning, opening it out to new possibilities of evaluation and tactical intervention. Thus *corruption* becomes *Corruption*, *catastrophe* is promoted—by being used 'badly'—to *Catastrophe*. (A word capitalized by Barthes is not necessarily positive: *Doxa* has the majuscule not because it is highly valued, but because it is a *barthème*, a word he has made his own.) In exposing his practice in this way, of course, Barthes demonstrates that he is not the only one to indulge in it: if all history depends on linguistic corruption, who can avoid it? But Barthes deliberately shows his awareness both by this exposé and by the stylistic marker of the capital.

The capitalization of words is, in any case, as I have said, a figure of writing, not of speech. 'L'Image' was first read aloud to an audience at the Colloque de Cerisy: Barthes's passage from corruption to Corruption will have been inaudible to them. Derrida's paper 'La Différance' (also first delivered as a paper) examines the difference between *différence* and *différance*: this difference resides in writing alone, not speech. (Or, more precisely, there is no phonetic difference between the two *words* when they are treated in isolation: their usage in context may well differ.) *Différance* thus becomes a key element in Derrida's investigation of the irreducibility of writing to speech. It is not the only term to perform this function in Derrida's work: what it points to is named in a variety of ways, and each term Derrida resorts to is itself an attempt to question the pretentions of meaning as

---

[42] *BL*, 396.

intended by a self-aware subject. These terms, all of which relay *différance*, in different ways, include *archi-trace, archi-écriture, réserve, brisure, articulation,* and *supplément.* 'J'essaie d'écrire la question: (qu'est-ce) que vouloir-dire? Il est donc nécessaire que, dans un tel espace et guidée par une telle question, l'écriture à la lettre ne-veuille-rien-dire . . . C'est en ce sens que je me risque à ne-rien-vouloir-dire qui puisse simplement s'entendre, qui soit simple affaire d'entendement.'[43] Not only can the difference not be heard, it may not be understood, or even understandable in the terms usually associated with philosophical discourse.

Derrida is sensitive to the fact that 'to mean' is, in colloquial French, 'to wish to say' (*vouloir dire*), and 'to understand' is frequently 'to hear' (*entendre*). This will be important at a later stage in my argument, when I show how Barthes tends to react against the privilege given to the voice as bearer of meaning. In 'L'Image', Barthes does not discuss the speech/writing opposition in such terms, but he does employ its effects, and capitalization is part of the *différance* of drift. The capital resists being translated immediately into the meta-linguistic terms of speech: it may thus be difficult to locate semantically. As Barthes notes of *corruption*, the effect can be both difficult to identify and (*ipso facto*) very attractive. The most beautiful example of this in Barthes's work comes at the end of his essay 'La Lumière du Sud-Ouest', written for *L'Humanité.*[44] Barthes evokes his own *pays*, its regional accent, its microclimate, its rivers, its smells, its craft industries. Many of the latter are now defunct, hence Barthes's nostalgia. But this is not a mere indulgence, since he notes that politico-sociological analysis (in other words, we might add, 'science') may miss some of the subtleties of *le pays*; and this observation leads Barthes to comment on the way he himself reads his native land.

Car 'lire' un pays, c'est d'abord le percevoir selon le corps et la mémoire, selon la mémoire du corps. Je crois que c'est à ce vestibule du savoir et de l'analyse qu'est assigné l'écrivain: plus conscient que compétent, conscient des interstices mêmes de la compétence. C'est pourquoi l'enface est la voie royale par laquelle nous connaissons le mieux un pays. Au fond, il n'est Pays que de l'enface.[45]

What is the difference between *pays* and *Pays*? How can we speak this difference? It can be paraphrastically interpreted, but this interpreta-

---

[43] 'Implications', in *Positions*, 9–24 (23–4). See also 'La Différance' in *Marges—de la philosophie* (1972), 1–29.
[44] *I*, 11–20.   [45] Ibid. 20.

tion will necessarily be both verbose and fragile. The land of childhood—we might say—is found and celebrated at the same time as its loss is recognized. It becomes a metaphor. The public *pays* of unemployment figures and declining cottage industries is not disregarded but supplemented by the subject's experience: Barthes gains access to the public *pays* via the private *Pays* whose very capitalization suggests that it is a *Fiction*. And this fiction is a necessary supplement to the objectivity of socio-political analysis: 'La Lumière du Sud-Ouest' shows how science may need the aesthetic to fill in the 'interstices mêmes de la compétence', and objective analysis may need subjective velleities and sensations to get at the truth. This is Barthes's version of the dialectic, his way of overcoming the antinomies of subjective and objective existence. By a trick of punctuation, he cancels, preserves, and raises *pays* into *Pays*—in writing. Barthes's return to the origin elevates it to a Utopian fiction. To compare small things with great, the eight pages of 'La Lumière du Sud-Ouest' are as suggestive as anything Barthes wrote of the work of Ernst Bloch, who ends *The Principle of Hope* with a vision of childhood generalized into a homeland that will be recognized as such only at the end of history.

True genesis is not at the beginning but at the end, and it starts to begin only when society and existence become radical, i.e. grasp their roots. But the root of history is the working, creating human being who reshapes and overhauls the given facts. Once he has grasped himself and established what is his, without expropriation and alienation, in real democracy, there arises in the world something which shines into the childhood of all and in which no one has yet been: homeland.[46]

Although capitalization is very Barthesian when it affects the boundaries between science and the aesthetic, its antecedents in Barthes's own literary tradition are of course innumerable. In Mallarmé's sonnet 'Le vierge, le vivace et le bel aujourd'hui, the *cygne* of the second stanza is apotheosized (and sublimated and 'disappeared') into the last stanza's *Cygne*.[47] And the reverse effect (degradation from capital to lower case) adds its melancholy to the end of Proust's *Du côté de chez Swann*: the narrator fails to recognize the ideal beauty he had once located in the Bois de Boulogne: 'le vent ridait le Grand Lac de petites vaguelettes, comme un lac; de gros oiseaux parcouraient

---

[46] *The Principle of Hope*, iii. 1376.
[47] Mallarmé, 'Le vierge, le vivace et le bel aujourd'hui', in 'Plusieurs sonnets', in *Poésies* (1945).

rapidement le Bois, comme un bois'.[48] My point is that Barthes is again appropriating the energies of a common device in imaginative literature for his own mixed mode of essayistic writing. This is allegorically staged in one of Barthes's more notorious essays, 'La Mort de l'auteur'. Whereas the reader whose advent is being celebrated remains, throughout, a lower case *lecteur*, the word *auteur* oscillates, for reasons never explained, between lower- and uppercase initial: but right at the end, as if (to risk an interpretation of the tone created) being consecrated *in articulo mortis*, the author returns with a firm if silent capital: 'la naissance du lecteur doit se payer de la mort de l'Auteur.'[49]

WRITING: FROM QUOTATION TO 'QUOTATION' AND BACK AGAIN

> This is *our* proletarian task, this is what we can and must *start* with in accomplishing the proletarian revolution. Such a beginning, on the basis of large-scale production, will of itself lead to the gradual 'withering away' of all bureaucracy, to the gradual creation of an order—an order without quotation marks.
>
> Lenin, *The State and Revolution: The Marxist Theory of the State and the tasks of the Proletariat in the Revolution*

Barthes's reference, in 'L'Image', to Montaigne also suggests that his way of using, mentioning, and re-evaluating words all at the same time has other antecedents: indeed, during a discussion of Montaigne earlier in the Colloque de Cerisy at which 'L'Image' was presented, Antoine Compagnon had pointed out how Montaigne quoted his authors—his authorities—without giving references.[50] This is a tactic which Barthes, too, frequently employs. A good example is the opening fragment, 'Affirmation', in *Le Plaisir du texte*. A slice of Bacon (though it does not seem to translate directly any single phrase in the *Essays*: *'ne jamais s'excuser, ne jamais s'expliquer'*) is followed by a quotation, unattributed to, but taken from, Nietzsche: 'Je détournerai mon regard, ce sera désormais ma seule négation': one English translation

---

[48] *Du côté de chez Swann*, ed. Bernard Brun (1987), 572.
[49] 'La Mort de l'auteur' (1968), in *BL*, 61–7 (67). In the pref. to the 1971 work *SFL* (13), Barthes is already insisting that 'le plaisir du Texte comporte aussi un retour amical de l'auteur', now in a dispersed and fragmented form—a paschal apparition, indeed, albeit after an absence not of 3 days but 3 years.
[50] *C*, 40–56.

of Nietzsche's words has: '*Looking away* shall be my only negation.'[51] The fact that we are not told, so to speak, viva voce, that the quotation comes from Nietzsche means that any interpretative choice is the reader's responsibility. (We might, for instance, focus on the pertinence of the highly affirmative end of Nietzsche's fragment—'And all in all and on the whole: some day I wish to be only a Yes-sayer'— especially since it is cited in a Barthes fragment itself labelled 'Affirmation'.) For Barthes obeys the injunction of pleasure, shows what he says, and performs what he quotes ('*ne jamais s'expliquer*').

While *Le Plaisir du texte* does not begin exactly in the Tower of Babel ('Babel' is the second fragment in it), it does, from the start, stage itself as writing—as a text in which voices will be mimicked polyphonically. (Barthes learnt about Bakhtin and his theory of the polyphonic text from his pupil Julia Kristeva.) *Le Plaisir du texte* will not just be a text about pleasure, but a text that gives pleasure. It is thus, according to Barthes, caught in a contradiction, since he thinks one cannot talk about pleasure and give it at the same time: his text will oscillate between giving pleasure (not talking about it or explaining it) and talking about pleasure (while not giving it, being forced to point elsewhere, anticipating or remembering pleasures had or to be had). While the text to pleasure can be commented on, pleasure as such seems to debar interpretation: Barthes will not explain other than allusively why he is writing *about* pleasure (it is a tactic aimed at affirming pleasure against the ideologies that censor it: as *paradoxa* its movement is merely that of detaching itself from the censorious and puritanical *doxa*.)[52] Above all, in its radical form of *jouissance*, that pleasure beyond pleasure in which all interpretive bearings are lost and the reader left adrift, the pleasure experienced in reading a text is not subject to literary criticism because 'la critique est toujours historique ou prospective: le présent constatif, la *présentation* de la jouissance lui est interdite; sa matière de prédilection est donc la culture, qui est tout en nous sauf notre présent'.[53] Is a dialectical subsumption of pleasure and criticism possible? Of course—what if, says Barthes echoing Brecht, knowledge itself were pleasurable?[54] According to psychoanalysis, the drive to knowledge is, after all, *derived* from the pleasure principle: epistemophilia is the Freudian Eros of the idea. But Barthes wobbles between this view and the notion taken

---

[51] *The Gay Science*, trans. Walter Kaufmann (New York, 1974), bk IV ('Sanctus Januarius'), Sect. 276.
[52] *P/T*, 31.   [53] Ibid. 37.   [54] Ibid. 39.

from Lacan that *jouissance* cannot be spoken, is a kind of subjectivity that cannot be objectified or expressed.

If we return to Compagnon's paper on Montaigne, we see that the interrelationship between pleasure and knowledge is indeed complex. Pleasure may come from being told the truth and thus enlightened; its source may be a certain *recognition* (of a quotation, an authority, or an orthodoxy). On the other hand, pleasure may come from mystifying and being mystified. Compagnon notes, in the discussion following his paper, that for Montaigne, authors such as Cicero and Plutarch gave added authority to his own texts. But he was also suspicious of this effect: why, he asks, should the reader accept as true something because it has been said by an authority (rather than by me, Montaigne)? Montaigne thus quotes, but without saying when he is quoting. A reader who attacks what seems to be Montaigne's opinion may in fact be attacking a consecrated classical author. Compagnon suggests that Montaigne's tactic, which has a powerful critical and enlightenment thrust to it, is none the less paradoxical: how will a reader know, without being told, that to reject Montaigne in fact means rejecting some hallowed authority? Even this, he suggests, adds to the fact that Montaigne derives from his practice 'une jouissance somme toute perverse'.[55]

This tactic, which amounts to making the quotation marks unlocatable, is peculiarly Barthesian. Not that Barthes frequently quotes without acknowledging the fact, for this is rare: the quotations may not be attributed, but they are almost always marked, at least punctuationally—by quotation marks or italicization. Rather, the writing and unwriting of quotation marks is characterized as a way of making the reader part of the citational interplay. The reader should not stop at hearing, or seeing, the language of the other (the author): rather than judging a language, we should ironize it.

Selon une première vision, l'imaginaire est simple: c'est le discours de l'autre *en tant que je le vois* (je l'entoure de guillemets). Puis, je retourne la scopie sur moi: je vois mon langage *en tant qu'il est vu*: je le vois *tout nu* (sans guillemets): c'est le temps honteux, douloureux, de l'imaginaire. Une troisième vision se profile alors: celle des langages infiniment échelonnés, des parenthèses, jamais fermées: vision utopique en ce qu'elle suppose un lecteur mobile, pluriel, qui met et enlève les guillemets d'une façon preste: qui se met à écrire avec moi.[56]

---

[55] C, 61.   [56] *RB*, 164.

L'imaginaire is Barthes's way (adopted from Lacan) of referring to the way we defend ourselves against the radically decentring force of a language we can never control by taking refuge in narcissistic images of totality and security with which we can identify. At first, the *imaginaire* is euphoric, since it grants us a relatively stable identity: it means we can recognize ourselves and others. Later, the *imaginaire* becomes a prison: we are unable to free ourselves from the images of ourselves that we, in collusion with others, have constructed. Barthes's fragment is about the struggle to free writing from its images (from the fact that it is identified as originating in a certain person—when that person may be writing precisely in order to escape from the sclerosis of personality and the mortifying grip of an imaginary order). We have to cease to identify the other's writing (to objectify it too readily), just as we have to distance ourselves from the ways the other may have objectified *our* writing (and turned us into an image—the problem discussed in 'L'Image').

Barthes suggests that mentally adding and subtracting inverted commas 'd'une façon preste' may help in this process of disoriginating writing, restoring its symbolic mobility (its polyphony and polysemia). Like all Barthes's suggestions, such a tactic may not always work—at least not in Barthesian ways. To take one example: the placing of inverted commas (around fragments from an article by the American philosopher John Searle) is, of course, one of the ways Derrida attempts to expropriate speech in writing in *Limited Inc abc* . . . .[57] But although Derrida is attacking Searle for believing that an author can control the meaning of texts, and also questioning Searle's notion that quotation is only a marginally pertinent example of language use, constituting at best what Searle's mentor the Oxford philosopher Austin considered an 'infelicitous' discursive operation, the effect is not as Barthesian as it ought to be, given that Derrida 'met et enlève les guillemets d'une façon preste'. This suggests that one needs to

---

[57] This is Derrida's response to Searle's objections to 'Signature événement contexte'. This latter essay, Derrida's discussion of J. L. Austin's theory of performatives (*How to Do Things with Words*, ed. J. O. Urmson and Maria Sbisà (2nd edn., Oxford, 1975)), is in *Marges—de la philosophie*, 367–93. In *Limited Inc abc* . . ., *Glyph*, 2 (suppl.) (Baltimore, 1977) Derida quotes Searle's copyright thus: ' """"Copyright © 1977 by John R. Searle""""' in an attempt to show how few rights Searle has over his copy and how he has failed to register that to say '©' is always to quote a code (3). Another technique used by Derrida is itself a way of quoting and changing at the same time (like Barthes's drift): he places certain key but problematic concepts *sous rature*, under erasure—figured in the text as a saltire cross overprinting the word in question. This typographical device was also used by Heidegger.

do rather more than scatter punctuational marks around to overcome the potential arrogance of one's text: *Limited Inc abc* . . . is still a satire on Searle, deprived of the far more complex effects Derrida achieves with intercitationality elsewhere (notably in the way he gets Hegel and Genet talking to, through, and across each other in *Glas*). When Barthes quotes his critics in *Critique et vérité* he is not resorting to citationality but engaging in an old-fashioned polemic: but even here, on at least one occasion, his use of quotation anticipates the way he will develop this tactic in the 1970s. He quotes a number of phrases that sound like the language used by Raymond Picard, author of *Nouvelle critique ou nouvelle imposture?* and scourge of the new criticism—*laborieusement inexact, bévues, subtilités de mandarin déliquescent* and so on. Barthes then points out that these vituperations were authored not by Picard but by Proust, in a pastiche of Sainte-Beuve and in M. de Norpois's dismissal of the writer Bergotte as described in the *Recherche*.[58] Barthes seems to take it for granted that to share a language mocked by Proust—in a very different context—is automatically to be shown up as a fake. Proust, in other words—and in the form of a pastiche and a fiction—is Barthes's authority here, defending, without knowing it, *la nouvelle critique*.

Despite the vulnerability of the procedure, Barthes quotes in other effective ways. For instance, in *Michelet par lui-même*, he places great emphasis on the body. But how could Michelet base his history on carnal values, rather than on a properly historical analysis? And how could Barthes duplicate Michelet's *parti pris*, in the post-war years when the ways of writing history were subject to close scrutiny? The problem was especially acute in that Barthes had dismissed Michelet's ideology, a major focus of any sustained historical critique, in fourteen lines. What Barthes does on one characteristic occasion is to emphasize Michelet's focus on the body ('Toute l'histoire repose en dernière instance sur le corps humain'), while deflecting attention from the potentially problematic phrase *en dernière instance*, with its weight of controversy, by dropping a footnote quoting Marx.[59] This quotation from *The German Ideology* is not merely a way of being both Micheletesque and Marxist: in that Marx is noting the importance of *l'organisation corporelle* of individuals in their relations to nature, Barthes's point may throw into relief the materialist aspects of Michelet's apparently outmoded and sentimental form of history. But the point is that the quotation (of an authority) is not a statement (of

---

[58] *CV*, 16 n. 1.   [59] *Mi*, 80.

the type: 'Michelet, like Marx, is materialist in that both show the importance of physiology and the priority of material factors over ideology')—it is an indirect hint, a sudden new perspective, that is not defended discursively. We are not, in other words, being invited to compare the Marxist and the Micheletesque views of history (though we may want to): we are allowed to savour a possibility. The quotation here is proleptic: it suggests that, if the text had time, it could tell us how two apparently conflicting views of history can be reconciled—but it does not do so itself. This art of the *elliptical citation* is one of Barthes's most constant tactics, and it alerts us to the fact that all citation is elliptical: selective and subjective, despite the presence of the *ipsissima verba* of the author or authority being discussed. Standard examples of the problem of quotation include the Bible and the works of Nietzsche: in the former case, questions of considerable concern may need to be decided by quoting words out of context, if only because the context is so huge and problematic. And in the latter case, as Karl Jaspers noted, we have to recognize that every quotation from Nietzsche could find its counter-quotation from elsewhere in his work. Furthermore, every quotation, torn from an original context (the *opera omnia* of Michelet or Marx, for instance, which as totalities exist only in the imaginary) creates a new context for itself.

Quotation, then, is one of Barthes's many prolepses, and every prolepsis a form of drift as openness to a future that may never, in the work, be realized. Other prolepses are catalogued in the 'Plus tard' section of *Barthes par lui-même*, where Barthes turns the tables on a self-critical voice which points out how his work promises more than it ever performs: this, claims Barthes, is the *essence* of writing: 'L'œuvre n'est jamais monumentale: c'est une *proposition* que chacun viendra saturer comme il voudra, comme il pourra; je vous passe une matière sémantique à courir, comme le furet'.[60] Barthes's word-play (and his reference to the child's game of pass-the-slipper) is here particularly malicious: the *proposition*, the scientific *énoncé*, is etymologically disarmed, tamed into a modest *proposal*.

Other forms of quotation are equally striking. In the 'Droite' section of *Le Plaisir du texte*, Barthes deploys quotation against the idea, found on the political left as well as the right, that pleasure is reactionary and self-indulgent. For the right, this means it can be welcomed with open arms, as a diversion from dangerous theory and the dry

[60] *RB*, 177.

abstractions of the revolutionary. 'Et à gauche, par morale, (oubliant les cigares de Marx et de Brecht), on suspecte, on dédaigne tout "résidu d'hédonisme".'[61] Marx and Brecht are thus cited as authorities: they will authorize Barthes's pleasures. To which an immediate response might be that Marx and Brecht did not only smoke cigars. But, as so often with Barthes, the immediate response is beside the point: it is the lightness of touch, the rapidity, the indirection of the citation that is effective: just as the Marxist theory of history is more than the body, there is more to Marx than a few personal habits: but drift disregards the totality, raises a scatter of questions—is there a Marxist theory of the historical body? Why is Marxism so often puritanical? What, in general, is the relationship between an intellectual's life (tastes, pleasures, manias) and thought?

Quotation is also a way of staging discourse, dramatizing science, and delegating signifieds. In a late lecture, Barthes notes how the novel allows not direct expression (which his own aesthetic debars, as lyricism), but indirect expression (attributed to some character).[62] And in an earlier essay, Barthes speaks of the need for science to abandon its privileged and sheltered metalinguistic exterritoriality, and enter 'cette "vie littéraire" dont Baudelaire nous dit, à propos d'Edgar Poe, qu'elle est "le seul élément où puissent respirer certains êtres déclassés".'[63] This quotation works as an indirect expression: what we realize on rereading it is that Barthes, who is advocating a move from science to literature, may be surreptitiously identifying with these literary êtres déclassés, but cannot say so directly without rousing the reader's suspicion of what would come across as a form of self-imaging pathos. He thus delegates his expression. We accept the quotation as a quotation—of the cultural doxa of romanticism—without asking to what extent Barthes may, in spite of this delegation of discourse, be speaking in propria persona.

There is another aspect to the way Barthes refers constantly to a certain intellectual intertext. His references are rarely, as is the case in more securely intellectual writing, to debate a point, query a notion, or question a fact. Barthes rarely quarrels with his intellectual intertext, or corrects a point made by a colleague, at least after his more technical semiological period. Does he then agree with all the people he quotes? No: but there is a sense in which he is placing his

[61] PlT, 38.
[62] ' "Longtemps, je me suis couché de bonne heure" ', in BL, 324.
[63] 'De la science à la littérature', in BL, 13–20 (19).

work under the aegis of so many other figures, all of them major presences in contemporary intellectual activity, especially but by no means exclusively in France: Gide, Sartre, Marx, Brecht, Saussure, Sollers, Kristeva, Derrida, Lacan, and Nietzsche, to name only those listed in 'Phases', a schematic and tabular display of Barthes' intertext on page 148 of *Barthes par lui-même*. In what Barthes says, any one or more of these figures may be speaking ventriloquistically through him, often in indirect ways ('l'intertexte n'est pas forcément un champ d'influences; c'est plutôt une musique de figures, de métaphores, de pensées-mots; c'est le signifiant comme *sirène*,' he adds). One of the effects of this table, as of an earlier fragment ('La chambre d'échos') is, however, to suggest that any truth content comes from the authorities and that the deviations are all his.[64] This is to claim drift (the possible misunderstandings and deviant swerves from systematic or conceptual correctness) as his own: he appropriates impropriety: the rest (the truth content) is theirs, and if we want to quarrel with the truth content, we will have to take on the authorities that propounded it (even if few of them would claim to be authorities in this archaic and doctrinaire sense). Barthes both stands apart from and defends his work by exposing its dependence, its lack of originality. His blurb on the back of the Seuil 'Points' edition of S/Z is characteristic.

J'ai pilé, pressé ensemble des idées venues de ma culture, c'est-à-dire du discours des autres; j'ai commenté, non pour rendre intelligible, mais pour savoir ce qu'est l'intelligible; et en tout cela, j'ai continûment pris appui sur ce qui s'énonçait autour de moi.

This is not just modesty (*S/Z* is perhaps Barthes's most challengingly experimental text, the one that frees him for the highly original work of his last decade): rather, as so often, Barthes is creating a space for himself by keeping the *discours des autres* at a distance, however much he is drawing on it. It is this Barthesian space (a *topos* which is *atopos*) that is difficult to describe. And yet to claim that one's own discourse is impure, unscientific, subjective, and derivative is in a sense merely to suggest that it is literary, perhaps, even, in rather traditional ways. For if literature is what Barthes sees as the realm of the signifier (the form to which each new generation brings a content, a signified), it cannot be epistemologically pure (it tends to encode a certain *doxa*—as Balzac tells us 'what people thought'—or what he thought they thought—in the first half of the nineteenth century), nor can it be conceptual or

---

[64] *RB*, 148.

objective like science. In Julia Kristeva's highly sophisticated theory, literary writing is seen as intertextual, functioning on the basis of other texts which it implicitly cites or plagiarizes: the fact that Barthes's writing does all these things (albeit more explicitly—like Lautréamont and Sollers, he is an avant-garde artist in this heightened self-consciousness) may be his way of trying to skew his work away from theory and towards the kind of literature that theory discusses. So the deliberate impurity of his discourse (it is scientific—'about' literature—but it is also literary), together with the fact that his writing defends itself by reflecting on its own presuppositions and procedures (he mimics the paranoia of commentary in various ways, such as referring to himself in the third person in *Barthes par lui-même*—so that a critique of Barthes is bound to echo many of the things he has already said or implied himself), may help to explain why Barthes is, now, caught in a difficult historical moment: the real polemics seem to centre on other figures (including most of those listed in Barthes's intertextual table). That Barthes is no longer here to engage in production and debate is irrelevant: the same is true of Sartre, Foucault, Lacan, and Althusser. The important thing is that it is drift which, by his own tenets, makes Barthes a writer, and it is drift which debars us from categorizing exactly what kind of writing he produced. We are, in other words, forced to oscillate wildly between (again in his terms) the signifier and the signified (Barthes as writer and theorist), without being able to reach more than local and far from dialectical accommodations.

Barthes thus theorizes in ways that approximate asymptotically to literature, which in the 1970s can almost be defined, it seems to him, as every discourse that is not theoretical. Or rather, since literature itself has become more theoretically self-aware, literature is everything that is not quite as theoretical as theory (or is even *more* theoretical, but in ways that institutional theory has not yet come to terms with). This problem is still with us, as one of the many paradoxes developed by Hegel: art is past, to be replaced, ultimately, by philosophy; literature is past, to be replaced by theory—but not quite yet. So triumphant do the human sciences become in the 1970s that when, in his inaugural lecture as 'Professeur de Sémiologie littéraire', Barthes asks what place there is for literary semiology, he finally decides that semiology—his kind of semiology—is there to pick up the pieces that are too impure to be dealt with by linguistics.

La sémiologie serait dès lors ce travail qui recueille l'impur de la langue, le rebut de la linguistique, la corruption immédiate du message: rien moins que les désirs, les craintes, les mines, les intimidations, les avances, les tendresses, les protestations, les excuses, les agressions, les musiques, dont est faite la langue active.[65]

He has already told us that literature works on 'ce qu'on pourrait appeler le grand *gâchis* du langage'.[66] It is therefore not surprising that he comes to see literature and semiology as coming together 'pour se corriger l'une l'autre'.[67] This professor of literary semiology almost identifies literature with semiology, in that they are both to some extent the left-overs, the rejects, the waste paper discarded from the clean formalizations of science.

This brings us back to 'L'Image' and corruption. Barthes presents a micronarrative which suggests that many of the words he uses are *derived* from scientific contexts. He says, in effect, that words can be seduced from the linguistic *innocence* of science into the *experience* of the aesthetic. This is evidently a simplification: Derrida has pointed out the mythical nature of any attempt to tell the story of the origin of a language.[68] But Barthes is not necessarily indulging in a myth of origins. The very example he cites in the above-mentioned passage of 'L'Image' ('"catastrophe" est un mot technique en mathématiques, chez R. Thom; je puis mal employer "Catastrophe", qui devient alors quelque chose de "beau"') is paradoxical: the usual meaning of the word *catastrophe* is not that associated with the theories of René Thom, but the more everyday sense of disaster.[69] If Barthes writes *Catastrophe*, how many readers will respond, without expository or metalinguistic guidance, to its mathematical connotations? As with Montaigne, how will we know that a certain subversion of sources is going on unless we are told? The *catastrophe* will not be heard, even if it is amplified to *Catastrophe*: the quotation marks around it will remain invisible.

This may explain why, when Barthes does use this word 'badly' he is forced to alert us to its 'good' scientific resonances. So he creates the very context—of science—which he can then enjoy subverting. For example, the section 'Catastrophe' of *Fragments d'un discours amoureux* seems to be devoid of references to the Thom intertext. But

---

[65] *L*, 31–2.
[66] Ibid. 19.
[67] Ibid. 35.
[68] *De la grammatologie* deals extensively with this problem.
[69] Catastrophe theory is a mathematical theory that classifies surfaces according to their form and extends to the explanation of abruptly changing phenomena. Thom has been criticized for using such an emotional term in a sober mathematical theory: see Alexander Woodcock and Monte Davis, *Catastrophe Theory* (Harmondsworth, 1980), 80–1.

when this intertext becomes pertinent, it is named, as in the section 'Dédicace'. Here Barthes says that anything (a book, a gift) dedicated to the loved one may reduce the loved one to silence, but ultimately this is not important:

dans *Teorema*, l''autre' ne parle pas, mais il inscrit quelque chose en chacun de ceux qui le désirent—opère ce que les mathématiciens appellent une catastrophe (le dérangement d'un système par un autre): il est vrai que ce muet est un ange.[70]

Pasolini's film is about a man (or rather an angel) who has a brief affair with every member of a particular family and changes them in various subtle ways. The angel may be silent but Barthes's text, in describing the angel's effect on those he meets, speaks that effect, calls it, clearly and metalinguistically, a catastrophe 'in the mathematical sense of the word'. (Significantly, the angel, the loved one, is a figure of writing: he inscribes his effects on the family in silence. Pasolini's *Teorema* is therefore a rather non-theoretical theorem.)

By pointing out, in 'L'Image', this aspect of his practice, Barthes is alerting us to the generalized citationality of language. Every *barthème* may have a secret resonance, an unvoiced intertext, but the secret is an open one, in that we do not necessarily gain anything (on the plane of the signified) by knowing the origin of the particular word. At any moment, the word *jouissance* in a Barthes text may vibrate in sympathy with that of Kristeva, Lacan, or Leclaire, but we cannot tell to what extent this may be pertinent. Again, this is typical of drift: Barthes invites us to go to other places, other texts, for a full explanation of what his terms signify, but by the time we return, we find that what we have learnt may be curiously irrelevant. Barthes insists that he has deformed the terms he appropriates, but the degree of deformation is difficult to determine. The difference between, for instance, Kristeva's *texte* and Barthes's *texte* (which he occasionally claims is at least partly derived from Kristeva) may be as difficult to locate as that between Thom's *catastrophe* and Barthes's *Catastrophe*. This is no doubt because both Barnes and Kristeva see *texte* as something very complex. But more problematically, Barthes especially, as we have seen, rarely writes about it theoretically, as opposed to the extremely sophisticated formalizations of Kristeva. Where Kristeva will refer to the text as a signifying practice, Barthes prefers to say the text is an onion, a piece of lace, or a television screen gone haywire.[71] Barthes's *texte* is more

---

[70] *FDA*, 94.   [71] *RB*, 78.

beautiful and corrupt than Kristeva's: the *barthème* is the Catastrophe of theory.

It would be too simple to suggest that a pure scientific discourse is innocent until corrupted by Barthes, although Mary Bittner Wiseman makes an interesting and far-reaching comparison between Barthes and Socrates, the latter accused of 'corrupting' the young men of Athens and believing in deities of his own invention instead of those recognized by the State.[72] For a science will habitually use words that do not belong to it *en propre*: it cannot always cleanse those words of the non-scientific connotations that adhere to them. In making the word *catastrophe* drift away from its scientific bearings, Barthes is recalling the process by which it first drifted into science to become a technical term. Again, Nietzsche provides parallels: Zarathustra's arch-enemy is *der Geist der Schwere*, 'the spirit of gravity': the connotations of that last word (seriousness, pomposity) suddenly cast a harsh light on its more scientific, and thus, supposedly, value-free connotations (the gravity of Newton).[73] There is thus another angle to Michel Butor's percipient comment that Barthes's activities as a writer are a tactic to win the right to use three modes of language forbidden to the young boy in contemporary French society: sexual language, learned language, and women's language.[74] For Barthes's right to use learned (or scientific) language in general is hard won, given the systematicity of his technical writings: but having served his apprenticeship and become a master he turns on that mastery, pointing out that technical terms are a form of writing and should be recognized as such.[75]

Furthermore, in using scientific terms in this way, corrupting them into something aesthetic, Barthes is reappropriating for literature a knowledge that literature always already had, in non-discursive form, for 'il n'est certainement pas une seule matière scientifique qui n'ait été à un certain moment traitée par la littérature universelle'.[76] In the preface to *Sade, Fourier, Loyola*, Barthes suggests that generalized theft is the most effective riposte in a war of the words in which all the words seem to have been appropriated by bourgeois ideology: it is

---

[72] *The Ecstasies of Roland Barthes* (London, 1989), *passim.*
[73] See 'Of the Spirit of Gravity' in *Thus Spake Zarathustra*, trans. R. J. Hollingdale (Hardmondsworth, 1969), pt. III, p. 210.
[74] 'La Fascinatrice', in *Répertoire IV* (1974), 371–97 (381).
[75] Science speaks, but it should learn to write itself: this is the message of 'De la science à la littérature', in *BL*, 13–20.
[76] Ibid. 13.

thus clear that Barthes's theft of such words as *catastrophe* is not a preliminary to handing them back to their 'proper' owners or their 'proper' meanings; there is no such propriety: both the historical ('Il n'y a d'Histoire que parce que les mots se corrompent') and the aesthetic are fields of dispossession. The technical word is lifted—at once stolen, and lightened of that spirit of gravity that attempts to keep it tied down to the reasonable Earth. The technical term becomes aesthetic: 'On pourrait dire que le champ de cette Corruption est l'esthétique, la littérature.'[77] These two quotations taken together link history and the aesthetic as modes of emergence. What literature reappropriates is a knowledge that, stranded in science, risks disappearing with every epistemological break, or, if the existence of such breaks is denied, every time a certain theory is disproved. The harmony of the spheres, scientifically dead, is saved as literature, as a metaphor. Indeed, a 'scientific' truth-value can re-emerge from such a metaphor after periods of eclipse: the Pythagorean belief in the harmony of the spheres, having been rejected by the mechanistic world-view, has a certain truth today, in that it views the universe as something that holds together in a way closer to a piece of music than to a piece of clockwork, and emphasizes the role of the subject in the appreciation of that music. (The Copenhagen interpretation of quantum theory, and the cosmic anthropic principle, both imply, controversially, that consciousness is built into the universe.) Science thus becomes for Barthes something ephemeral because its discourse is determined by the historicity of truth (sciences are born and die, 'il en naît quelques-unes par siècle, dont certaines passagères').[78] But this 'Heraclitean' trend in Barthes is, again, not merely a fetishization of the archaic notion that the literary monument stands *aere perennius* while mere ideas come and go: rather, it is never certain *what* is transmitted by literature: ideas may take refuge in the aesthetic, as signifiers that both preserve and cancel their signifieds, only to become true in different ways at a later turn in the spiral. Despite his mistrust of science, then, Barthes does not reify it to reject it *en bloc*: he is convinced that it is interwoven with other languages, both fictional and ideological, and that it becomes domineering only if it identifies truth with a hermetic isolation from such profane discourses. Barthes's view is thus, ultimately, holistic: he is attempting to see how all these discourses cannot be divided from one another. That is why

---

[77] *BL*, 396.   [78] Ibid. 17.

he sees the truth in fiction and the mythology in science.[79] (This latter insight may well be derived from the epistemology of Bachelard, who acknowledged the importance of imagery and metaphor in the development of science.)

The relations between science and the aesthetic are thus of crucial importance to Barthes. In a fragment of *Barthes par lui-même*, Barthes tells an anecdote which casts light on his notion of the aesthetic. An interlocutor, named only as X, criticized by Barthes for not protecting his essay on television 'aesthetically', strikes back by claiming that *Le Plaisir du texte* 'frôle sans cesse la catastrophe': on which Barthes comments: 'la catastrophe, sans doute, à ses yeux, c'est de tomber dans l'esthétique'.[80] Again the interrelationship of catastrophe and the aesthetic that we have noted in 'L'Image'—Barthes is both defensive and defiant not only about his use of the term 'aesthetic' but also about his refusal to jettison aesthetic modes of experience and analysis: the aesthetic is still in his work a necessary category, the fall into the aesthetic a *felix culpa*. For him, above all, the aesthetic is less a question of sensation, contemplation, or evaluation than a way of behaving, a practice. His decision to corrupt the word *catastrophe* is an example of an aesthetic tactic: the word is cut out of its scientific context, the signifier floats above the signified: this drifting (still against a tacit background of scientific usage, and thus inscribed in the forcefield between practice and knowledge, according to Barthes) is the aesthetic.

This aesthetic activity can take a variety of forms. Barthes mentions his hobby of painting: when he buys paints he is captivated by the name ('jaune indien, rouge persan, vert céladon') as much as by the colour itself: 'le nom est alors la promesse d'un plaisir, le programme d'une opération: il y a toujours du *futur* dans les noms pleins.'[81] Stendhal's beauty as 'une promesse de bonheur' is being echoed here. And Barthes concludes his anecdote by suggesting that his attitude to words themselves is similar to that he shows towards the names of colours. A beautiful, pleasing word is seductive because Barthes thinks he can do something with it. As he says in the same fragment: 'Le

---

[79] Psychoanalysis was a major influence in this revision: for psychoanalysis, the truth has to be reached via many detours, and appropriated by the subject. Knowledge about psychoanalysis may actually hinder the progress of any one analysis. The fact that the science of the subject is restated by Lacan in metaphorical and polyphonic ways, rather than as a mere body of doctrine, was seen as a great liberation by Barthes, in the development of his own science of the text.

[80] *RB*, 108–9.   [81] Ibid. 133.

mot m'emporte selon cette idée que *je vais faire quelque chose avec lui*: c'est le frémissement d'un faire futur, quelque chose comme un *appétit.*' Barthes thus accepts the psychoanalytic view that aesthetic activity is a dynamic and libidinal drive, one in which corruption and perversion are always implicated. I want now to examine this psychoanalytic theme in more detail.

WRITING: FROM NEED TO DESIRE

Dérive is an openness to the future rather than a reference backward to derivation. But since Barthes frequently tells the story of the coming-into-being of the aesthetic in anecdotal terms, presenting this phenomenon as a micronarrative in which background material (science) is foregrounded in certain poetic ways, we may see a parallel here with another teller of stories—Freud, who narrates the *emergence* of sexuality. For while, according to Freud, sexuality relies on something prior—those somatic processes which ensure basic self-preservation—, sexuality, as Jean Laplanche puts it, 'is simultaneously entirely *in the movement which disassociates it* from the vital function'.[82] This movement is one of propping: Laplanche cites Freud's use of this term (*Anlehnung*, a 'leaning against', frequently translated in *The Standard Edition of the Complete Psychological Works of Sigmund Freud* by the neologistic 'anaclisis') from the second of Freud's *Three Essays on Sexuality*: at its origin, an infantile sexual manifestation '*attaches itself to* [or 'props itself upon'; *entsteht in Anlehnung an*] one of the vital somatic functions'.[83]

This story of the birth of sexuality (in Freud's example, the way the child's impulse to suck in order to feed and thus survive is rapidly placed at the disposal of the sexual urge to suck for pleasure) is not something which happens once and for all. Sexuality originates in a vital order of self-preservation and need—an order which it both mimes and perverts. Sexuality is not something that may or may not become perverted, depending on the vicissitudes of the life of the psyche: it is always already perverted in so far as it is founded in the moment of mimicry and separation that begins in the process of anaclitic propping. And mimicry and separation together comprise the process I have been calling drift.

---

[82] *Life and Death in Psychoanalysis*, trans. Jeffrey Mehlman, (Baltimore, 1976), 15.
[83] Ibid: the comments in square brackets are Laplanche's.

Sexuality, according to Laplanche's reading of Freud, is something which is always emergent: furthermore, it shares with perversion a certain gratuitousness: it has no 'proper' source or object, being able, says Laplanche, to take as its point of departure 'absolutely anything'. According to Freud, the process of propping introduces into the psychic economy a 'fringe benefit' of supplementary pleasure (*Lustne-bengewinn*). This process of propping contains no immanent control mechanism within itself, so that psychoanalysis has to rely on non-scientific, social norms of conduct if it is to classify sexuality as 'normal' or 'perverted'. Sexuality as such need stop nowhere. (Laplanche tends to neglect the fact that Freud sees sexuality as more or less fixed by puberty: Freud was still concerned to tie the emergence of sexuality down to biological periods in the life of the subject. But Laplanche might want to suggest that this is a weak point in Freud's theory.)

Barthes frequently uses the idea of 'perversion' in his discussions of the aesthetic. In psychoanalysis, of course, the perverse is that which is not useful for procreation. Barthes's provocatively positive evaluation of this term has to do with his view that the aesthetic likewise is useless, gratuitous, and in some sense, therefore, free. And a perversion is close to *schize*, implying a split in the ego. For instance the activity of reading which, as *Le Plaisir du texte* points out repeatedly, may be split, fetishistic, and pleasurable, is itself, according to Barthes, the locus of perversion *par excellence*: it is 'ce geste du corps (car bien entendu on lit avec son corps) qui d'un même mouvement pose et pervertit son ordre: un supplément intérieur de perversion'.[84]

When Barthes talks of perversion, he frequently sees it as adding a supplementary pleasure—a halo of aesthetic interest and activity—to something that would otherwise be too tediously 'straight' to arouse desire. Here, for instance, is a fragment, entitled 'La Déesse H.', in which Barthes characteristically personifies two figures of perversion and demonstrates how this perversion creates a surplus pleasure:

Le pouvoir de jouissance d'une perversion (en l'occurrence celle des deux H: homosexualité et haschisch) est toujours sous-estimé. La Loi, la Doxa, *la Science* [*my emphasis*] ne veulent past comprendre que la perversion, tout simplement, *rend heureux*; ou pour préciser davantage, elle produit un *plus*: je suis plus sensible, plus perceptif, plus loquace, mieux distrait, etc—et dans ce *plus* vient se loger la différence (et partant, le Texte de la vie, la vie comme

[84] 'Sur la lecture', in *BL*, 37–47 (40).

texte). Dès lors, c'est une déesse, une figure invocable, une voie d'intercession.[85]

It is noteworthy that Barthes does not here see perversion as transgressive (as he largely does in, for instance, the essays on Sade in *Sade, Fourier, Loyola*): perversion merely goes beyond what is normally accepted as good sexuality by exaggerating that sexuality's fundamental tendencies, by refusing to stop. But only the smallest difference need be necessary, for those who can register such differences. Perversion, like the aesthetic, like drift, is a difference, a plus, a separation that stands in an oblique rather than a contestatory relation to that from which it springs.

In a sense, science for Barthes plays much the same role as psychic need for Freud. And just as the aesthetic comes into being by a process of drifting away from science, the sexual comes into being by drifting away from vital somatic needs. This gives us one narrative version for the emergence of the avant-garde, which positions the tradition it subverts and can begin absolutely anywhere, with Lucan or La Bruyère.[86] The parallel would be too loose to be worth making, however, were it not for Barthes's particularly sensitive relations to the 'science' of psychoanalysis. 'Son rapport à la psychanalyse n'est past scrupuleux (sans qu'il puisse pourtant se prévaloir d'aucune contestation, d'aucun refus). C'est un rapport *indécis*.'[87] For Barthes's texts after 1970 bristle with the terminology of psychoanalysis. Sometimes Barthes's insights are creatively based on psychoanalysis: sometimes, as he himself points out, he has deformed the technical terms associated with that science (as is the case with *imaginaire*). He has been cruising after terms to use in his own texts: hence the Barthesian theme of *la drague*, with its connotations of the body on the alert to passing people and words.[88]

[85] *RB*, 68.

[86] On Lucan as a Flaubertian *avant la lettre*, see Barthes's 'Une leçon de sincérité', *Poétique*, 47 (Sept. 1981), 259–67 (267); on 'cette modernité qui commence avec La Bruyère', see 'La Bruyère', in *EC*, 221–37 (236).

[87] *RB*, 153.

[88] *Draguer* in French, meaning to dredge, or to sweep (as for mines), is another marine metaphor like drift. Colloquially it means to 'pick up' somebody. The English verb 'to cruise', originally part of gay usage, preserves the seaborne connotations. Barthes notes the emphasis the word places on the encounter, the first time, in an interview with *Le Magazine littéraire*: 'Vingt mots-clé pour Roland Barthes', *GV*, 194–220 (218). The fragment 'La mollesse des grands mots' in *RB* notes how 'd'autres mots, enfin, sont dragueurs: ils suivent qui ils rencontrent' and suggests that *imaginaire* is vaguely Bachelardian in 1963 (a set of poetic images that convey attitudes to the material world), and rebaptized as Lacanian in *S/Z*, where *imaginaire* is the way a subject is condemned to self-images that disguise the real nature of unconscious desire (*RB*, 129).

There is a paradox implicit in Barthes's perversion of words taken from psychoanalysis. By giving positive overtones to such notions as perversion, fetishism, voyeurism, and so on—as he often does ('la perversion, tout simplement, *rend heureux*')—Barthes is miming and displacing the discourse of psychoanalysis.[89] In so doing, he is *repeating* the fundamental myth of the origin of sexuality that is part of psychoanalysis. Barthes can only drift away from psychoanalysis (and not negate it) because the *figure de système* of that science means that both outright acceptance and outright rejection are forms of miscognition. And he can only drift out of psychoanalysis in so far as psychoanalysis itself accompanies him in that drift. By taking psychoanalysis as a point of departure, and therefore constituting it retroactively as law, origin, science, an economy of need rather than of desire (as a theoretical *gendarme*, he suggests in *Le Plaisir du texte*), Barthes is propping his own discourse on that which is itself a general discourse on and of propping.[90]

This is symptomatic of the fact that his discourse never quite stops being, to some extent, scientific. Like all forms of drift, the tension involved is clear. Confronted with the final illness of his mother, Barthes notes in his diary: 'Sombres pensées, peurs, angoisses: je vois la mort de l'être cher, m'en affole, etc.'[91] Where is the science here? In the 'etc.': Barthes knows that however intense his emotion may be, it can be written only as a stereotype ('fear for the loved one'): he is, even here, quoting a code, imprisoned by his own scientific awareness of stereotypes.

As far as the lexicon is concerned, Barthes's semantic slippage is, again, already there in psychoanalysis. Laplanche refers to propping (Freud's *Anlehnung*) as a good example, being a word found in common non-scientific discourse before Freud took it up and gave it a more scientific twist in his own theory of sexuality. The slippage of conceptual oppositions in Freud 'is nothing else than the slippage effected, within the genesis of the sexual drive, by the movement of anaclisis or propping'.[92] The story of the emergence of sexuality is thus, also, the story of the emergence of the *discourse* on sexuality.

One last point: by coining neologistic terms such as anaclisis, cathexis, and parapraxis for what in the German are words of less

---

[89] Freud's paper 'Fetishism' emphasizes the fact that fetishists are happy—or rather, that their fetish is not a source of anguish to them (in *Pelican Freud Library*, vii. 345–57 (351).

[90] *PlT*, 91.

[91] 'Délibération', in *BL*, 402.

[92] *Life and Death in Psychoanalysis*, 87.

esoteric resonance, the translators responsible for the *Standard Edition* of Freud's work show both a (remarkably Barthesian) love of hellenistic verbal creativity and also a desire to make Freud sound more technical than he does in German. Bruno Bettelheim has pointed out that Freud's language is less technical in the original—more concrete and metaphorical, happy, one might say, to drift within the words already at his disposal in the German language.[93]

Bettelheim's criticisms are quite valid, stemming as they do from the desire to save psychoanalysis from being a mere psychic technology. But the coinages of the *Standard Edition* have their own merits. In a sense, whether we translate *Anlehnung* as 'anaclisis' or as 'propping' depends on a particularly Barthesian choice, between neologism (Saussure's 'partial analogy' applied to an ancient language) or drift (keeping an old word and giving it a new meaning). Psychoanalysis has shown that its effectiveness as a science of the subject cannot be isolated from its linguistic techniques: and the language of psychoanalysis ends up mimicking some of the discoveries of psychoanalysis—so that both 'anaclisis' and 'propping', in their different ways, suggest some of the force of the theory: the former emphasizing the way language itself can be twisted into new shapes by the perverted and creative drives laid bare by psychoanalysis; the latter by emphasizing how drives rise from somatic impulses in a way which is paralleled by the emergence of a new technical meaning to the term 'propping' from its former, ordinary-language use. Robert Young, to give one further example of how unstoppable this process is, suggests that theory after Barthes and Foucault becomes the critic's permanent autocritique, 'a form of *antanaclasis*, the rhetorical term for a self-reflexion or bending back. I would go further and modify this to form the neologism *antanaclisis*, thus introducing from the psychoanalytical term *anaclisis* the Lucretian swerve or "leaning" of error or desire.'[94] This Lucretian swerve is also a Barthesian drift.

[93] *Freud and Man's Soul* (London, 1983), 8. 'Anaclisis' translates *Anlehnung*, 'cathexis' is *Besetzung*, and 'parapraxis' is *Fehlleistung*. Even more problematic are the equivalents 'psyche' for *Seele*, 'ego' for *Ich*, 'super-ego' for *Über-Ich*, and 'id' for *Es*. The trans. of Barthes's terms into English mobilizes equally sensitive forces: thus Stephen Heath objects, with some justification, to *jouissance* being trans. (by Richard Howard) as 'bliss', since the latter term has undesirable connotations of 'religious and social contentment' (see the 'Translator's Note' with which Heath prefaces *Image-Music-Text* (London, 1984) 9). It is the note of contentment that is wrong. 'Ecstasy' is closer—and yet *jouissance* has perfectly ordinary connotations of simple enjoyment, too.

[94] 'Post-Structuralism: The End of Theory', *Oxford Literary Review*, 5: 1 and 2, 'Papers from the OLR/Southampton Conference (1982)' 3–20 (pp. 6–7).

Thus it is clear that one of the reasons why Barthes finds the notion of drift potentially liberating is that it enables him to distance himself from *within* a system (psychoanalysis) that he might otherwise have found too overpowering, and that could not, because of its alleged capacity to recuperate opposition, be countered directly. Drift is thus not solipsistic, but a form of mediation. It recognizes the force of the *figure de système* that sees denial of the unconscious as proof of its existence. It recognizes that, for a psychoanalyst, psychoanalysis has no outside (which is the characteristic of all ideologies). But it moves into the system only to undermine it by mimicking the processes it describes (here, drift). Barthes's constant praise of indirect modes of writing, itself part of the general area of drift, should not be seen as merely aesthetic, but as a deliberate tactic of immediate importance for the life of the subject in an overcoded world (the *logosphère*).

Or rather, what emerges from this discussion is that the aesthetic itself cannot be dismissed as merely aesthetic: for it too is a necessary tactic in the war of languages. Barthes points out that Brecht had suggested that whatever the polemical force of revolutionary language, the transformative energies of revolutionary praxis, there might be one delicate tool that alone can accomplish certain fundamental tasks. What Barthes seems to suggest is that aesthetics might play such a role.[95] But it is not a contemplative but an active aesthetics, akin to the semantic entryism Barthes praises and practices. According to 'Écrivains, intellectuels, professeurs', for instance, a completely free-wheeling semiosis, an untrammelled play of signs and languages, is socially and historically premature: what we must practise is a form of trickery: 'dans une société soumise à la guerre des sens, et par là même astreinte à des règles de communication qui en déterminent l'efficacité, la liquidation de l'ancienne critique ne peut progresser que *dans* le sens (dans le volume des sens), et non hors de lui. Autrement dit, il faut pratiquer un certain entrisme sémantique.'[96]

For what Barthes does not suggest in 'Écrivains, intellectuels, professeurs', but what his work clearly suggests elsewhere, is that unlimited semiosis is not just Utopian, but easy to recuperate: its oppositional stance to the institutions and practices in power is overt, and its extremism may be easily read within the terms of that power— a problem that we earlier identified at work in the politics of the avant-garde. Barthes is aware of the fact that any freedom of the signifier will be contaminated by the fact that it is merely a freedom

[95] *RB*, 111.   [96] *BL*, 361–2.

from the constraints of social meaning—it is a reaction against them. For Nietzsche, new forces that are going to have a chance of survival tend to mimic rather than oppose the old. This still involves a certain reactivity, but one that is masked and less overtly concerned merely to overturn a binary set of evaluations than to do something more insidious. Thus, says Nietzsche, the philosopher, as type, came slowly into existence by mimicking a previously well-established type (the religious) and, in a sense, this mimicry has never ended, the mask has stuck: every philosopher still, says Nietzsche, is something of a prophet, an ascetic, or a contemplative.[97] Barthes's frequent references to the mask should be seen as part of a similar tactic: like Nietzsche, he imagines new cultural forces as coming into being by imitating forms that are already in position, and then slowly detaching themselves from those forms.

Narratives of emergence are also important in sociological and historical terms: rising classes mimic those in power. As Raymond Williams notes, even when an emergent culture has new things to say, it may find that the more oppositional it is, the greater are the attempts to recuperate it made by the dominant culture.[98]

These large-scale typological and historical considerations are, however, less important than the fact that, in psychoanalytical terms, drift is a form of anaclitic object-choice. Anaclitic object-choice is distinguished, by Freud, from narcissistic object-choice. Narcissistic object-choice occurs when a person chooses as love-object someone or something that resembles that person. In the case of anaclitic object-choice, the object is different—as is the case in infantile dependence, where the mother is loved by the helpless baby because she is strong. Anaclitic and narcissistic object-choices can never be securely distinguished (the infant will eventually want to become *like*

---

[97] Nietzsche's view of emergence is clearly expressed in *On the Genealogy of Morals*, Ch. 3, Sect. III. 10: 'To begin with, the philosophic spirit always had to use as a mask and cocoon the *previously established* types of the contemplative man—priest, sorcerer, soothsayer, and in any case a religious type—in order to be able to *exist at all*' (pp. 115–16).

[98] Raymond Williams has proposed a theory of emergent cultures which always risk recuperation (or, as he puts it, 'incorporation') into the dominant culture. He notes the difficulty (an essential part of our 'drift') of deciding what is really emergent, and what is just novel; and he shows how definitions of the emergent can be made 'only in relation to a full sense of the dominant' (see *Marxism and Literature*, 121–7, esp. 123). There are of course major *differences* in all these stories of emergence, but they help to place Barthes in a wider context, and suggest that his apparently playful mimicry and perversion are often a fraught response to historical conditions.

the mother—independent like her), just as need can never be separated entirely from desire.[99]

Because of the mixed mode of Barthes's writing, we can see his drift (his emergence) in two ways. Firstly his choice of science (Marxism, semiology, psychoanalysis) is anaclitic: as a *littérateur* he props himself against these strong discourses, and mimics them because he cannot ever identify with them: his trajectory is fuelled by their energy, but ultimately, as love-objects, they are, like all such objects, lost. (But they are not entirely shaken off, since for psychoanalysis what is lost is, in mourning, introjected.) 'Il avait toujours, jusqu'ici, travaillé successivement sous la tutelle d'un grand système (Marx, Sartre, Brecht, la sémiologie, le Texte). Aujourd'hui, il lui semble qu'il écrit davantage à découvert; rien ne le soutient, sinon encore des pans de langage passés (car pour parler il faut bien prendre appui sur d'autres textes).'[100] In this case, Barthes is slowly moving towards a maturity of his own, one that will no longer involve the proppings of science.

A second, different way of telling the story is to suggest that Barthes is anaclitically propping his theoretical discourse on the very different languages of literature. But in this case, the object-choice becomes narcissistic: he increasingly chooses literature as that which his own discourse would resemble. At the Colloque de Cerisy based on Barthes's work, Robbe-Grillet noted how it was easier for Barthes to drift (in his word, *glisser*) in material that was relatively stable and fixed—in other words he suggested that Barthes's best work was the result of anaclitic object-choice: Barthes chose texts whose difference posed a challenge to him.[101] But he could also have pointed out that this anaclitic choice is, as a project, narcissistic: Barthes increasingly wants his discourse to resemble the texts on which he writes—to lose their infantile dependence and gain the autonomy of literature. This trend was in a sense never brought to completion (Barthes never wrote his 'novel'), but it is as important as the different trend to see the world as it is which dominates Barthes's last major work, *La Chambre claire*, in which Barthes works his way beyond the world's images (especially its photos) in order to respond, in the book's last

---

[99] In Lacan's terms, the infant needs the mother: as a result of expressing that need in the signifiers of the demand for love, the infant's need is inscribed in the symbolic system of language: but need does not fit entirely into the mould of language, and the leftover is what becomes an unsatisfiable desire.

[100] *RB*, 106.   [101] C, 264.

words, to 'l'éveil de l'intraitable réalité'. Indeed, Barthes's final drift was towards a Utopian reconciliation of the world in its contingency (represented by the facticity of photographic images) and the world as it appears in a fiction. It is as if he wanted to take Wittgenstein's image seriously, making his way up the ladder of discourse to reach an insight into reality that would no longer be expressible in discursive, theoretical terms (but could be staged, perhaps, in the aesthetic terms of a fiction).

My propositions serve as elucidations in the following way: anyone who understands me eventually recognizes them as nonsensical, when he has used them—as steps—to climb up beyond them. (He must, so to speak, throw away the ladder after he has climbed up it.)

He must transcend these propositions, and then he will see the world aright.[102]

Barthes's writing too tends to borrow ladders from the discourses around him, as a mode of self-discovery. But he is aware that, given his own model of language as many-levelled and multi-layered, it is not going to be easy to throw the ladder away: it may have an infinite number of rungs. 'En un mot, l'œuvre est un échelonnement; son être est le *degré*: un escalier qui ne s'arrête pas.'[103]

DRIFT: WRITING ITSELF

But what does Barthes mean when he sometimes sees his work as moving 'from science to literature'—what is the *Fiction* to which he aspires? To situate such a word, we need to place it within some opposition. Fiction rather than—what? Fact? Theory? Science? Fragment? Fiction? (That is, fiction in the 'old' sense?) Fiction itself is a drifting term: sometimes Barthes sees it as different from theory, sometimes he sees theory as a fiction in that both share the readability, coherence, and systematicity of a classical novel—as when he identifies psychoanalysis as a fiction, 'comme les voies admirables d'une très grande ville, voies à travers lesquelles on peut jouer, rêver, etc.'.[104] Barthes no longer locates truth in the factual correctness of science: he sees science itself, a historical and transitory human construct, as

---

[102] Ludwig Wittgenstein, *Tractatus Logico-Philosophicus*, trans. D. F. Pears and B. F. McGuinness (London, 1961), 6. 54.
[103] *RB*, 177.   [104] *P/T*, 93.

generated by the same drive to organize the world as is a novel. Indeed, he turns the tables: since a science strives for coherence, it is more fictional than a novel, which can admit contingency. Since 'la vérité est dans la consistance' he says, quoting Poe, consistency itself means the abstract truth of science that he rejects.[105] The deeper, more subjective truth he espouses has to be reached not so much through the consistent fictions of theory, but through the intractable and singular facticity of Fiction.

Drift, then, is a figure of writing. I have not been able to define it, though I have shown some of the ways it works in Barthes's texts and elsewhere. But neither have I failed to define it—failed, that is, in the way drift actively seeks to fail to be defined. In my treatment, drift stagnates, is recuperated, made part of the public discourse it always potentially was: it gains 'a certain conceptual currency', becomes a *theme*.[106] I can neither be faithful to drift, nor unfaithful: in being one I am automatically the other. In order not to understand drift I have had to understand it—by assigning signifieds to its various uses. In order to respect its silence, as writing, I have had to make it speak. In this sense *dire la dérive* is indeed *un discours suicidaire*, since if you succeed in defining it (or even in discussing it in cogent metalinguistic terms), you fail. Hence the double bind we found at work in the 'Dérive' of *Le Plaisir du texte*, discussed at the end of Chapter 1.

But many of the things I have said of Barthes could have been said about writing in general, especially as we encounter it in the genre of the essay.[107] Furthermore, the fact that I can be neither direct nor indirect in my treatment of drift was early identified by Barthes as the quandary of the critic, who uneasily straddles the distinction between *écrivant* and *écrivain*.[108] But that unease, the dissolution of metalanguage, is part of the more general uncanniness of writing in general. As Barthes shows of Queneau, 'il ne s'agit pas de faire la leçon à la Littérature, mais de vivre avec elle en état d'insécurité'.[109] The unremitting examination of this insecurity is one of Barthes's greatest services to literary studies. Theoretical responsibility itself can no

---

[105] *RB*, 63.

[106] See Christopher Norris, *Derrida* (London, 1987), 16–17, for Richard Rorty's noting of the fact that complex notions such as *différance* always end up as modish and easily usable buzz-words.

[107] For Barthes as elaborating a new theory and practice of the essay, see Réda Bensmaïa, *Barthes à l'Essai: introduction au texte réfléchissant* (Études littéraires françaises, 37; Tübingen, 1986).

[108] See the pref. to *EC* and the essay 'Écrivains et écrivants', ibid. 147–54.

[109] 'Zazie et la littérature', ibid. 125–31 (130–1).

longer be predicated on systematicity, as was the case in *Critique et vérité*, since the whole is the false, the systematic a fiction.[110] Nor, since the subject of reading and writing can no longer be isolated in self-present authenticity, can it be located in the intention to mean, to wish to say: *vouloir-dire*. This notion of responsibility is too phonocentric, centred on the voice: writing (*larvatus prodeo* wrote the secretive Descartes, frequently quoted by Barthes) points to its *mask* in silence. It may take the form of a punctuational quirk, an unacknowledged citation, an allusion to science, or a lexical impurity: it may fulfil its responsibilities precisely by refusing to respond: its sociability lies in its distance and otherness.

'Et la marquise resta pensive.'[111] Barthes takes the marchioness's silence, at the end of *Sarrasine*, as an emblem of the classical text, which creates the illusion that if the text wanted to, it could tell us everything. But the marchioness can stand allegorically for Barthes's text, too, in which his voice continually falls silent so that we can say what he writes. Barthes positions his readers as wanting to know what drift, which says it does not mean anything, means: that is why drift is an exemplary figure of writing.

[110] 'The whole is the false': Adorno, *Minima Moralia*, 50.
[111] These are the last words of Balzac's *Sarrasine*, reproduced in *S/Z*, 258: see Barthes's discussion of *Sarrasine*, ibid. 222–3.

3

FRAMES AND NAMES

What is the effect of a frame? The frame opens up and controls a space of representation, positioning the spectator as looking into a field of vision. According to Barthes, representation is defined by its reliance on a geometrical figure rather than by its attempt to copy the real. In 'Diderot, Brecht, Eisenstein', he notes: 'il restera toujours de la "représentation", tant qu'un sujet (auteur, lecteur, spectateur ou voyeur) portera son *regard* vers un horizon et y découpera la base d'un triangle dont son œil (ou son esprit) sera le sommet'.[1] This applies to classical painting, theatre, cinema, but also to 'le discours littéraire classique (lisible)', which, 'abandonnant depuis longtemps la prosodie, la musique, est un discours représentatif, géométrique, en tant qu'il découpe des morceaux pour les peindre'.[2]

Art also frames in so far as it detaches an object from the social totality. Art is not the only activity in which this detachment occurs, but detachment itself will tend to have an aesthetic aspect to it. The modes of that detachment are multiple: frame, book, musical score, concert-hall, museum ('do not touch the exhibits'), cinema screen. Even prehistoric wall-paintings can be seen as detached in this way, according to Georges Bataille, who sees them as forming 'une œuvre d'art détachée', despite the fact that they are not materially detached from any support or context.[3] It is this detachment, claims Barthes, which differentiates art, which detaches, frames, and fetishizes, from sociology, philology, and politics, which are paranoid, integrative, and totalizing.[4]

Paradoxically, however, Barthes suggests that, while detachment is perverse and fetishistic, its necessary consequence, framing, is progressive. He himself likes things framed, as the fragment 'Le goût de la division' notes.

---

[1] *OO*, 86–93 (86).
[2] Ibid. 86–7.
[3] *La Peinture préhistorique: Lascaux ou la naissance de l'art*, in *Œuvres complètes* (1970–87), 7–101 (14).
[4] 'Détacher' in *RB*, 72–3.

Goût de la division: les parcelles, les miniatures, les cernes, les précisions brillantes (tel l'effet produit par le haschisch au dire de Baudelaire), la vue des champs, les fenêtres, le haïku, le trait, l'écriture, le fragment, la photographie, la scène à l'italienne, bref, au choix, tout l'articulé du sémanticien ou tout le matériel du fétichiste. Ce goût est décrété progressiste: l'art des classes ascendantes procède par encadrements.[5]

At the Colloque de Cerisy, Barthes emphasizes his resistance to open-air theatre, theatre in the round, and other experimental disruptions of theatrical space: he likes the action to take place on stage, and to be brilliantly illuminated. He also likes, in painting, the *veduta*.[6]

The fragment I have quoted contains a number of surprising inclusions. All the items catalogued involve, in the simple, visual sense of the word, framing, that *encadrement* Barthes calls progressive, with the exception of four in which the frame is more difficult to imagine. In so far as a haiku and a fragment are both seen as detached (in that one haiku does not 'communicate' with the next, and a collection of fragments must ensure that each fragment can stand by itself), they too involve framing. But *le trait* and *l'écriture* are more puzzling, and thus demonstrate that at this point Barthes is making an evaluative point: he likes *le trait* and *l'écriture* in so far as they are gestures of division, in so far, that is, as they resist being absorbed · entirely into any context (of the kind described in 'Détacher': sociology, philology, politics). I will be looking more closely at a ·potential equation between *trait* and *écriture* in the next chapter: here, what is important is Barthes's equivocation between *division* and *encadrement*. For the fragment 'Le goût de la division' ends by affirming framing as politically progressive, a form of analysis, whereas the fragment 'Détacher' sees politics (presumably including progressive politics) as that which detaches only in order to integrate, a form of synthesis.

While it would no doubt be possible to save Barthes's argument by mediating between the two fragments (suggesting that the difference between political theory and political practice, especially in its artistic forms, is here pertinent, so that the former is hostile to the framer's fetishism which the latter can exploit in progressive ways), this would raise questions of its own. In any case, since the fragment is a mode of detachment, how can I mediate between two fragments? Attempting to do so places me in the unhappy position of the paranoid, attempting to smooth out the difficulties and integrate (mediate between) appar-

[5] *RB*, 74.   [6] *C*, 125–7.

ently different positions, trying to make Barthes's text perfectly *lisible*. Ultimately, the paranoid wants to frame everything, to keep everything in view from one, all-controlling, panoptic point of absolute visibility.[7] But on the other hand, to respect each fragment as fragment is impossible, since no fragment can be read outside some context, and the very fact that I understand what each one says means that the possibility of comparing them will arise. In both cases, I have to choose my frame of reference while being aware of how the effects of framing and unframing are difficult to control.

What are the paradoxes of the frame? Taking Barthes at his word, I will concentrate first on the frame as something positive, and framing as an activity that he enjoys.

This is true, for instance, of his treatment of Balzac's *Sarrasine*. In *S/Z*, he cuts the text into *lexies*, units of reading, each of which can be scrutinized for the semes (the ideological connotations) within it. The cutting of Balzac's text is compared to the way an augur, a priest who practised divination by examining the flight of birds, first marked out a rectangular area in the sky by pointing with his wand.[8] In *Barthes par lui-même*, Barthes claims how much he likes this image: the augur, like the textual commentator, has to begin somewhere, and therefore arbitrarily frames a rectangle within which he will be able to observe the migration of birds or meanings: for without framing, no meaning can be observed: we are faced with the empty and infinite sky, or the other sky, 'plat et profond à la fois, lisse, sans bords et sans repères', of the text.[9] Tracing a frame is one way of overcoming the fear felt at the prospect of this infinity, at the text's plenitude. Barthes constantly has recourse to the frame in order to overcome the sense of panic that his object inspires in him. What is tamed by the frame would otherwise risk being endowed with the frightening, monstrous power of nature, in its guise both as 'the way things are', and as totality. In *S/Z*, Barthes needs reading units but he claims that his reasons for dividing up the text in the way he does are relatively arbitrary. (The augur must not have *too* clear an idea of what will result from his framing of the sky, otherwise his prediction will lack the necessary divine objectivity.) So

[7] The demand for *lisibilité* is characterized in terms that make it sound particularly paranoid in *S/Z*, 161–2. The panopticon, a tower from which the population of an entire prison could be kept under surveillance, was imagined by Bentham and is discussed by Michel Foucault in *Surveiller et punir: naissance de la prison* (1975).

[8] *S/Z*, 20.

[9] *RB*, 52. In this passage, Barthes in fact replaces the augur, who observed birds, with the haruspex, who examined entrails. But it is the former he means, not the latter.

the units need to be short enough to be manageable and long enough to contain enough material (enough connotations) for him to have something to write about in each *lexie*.

But a paradox of the frame is that it can be jettisoned once it has been used to start the detection of meaning: the *augur* traces out a rectangle in the sky, but 'ce geste est fou: tracer solennellement une limite dont il ne reste immédiatement *rien*, sinon la rémanence intellectuelle d'un découpage, s'adonner à la préparation totalement rituelle et totalement arbitraire d'un sens'.[10] The frame does not remain—is invisible (operationally, this is quite correct: we soon forget that Balzac's text is not *in fact* cut into fragments and that Barthes's divisions may actually affect the different meanings we find in each fragment). But the frame is essential none the less, and Barthes emphasizes the fact that meaning may be an effect of framing. For to frame is to provide a context: and while every context reduces meaning, it also makes meaning possible. According to 'Écrivains, intellectuels, professeurs', 'le contexte est par statut réducteur du sens'.[11] This statement, if taken out of context, makes a large claim that can be objected to on the grounds that meaning as such may in fact depend on a context: a black pebble may mean little on a beach, but a sentence of death if it emerges from the urn of a jury in Periclean Athens. But if read in context, Barthes's suggestion makes more sense: he is comparing the context-bound nature of speech as opposed to writing, which is always, for him, susceptible to being read out of context. One corollary of this is that, for Barthes, meaning is always a reduction of something else. (Framing, one might say, reduces *signifiance*, in which the signifiers are in spectacular excess of any signified, while making possible *signification*, in which the textual signs are more stable.)

Furthermore, this *découpage* is already inscribed within the procedures of Balzac's realism. Barthes goes to some lengths to draw a parallel between what is contained in the frame and classical perspective: 'La suite des actions . . . est un espace perspectif: la matérialité du discours est le point de vue; les codes sont les points de fuite; le référent (l'orgie) est l'image encadrée.'[12] But Barthes's manic reframing fragments Balzac's own more large-scale and stable framing, creating new, paradoxical perspectives in which the overall *institutional* frame is now no longer Balzac, or *Sarrasine*, but, ideally, literature

---

[10] *RB*, 52.   [11] *BL*, 346.   [12] *S/Z*, 164.

itself, whose perspective is based on a 'point de fuite . . . sans cesse reporté, mystérieusement ouvert'.[13]

The essential thing about the equation of the commentator with the augur is that the meanings the commentator discovers are, in Barthes's image, completely dependent on the way the augur's wand points in silence to something which thereupon becomes meaningful. The augur's wand is a pen silently tracing a rectangle in which the text will be able to speak. In other words, what Barthes's image suggests is that the augur is a figure of writing (of division, of *le trait* and *l'écriture*) in a very radical sense, more concerned with the ostensive, deictic drawing of a limit than with identifying what comes within that limit. For while Barthes's image does not apply in operational terms (for in fact, as he says, the commentator's choice of *lexies* is not *totalement arbitraire*, being dependent on the possible senses that are already intuited), it does apply to a hypothetically pure writing that would be an act of inscription, the tracing of a boundary, the framing of a space. This pure writing points but does not name. It presents without presenting its presentation.[14]

So although Barthes begins with a common-sense view of the frame, he soon develops it to the point where any frame can be seen as a fundamental mode of articulation—as the writing that lies behind that isolation of any visual field (in painting) or behind the identification of meanings (in the case of other contexts). When he talks of the frame, it is sometimes of the frame in the first sense (that which surrounds an object, drawing our attention to it), sometimes the second (in which the frame is a division and we have to pay especial attention to what may be outside it). In the first sense, Diderot, Brecht, and Eisenstein are all framers aiming at the production of *tableaux* full of explicit meaning, seizing an action at what Lessing called the 'pregnant moment'.[15] It is this meaning on which we concentrate. For instance, the *Gestus* in a play by Brecht is a kind of *tableau vivant* in which the underlying meaning of a constantly developing situation is made clear to us. It is as if Brecht has arrested the action to provide us with a picture. Each *Gestus*, suggests Barthes, is rather like a painting by Greuze (a painter celebrated by Diderot) in the clarity of its signified. In the same way, Eisenstein dwells on certain scenes in order to make their political importance stand out

---

[13] *S/Z*, 19.
[14] On the way that presentation (the act of presenting) may itself be unpresentable, see Jean-François Lyotard, *Le Différend* (1983).
[15] *OO*, 89.

from the film—so much so that when Barthes writes a lengthy essay on Eisenstein, he finds all he wants less by watching an Eisenstein film than by examining film stills: indeed, these framed and quasi-fetishistic images give him his main insights into the essence of Eisenstein's art as a revolutionary cineast.[16] But there is already a sense in which the three figures Diderot, Brecht, and Eisenstein are framers in the second sense: it is the act of framing (the deliberate performance of a gesture in which meaning is produced before our eyes so that we see the process as well as the product) that is politically progressive, as well as the fact that what is framed is a clear political statement. So although it is the meaning which is valued ('fetishized', says Barthes), the act of meaning is almost as important: the frame (framing as a performance) is starting to draw attention to itself.

Derrida has shown considerable interest in the duplicity of the frame, notably in his essay 'Parergon', in which he concentrates on the way it plays an apparently marginal but in fact deeply unsettling role in the aesthetics of Kant as set out in *The Critique of Judgement*. The frame is important for Kant: it excludes the spectator in two ways—it suspends the reality of what is framed (turns it into a representation), and it also ensures that the spectator's self-interest does not come into play. But, as Derrida points out, it is difficult to draw this framing boundary between what is part of the spectator's interest and what is disinterested contemplation, or between what is outside the frame of representation and what is inside. An entire history of aesthetic thought has been preoccupied with this question.[17] But, as he points out, no frame is ever entirely sealed off from external disruption: frames are heuristic fictions—a role they play, as we have seen, in Barthes's discussion of the *lexie*.

The frame is also implicated in Kant's position that, for instance, a wild tulip is beautiful because it is 'cut off' from any finality: here again we have a limit, difficult to locate in topological terms but essential for Kant's definition of beauty. This *de-finition* of beauty is ultimately dependent on something (the frame as a cut or limit, a *finis*)

---

[16] 'Le Troisième Sens', Ibid. 43–61.

[17] As Derrida notes, by 'representing' Kant's argument he is in effect framing Kant (*La Vérité en peinture* (1978), 57). Derrida also insists that the need to 'distinguer entre le sens interne ou propre et la circonstance de l'objet dont on parle' organizes the tradition of aesthetic debate from Plato onwards. It is a need which 'présuppose un discours sur la limite entre le dedans et le dehors de l'objet d'art, ici un *discours sur le cadre*' (ibid. 53).

that the *Critique of Judgement* tries to keep in its lowly place, as a 'parergon', something extraneous and superfluous. In so far as the frame is a trace, and beauty dependent on it, beauty itself, notes Derrida, is difficult to *say*: the drawing of the trace (the *trait*, the frame) is itself beautiful, as a writing that resists translation into speech.[18] Derrida also suggests how quickly frames become invisible. 'Un cadre est essentiellement construit et donc fragile'; furthermore, attempting to think away the frame is not 'romanticism' so much as a way of making God the ultimate frame: 'ce qui a produit et manipulé le cadre met tout en œuvre pour effacer l'effet de cadre, le plus souvent en le naturalisant à l'infini, entre les mains de Dieu (on pourra le vérifier chez Kant)'. [19] Deconstruction, according to Derrida, cannot stay content either with reframing or with trying to abolish frames altogether. In other words, deconstruction is about frames (and about contexts) in both the senses I identified at the beginning of this chapter: the frame focuses attention on what is framed, the striking image or the clear meaning, but it can also raise the question of context—of what is left outside, and why: in this later question we start to see the frame as well as what it frames.

On the basis of this duplicitous nature of the frame, Barthes shows how the framing devices operative in the process of reading can be many and varied. The material existence of a text (its nature, usually, as a book) is one: another is the proper name (of the text, of its author). These are framing effects in so far as they attempt to pose limits to the way in which reading takes place: for example, the author's proper name ensures that we will read the text 'within' a horizon of expectations aroused by that name—a horizon of expectations that is relatively fluid and open to modification, but that governs our reading none the less, ensuring that we do not read *The Imitation of Christ* as if it were written by James Joyce.[20]

According to Michel Foucault, the author's name acts as a frame that reduces the proliferation of meaning, which is seen as being a 'great danger' unless it is controlled. We are mistaken, says Foucault, to see the author as the producer of rich and proliferating meanings.

[18] *La Vérité en peinture*, 101–3.

[19] Ibid. 85.

[20] The term 'horizon of expectations' is taken from the work of Jauss, where it refers to the mind-set a reader brings to a literary work. See Robert C. Holub, *Reception Theory: A Critical Introduction* (London, 1984), 58–63. For the way we *can* conflate Thomas à Kempis with the author of *Ulysses*, see Jorge Luis Borges, 'Pierre Menard, Author of the *Quixote*', in *Labyrinths, Selected Stories and Other Writings*, ed. Donald A. Yates and James E. Irby (Harmondsworth, 1970), 62–71.

The truth is quite the contrary: the author is not an indefinite source of significations which fill a work; the author does not precede the works, he is a certain functional principle by which, in our culture, one limits, excludes and chooses; in short, by which one impedes the free circulation, the free manipulation, the free composition, decomposition, and recomposition of fiction. . . . The author is therefore the ideological figure by which one marks the manner in which we fear the proliferation of meaning.[21]

While we may now be moving into a period when this ideological framing will lose its importance, Foucault argues it would be pure romanticism to expect the author-function to disappear without being replaced by some other form of constraint. One frame, it seems, will inevitably be replaced by another. The question is one of knowing where the new limits will be drawn.

Frames, in other words, can be described as any of those modes of the classification of the text that assign it to a certain place: frames are part of the study of places, the topology of writing, that so much of Barthes's work is concerned to establish. But Foucault's article helps to put into perspective (to frame, perhaps) Barthes's celebration of the death of the author. For, as Foucault points out, author and work frame and control each other: to talk of a 'pure work' without an author is meaningless since the work is partly defined by its authorial frame: what is a work if not what an author has written? (This is true even if we *then* disregard—or pretend to disregard—the author's authority and abandon the hermeneutic quest to recover authorial intentions.) Barthes's essay 'La Mort de l'auteur' suggests in any case how the removal of one frame, in the topology of reading and writing, is accomplished only with the establishment of another. The disseminated identity of the author is recomposed in the reader, however split and riven by contradiction that reader may be. The text is indeed plural and polyphonic (in other words needs to be read outside the frame of reference of authorial intent):

mais il y a un lieu où cette multiplicité se rassemble, et ce lieu, ce n'est pas l'auteur, comme on l'a dit jusqu'à présent, c'est le lecteur . . . l'unité d'un texte n'est pas dans son origine, mais dans sa destination . . . le lecteur est un homme sans histoire, sans biographie, sans psychologie; il est seulement ce *quelqu'un* qui tient rassemblés dans un même champ toutes les traces dont est constitué l'ecrit.[22]

[21] 'What Is an Author?', in Josué V. Harari (ed.), *Textual Strategies: Perspectives in Post-Structuralist Criticism* (London, 1980), 141–60 (159).
[22] *BL*, 66–7.

Foucault, in other words, enables us to see that Barthes is still in this essay ignoring the fact that the author-function of framing has merely been delegated to the reader. A further twist to the argument would lie in suggesting that Barthes's reader is hypothetically a rather empty frame—a mere place in which the writings of the text intersect the writings of the reader's world.

In Barthes's own work, the proper name of text and author do act as frames: if we open *Le Plaisir du texte*, for instance, we do so with the expectation that this slim volume is going to tell us something about the pleasure of the text. It will, that is, represent textual pleasure for us. But pleasure where? In this frame (this book) or somewhere else? In 'the text' in general (and thus in Sollers, Sarduy, Flaubert, Stendhal—all places of pleasure indicated or cited by the text)? Or in those texts only in so far as they are kept securely within the benign purview of *this* frame, the book called *Le Plaisir du texte*? But the fragmented presentation and the constant *renvois* outside, as well as the questioning of the extent to which pleasure can be represented ('Un texte sur le plaisir ne peut être autre chose que *court* . . . tout texte sur le plaisir ne sera jamais que dilatoire; ce sera une introduction à ce qui ne s'écrira jamais') all imply that pleasure can be framed only imperfectly.[23]

Other framing devices operate in *Le Plaisir du texte*. Shortly after the title-page, arousing expectations of pleasure either as something we are going to experience or something we are at least going to hear about, we encounter another framing device—the epigraph: '*La seule passion de ma vie a été la peur.*' Why does *fear* suddenly loom up before us, like an unexpected mountain blocking our prospect (our *veduta*) of the cities of pleasure? This epigraph, from Hobbes, is itself framed by an otherwise empty page, detached as it is from the rest of the text. And it acts as a frame for our reading: if the first frame was pleasure, fear forces us to reframe our expectations. Will pleasure 'contain' fear—mastering and disarming it, including it within itself? The tension between these two framing devices—title and epigraph—plays a major part in our reading of *Le Plaisir du texte*: the epigraph has opened up a place for fear, but that place is not located until page 77, when we learn that fear and *jouissance* may be close or even identical to each other. But the force of the brooding epigraph is not contained by the fact that its referent, fear, is discussed in the text in relatively discursive terms. We learn there that fear too is an outcast: it is not

[23] *P/T*, 31–2.

discussed by the contemporary philosophies on which Barthes draws and from which he is distancing himself. But the epigraph still seems to emphasize rather enigmatically an apparently minor aspect of the text. A history of epigraphs would be useful. When did the habit of using epigraphs become widespread? Did it begin as an appeal to authority and rapidly become ironic, as in Stendhal, whose play with epigraphs is a major feature of *Le Rouge et le Noir*? What effect does it have when it is used in discursive writing? Or when it is used in fiction or poetry? An epigraph can play an extremely large part in determining the ways we want to interpret a text. 'Vengeance is mine and I will repay': these words track down Anna Karenina from the very start of the novel of which she is the protagonist.

Barthes frequently experiments with the effects such framing and reframing may have: for him, framing is a figure of writing in that it is a formal feature (the drawing of a *trait*) which forces us to say and resay what we read, each time in different ways. Framing and reframing may enable us to identify trends in the history of an artistic form: as he suggests, if we frame two square centimetres of Cézanne and enlarge the result, we end up with Nicolas de Staël.[24] Furthermore, the more frames we introduce, the more we will succeed in seeing the text as an onion, surrounded by layers of skin (each one a frame), but with nothing substantial in the middle: to multiply frames can thus help to create that art of multiple surfaces and interstices that he sees as particularly Japanese and celebrates in *L'Empire des signes*, noting for instance that when you receive a Japanese present, the important thing to notice about it is not the present itself (usually trivial) but the way it is wrapped up (layer upon layer of wrapping: the pleasure lies in taking each one off, even if what is left is not itself very exciting).[25]

One of his experiments with framing can be found in his book 'about' himself, *Barthes par lui-même*, and among the particular frames he plays with are: the name of the book; its epigraph; and the book as material object.

I will be looking at the book (and its writing) as material objects in the next chapter. First, what about its title? The book in fact has at least three titles. One is, simply, *Roland Barthes*. This is a book written by Roland Barthes (*par Roland Barthes*). Curiously, no bibliography gives this as the title. Instead, bibliographies name the book as *Barthes par lui-même*, or as *Roland Barthes par Roland Barthes*. What are the implications of these different titles?

The format of the series is such that all titles in it follow the type: *X par lui-même*, and vary in the way they are set out, while generally dividing into biography and commentary on the one hand, interspersed or followed with extensive extracts from the author's work on the other. The title of the series is meant to suggest that the author in question is being presented through the intermediary of a guide—the (contemporary) scholar, there to act as a friendly and knowledgeable mediator.[26] However, Barthes takes the series title literally (the only author so far to have had the opportunity to do so): his book is indeed himself by himself: he is his own mediator. Which Barthes will frame which? Will metalinguistic Barthes frame object-language Barthes? The title *Roland Barthes par Roland Barthes* suggests the dizzying specularity that brings out neatly the point I am making about Barthes's subtle use of frames: the framer and the framed keep exchanging attributes. The frame (Barthes 2 as commentator on a body of writing produced by Barthes 1, who is and is not the same as his critic) creates the framed (it is Barthes 2 who is allowed to do most of the talking, rarely if ever quoting Barthes 1—which is what the series format is supposed to encourage its contributors to do). In other words, Barthes 1, although chronologically prior to Barthes 2 (even though Barthes 2 does not deprive himself of the pleasures of anticipating what Barthes 3 might one day like to write), is in fact positioned as subsequent to Barthes 2. For Barthes 2 is after all still Barthes, and when he comments on his past writings he is not out to view them from some metalinguistic position (outside the frame): he is adding to them, prolonging them and deforming them, emphasizing certain aspects at the expense of others (so that, as Annette Lavers has observed, Barthes 2 is very tough on Barthes 1's pretensions to scientific competence, dismissing his technical works as the result of a (pseudo-)scientific delirium).[27] And it is thenceforward difficult to read Barthes 1 without being aware of the way he has been dismissively framed and abusively represented by Barthes 2. But because Barthes 2 is, even in the act of discussing Barthes 1's work, adding to it (adding to the work of 'Barthes' *tout court*), Barthes 2 is not just a framer, but a writer who moves into the same picture as what he is

---

[26] The series is also an interesting ex. of a canon (who counts as an *écrivain de toujours?*): and the framing effects of a canon (as selection and exclusion) always need to be taken into account.

[27] See, *Roland Barthes: Structuralism and After* (London, 1982), 209, and *RB*, 148.

supposed to be framing. (And Barthes 2, even at his most metalinguistically protected, can still be framed by the nascent Barthes 3, as
well as by us as readers). So Barthes uses the context of the 'Écrivains
de toujours' series, its *institutional* frame and its protocol title to
question and split that frame—how can we have a book called *X par
lui-même*, when there is another author, Y? (Barthes is here both X
and Y.) Barthes's own self-inscription as an *écrivain de toujours* has
occasionally been the cause of ironic comment. But his own irony
towards such a notion is evident.[28] Remembering his own distinction
between the *écrivain* for whom writing is a problem in itself, and the
écrivant for whom writing is the medium of a message (so that,
traditionally, the critic is an *écrivant* writing on *écrivains*), we can see
him as occupying variants of both roles, multiplying his writing selves,
less as an aspiring great writer than as one who just keeps writing,
toujours un écrivain, always writing on, *(un) écrivant toujours*.

The other way in which Barthes here uses a framing device in a
deliberately paradoxical way is the epigraph: on opening the cover of
Barthes par lui-même, we find the left-hand page is black: and in white
handwriting we read 'Tout ceci doit être considéré comme dit par un
personnage de roman.' This voice 'off' (off-stage, off-frame) authori-
tarianly subverts the text's authority, as well as the expectations
aroused by its proper name (or rather its proper names—that of
author and title, which in this case happen to be the same): how can
'Barthes' be speaking as, or about, a *personnage de roman*? It opens up
a new level of indeterminacy. For where does the voice that says 'Tout
ceci . . .' come from? What is its place? If it is outside the text, from
where does it derive its authority? Why should we believe it? The
dogmatic tone of this interruption of our expectations is an attempt to
frame—to bracket, like an algebraic factorization—everything it
stands outside of. It is thus, at the same time, an attempt to keep
everything troublesome (like truth) off-frame. We are not going, it
warns us, to meet the 'real' Barthes.

There are philosophical precedents for this attempt to bracket
extraneous material. In Husserl's phenomenology, the eidetic reduction, a move meant to purify the apperception of a mental phenomenon, consists of bracketing out the world of ordinary determinations
(the bracketing is what is called the *epochē*, meaning 'suspension of
judgement'). This is, simultaneously, an attempt to purify the *language*
of phenomenology, by bracketing out earlier meanings. But Derrida

---

[28] See 'L' Écrivain en vacances', in *My*, 30–3.

asks whether, when the *epochē* is applied to language, it can work in the way Husserl wants.[29] Bracketing, in any case, can never operate in language as it does in mathematics. So Barthes's instructions ('Tout ceci . . .') cannot factorize discourse in this way, multiplying everything in the text by the factor of fiction.

And, taking the other possibility, if 'Tout ceci . . .' includes itself *within* the text, as part of the 'all this' that it is trying to control, then it too must be spoken as if by a character in a novel, and thus no longer as a metalinguistic instruction but as one voice among a polyphony of others. And in a sense, the 'Tout ceci . . .' certainly *is* in the text (just as the epigraphic fear cropped up in the middle of *Le Plaisir du texte*): we find it on page 123: 'Tout ceci doit être considéré par un personnage de roman—ou plutôt par plusieurs.' We cannot locate with any precision the 'all this': it is a shifter ('this—where, this?'): it multiplies places. Magritte's painting *Ceci n'est pas une pipe* likewise tempts us to obey the injunction of the title: to do so we have to ask what *ceci* means (the *repraesentamen* is indeed a pipe: but the agents of representation (paint, canvas), and the word *ceci* itself, are not).[30]

There is a similar problem with the title of Philippe Roger's stimulating study of Barthes: *Roland Barthes, roman*. How do we read this title? Is Barthes a novel, or is Roger's book? If so, as seems to be the claim, why?[31] Again, the frame may not succeed in controlling its contents. The attempt to remodel genres merely by exchanging their names frequently fails to reckon with institutional and material frames that, even when silent, exercise their power. Barthes is always remodelling genres in this way, suggesting that the essay is 'almost' a novel—a novel without proper names.[32] But although he manages to loosen our preconceptions about genre, it is not clear that he destroys them: rather, he transgresses them. For he needs frames *so that* he can cross them.

Sometimes it is difficult for us to follow him in this crossing, just as it is difficult for us to obey the instructions for drifting reading that he gives us. A novel cannot lay down the law about how it is to be read,

[29] *La Voix et le Phénomène. Introduction au problème du signe dans la phénoménologie de Husserl* (1967), 6.

[30] Magritte's painting is discussed by Foucault in *Ceci n'est pas une pipe* (Montpellier, 1973), which also investigates the problem of the frame.

[31] Roger cites Aragon's *Henri Matisse, roman* as a precursor *Roland Barthes, roman* (1986), (11): Aragon's point is that his study is 'ni un récit ni un discours', but a *roman*.

[32] *RB*, 124.

except in the burlesque mode of Beckett's conclusion to *Watt*: 'no symbols where none intended.' Nor can a dissertative work claim unproblematically to be a fiction. Ultimately, the frame of institutional expectations frames Barthes's own attempt to frame his work as fiction. You cannot frame by fiat: in his essay on the progressiveness of the frame, Barthes ignores the constraints (of context and institution) that framers face. Furthermore, undermining the authority of frames creates its own authority. What is more authoritarian than to tell us to read a particular work as a fiction? For while, in general, a fiction does not tell us to read it as such, and thus makes it possible for us to register ways in which it may not be 'just made up' (can show us how things are in the world), the instruction to read *Barthes par lui-même* as a fiction forces us, if we obey it, into a position where we cannot contradict the text (which is avowedly meant not to be truthful). Or rather we can, but we are contradicting only one voice, that of only one character in a novel. In any case, another potential consequence of the 'Tout ceci doit être considéré comme dit par un personnage de roman' is that any Barthes we as readers construct from the book will be novelistic (will be a character in a novel that we, collaboratively, write with the author, and call *Roland Barthes*). None the less, since we cannot suspend the truth-claims of all Barthes's fragments, they retroactively force us to re-evaluate, tentatively, what we mean by *roman* and *fiction*: Barthes is reminding us that a novel is not absolutely untrue. So Barthes does not say *Barthes par lui-même* should be read as a novel, but as being spoken by characters in a novel. And fictional characters may well say things that are true. This is why Barthes notes how the third person *il* or 'R. B.' complicates things further. For while his book functions by alternating *bouffées d'imaginaire simple* with *accès critiques*, the latter, too, are still mired in his own imaginary self-identity.

La substance de ce livre, finalement, est donc totalement romanesque. L'intrusion, dans le discours de l'essai, d'une troisième personne qui ne renvoie cependant à aucune créature fictive, marque la nécéssité de remodeler les genres: que l'essai s'avoue *presque* un roman: un roman sans noms propres.[33]

Somebody in *Barthes par lui-même* is saying *il*, framing Barthes: that somebody is a fictional character (according to the 'Tout ceci . . .') but the *il* is not a *créature fictive*: Barthes has thus ensured that in such

---

[33] *RB*, 124.

passages he has written a fiction whose (unnamed and unreal) soliloquist does nothing but discuss the (real) *il*. Given that Barthes notes that the use of *il* is sometimes paranoid ('the way they talk about me'), he has also drawn the one who says *il* (here identified with the critic) into the frame, positioned the potentially hostile speaker firmly within the fiction. In other words, all speakers who might wish to criticize Barthes are positioned as fictional characters: in so far as he speaks (as a *je*), he is fictional too: but in so far as he is positioned as a referent, he is real.

A later fragment in *Barthes par lui-même*, 'Moi, je', which discusses Barthes's use of shifting pronouns in some detail, adds yet a further complication. The *il* may be Brechtean (a mode of epic distancing and thus, potentially, of self-critique); it may also, as we have seen, be paranoid. In either case, using *il* is an act of aggression: it is 'le mot le plus méchant de la langue: pronom de la non-personne, il annule et mortifie son référent'.[34] If we then discuss (as we are doing here) Barthes in the third person, we are positioning him as a referent (and thus as real), but also as an unperson, as dead. The subject Barthes will be somewhere else: we are always left with a corpse on our hands. This is a curious foreshadowing of the discovery, in *La Chambre claire*, that just as a photograph shows us a reality that is now, necessarily, past (the one moment of photographing the object cannot be recovered), so the referent of language seems to be forced into the past too. Umberto Eco tells us that the Oulipo group, which performs sophisticated formal experiments on literary genres, has discovered that, in a matrix of all possible murder-story situations 'there is still to be written a book in which the murderer is the reader'.[35] Barthes shows that this situation is not uncommon: for while, in everyday life, reference to a third person merely distances that person from the immediate circuit of communication, the life of the writing subject (as writing) is dependent entirely on the reader, whose metalinguistic dismissal may be deadly: the writing subject never answers back. In *this* murder story (the one set up by the reading of *Barthes par lui-même*), the reader is invited into the frame of the book to find R.B.: what we find is that we have been turned into fictions, our role already written for us by the object of our quest (the object-language of our metalanguage), who is now dead, has vanished off-frame. If anyone has murdered R.B. it is the commentator, by positioning him as a

---

[34] *RB*, 171.
[35] *Reflections on 'The Name of the Rose'*, trans. William Weaver (London, 1985), 78.

referent. But the murder of *one* R.B. (the imaginary R.B., the Barthes of his public image) is salutary for the writing of Barthes, since he thinks that writing, if it is to be a successful escape from the immobility (itself 'funereal') of the subject's imaginary, needs the co-operation of the reader. The imaginary Barthes (*Barthes imaginaire*) needs us to disperse him, by reading him with full attention to the symbolic ambiguities, the shifts, drifts, and multi-layered ironies of his writing (*Barthes écriture*, so to speak). If we fail to help *Barthes imaginaire* to commit suicide so as to become *Barthes écriture*, we are guilty of killing off the latter. This is a dire consequence to draw from Benveniste's observation that the third person singular is the pronoun of the non-person. But Barthes takes it perfectly seriously, and it is merely a consequence of the view which has now become commonplace, that writing releases meanings because it is *not* constrained by an author. Barthes has thus successfully framed his commentators: in discussing him in his absence we are forced to mimic a voice that has come before: thinking we are outside the frame, we suddenly find ourselves within it: thinking we are real, we discover we are creatures in a fiction: imagining ourselves to be innocent, we suddenly catch sight of our own face in the identity parade of the principal suspects.

The reader's responsibility in this business thus turns out to have an Oedipal irony, and it is *l'Œdipe*, the Oedipus complex, that determines the way Lacan sees the child as appropriating language. Even the pronoun of absolute subjectivity has nothing absolute about it: the word 'I' is part of a code, and learned as such (even though it may merely be acting as a stopgap for the real 'I', the 'subject'). Since 'I' have to take place in a language that 'he' (in Lacanian theory, the father, whose name is the origin of all onomastic co-ordinates) has already written, 'I' always takes place as a character in a fiction beyond whose frame 'I' can never step. *Barthes par lui-même* is a particularly effective staging of these tensions, conflicts, and frustrations.

The 'Tout ceci . . .' positions (and frames) potential readers in another way. For example, somebody who decided to elaborate, on a Barthesian basis, a 'philosophy of preferentialism' would risk attracting charges of naïvety and misreading—for Barthes explicity tells us that he dreamt up this chimera to pass the time on a boring car journey.[36] And is he not, in any case, a character in a novel? One extension of this would note that, since there is a powerful totalizing thrust to the book's title, *Barthes par lui-même*, we may expect Barthes's discussion

<hr>

[36] 'Entre Salamanque et Valladolid', in *RB*, 160.

to include all his work hitherto—which, by virtue of the 'Tout ceci
. . .', is thus spoken by a character in a novel: even *Système de la mode*.
It is thus not only the budding preferentialist who is maliciously
viewed by the text as a naïve referentialist, but all those who have read
Barthes's technical semiological works and learned from them.

If framing is an attempt to control, what about other ways in which
that control is subverted? Frame and representation imply each other.
'La représentation, c'est cela: quand rien ne sort, quand rien ne saute
hors du cadre: du tableau, du livre, de l'écran.'[37] Thus non-representational art and writing are attempts to allow the force of the work to
cut across frames, institutional and other—to achieve 'the condition
of music', an art which Barthes sometimes views as sovereign in its
refusal of representation. The conclusion of 'Diderot, Brecht, Eisenstein' ties representation to metaphysics, to fetishism, and to a class
society—or as Barthes puts it 'une société qui n'a pas encore trouvé
son repos'—and asks 'A quand la musique, le Texte?'[38] This transgressive, non-representational force of music (that which allowed
Nietzsche, in *The Birth of Tragedy*, to identify it as a Dionysian art,
while he sets the plastic arts under the patronage of Apollo), is figured
in Balzac's short story *Sarrasine*. Here the music gets out of hand,
overwhelming the protagonist (a sculptor—one who ought to be
protected by Apollo) with its Dionysian power, and even tears up the
contract established between narrator (another re-presenter) and
narratee. This music is the singing of a castrato: there is therefore a
sense in which it springs from 'nothing'. When Sarrasine sketches the
singer (Zambinella) and then attempts to sculpt him/her, he is creating
fetishes. But this attempt to turn music into representation, and
castration into a fetish (the urge to frame, yet again, the unrepresentable), leads to the collapse of the contract on the basis of which the
narrator is telling the story: the marchioness whom he is trying to
seduce with his neat narrative (itself a framed fetish) is horrified at
what the frame is trying to contain (the force of castration). That is
why, in the end, the content of the frame bursts through, turning
Sarrasine into a *texte-limite*, on the edge of Balzac's art as a storyteller
in that it figures forces that no story can completely contain.[39]

[37] *P/T*, 90.
[38] *OO*, 93.
[39] See *S/Z*, 218–19, for a discussion of how the contents of the picture burst out of
their narrative framework. Again, on a Derridean view, castration is strictly speaking
unrepresentable as such, being the trace of a difference between the presence and
absence of the phallus.

A photograph would seem to be a perfectly framed cultural form. The *studium*—the general cultural or anecdotal interest Barthes takes in any one particular photo—is restricted to its frame in this way. But the force of the *punctum*, the poignant or arresting detail in the photograph, cuts through the photo's frame, through all mediations, to me.[40] This musicality (the *punctum* is not representational and Barthes finds it difficult to talk about it in theoretical terms) is partly why Barthes's last book is less an essay than a musical note (its subtitle is 'Note sur la photographie'), or series of notes, a sonata or a fugue (*punctum contra punctum*).[41]

I mentioned the fact that frames and fetishism are inseparable. That which is framed, as a part-object that comes to stand for the whole (or as a detached fragment related by metonymy to that from which it has been detached), is a fetish. Both psychoanalysis and Marxism resort to the category of fetishism (different in each case, but sharing a certain logic), and generally evaluate it negatively. The 'fetishism of commodities', according to Marx, is a magical way of thinking which grants a kind of charismatic autonomy to the commodity, thereby failing to take account of the structures of production and exchange that are at work. And for Freud, fetishism is a perversion, not an expression of mature sexuality.[42] Barthes's questioning of the frame as representation is complicated by the frame as writing. His use of the term 'fetish' is varied and ambiguous, never securely situated in evaluative terms. He does, however, question the usual condemnation to which the fetishist is subject. Why?

THE FETISHIST

I have never taken part in polemics. My habit is to repudiate in silence and go my own way.[43]

---

[40] *CC*, 90–1.

[41] For the book as a sonata: see ibid. 49. Derrida talks of a fugue in 'Les Morts de Roland Barthes', in *Psyché*, 273–304 (281).

[42] Theodor Adorno suggests that even music can be fetishized. See 'On the Fetish Character in Music and the Regression of Listening', in Andrew Arato and Eike Gebhardt (eds.), *The Essential Frankfurt School Reader* (New York, 1977), 270–99. His *Aesthetic Theory* catalogues the mechanisms by which fetishistic modes of artistic production and consumption are determined by historical forces they deny.

[43] Freud, letter to Ferenczi, 8 May 1913, cited in Alfred Ernest Jones, *Sigmund Freud: Life and Work* (London, 1953–7), ii. 168. This was shortly before the final secession of the Zurich group from Freud's orthodoxy.

Cutting and framing is the gesture of the fetishist, and the fetish is a place of pleasure *par excellence*. Pleasure does not deny: it merely, says the opening of *Le Plaisir du texte*, citing Nietzsche (and echoing Freud), averts its gaze and goes its own way. So does the fetishist. He does not deny: indeed, he fails to make the intellectual judgement of negation in so far as he refuses to abandon his belief that his mother has a penis.[44] The fetishist cuts and frames so as not to have to deny: he cuts off his perception of absence (of the fact that the mother seems to have been cut by some castrating knife), and he frames the whole scene (he deludes himself into thinking that he has not seen the absence he has, and he lovingly frames the fetish—frequently the last thing seen before the dreadful absence—that is metonymically going to replace the missing organ). In so far as fetishistic mechanisms are characteristic of the ego as split, they serve Barthes as a general category for the reader, who both knows and does not know (that what is being read is 'mere' fiction).[45] Fetishism does not rely on repression, but on division. The reader's self-division, itself a source of pleasure according to Barthes, is thus seen as a mode of dissociation close to that which affects the fetishist (who knows that the mother has no penis, but keeps that knowledge in another, split-off part of the ego). By admitting that this dissociation of response is characteristic of the pleasure of reading (rather than the fact that in reading, we can allow—with impunity—ideas which are usually repressed to rise to consciousness, which is the way Freud tends to see things), Barthes also limits dialectical or dynamic models of reading. What we enjoy about reading is that the many languages co-exist (as in some *Babel heureuse*): they do not struggle with each other (and Barthes has a tendency to underestimate the degree to which reading *is* an *agon*: ideally, for him, this struggle in reading should not take place). The different languages encountered in reading cannot (or need not) be

---

[44] The fetishist tends, in classical psychoanalysis, to be a male figure. Barthes does not explicitly question the possible gender specificity of the modes of reading he describes, though his work does blur gender stereotypes in an interesting way. Freud's theory of fetishism is most succinctly set out in 'Fetishism', in *The Pelican Freud Library*, ed. Angela Richards (Harmondsworth, 1973–86), vii. 345–57: on the fetishistic mechanisms of disavowal and splitting, see 'Splitting of the Ego in the Process of Defence', ibid. xi. 457–64. Is the fetishist an artist? Freud in his paper on 'Splitting' admits to a certain admiration for the way the fetishist solves the problem of castration, calling it 'very ingenious' (462) and saying the fetishist's way of dealing with reality 'almost deserves to be described as artful' (464). Barthes quotes from this paper in *PlT* (40–1), in the course of an argument on society's split attitude to art (which it values—commercially— because of art's apparent superiority to commercial values).

[45] *PlT*, 46–7.

synthesized (the split need not be overcome). Furthermore, this split also suggests a limit to theoretical models of reflexivity, for the self-conscious or reflexive reader, in trying to keep everything in view all at once, both what is read and the act of reading, may end up being systematically paranoid—may try to get everything into one frame, see from one perspective, rather than enjoying the cracks that run through the field of vision.

Sometimes Barthes falls back on the category of the fetishist in order to describe one particular kind of reading. The obsessional is literal-minded, the paranoiac is systematic to a crazy degree, the hysteric believes everything and is projected wholesale into the text: but 'le fétichiste s'accorderait au texte découpé, au morcellement des citations, des formules, des frappes, au plaisir du mot'.[46] But the fetishist is, on a deeper level, the reader *tout court*. Since the fetishist knows (in one part of the ego) and does not know (in another)—knows about castration, that is—, the fetishist's logic has no room for the law of the excluded middle. The fetishist is indifferent to logical contradiction. So is the reader in *Le Plaisir du texte*.[47] This logical indifference means that any boundaries Barthes tries to establish between *plaisir* and *jouissance* will never be secure: 'la faille, la coupure, la déflation, le *fading* qui saisit le sujet au cœur de la jouissance' is the crossing of the line between culture (framed and secure) and its other (which can never be named, except as '*un autre bord*, mobile, vide').[48] It is the fetishist who most effectively allegorizes reading as the enjoyment of dissociated languages which cannot necessarily be all seen from one perspective.

In his discussions of other art-forms, Barthes also shows how fetishism and the question of the frame are linked. In an essay on the artist Réquichot, Barthes demonstrates a certain suspicion of fetishism in that the fetishized object (the work of art itself, or the objects in it—the objects, for instance, from which Réquichot constructed his collages) is isolated from production and overvalued (commodified). In other words, he repeats Marx's critique of commodity fetishism. But he then turns to Freud for a more positive view of fetishism of this kind. (For as we have seen, although Freud viewed fetishism as an evasion of the real task of coming to terms with castration, he showed some admiration for the ingenuity of the 'almost artful' fetishist, whose 'perversion', he noted, was rarely a source of anguish.)

---

[46] *PIT*, 99–100.   [47] Ibid. 9–10.   [48] Ibid. 10, 14.

The fetishist is able to *displace* his feelings, from the sexual organs to something which stands in for them, and the energies of displacement that are released in this process are ultimately liberating. Réquichot hijacks curtain rings and isolates them from use-value and exchange-value: he frames them. At first, they seem to constitute a fetish, immobilized and reified.[49] But the result of the fetishization is a defetishization: by displacing his curtain rings, Réquichot suggests that the raw material of art is always displaceable—can always be shifted. To frame is to show that framing need never stop. Again, Barthes uses an apparent figure of immobility to show the mobile nature of artistic raw materials.

La conséquence ultime (peut-être encore imprévisible) de ce détournement est d'accentuer la nature matérialiste de l'art. Ce n'est pas la matière elle-même qui est matérialiste (une pierre encadrée n'est qu'un pur fétiche), c'est, si l'on peut dire, l'infinitude de ses transformations; . . . l'artiste . . . sait que la matière est infailliblement symbolique: en perpétuel déplacement.[50]

Barthes adds that the framing (for sale and exhibition of the art work) is an arrest of this displacement, a new fetishization. But this need not be so—it depends on the spectator's ability to reframe the art object, to resymbolize it. In other words, what is materialist is an attention to the institutional frames that govern our perception of the art object: that attention can help to reframe, again and again, the framed fetish. The essay on Réquichot also suggests that a term like 'fetish' is never one whose value (positive or negative) can in Barthes be securely identified. Here again, Adorno is a useful parallel, pointing out that to defetishize the artwork by integrating it (making it, in his example, politically progressive in an interventionist way) is as dubious an oversimplification as is an exaggerated emphasis on art's fetishistic autonomy.[51]

---

[49] *OO*, 189–214 (202).

[50] Ibid. 202–3.

[51] *Aesthetic Theory*, trans. C. Lenhardt, ed. Gretch Adorno and Rolf Tiedemann (London, 1984), 324. See Derrida, *Glas* (1981) for a critique of the metaphysical assumptions behind the concept of the fetish as a mere illusion that can be contrasted either to truth, reality, or totality. See too 'Au séminaire', in *BL*, 369–79, in which Barthes suggests that we are condemned to fetishism at this historical juncture: the Utopian seminar whose frame Barthes fetishistically draws in his essay (which itself is neither fact nor fiction, as his opening remarks make clear) is fantasmatically isolated from the alienated world outside: 'à sa façon, le séminaire dit *non* à la totalité', and in any case we are condemned, now, to a purely anthological culture, 'sauf à répéter une philosophie morale de la totalité' (379). Vincent Descombes, in 'An Essay in Philosophical Observation' (trans. Lorna Scott Fox, in Alan Montefiore (ed.), *Philosophy in France Today* (Cambridge, 1983), 67–81), presents a less indulgent picture of the seminar as

The pleasure of reading Barthes may well be fetishistic. It is easy to fetishize certain aspects of Barthes we extol above others (Barthes as Marxist, as semiologist, as autobiographer). But if we try to fetishize Barthes himself, which means, in effect, trying to get everything within the one frame that we will label 'Roland Barthes', we are forced to systematize differences and contradictions, and fall prey to the totalizing drive of the committed paranoiac. But this is far less pleasurable. In reading Barthes, it is essential to find as many frames as possible, as he did when he decided that the writing that gave him most satisfaction was the writing of fragments. The overall frame (the name 'Roland Barthes') has to be shattered.

THE NAME

—Mais qui est-ce?
J'hésitai.

Balzac, *Sarrasine*

The proper name of an author or text is, as we have seen, a frame that gives the text a legal identity, implicates it in an economy of commodity exchange, and assigns it a place in the bibliography. Especially important is the name of the author (it is noteworthy that catalogues and bibliographies privilege this over the name of the book itself.)

Why does one sign a book? Partly, as Lyotard says in the preface to *Dérive à partir de Marx et Freud*, to establish that bizarre thing, one's 'intellectual property': a signature is a frame too—it poses limits.

La signature est la clôture du terrain scripturaire, la main-mise par un supposé sujet sur des produits élevés *ipso facto* à la dignité d'œuvre. En fait le sujet comme 'auteur' de cette œuvre est institué grâce à l'exclusion d'autrui par la signature. Étrange exclusion: du moment que je signe, qu'est-ce qui *vous* est interdit?[52]

---

the place that *cannot* be isolated from a certain totality. Gregory L. Ulmer's detailed examination of 'Fetishism in Roland Barthes's Nietzschean Phase' (*Papers on Language and Literature*, 14: 3 (summer 1978), 334–55) suggests how problematic it is to discuss the possible effect of Barthes's fetishism when fetishism itself is a thought of the effect. And as Ulmer says, the fictional force of fetishism is such that to affirm fetishism is to deny it (346).

[52] *Dérive à partir de Marx et Freud* (1973), 7. See also Foucault, 'What Is An Author?'

The name constitutes by excluding. And, says Lyotard, the very act of signing and framing gives the work value: 'la plus-value est ce potentiel contenu dans une forme d'objet (un livre, un tissue, des plaques d'acier), isolé, arrêté, suspendu et attribué-réservé à un supposé sujet'.[53]

What if I refuse to sign? Lyotard had entertained the possibility of an anonymous book, before realizing that the frame could not be kept open for very long: it would have framed such a book as a rarity, named its anonymity. Réquichot, according to Barthes, wondered why he need sign only the finished work: why not sign the object that moved him to create (like an *objet trouvé* or a 'ready-made')? Anonymity in art is unnecessary—one need merely *déplacer son objet*, in other words sign things one has not made.[54]

But there are names other than proper names. Plato's Socrates asks: 'A name is, then, an instrument of teaching and of separating reality, as a shuttle is an instrument of separating the web?' and decides: 'The weaver, then, will use the shuttle well, and well means like a weaver; and a teacher will use a name well, and well means like a teacher.'[55] Barthes loves names and devotes much of his theoretical time to the Adamic or onomatourgic activity of giving names to hitherto anonymous textual effects that he has located, separating out (but not cutting) the strands in the web of the text. Are the names he gives these effects 'proper'? What is the difference between a proper name and a name in general (a noun, a substantive)?

In Chapter 2, I suggested that Barthes's capitalization of certain key nouns has the effect of turning them into proper names. Derrida asks whether a proper name can be translated: in common practice, of course, the proper name is what is transferred intact (or largely so) from one language to another.[56] As Derrida also says, making a rather different point, 'tout signifié dont le signifiant ne peut pas varier ni se laisser traduire dans un autre signifiant sans perte de signification induit un effet de nom propre'—the question then being whether

---

[53] *Dérive à partir de Marx et Freud*, 8.
[54] *OO*, 213.
[55] *Cratylus*, 388B–C.
[56] The theory of naming is an important topic in contemporary philosophy and literary criticism: Barthes's references to such discussions (Frege, Russell, Wittgenstein, Genette, Derrida) are scattered and oblique, so that there is no Barthesian theory of the proper name: the name is, however, as I shall be showing, a *barthème*. For the proper name as that which survives translation, see Derrida, *Glas*, 27*a*. (My references to *Glas* use, if necessary, *a* to refer to the left-hand side of the double-page, *b* to the right.)

there are such signifieds.[57] This helps explain the difficulty of translating (of manipulating metalinguistically) such proper names as *Dérive*. For while to name is to attempt to control, the name itself may resist being incorporated into any new metalanguage: it may insist on remaining in some sense proper.

In an essay on Proust and names, Barthes suggests that names are signs, not indices (in other ways they do not just label a referent: they act as signifiers), and lists different ways in which Proust treats proper names: essentialization (they name one referent), quotation (all the essence locked in the name can be released if it is cited), and exploration (it can be unfolded, broken up into other names).[58]

Like the 'barbaric' names of classical rhetoric, however, the names Barthes gives to textual phenomena are an (impossible?) attempt to codify *parole*.[59] In reading, we name and rename (for instance, sequences of actions in a narrative). In *S/Z* these action sequences are subsumed under names such as *entrer* which can in turn be subdivided (unfolded) into further named divisions such as *s'annoncer* and *pénétrer*: 'lire (percevoir le *lisible* du texte), c'est aller de nom en nom, de pli en pli'.[60] This naming may be unconscious, but it is essential; it may be an act of *māyā* (the name Indian philosophy gives to the world of appearances) but if it is interrupted (if we cannot name, even unconsciously, what is happening), the text's readability is threatened.

However, in Barthes, the name is a highly ambiguous phenomenon. In general, what he suspects as potentially malevolent is every name (especially when applied to text or subject) *except* the proper name. And even the latter is saved only in so far as it acts as a tentative and fragile unit, an empty frame. What formed the unity of the ship *Argo*? Only its name. Within the frame created by the name, the material structure of the vessel could be broken down, its elements recombined: 'à force de combiner à l'intérieur d'un même nom, il ne reste plus rien de l'*origine*: Argo est un objet sans autre cause que son nom,

---

[57] Id., 'Spéculer—sur "Freud"', in *La Carte postale de Socrate à Freud et au-delà* (1980), 275–437 (331).

[58] 'Proust et les noms', in *NEC*, 121–34 (124–5).

[59] Why was so much energy invested in the rhetoricians' quest? Why so much cutting, framing, and naming? 'Pourquoi cette furie de découpage, de dénomination, cette sorte d'activité enivrée du langage sur le langage?' No doubt, answers Barthes in order to codify *parole*, which is where the codes cease: rhetoric was an attempt to 'maîtriser l'immaîtrisable' ('L'Ancienne Rhétorique: aide-mémoire', in *AS* 85–164 (157)).

[60] *S/Z*, 89.

sans autre identité que sa forme'.[61] In *S/Z* the name is that frame in
which all the semes of a *personnage* (that is, signifiers of character) are
kept: the name is a supplement, in Derrida's sense of the term—both
necessary and superfluous. 'Le nom propre permet à la personne
d'exister en dehors des sèmes, dont cependant la somme la constitue
entièrement.'[62] Similarly, in *Barthes par lui-même*, Barthes relies on his
proper name in order to transcend the impossibility of writing 'about'
himself. 'Je ne dis pas: "Je vais me décrire", mais: "J'écris un texte, et
je l'appelle R.B." Je me passe de l'imitation (de la description) et je
me confie à la nomination. Ne sais-je pas que, *dans le champ du sujet,
il n'y a pas de référent?*'[63]

There are other uses of the proper name that are problematic.
Foucault suggests that the proper name of an author is, despite the
importance we have seen him give it, never entirely proper. It always
acts as a frame for 'a certain discursive set', and Foucault points out
how (because, we might say, of the institutional framework within
which reading and writing take place in our society) the author's name
does not act in the same way as proper names in general. The name
'Barthes' now acts as a similar frame. By making a name for himself,
Barthes has lost the 'properness' he seems to want names to have:
there is an identifiable Barthesian style, so that 'Barthes' is never just,
if it ever was, an index, but a signifier.

This fall from some hypothetical propriety of names is discussed by
Socrates and Hermogenes in Plato's *Cratylus*. Who has the authority
to name? Socrates reduces Hermogenes' position to the position that
names (in the general sense of substantives) can be given by anybody.
Socrates himself suggests that to name requires a certain competence:
only the *onomatourgos*—a specialist namer—can name. The fact that
the original *onomatourgos* may have made mistakes allows for such later
name-givers to attempt to restore to language a propriety it may never,
in absolute terms, have had.

In the case of the *Cratylus* there is a constant slippage between the
name as substantive and the name of a person or a place. This may
lead to paradoxes: why do we give the name 'name' to the name? The
answer proposed in the Cratylus is etymological: the name *onoma* is so

---

[61] *RB*, 50. Roger, in *Roland Barthes, roman*, sees the myth of Jason and the Argonauts
as of great explanatory power in discussing Barthes's writing.

[62] *S/Z*, 197.

[63] *RB*, 60. The proper name remains proper in so far as it is not reduced to a
signified or a referent: even as a signifier it is, as it were, held in suspense. It is of
course not easy for a proper name to avoid this reduction.

named because it is 'being of which the search is' (*on hou masma estin*); this already suggests that the name comes at the end of a search, and that naming is thus inseparable from a narrative, a quest.[64]

Barthes's main concern is to prevent names from being used as signifieds (as evaluative labels). He thus deploys various techniques to use names while keeping them at a distance. In *Le Plaisir du texte*, the fragments are not named as they appear but only at the back of the book, where by convention the contents list appears in French publications. How then do we read the fragments? The name of each fragment may seem somewhat idiosyncratic if we read the fragment according to its name: this suggests the name may be relatively arbitrary—a contingent element picked from the text it then names. Schematically speaking, we are given a choice between two micronarratives of reading: either the fragment and then, by referring to the back of the book, its name: or name first and then fragment.

In the first case, there is a sense in which the name comes to the reader as the solution of the fragment's riddle (for it is undeniable that, read *en suite*, the fragments can be baffling: they constantly change focus, run into each other, break apart into subsections, swerve off in new directions). There is thus a temptation to read the name as the text's signified: on consulting the name, we know that the fragment on pages 26 to 28 is 'about community'.

The converse narrative of reading gives us the name first, its fragment later, as if we were invited to see the fragment in the context (the frame) of its name, make it fit. The first order of reading will tend to lead to the second, the discovery of the name to a re-evaluation of the fragment. In his article on 'L'Ancienne Rhétorique', Barthes notes that in rhetorical analysis, it is easy to understand how the figures work, to look up *chleuasme, épanalepse, paralipse*, and go from name to name to example. But the converse is not so easy: it is notoriously hard to discover, without knowing already what hypallage is, that 'tant de marbre tremblant sur tant d'ombre' is a fine example of it.[65] In *Le Plaisir du texte*, what is the effect of having all the names printed separately, in almost alphabetical order, as an appendix? (The alphabetical order temporarily breaks down in the Cs, where we have *communauté—corps—commentaire*, instead of *commentaire—communauté—corps*, perhaps because the communal commentary of theory is

---

[64] *Cratylus*, 421A. On this Cratylean theme, see Gérard Genette, *Mimologiques: voyage en Cratylie* (1976), 34–5.
[65] *AS*, 158.

out of place when the body is at stake.) The effect is like the tension aroused by the frequent difficulty in getting name and fragment to coincide: like the visitor to an exhibition of modern art, the reader may well look at the fragment (the picture), then, for clarification, at the name (on, or near, the frame), then, frequently still (or even more) mystified, back to the text or painting. Twentieth-century art has derived many of its effects from a deliberate tension between what a painting is called and what it seems to represent (or be). Magritte is the most entertainingly provocative of these artists: one need only remember his painting of a ghostly table, draped with a white cloth, painted on a blank wall. It is called *La Vérité aimable*—why? This tension is defused completely when the name is explicitly an attempt to arrest the process of naming: all the canvases entitled 'Untitled', for instance.[66]

Barthes suggests, by an attention to the effects of the way his writing is disposed on the page and through the book, that the name should not sink to being a mere signified: it is not a condition of intelligibility, but rather something to be understood *in addition* to what it might seem to be explaining. In the fragment 'L'alphabet' of *Barthes par lui-même*, a certain order is proposed. It is not an order that follows the apparent chronological genesis of the work: the last-written fragment is presented in the middle ('Les amis', 69) and what may well be the earliest-written, 'Le monstre de la totalité, (we are given the date but no year), comes last (182). Nor is it an order of ideas (of discursive exposition). It is an order of writing—the order *par excellence*, that of the alphabet. After discussing the alphabetical order his later work so often adopts, Barthes comments:

Il ne définit pas un mot, il nomme un fragment; il fait l'inverse même d'un dictionnaire: le mot sort de l'énoncé, au lieu que l'énoncé dérive du mot. Du glossaire, je ne retiens que son principe le plus formel: l'ordre de ses unités.[67]

Barthes's essays increasingly take the form of fragments which are then given names. *Le Plaisir du texte* is a case in point—a kind of inverted dictionary in so far as the word is not so much the starting-point as a product of the fragment. And it goes to the back of the book, to the place of the index: we consult an index to find where to go: the index, like a finger, points back to the text. There is nothing

---

[66] For an ex. taken from a painter admired by Barthes, see Cy Twombly's *Untitled* (1967), reproduced in Herbert Read, *A Concise History of Modern Painting*, (new edn., London, 1974), 362.

[67] *RB*, 151.

peculiar about this: it is a feature of any book with an index. But as so often, Barthes, the novelist of the intellect, foregrounds (and thus makes strange) commonplace discursive operations. His practice frequently takes the form of a multiplication of these indices, a good example being the structure of *S/Z*. The interweaving of a section of general comment with the *pas à pas* reading of the *lexies* (those elementary reading units, or frames for meaning, that we have already glanced at) is followed by 'Annexes' in which Balzac's text is presented in its totality, followed by a list of the action sequences (what Barthes calls the proairetic code, the code governing narrative), then by a 'table raisonnée' which restructures Barthes's commentary in a more overtly thematic way than was possible in the main body of his analysis (which followed the narrative order of Balzac's story). These two 'Annexes' are as much rereadings (reorderings) of the story and Barthes's analysis of it as they are summaries.

In *Barthes par lui-même*, the subject index or, as it is called, 'Repères', is again a curious rewriting of many of the book's themes: Marrac is included, as the site of a *souvenir d'enfance* whose geographical situation (it's the name of an area just outside Bayonne where Barthes lived as a child) seems relatively contingent: but Tokyo, mentioned in an important fragment on an image which Barthes had already used in *L'Empire des signes* (the capital city as suggesting the structure of the subject in Lacan's topological model), is not. Such statements, of course, beg the question of what is important and what is not—the question that naming and framing constantly raise. Any such index, Barthes suggests, is a redistribution of the value and intensity allotted to different themes. In *Barthes par lui-même*, this feature makes it difficult to use the 'Repères' to find out 'what Barthes thought' about this or that topic. The 'thought' slides between topics (between the places identified by the indexical names), or else attaches itself (usually metonymically) to an apparently contingent and thus unindexed name. Barthes's 'thought' refuses to separate itself from his 'life'. We cannot be sure what the indexical function of these names may be. They raise the possibility of meanings they never underwrite.

One of the fragments indicated by the 'Repères' under the name 'Bayonne' thus seems to be 'about' the way memory for Barthes is mediated most often by smell.[68] But 'Repères' notes neither *odeurs* nor *mémoire* nor *souvenir*. A triviality? Why not let Barthes index his own

---

[68] *RB*, 139.

books in his own way? But that is the point—the indices are made
(are not natural): and they are made public: one of their effects—part
of the work they do—is to draw the reader in, make us question why
one item has been selected rather than another, in a small way
rewriting the book.

I thus find surprising the absence of references to those key
Barthesian themes *plaisir, jouissance, nature, lisible,* and *scriptible*: and,
despite being major topics discussed at some length in the book, *atopie*
and *utopie* are nowhere. It is equally surprising to see included such
elements as *tableau noir, excoriation, chahut,* and *Céline et Flora.* But any
surprise is due to the pious hope that an index will tell the reader
where to go to find out what the text says. At all events, by choosing
names (indices) that are not obvious, Barthes again shows there is
nothing natural about naming, and creates a gap between the different
layers of his text. *Barthes par lui-même* thus resembles at least one
particular post-modernist novel that playfully disappoints the reader's
expectations that the sections of the text will all cohere. Nabokov's
Pale Fire consists of an epic domestic poem by John Shade, followed
by an apparent commentary on it by Charles Kinbote. But the
commentary in fact uses the poem 'Pale Fire' as a springboard into
the telling of another story (a fantasy of the commentator's?): the index
fails to act as a reliable guide to either poem or commentary, and
underlines the (vicious) circularity of the whole procedure in its 'Word
golf' sequence, where the reader becomes caught in a loop.[69]

Ultimately, these distanced names make it difficult to paraphrase a
book such as *Barthes par lui-même,* to say what it writes. Barthes
himself refers in the text to the process of making an index: it involves
working on and with names, revealing their arbitrariness, their limita-
tions, and their power to frame reading and writing. A list of contents
to such a book will become parodically encyclopaedic: it is both a
skeletal but tyrannical correspondent to the text, and, at the same
time, another text. He analyses, in the fragment 'Le cercle des
fragments', that fragment itself.

Non seulement le fragment est coupé de ses voisins, mais encore à l'intérieur
de chaque fragment règne la parataxe. Cela se voit bien si vous faites l'index
de ces petits morceaux; pour chacun d'eux, l'assemblage des référents est
hétéroclite; c'est comme un jeu de bouts rimés: 'soit les mots: fragment,
cercle, Gide, catch, asyndète, peinture, dissertation, Zen, intermezzo; imagi-

---

[69] 'Word golf . . . see Lass', 'Lass, see Mass', 'Mass, Mars, Mare, see Male', 'Male,
see Word golf'.

nez un discours qui puisse les lier.' Eh bien, ce sera tout simplement ce fragment-ci. L'index d'un texte n'est donc pas seulement un instrument de référence; il est lui-même un texte, un second texte qui est le *relief* (reste et aspérité) du premier: ce qu'il y a de délirant (d'interrompu) dans la raison des phrases.[70]

The names we find in Barthes's index are like the augur's wand 'pointé vers le ciel, c'est-à-dire vers l'impointable'.[71] Discourse is what binds the erratic energies of these names into a cohesive, systematic, and perfectly imaginary identity.

Problematizing our perception of the name is linked to Barthes's constant suspicion of science. Science, he suggests, is the drive to name and classify the unruly phenomena that it wants to bring under its control. Like Foucault, he is sensitive to the fact that methods of naming and classifying involve questions of power. But in the following fragment he stages his suspicions in an indirect and anecdotal form.

A. me confie qu'il ne supporterait pas que sa mère fût dévergondée—mais qu'il le supporterait de son père; il ajoute: c'est bizarre, ça, non?—Il suffirait d'un nom pour faire cesser son étonnement: *l'Œdipe!*[72]

The fragment from which this comes is named, pertinently, 'Nomination'. 'Oedipus' is the name of names as far as the science of psychoanalysis is concerned: it is passage through the Oedipal crisis which constitutes the subject as subject in and to the symbolic order. 'Oedipus' is a proper name which has become a scientific concept. Psychoanalysis uses it to explain—and defuse—the astonishment shown by A.

Barthes continues:

A. est à mes yeux tout près du texte, car celui-ci *ne donne pas les noms*—ou il lève ceux qui existent; il ne dit pas (ou dans quelle intention *douteuse?*): le marxisme, le brechtisme, le capitalisme, l'idéalisme, le Zen, etc; *le Nom ne vient pas aux lèvres*, il est fragmenté en pratiques, en mots qui ne sont pas des Noms. En se portant aux limites du dire, dans une *mathésis* du langage qui ne veut pas être confondue avec la science, le texte défait la nomination et c'est cette défection qui l'approche de la jouissance.

The text resists the metalinguistic name, the identification (of themes, semes of ideology). 'C'est bizarre, ça, non?' Psychoanalysis above all, Barthes is suggesting, should not be that practice of interpretation

which, calling on the subject to assume a proper name and place (a
place within the symbolic order whose co-ordinates are plotted with
reference to the Origin, the Name of the Father) reduces the bizarre
displaceability of *ça*, 'Sa' (*le signifiant* in Saussure's shorthand), the S,
das Es, the id. 'Then there's life in't. Nay, an you get it, you shall get
it by running. Sa, sa, sa, sa.'[73]

In other words, the text holds names in suspense. Balzac's Sarrasine
is not allowed to discover that Zambinella is a castrato until towards
the end of the story, when we in turn finally learn that the old man we
saw at the de Lanty ball is this very same castrato. One of the ways
Balzac's story is approaching Barthes's ideal of textuality is that it
shows great sensitivity about identities, so much so that it never
actually *names* Zambinella as a castrato, leaving us to fill in the blank.
Barbara Johnson has suggested indeed that Barthes himself destroys
this delicacy by insisting so heavily on the fact that Zambinella *is* a
castrato—he has named where Balzac does not.[74] Another critic in
the deconstructive tradition, Paul de Man, sees romantic literature as
a process of naming and renaming a central void (this would make
Sarrasine, whose central void is that of castration, a crucial romantic
text): 'The romantic consciousness consists of the presence of a
nothingness. Poetic language names this void with ever-renewed
understanding and . . . never tires of naming it again. This persistent
naming is what we call literature.'[75] But even the word 'nothing' is still
a name, of course, and de Man is perhaps a little too prepared to jump
romantically into the void.

In *Sarrasine*, as in all classical texts, as long as the story lasts, we
read with the name 'just on the tip of our tongue'.

Le signifié de connotation est à la lettre un *index*—il pointe mais ne dit pas;
ce qu'il pointe, c'est le nom, c'est la vérité comme nom; il est à la fois la
tentation de nommer et l'impuissance à nommer . . .: il est ce *bout de la langue*,
d'où va tomber, plus tard, le nom, la vérité.[76]

The arrival of the name can never be prevented absolutely, but if the
text can be exhausted by its name, the astonishment fades, the text
dies. For the name shows, yet again, Barthes's fear of the speaking
voice in so far as it says something (conveys signifieds). The tip of the

---

[73] *King Lear*, IV, vi.
[74] 'The Critical Difference: Balzac's *Sarrasine* and Barthes's *S/Z*', in Young (ed.),
Untying the Text: A Post-Structuralist Reader (Boston, 1981), 162–74 (172).
[75] 'Criticism and Crisis', in *Blindness and Insight: Essays in the Rhetoric of Contemporary
Criticism* (2nd edn., London, 1983), 3–19 (18).
[76] *S/Z*, 69.

tongue is the locus of the aesthetic effect *par excellence*: the text is always just about to tell us (what it really means and wants to say): we, as readers, are always just about to name the text—with such names as those Barthes suggests for Zola's *Fécondité*: *naturisme, familialisme, colonialisme*.[77] But what the speaking voice finally says, if we follow Barthes premisses is, in a sense, nothing but the explosive 'Dead! dead!' ejaculated by the quivering tongue of the protagonist of Poe's short story 'The Facts in the Case of M. Valdemar', as his body finally disintegrates before the eyes of the horrified spectators.[78]

In this way, Barthes rewrites a major theme in the aesthetics of the last two centuries, one that has different resonances and different consequences every time it is stated. We find it in Stendhal. 'Ne jamais dire: "La passion brûlante d'Olivier pour Hélène." Le pauvre romancier doit tâcher de faire croire à la passion brûlante, mais ne jamais la nommer.'[79] We find it in Mallarmé: '*Nommer* un objet, c'est supprimer les trois quarts de la jouissance du poème qui est faite du bonheur de deviner peu à peu; le *suggérer*, voilà le rêve.'[80] The early Wittgenstein's notion of 'showing' rather than 'saying' had important consequences for his view of aesthetics and his hostility to any view of philosophy as a metalanguage capable of saying what is in the object-languages with which it deals.[81] And a similar fascination with the aesthetic as being the realm of 'almost naming' is clearly expressed in a short essay by Borges, 'The Wall and the Books', which, significantly, is also about one of the greatest framing devices ever seen, the Great Wall of China. Shih Huang Ti built the wall to frame his empire, protect it from outside marauders: he also had all books prior to him burnt. He said 'History begins with me.' He took the name of the legendary emperor who invented writing and who had given things their true name: 'in a parallel fashion, Shih Huang Ti boasted, in inscriptions which endure, that all things in his reign would have the name which was proper to them'.[82] Borges entertains various conjec-

---

[77] *P/T*, 52.

[78] See Barthes's essay on this story: 'Analyse textuelle d'un conte d'Edgar Poe', in *AS*, 329–59 (354). This essay more than any other stages Barthes's mixture of attraction and repulsion for the voice.

[79] Letter to Mme Jules Gaulthier (1834), in *Correspondance*, ed. ii. H. Martineau and V. del Litto (1962–8), 643.

[80] 'Réponses à des enquêtes: sur l'évolution littéraire', in *Igitur, Divagations, Un coup de dés* (1976), 387–95 (392).

[81] The distinction between 'showing' and 'saying' is perhaps the most constant theme in Wittgenstein's work: it is first found in the *Tractatus Logico-Philosophicus*, e.g. at 4. 1212: 'What *can* be shown, *cannot* be said.'

[82] *Labyrinths*, 221–3 (222).

tures as to the power of this conjunction (walling off the empire, burning the books): he tries to name a meaning. But his conclusion lies in a suspension of the name: the idea of the coincidence of the two activities 'moves us in itself'.

Music, states of happiness, mythology, faces belaboured by time, certain twilights and certain places try to tell us something, or have said something we should have missed, or are about to say something; this imminence of a revelation which does not occur, is, perhaps, the aesthetic phenomenon.[83]

The revelation would be spoken, but the aesthetic effect relies on the absence of speech.

In Barthes, speech is an object of suspicion for other reasons that have to do with the ways he figures social relationships: speech is the locus of alienation par excellence, and I will be examining this theme in more detail later on. But while his fear of the name as exemplifying the deadly powers of speech (of the signified) is taken to idiosyncratic lengths, it is not entirely eccentric. The sociologist Bourdieu makes a valid point about academic life: to identify a writer as a Marxist or a Weberian may be both an act of surreptitious evaluation and ultimately uninformative.[84] And Derrida is attempting to limit the definitional, framing and naming power of predication.

Toute phrase du type 'la déconstruction est X' ou 'la déconstruction n'est pas X' manque a priori de pertinence, disons qu'elle est au moins fausse. Vous savez qu'un des enjeux principaux de ce qui s'appelle dans les textes 'déconstruction', c'est précisément la délimitation de l'onto-logique et d'abord de cet indicatif présent de la troisième personne: S est P.[85]

Indeed, Derrida goes on to say that he does not much like the name given to the kind of philosophical activity he does—the word déconstruction is not beautiful.[86]

Barthes suggests two possible objections to the compulsion to name. The first is this: by naming the text we run the risk of thinking that we have exhausted it—that there is nothing in Verne except colonialism. The second objection is that names are always themselves part of a code: the way we name is a way of naming ourselves (as ideology

[83] *Labyrinths*, 223.
[84] 'Fieldwork in philosophy', in *Choses dites* (1987), 13–46 (39).
[85] 'Lettre à un ami japonais', in *Psyché: inventions de l'autre* (1987), 387–93 (392).
[86] Ibid. The fact that Derrida's hostility to statements of the kind 'S is P' is sometimes—but not always—conveyed by various statements of the kind 'S is P' no doubt adds further complications, though this by no means destroys his critique of ontology.

critics, for instance): and the names we use cannot be taken for granted. Where names exhaust what they name, we have Stalinism, in which fact and value are crushed together: 'il n'y a plus aucun sursis entre la dénomination et le jugement'.[87] 'Stalinism' is itself an effective name, which suggests that Barthes's hostility to the name is a difficult option: it is not a simple matter to produce an intellectual discourse which manages entirely without such name-calling. But Barthes constantly attempts to distance himself from its effects. His last work thus drifts away from the detection and identification of ideological semes. He imagines an intellectual 'gagné par le dégoût des noms' abandoning critique altogether and deciding to write novels instead.[88]

Colonialism, for instance, is a signified that can be extracted from the text (of Verne and others): when Barthes carries out his analysis of the myths of modern life, it is signifieds of this kind he detects (the signifieds of connotation, as he later calls them, most of which end in -ité, as in the celebrated socio-gastronomical pronouncement that concludes 'Le Bifteck et les frites': 'la frite est le signe alimentaire de la "francité." '[89] But colonialism can itself act as a signifier, in at least two ways. First, we can ask what exactly are its signifieds: what complex of assumptions, prejudices, and practices does it cover? ('nous ne pouvons manier les signifiés d'un signe ou des signes qu'en nommant les signifiés, mais, par cet acte même de nomination, nous reconvertissons le signifié en signifiant').[90] What kind of colonialism are we dealing with here? Secondly, the word 'colonialism' itself is not a neutral, scientific term: depending on the multiple contexts (or institutional frames) that operate, it marks its user, who is thereby situated, in general, somewhere within a certain political and intellectual class, though one that is never more than loosely defined: 'dès que je nomme, je suis nommé: pris dans la rivalité des noms'.[91] An accusation of 'logocentrism' (as in 'this move is still deeply logocentric') identifies its utterer as a deconstructionist; of 'phallocentrism' as a feminist; of 'reactionary' as a progressive, and so on. The dismissal

---

[87] DZ, 21.
[88] 'Le théâtre oblige à défaire le Nom. J'imagine très bien quelque théoricien, gagné à la longue par le dégoût des Noms, et, cependant nullement résigné à verser dans le refus de tout langage, j'imagine donc cet épigone brechtien renonçant à ses discours passés et décidant de n'écrire plus que des romans', 'Brecht et le discours: contribution à l'étude de la discursivité' in BL, 243–52 (250).
[89] My, 79.
[90] 'Sémiologie et médecine', in AS, 273–83 (280).
[91] PlT, 50.

of a position as 'pious', 'theological', and 'nostalgic' might well indicate
that the speaker is the Lyotard of the 1970s, for the more names we
have the more closely we can identify the name-callers: for example,
the names *opportuniste, dogmatiste, empiriciste, révisionniste,* taken
together, suggest that the writers using these names can be identified,
as it were, by antithesis—they are in fact signatories of the 'Déclara-
tion' of the Maoist June 1971 movement.[92] Although Barthes shows a
certain weariness with this, he does not say that theory can do without
it, and at least one of his own names, *doxa,* as the loose and amorphous
but all the more insidious category of petty-bourgeois ideology, has
passed into common theoretical usage. However, Barthes suggests
that to avoid the essentializing drive of such names, it is a good idea
to see them as partitives. He rarely does this with his negative values
and is still content to identify the massive presence of *la Doxa* in a
cultural practice, but he does see *du texte* or *de l'écriture* in types of
writing, and goes so far as to see *petit-bourgeois* itself, one of his earliest
acts of vituperation, as a partitive: there is *du petit-bourgeois* in the
revolutionary, in his friends, and in himself, just as *il y a du Texte* in a
particular work.[93]

   This qualification of the name is why the attempt to 'name' Barthes
can seem beside the point: he has named himself so often and in so
many ways that he has pre-empted us, and cast doubt on what is
achieved by focusing on the hidden signifieds of his texts. One
particular fragment of *Barthes par lui-même,* 'La personne divisée?',
shows the impossibility of finding one name that fits more than a
fraction of his work. And this is not Barthes's way of complacently
drawing attention to the variety and richness of that work: rather, he
is pinpointing his own contradictions; and these contradictions are
those of any subject, of the *sujet divisé* described by his own theory,
diffracted, scattered, and dispersed. Adopting, as frequently, dialogic
form (as if to emphasize *that* aspect of the split self), he says to
'himself': 'Philosophiquement, il semble que vous soyez matérialiste
(si ce mot ne sonne pas trop vieux); éthiquement, vous vous divisez:
quant au corps, vous êtes hédoniste, quant à la violence, vous seriez
plutôt bouddhiste!'[94] Any classification he reads makes him wonder
where he fits in it. But like Harpo Marx pretending to be a heroic
Russian aviator in *A Night at the Opera,* drinking more and more water
to conceal his inability to speak (an aphasia that particularly endears

---

[92] *Tel Quel,* 47 (autumn 1971), 133–41 (135).   [93] *RB,* 147.   [94] Ibid. 146.

him to Barthes), but succeeding only in dissolving the glue of his fake beard, Barthes finds that his own identity dissolves the more he tries to pin it down. Take psychoanalysis: he discovers that he is 'obsessionel, hystérique, paranoïaque et de plus pervers (sans parler des psychoses amoureuses)'. And in overall *Weltanschauung*, he tells himself, 'vous additionnez toutes les philosophies décadentes: l'épicurisme, l'eudémonisme, l'asianisme, le manichéisme, le pyrrhonisme'.[95] And he derives considerable satisfaction from transgressing the names his own image has been identified by: the lifelong 'materialist' wonders what difference it makes on which side of the divide (materialism/idealism) he ultimately comes down, and resurrects one of his own most powerful taboo words (*âme*), in *La Chambre claire*. Indeed, at a time when theory was particularly and fruitfully polemical, Barthes showed an increasing tendency to use classifications of his own making, rather than to try to fit into those being bandied around in the intellectual *agora*: hence his interest in developing the Guelph/Ghibelline opposition elaborated by Michelet, and naming himself not where we would have expected, as a Guelph (given Michelet's own identification of the Guelph with the enlightened intellectual) but as a Ghibelline.[96] Both categories challenge current labels: the Ghibelline, alarmingly, is 'l'homme du lien féodal, du serment par le sang, c'est l'homme de la dévotion affective, l'Allemand', as if Barthes were going the way of the German Romantics. But he resists this metonymic contagion (and would have been repelled by the anti-Semitism of some of the Romantics): rather, he shows an increasing interest both in the mysticism associated with that movement and in the ways the German Romantics initiated the main trends of modern literary theory. Hence what *he* understands by the name 'Ghibelline' is something rather different, implying 'une précellence du corps sur la loi, du contrat sur le code, du texte sur l'écrit, de l'énonciation sur l'énoncé'.[97] Another case of drift, this time in a quasi-proper name: indeed, this habit of retrieving old names and sheering them in accordance with his passing interests is one of Barthes's most attractive habits.

So sometimes it seems as if the best way of commenting on Barthes is not to attempt to rise in metalinguistic level, to a greater and more

---

[95] *RB*, 147.

[96] According to Barthes, the intellectual as seen by Poujade is like the Jesuits (and thus the Guelphs) as seen by Michelet: see *My*, 189.

[97] *BL*, 378.

all-encompassing degree of abstraction and conceptual power, but to descend to the level of primary, literary texts of the sort he himself commented on. In other words, we may choose to observe Barthes's precept that literature is its own best metalanguage, or, as he puts it, that 'la science de la littérature, c'est la littérature'.[98]

The literary text I am proposing as an illustration is itself part fiction, part essay: again, it is from Borges. His short story 'Averroes's Search' suggests a definite preoccupation with the name. It tells the story of the great Arab philosopher Averroes—or rather, of Abulgualid Muhammad Ibn-Ahmad ibn-Muhammad ibn-Rushd, also known as Benraist, also known as Avenryz, also known as Aben-Rassad, also known as Filius Rosadis: our hero's very name is problematic.[99] Averroes, locked within a civilization (a frame: medieval Islam) that has no theatre (and constantly questions what can be represented), is arrested by the words 'tragedy' and 'comedy' in Aristotle, whose *Poetics* he is translating. What do these names, in the text of one of the founders of Western thought, mean?

In the story, Averroes is given two chances to gain some insight into the meaning of theatre. Looking out of his study window he sees children playing a game in which they pretend to be a muezzin, a minaret, and a worshipper respectively. And later, after dinner, the fatuous and mendacious traveller Abulcasim recounts an episode of his adventures in China: in 'a house of painted wood' he saw a group of masked people, who 'suffered prison, but no one could see the jail; they travelled on horseback, but no one could see the horse; they fought, but the swords were of reed; they died and then stood up again'.[100] Averroes cannot see (how could he?) that the children playing are acting out a theatrical representation; and he does not realize that there is a link between the spectacle witnessed by Abulcasim and the notion of theatre he finds in Aristotle. For the whole of Islam, the words 'tragedy' and 'comedy' are signifiers without signifieds.

When Abulcasim attempts to explain what he thought he had seen ('they were representing a story'), he is met with blank incomprehension—the *étonnement* of A. in Barthes's fragment 'Nomination'. And

---

[98] Interview with Raymond Bellour, 'Sur le *Système de la mode* et l'analyse structurale des récits', in *GV*, 45–56 (53). I have already suggested the ambiguity of this statement, which is difficult to locate as being either theoretical or fictional, and so forces us to rethink that opposition.

[99] 'Averroes's Search', in *Labyrinths*, 180–8 (180).

[100] Ibid. 184.

when Averroes returns to his translation, and on impulse decides he has discovered the meaning of the names 'tragedy' and 'comedy', he gets them completely wrong, defining them in terms 'we' can recognize as ethnocentric and anachronistic: 'Aristu (Aristotle) gives the name of tragedy to panegyrics and that of comedy to satires and anathemas. Admirable tragedies and comedies abound in the pages of the Koran and in the *mohalacas* of the sanctuary.'[101]

We know this is wrong because we know what Aristotle meant, the meaning of his names. Or do we? Having told his story, Borges suggests that his attempt to imagine a day in the life of Averroes on the basis of minimal scholarly information is as deluded as Averroes's attempt to imagine drama from inside a conceptual world that had no place for theatre. What happens when Borges tries to imagine the mind of someone from a culture distant in space and time from his own? In a further raising of the ironical stakes, we might suggest in turn that our attempt to imagine the original form of *Greek* drama (part of 'our' culture) is perhaps almost as deluded: are we perhaps more sure than we should be about the meaning of the words 'tragedy' and 'comedy' as they occur in Aristotle? Who is closest to the text in this story of the three As, Aristotle, Averroes, and Abulcasim? Ultimately, for us, it is perhaps Abulcasim, whom Borges makes out to be vain, pompous, and stupid: his narrative admirably makes strange a practice (theatre) which it does not name. This A. too is 'tout près du texte'—a lot closer, perhaps, than the philosopher Aristotle whose characterization of tragedy controlled theoretical speculation on drama for so long; closer too than the more sympathetic philosopher Averroes, who tries to define but gets his definitions grotesquely wrong. There are other modern texts that suspend the name, or give us names and no identities. Who is the man in the brown mackintosh? Who is V?[102]

If Barthes wants to write a text, therefore, one which 'ne donne pas les noms', or which does not give names without a struggle, he will have to construct a narrative—not, necessarily, by writing a story, but by forcing the reader to become aware of the narrativity of reading, to struggle against onomastic aphasia, to wait and work for the name. Barthes in turn will have to struggle against the metalinguistic identification he dreads. Mystification? But the aesthetic effect (the

---

[101] Ibid. 187.
[102] The man in the brown mackintosh walks through the Dublin of *Ulysses*: V is in Pynchon's novel of that name.

suspension of names) may be politically progressive: Chaplin and Brecht, two artists admired greatly by Barthes, show us people not quite able to see the conditions of their slavery: the 'not quite' is necessary for *us* to see and understand the frame that controls these subjects (Chaplin's *adorable* prisoner is cosseted by his wardens and reads the paper under a portrait of Lincoln: what we see, and what he shows his prisoner as blind to, is the fact that the petty-bourgeois lifestyle he incarnates is a way of being perpetually imprisoned).[103] Brecht too shows us 'l'homme à la veille de la Révolution'—about to step outside the frame in which he is held, decipher the name ('capitalism') inscribed on it.[104] The name is always just about to be spoken, but this must not happen in the work of art itself, for it would then, says Barthes, lose its *force esthétique*.

There are two possible ways in which we can respect Barthes's fear of being named. One is by naming him in a variety of ways. In 'Réquichot et son corps', Barthes contrasts two modes of modern art (the ready-made, and conceptual art). They have one feature in common: both are activities of classification.

> Prenons deux traitements modernes de l'objet. Dans le ready made, l'objet est *réel* (l'art ne commence qu'à son pourtour, son encadrement, sa muséographie)—ce pour quoi on a pu parler à son sujet de réalisme petit-bourgeois. Dans l'art dit conceptual, l'objet est *nommé*, enraciné dans le dictionnaire—ce pour quoi il vaudrait mieux dire 'art dénotatif' plutôt qu''art conceptuel'.[105]

If the object is real, its name can be uncertain: if it is named exactly, it does not need to be real. Both these activities are activities of the realm of appearances (the Indian *māyā*): Réquichot attempts to go beyond the veil, but not directly. For his attempt to 'défaire le Nom' passes first through a 'sur-nomination exubérante': since each of his objects can be compared with a great number of others, metaphor proliferates out of control and we are forced to realize that if each object can resemble anything, it overall resembles nothing in particular.[106] This parallels Barthes's frequent assertion that we cannot just leap into Utopia: it has to be won, through the purgatorial and initiatory process of meaning *jusqu'au bout* ('il faut traverser, comme le long d'un chemin initiatique, tout le sens, pour pouvoir l'exténuer,

[103] *My*, 41.   [104] Ibid.
[105] *OO*, 189–214 (204).   [106] Ibid. 205.

l'exempter').[107] This polynominal treatment is a way of overcoming the power of one name. The young Stephen Dedalus reflects on the names attributed to the Blessed Virgin in the liturgy, the subject of mockery on the part of his protestant neighbours: '*Tower of Ivory*, they used to say, *House of Gold*! How could a woman be a tower of ivory or a house of gold?'[108] But the risk of idolatry is lessened by the diffraction of metaphorical naming: hence Barthes's liturgy of the / separating SarraSine from Zambinella: 'c'est la barre de censure, la surface spéculaire, le mur de l'hallucination, le tranchant de l'antithèse, l'abstraction de la limite, l'obliquité du signifiant, l'index du paradigme, donc du sens'.[109] The Kabbalist Ezra ben Solomon wrote: 'the five books of the Torah are *the Name* of the Holy One, blessed be He': this comment is cited by Gershom Scholem, who notes that in this kind of speculation the Torah is both made up of the names of God and is also as a whole 'the one great Name of God'.[110] Here idolatry is avoided by making the name too vast, too full of folds and complications, for human comprehension—a theme that has recently been exhaustively exploited by Umberto Eco in *Foucault's Pendulum*.

So Barthes's questioning of the name ultimately draws on considerations of a theological nature, hence his feeling that an alternative to being named many times over is not to be named at all. But hitherto only God has been granted such a privilege: hence Barthes's fascination for the tussles theologians have had with, as he puts it at the Colloque de Cerisy, the '*nomen innominabile* de Dieu, le nom innommable. Si Dieu n'a pas de nom, donc si on ne peut pas l'enfermer dans un nom, il est innommable, mais "innommable" devient le nom de Dieu, et on s'enferme donc dans une aporie.'[111] But the fact that the

---

[107] 'L'exemption du sens', in *RB*, 90. This idea gives us a micronarrative (from names to namelessness) that counters the usual micronarrative followed by hermeneutic or analytical procedures (from namelessness to the name).

[108] Joyce, *A Portrait of the Artist as a Young Man*, in *The Essential James Joyce*, ed. Harry Levin (Harmondsworth, 1963), 76.

[109] *S/Z*, 113.

[110] Gershom Scholem, *On the Kabbalah and its Symbolism*, trans. Ralph Manheim (New York, 1965), 39.

[111] *C*, 22. A theologically inspired theory of names that parallels Barthes's mistrust of them is Walter Benjamin's essay 'On Language as Such and on the Language of Man', in id., *One Way Street and Other Writings*, trans. Edmund Jephcott and Kingsley Shorter (London, 1979), 107–23. Since the Fall, when proper names lost their purity, there has always been something judgemental about the name (120): the languages of humanity have to 'overname' in a failed attempt to repair the loss of the divinely given proper name. 'To be named . . . perhaps always remains an intimation of mourning' (121). Significantly for our parallel with Barthes, the tragic aspect of human alienation resides mainly in speech, esp. speech as knowledge (that debased form of knowledge

subject too is treated as that which resists names suggests that
Barthes's refusal of all names, including adjectives, is part of an assault
on predication that aims to keep a place—an unlocatable, forever,
shifting place—open for subjectivity. Antoine Compagnon notes that
'atopos', the adjective applied to Socrates in the *Symposium*, and
appropriated for himself by Montaigne, is an ambiguous word:
claiming it for oneself may be to strive to be, not nowhere, but
everywhere.[112] Since Barthes too cultivates 'atopia', he may be saving
the subject from reification at the risk of ensuring that it partakes in a
certain deification.[113] The risk is that Barthes's ploy is ultimately one
of Socratic mastery: in giving himself away ('à l'Autre, au transfert, et
donc *au lecteur*', as he puts it in *Barthes par lui-même*) he is in fact giving
us an empty frame, a pure surface without depth or perspective.[114] By
naming his own writings so exhaustively, he has forestalled us, and we
have to think of some other tactic. Since the impulse to name (here
he is reactionary, there progressive: here fetishistic, there paranoid:
this text is structuralist in orientation, that one post-structuralist) is so
insuperable, one result is an initial bewilderment. But this is always

---

that obtains since the Fall): 'Overnaming as the linguistic being of melancholy points to
a curious relation of language: the overprecision that obtains in the tragic relationship
between the languages of human speakers' (122).

[112] C, 53. Compagnon claims that both Montaigne and Socrates ultimately avoid the
pretence of ubiquity: Barthes, in reply, has a harsher view of Socrates' arrogance (58).
Irène Pagès suggests that the suspension of names at the colloquium (the general
refusal to discuss Barthes's work in traditional evaluative ways) makes of him 'le dieu
de ce colloque' (313). Barthes states at the Colloque: 'Je souhaite, je soupire après
l'Abstinence des Images car toute Image est mauvaise.' But to refuse the name is to
constitute oneself as he who refuses names. 'Donc, ne pas détruire les Images, mais les
décoller, les distancer. Dans la "Méditation" Tao, il y a une opération initiatique, qui
est le *Wang-Ming*: perdre conscience du Nom (je dis: de l'Image). L'Abstinence du
Nom est le seul problème réel de ce Colloque' ('L'Image', in *BL*, 389–97 (395)). And,
in 'L'Adjectif' (in *RB*, 47): 'Il supporte mal toute *image* de lui-même, souffre d'être
nommé. Il considère que la perfection d'un rapport humain tient à cette vacance de
l'image: abolir entre soi, de l'un à l'autre, les *adjectifs*: un rapport qui s'adjective est du
côté de l'image, du côté de la domination, de la mort.' These statements again suggest
that when Barthes offers the truth of his writing to the reader as Other, it is not in
order to be identified: truth, that is, need not be of the order of identity at all. The
commentary Barthes aspires to, as far as his own work is concerned, would be close to
a psychoanalytic or transferential encounter in its suspension of names (which are
always, in a sense, a relegation of the subject-text to the *third person*): this is suggested
by the title of Julia Kristeva's article on Barthes, 'Comment parler à la littérature', in
Polylogue (1977), 23–54. The question is what forms such new modes of commentary
and analysis might take.

[113] 'Atopos' in Greek means, however, 'out of place' (rather than nowhere), and thus
'strange', 'unwanted', 'extraordinary', 'eccentric', 'paradoxical'.

[114] *RB*, 156.

the case when new discursive forms come into being, and the old classifying systems no longer fit. 'Socrates, even before I met you they told me that in plain truth you are a perplexed man yourself and reduce others to perplexity. . . . My mind and lips are literally numb, and I have nothing to reply to you.'[115] There is, after all, always the fiction of the proper name to fall back on, 'ce plus éprouvé des pseudonymes' as Barthes calls it.[116] All names are catachrestic and all proper names improper, but sometimes they are all we have left to work with, 'le dernier soupir qui reste des choses'.[117] This applies to the commentator as well as the story-teller. 'It is cold in the scriptorium, my thumb aches. I leave this manuscript, I do not know for whom; I no longer know what it is about; stat rosa pristina nomine, nomina nuda tenemus.'[118] And even the commentator who attempts to suspend naming, as Barthes believes names, images, and adjectives should be suspended, may end up by telling stories that themselves are merely deferred names. Even here, 'l'aventure a des passages dangereux' for the narrator discussing the career of Roland Barthes, Marxist, reactionary, structuralist, post-structuralist, idealist, materialist, teacher, hedonist, man of letters, moralist, philosopher of culture, connoisseur of strong ideas, protean autobiographer, polemicist, semiologist, critic, and writer.[119] For Barthes's dislike of such names— such images—is the result of a feeling that the truth of writing is elsewhere: not in the voiced name, the recognizable identity, but in a practice of writing that cannot be voiced—that is unpronounceable, like a scribble.

[115] Meno, in Plato, *Meno*, 80A–B.

[116] In his 'review' of RB, 'Barthes puissance trois', *Quinzaine littéraire* (1–15, 1975), 3–5 (5).

[117] Cited by Barthes in 'Noms propres', in *RB*, 55. In *all except you*, Barthes suggests that the truth of Steinberg's work is his 'Nom propre' (Ibid. 57).

[118] These last three sentences are the end of the story told by Adso in Umberto Eco, *The Name of the Rose*, trans. William Weaver (London, 1984), 502.

[119] I include the ch. headings of Culler's *Barthes*, as well as the list with which Susan Sontag begins her pref. 'Writing Itself: On Roland Barthes', in *A Barthes Reader*, (London, 1982), vii–xxxviii (vii), in this list of names.

4

THE SCRIBBLER

The scribbler is never satisfied: he is as insatiable as ever . . .

> Peter Greenaway, *The Draughtsman's Contract*

Avoid haphazard writing materials. A pedantic adherence to certain papers, pens, inks is beneficial. No luxury, but an abundance of these utensils is necessary.

> Walter Benjamin, 'The Writer's Technique in Thirteen Theses'

Là, je considère mes instruments de scripture. Vous le savez, j'ai un rapport très déterminé avec les instruments de scripture proprement dits, le crayon, la gomme (que je nomme *l'anti-crayon*, par manière de plaisanterie).

> Michel-Antoine Burnier and Patrick Rambaud,
> *Le Roland-Barthes sans peine*

I often think I overall resemble the scribble drawn by an unknown power across the paper, in order to try out a *new pen*.

> Nietzsche, letter to Peter Gast (August 1881)

INTERPRETATION: VIA DI LEVARE

To scribble: to write or draw in a hasty or illegible manner; to make meaningless or illegible marks; and, in derogatory or facetious contexts, to write in general—novels, poems, plays. The etymology of 'scribble' is from the medieval Latin *scribillare*, meaning to write hastily, from Latin *scribere*, to write. But there is another meaning too: to scribble can be to card (wool, for example). Its etymology in this case is probably from a Low German cognate of *schrubben*, which gives us the verb to scrub—to rub a surface hard in order to clean it; to remove dirt; and, in informal contexts, to delete or cancel.

These etymological notes introduce the theme of this chapter: is writing addition or subtraction, scribbling or scrubbing—or, indeed, the other form of scraping known as sculpting? Barthes's work plays off these figures of writing against each other.

Barthes frequently cites a comment made by Leonardo da Vinci: painting is a process of accumulation, a *via di porre*, and sculpture a process of subtraction, a *via di levare*. (I will be noting some of the contexts for Barthes's quotation of this remark later.) Leonardo's distinction between these two arts had already been noted by Freud, who says that psychoanalysis, as a mode of interpretation, is closer to sculpture than to painting, in so far as it operates by a process of removal: the analyst has to clear away the rough-hewn exterior of the patient's discourse, the stony resistance of its layers of untruth, in order to reach the hidden form within. Michaelangelo, in another phrase that continues to serve literary critics, says that sculpture amounts to freeing from the block of stone the figure already defined in it.[1]

A more insistent metaphor for psychoanalysis in Freud's text is that of archaeological excavation: but what is important here, as in sculpture, is the idea that interpretation is seen as progressing only through the removal of layers of obstructing rubble. At all events, the psychoanalyst as interpreter is a heroic transformer of raw materials, wielding the sculptor's chisel or the hammer and pickaxe of the archaeologist in an attempt to rediscover a truth that is already there, albeit concealed. These somewhat masculine, aggressive images suggest that all interpretation, when figured as the uncovering of a latent and necessarily resistant meaning, is violent: it is forced to work through and discard the outer protective layers (of the stone block to be sculpted, the archaeological site to be excavated, or the discourse to be analysed) in order to reach the form hidden beneath. I will later suggest how Barthes questions the aggressiveness inherent in a hermeneutics imagined in these terms.

Any quest for lost origins will be tempted by the sculptural or archaeological ideal of freeing an imprisoned form. When it comes to writing, however, we need a new metaphor: that of the palimpsest.[2]

---

[1] Freud refers to the distinction between *via di porre* and *via di levare* when he discriminates between the techniques of suggestion, which he now wants to move away from, and analysis (psychoanalysis in its mature mode): suggestion adds, analysis removes ('On Psychotherapy', in *The Standard Edition of the Complete Psychological Works of Sigmund Freud*, trans. and ed. James Strachey *et al.* (London, 1953–74), 257–68 (260). For a recent use of Michelangelo's metaphor, see Umberto Eco, *Reflections on 'The Name of the Rose'*, trans. William Weaver (London, 1985), 12.

[2] The image of psychoanalysis as archaeology is examined in detail by Malcolm Bowie, *Freud, Proust and Lacan: Theory as Fiction* (Cambridge, 1987). Freud frequently compared the analyst's uncovering of repressed material to the excavation of Pompeii, as in 'Notes upon a Case of Obsessional Neurosis' (the 'Rat Man' case), in *The Pelican Freud Library*, ed. Angela Richards (Harmondsworth, 1973–86), ix. 33–128 (57).

History, both as the unfolding of events in time and as the writing of those events into time, appears as a palimpsest, but one in which no layer of writing is ever entirely scraped away, so that the result consists of a long accretion of glosses, marginalia, and footnotes, interpretations that cover over some original text. This text may still be there, but it tends to be obliterated by its commentaries. When the original text is sacred but needs to be interpreted, as does the Torah, a different problem arises: that of a commentary which must not tamper with the original words. But in any case, the authors of such glosses or *midrashim*, claims Frank Kermode, considered that 'they were not really adding at all, but merely working towards the restoration of the full original meaning, a plenum that human endeavour can never hope to achieve'.[3] If we scrape away these superimposed interpretative layers, will we reach the original text, or just a blank page?

Barthes frequently uses metaphors that lead us to imagine that what is new about *la nouvelle critique* is its capacity for re-experiencing the text in its pristine purity, scraping away years of ideological accretion. In the preface to *Essais critiques*, for instance, criticism may not indeed *add* a new layer to the text, but it does have the virtue of working through earlier layers: criticism is there 'moins pour donner un sens à l'œuvre énigmatique que pour détruire ceux dont elle est tout de suite et à jamais encombrée'.[4] When, in *Critique et vérité*, Barthes hypothesizes about some potential science of literature, he suggests that its task would be not to interpret the text's symbols in new ways, but to uncover 'le sens vide qui les supporte tous'.[5] He thus demonstrates that there may be a transcendental drive at work in the archaeological or sculptural impetus of *la nouvelle critique*: such a project aims not merely to discover new meanings latent in the text, but to lay bare the conditions of possibility for all literary meaning as such. (A similar endeavour is manifest in some of Foucault's epistemological metaphors, notably, of course, that of the *archaeology* of knowledge.)

But while the transcendentalizing drive aims to stand above all interpretations in order to see the conditions of possibility that determine the set of all such interpretations, it is also a 'foundationalist' desire to dig down to the thing being interpreted, even though in so doing it cannot help but discover new meanings as well as remove old ones. There is a sense in which even scraping away meaning is never just a *via di levare*, but inescapably also a *via di porre*. We have

[3] Frank Kermode, *Essays on Fiction 1971–1982* (London, 1983), 25.
[4] *EC*, 10.   [5] *CV*, 57.

already seen, for instance, how Barthes's *Mythologies* attempt to *levare* the obfuscating interpretations made by petty-bourgeois ideology. But he does not aim to restore any original, value-free objectivity to the objects and practices he discusses. His success is inseparable from his own ability to *porre* various myths and figures—and these in their turn demand interpretation, as I have shown in the case of 'drift', where a local political point about media imagery was connected to a far-reaching system of metaphors running through Barthes's work sometimes in idiosyncratic ways.

One of the figures of modernism who demonstrates this problem of interpretation and its drive to reach bedrock is Nietzsche. I will take just one example of the way the attempt to interpret a phenomenon back to its origin runs into problems. Nietzsche constantly demonstrates how the ideological moment of interpretation produces a culturally determined reading. In *Beyond Good and Evil*, he correspondingly asserts that the cultural readings of the phenomenon 'man' must be torn away, that the superimposed layers of interpretation must be scraped off to reveal a hidden 'basic text' (an 'original text'—*Grundtext*, that text which is the ground and foundation for all subsequent interpretations). The idealistic words with which humanity has characterized its own activity—'honesty', 'love of truth', 'sacrifice in the service of knowledge'—are all so much flattering colour, painted over an original image in layer after layer of what Nietzsche calls 'colour and over-painting' (*Farbe und Übermalung*), under which 'the terrible basic text *homo natura* must again be discerned'. Humankind has to be transposed back into nature, metaphysics is a delusion, the only worthwhile discipline is science: this seems to be Nietzsche's message.

But the passage needs to be quoted in full for its complexity as writing to be appreciated:

For to translate man back [*zurückübersetzen*] into nature; to master the many vain and fanciful interpretations [*Deutungen*] and secondary meanings [*Nebensinne*] which have been hitherto scribbled and daubed [*gekritzelt und gemalt*] over that eternal basic text *homo natura*; to confront man henceforth with man in the way in which, hardened by the discipline of science, man today confronts the *rest* of nature, with dauntless Oedipus eyes and stopped-up Odysseus ears, deaf to the siren songs of old metaphysical bird-catchers who have all too long been piping to him 'you are more! you are higher! you are of a different origin!'—that may be a strange and extravagant task but it is a *task*—who would deny that?[6]

6 Nietzsche, *Beyond Good and Evil*, trans. R. J. Hollingdale (Harmondsworth, 1973), sect. 230.

This apparent demand for a scientific, naturalistic examination of man in nature (and as nature) is conveyed in a text that suddenly bristles with mythological references and thickens with metaphors. 'Translate', 'interpretations', 'scribbled', and 'basic text', as figures of writing, coexist uneasily with a figure of painting, 'daubed'; and both these visual activities are echoed by the aural 'siren songs' and the 'piping' we hear at the end of the section. I will be showing that the depiction of a similar tension between different artistic modes also affects a key Barthes text, *S/Z*.

As a programme, Nietzsche's plea is for a clearing away of the idealistic dross of centuries of interpretation. It has often been noted how close much of his philosophy is to certain forms of phenomenology, a mode of thought which too aspires to starting afresh, whether it be Descartes clearing away the clutter of scholasticism in the *Discours de la méthode*, or Husserl appealing for a return *zu den Sachen selbst* ('to the things themselves'). Husserl indeed resorts to the metaphor of the clean white page that needs to be restored to its original blankness. Derrida notes this metaphor and summarizes its consequences in these terms: 'The expressive noema must present itself . . . as a blank page or a clean slate, at least as a palimpsest restored to its pure receptivity.'[7] The rest of Derrida's discussion fastens on the problems this metaphor creates: returning to Nietzsche's text, we can likewise see how mythical metaphorical figures create a resonance that disturbs the purity of such a programme. 'Man' is not going to be a clean page.

For instance, we are enjoined to see the world through 'dauntless Oedipus eyes'. But Oedipus's insights were always inseparable from blindness: metaphorically blind to the situation (parricide and incest) into which his successful solving of the Sphinx's riddle led him, his realization of guilt caused him literally to put out his eyes. The myth's ironies, its entwining of blindness and insight, of nature and unnature, cannot help but disturb Nietzsche's message, for what the Oedipus myth suggests is that humanity is indeed part of nature, but of a nature that can only be retroactively reconstructed as the other of humanity's *un*nature. For the ban on incest is the mark of humanity as emerging from the state of nature, and it is this ban that Oedipus both transgresses in incest, and whose binding force he acknowledges in his self-inflicted punishment. Translating man back into nature, as

---

[7] 'Form and Meaning: A Note on the Phenomenology of Language', in *Speech and Phenomena and Other Essays on Husserl's Theory of Signs*, trans. and introd. David B. Allison (Evanston, Ill. 1973), 107–28 (117).

Nietzsche suggests we do, is thus bound to lead to an unreadable text, since 'man' and 'nature' are not two entirely separate languages that can be translated 'into' each other. To read through the interpretations scrawled over the original text of *homo natura*, to attempt to fix one's gaze on the lineaments of that obliterated but terrible original figure, is to run the risk of realizing that nature and unnature may be difficult to separate (incest is both forbidden *and* desired), and indeed, as a result of that insight, of never being able to see anything again. To attempt to get back to a state of affairs 'before' interpretation is to risk being blinded by an original text—that *ipso facto* becomes definitively illegible, indeed, invisible. Nietzsche suggests that 'man' has been translated out of 'nature' and proposes to retranslate him back again: although the German *übersetzen* has less purely linguistic connotations than the English 'translate', the metaphor tends to lead us to see 'nature' as a language, in other words a *cultural* construction, rather than a pure 'state of affairs' or *Tatbestand*. One of the masters of hermeneutic suspicion, who himself has enabled us to remove some of the constructions of culture and see through to deeper, more problematic levels, cannot help, in one of his most 'enlightening' texts, but add a new and difficult gloss to an age-old text that retains its stubborn indecipherability. Who *can* read *homo natura*?

A similar problem underlies Barthes's project as a *mythologue*: he is prepared to see myth itself as language, and the process of myth-formation as formalizable in terms of one language that acts as a metalanguage for another language—such is the position he sets out in 'Le Mythe, aujourd'hui'. He is concerned to show that 'History' is a language whose sentences have been translated into another and different language, called 'Nature', so that the task of the *mythologue* is to translate them back again (*zurückübersetzen*, as Nietzsche puts it) into 'History'. But what Nietzsche seems to have wanted to establish as a bedrock, namely nature, and what Barthes wishes to establish as a bedrock, namely History, are both in a sense 'languages', and to translate a phenomenon back into a language implies that it was potentially translatable out of that language in the first place—in other words, that it is not in the least foundational, but linguistic, and thus capable of occupying different places in different languages. (I will be discussing Barthes's interest in apparently untranslatable phenomena in Chapter 6.) The difference in Barthes's text is that to see History as a language leads to an increasingly general attack on myths, but one which extols, as the opposite of a repressive nature, not so much History as *writing*.

The critique of interpretation is thus stated in terms that are themselves subject to interpretation. One way in which Nietzsche deals with this problem is not by attempting to destroy interpretations, but by multiplying them. Thus the 'Oedipus eyes' that always risk blindness are replaced by another optical figure: we must have, he says, as many eyes as possible to read the complexities of the text of the world.[8]

In Barthes too, there is a revolt against the kind of purism that declares all interpretation to be illicit. Such purism frequently takes religious forms, as in iconoclasm, the ban on images. But such a ban tends to generate images of a different kind, verbal or conceptual: and in any case, to interpret transcendence in human ways seems unavoidable. The only escape is to loosen the hold of any one imaginative interpretation by ensuring that it is not the only one available, as I suggested in the discussion of names.

So Barthes decides that interpretation should be plural. He thinks, in *Critique et vérité*, that the critic's job, now, is to apply the interpretative modes of our own age—Marxism, psychoanalysis, structuralism, and so on—to both contemporary and past texts. This is what he does in *Sur Racine* and *S/Z*. But, especially in the latter, not only do the different systems interfere with each other: they also are not separable from the text they are being used to analyse. In the first case, Barthes draws on the energies of psychoanalysis with its fundamental category of castration, to explain why *Sarrasine* should show such preoccupation with the topos 'something out of nothing' in the economic sense. A purely Marxist analysis of *Sarrasine* would probably decide that the de Lanty family is not really representative of the nascent capitalism that Balzac is so anxious about, and in which there is indeed a way of producing something out of nothing (or almost nothing)—by speculation on the stock exchange. For the de Lanty's have not made their money like that: their fortune is that which Zambinella the millionaire castrato has left them. But Barthes allows the psychoanalytic theme of castration to inflect his 'economic' reading of *Sarrasine* as staging Balzac's nostalgia for an economy of landed property, or at least one based on a stable gold standard, rather than the 'big bang' of the 1830s. This allows him to suggest a symbolic equivalence between the 'nothing' of castration (as absence of the phallus) and the 'nothing' from which the de Lanty fortune

---

[8] See Nietzsche, *On the Genealogy of Morals*, trans. Walter Kaufmann and R. J. Hollingdale (New York, 1967), ch. 3, sect. 12. (119).

(and perhaps, potentially, all the money of the capitalist parvenus making a killing on a bull market) springs. But this is more to prolong Balzac's own symbolic obsessions than to do justice to the deeper ambiguities of the text—ambiguities that, as Barthes recognizes, complicate such an interpretative manœuvre. For Sarrasine decides, in disgust, that he has been in love with a 'nothing'. ('Tu n'es rien', he tells Zambinella once he has discovered that he/she is a castrato.)[9] But there is a sense in which this nothing is saying too much. Barthes at first suggests a neat and symmetrical schema on loosely Lacanian bases in order to map the networks of power and desire running through the story (a subject can 'have' the phallus—like the men, or 'be' the phallus—like the women).[10] But he soon complicates this by showing that the women in the story are more 'virile' (more 'active') than the men, so that a purely biological sexual binary paradigm is insufficient: one needs to look at the question of symbolic sexuality, or gender.[11] Furthermore, just as Balzac's horrified fascination with a fortune coming from 'nothing' makes a metaphysical symbol out of something that is quite definite (for in speculation on the money markets, you need something—a stake, however small—to gamble: you need some initial capital), so the 'nothing' of castration is a definite absence of the phallus. In other words, Barthes sometimes agrees with Sarrasine (and Balzac) that the castrato is a metaphysical threat (like death). If he did not *porre* the equation 'castrato' = 'nothing', he would not be able to suggest that, for Balzac, 'small capital stake' (of the sort which can generate a fortune) = 'nothing', and he would thus not be able to see how the symbolic forces of desire and political economy mesh in Balzac's fiction. But at the same time, he realizes that the castrato is not 'nothing', but, rather, a castrated male. (The axis of castration does not divide subjects up symmetrically: what would a castrated female be? A frigid woman? But the story is about a *real* castration as well as a symbolic castration). To imagine a counterpart to Zambinella, we would need to imagine a female eunuch, a 'Zambinello'. And despite his large-scale metaphorical equating of libidinal with monetary economies, Barthes also knows that the castrato does not fit into this scheme: 'quand au castrat lui-même, on aurait tort de le placer de droit du côté du châtré: il est la tache aveugle et mobile de ce système; il va et vient entre l'actif et le passif: châtré, il châtre; de même pour Mme

---

[9] Cited in *S/Z*, 256.   [10] Ibid. 42.   [11] Ibid. 43.

de Rochefide: contaminée par la castration qui vient de lui être racontée, elle y entraîne la narrateur'.[12] So it is less an absence or 'nothing' that the castrato represents, but a semantic wobble, a haze of meaning—and only this indeterminacy enables Barthes's imaginative metaphorical leap to the economies of money and meaning, which are afflicted by a similar instability.

So Barthes applies various current interpretative languages and shows how they interact with each other and with Balzac's text: he is prepared to *porre*, to pose, the equivalence, for instance, of the word *cœur* with the *sexe* that it euphemistically replaces. (When Sarrasine hears Zambinella sing for the first time, Balzac tells us that 'il sentit un foyer qui pétilla soudain dans les profondeurs de son être intime, de ce que nous nommons le cœur, faute de mot!')[13] A more deconstructive reader, Barbara Johnson, wants to *levare*, take away even this gloss and expose the blanks in Balzac's text for what they are—blanks. She thus wants to restore to Balzac's blanks (especially the absence of the word 'castrato') a certain purity: it is over these blanks that Barthes is prepared to write his own interpretation.[14] To leave a blank, of course, is to make the text less legible than it is, in that it forecloses the possibility of demonstrating how symbolically complex are its manœuvres—a blank as such can no longer be equated with anything else (and thus not with the 'nothing'—the very definite absence of landed property, for instance—from which wealth in Balzac's Paris seems to spring). Johnson's reading is an interesting corrective to what is sometimes an over-enthusiastic use of the topos of castration on Barthes's part, but she fails to note either that the maintenance of the blank as such is ultimately impossible and makes the story unreadable, or that Barthes shows considerable scruple in demonstrating how much more complex the text is than the interpretative languages (those of psychoanalysis and political economy, for instance) that he applies to it. By being prepared to follow Balzac's complexity, to prolong the symbolic force of his obsessions, Barthes is ultimately very faithful to the ambiguities of the text. His way of 'writing on' Balzac is to 'write on', continue, Balzac's own terms: his

---

[12] *S/Z*, 43.

[13] Discussed, ibid. 122.

[14] Ibid. Johnson's discussion of this and other places where Barthes is too prepared to *porre* an interpretation is in 'The Critical Difference: Balzac's *Sarrasine* and Barthes's *S/Z*', in Robert Young (ed.), *Untying the Text: A Post-structuralist Reader* (Boston, 1981), 162–74 (172–3). But is not even the word 'blank' still a mode of *porre*, of adding to a silence signified by the '. . .' in Balzac's text? (Naming is of course, as this ex., which I referred to in Ch. 3, above, shows, a mode of *porre*.)

metalanguage and the Balzacian object-language cannot be entirely separated.

So when Barthes advocates a 'plural' interpretation, he has two main things in mind. The first is a historicist vision in which each age produces new metalanguages (new sciences and epistemologies): all these are mortal, so that each such interpretative language is scribbled over by the one that succeeds it in history's next palimpsestic inscription.[15] The second is the breakdown between different levels— between text and context or interpretative gloss on the one hand, and between the different symbolic levels of both text and interpretative system on the other hand—as when psychoanalysis and political economy turn out to interfere with each other, to mimic each other's characteristic terminology and tactics. (This is perhaps most clearly seen in the word 'fetishism', a key term in both psychoanalysis and Marxism, as we saw in Chapter 3.) This second and more challenging kind of pluralism in interpretation is closer to deconstruction than the first and more historicist kind, but it is difficult to find any example of sustained deconstructive analysis (as in the deconstructionism of Derrida and de Man) in Barthes's work: *S/Z* is less a work of deconstruction than an exploded structuralism, an *analyse structurale du récit* in which we watch the analysis destructuring, rather than deconstructuring, itself. Where deconstruction is committed to a relatively negative mode, trying to unsay rather than say again, Barthes is prepared to add his own scribble, to *porre* as well as *levare*. (And of course, in practice, deconstruction tends to mix its negative moment of suspending meanings with a considerable palimpsestic zest in creating, in deliberately parodic and unbridled form, its own mock interpretations—as in Derrida's *Glas* where, as I have already mentioned, Hegel and Genet are read in and across each other.)

For Nietzsche, then, interpretation was something 'scribbled and painted' over the original text, so that our task is to try and read that text through the obstacle posed by this palimpsestic overlay. The progressive gesture is one of removing such accretions. But in Barthes, as to some extent in Nietzsche when, at other times, he too advocates

---

[15] This appears e.g. in the metaphor which concludes *SM*: 'un jour viendra inévitablement où l'analyse structurale passera au rang de langage-objet et sera saisie dans *un système supérieur* qui à son tour l'expliquera' (*SM*, 293, my emphasis). Barthes's vision of a metalanguage as a new layer lying on top of its language-object is somewhat simplistic when stated baldly, but runs throughout his work. It may become more complex, as in 'Le second degré et les autres' where the *échelonnements de langage* are not reducible to degrees of metalinguistic superiority (*RB*, 70–1).

plural readings of the world, a countervailing strategy of *adding* to the pre-existent text emerges, even if—perhaps especially if—this means disfiguring that text, making it unreadable.

SARRASINE: FROM SCRIBBLER TO SCULPTOR

Freud's interpretation of the Oedipus myth makes the hero's self-blinding a symbol of castration. In *Sarrasine*, the eponymous hero is depicted as in blind pursuit of the evasive object of his desire. Sarrasine is an artist and Balzac's text stages an intense struggle between various modes of artistic production—drawing, sculpting, singing, painting, writing, and telling fireside stories.

Sarrasine is a scribbler (a drawer) and a sculptor, but both, at first, in destructive ways. His art is founded on transgression. Here is the passage in which Balzac paints his portrait of the artist as a young vandal:

> Au lieu d'apprendre les éléments de la langue grecque, il dessinait le révérend père qui leur expliquait un passage de Thucydide, croquait le maître de mathématiques, le préfet, les valets, le correcteur, et barbouillait tous les murs d'esquisses informes. Au lieu de chanter les louanges du Seigneur à l'église, il s'amusait, pendant les offices, à déchiqueter un banc; ou quand il avait volé un morceau de bois, il sculptait quelque figure de sainte. Si le bois, la pierre, le crayon lui manquaient, il rendait ses idées avec de la mie de pain.[16]

Sarrasine's revolt—part of the cultural code which has as one of its items the image of the tempestuous romantic artist, the *cancre génial* as Barthes calls him—shows itself in two ways: he reacts against his environment by scribbling over it, but also by tearing it apart, trying to find behind its surfaces a truth of his own.[17]

Barthes suggests that a similar process operates when Sarrasine in Rome mentally undresses Zambinella in order to find the truth of 'her' body so as to appropriate it by drawing it. Having fallen prey to the fascination of Zambinella because of the rapture induced by her voice, Sarrasine goes back to his lodgings and fantasmatically attempts to recreate her, drawing her from memory in a variety of poses, both academic and free. 'Mais sa pensée furieuse alla plus loin que le dessin.'[18] The scribbler is not satisfied with surfaces, and Barthes

---

[16] Reproduced in *S/Z*, 240.   [17] Ibid. 100.   [18] Ibid. 128.

reads this as connoting *déshabillage*: an attempt to get to the naked reality behind the drawing. Sarrasine thus, in his desire, unites scribbling with sculpture: this kind of subtractive scribbling is close to sculpting in that both activities aim at reaching the reality behind the appearances, the body behind its clothes. In this way scribble (*porre*) is overcome by sculpture (*levare*): it is turned into another lifting of the veils.[19] The more masculine, aggressive figure of the apprentice sculptor dominates that of the scribbler.

Barthes's section liv of *S/Z* cites Freud on Leonardo to drive home the point that psychoanalysis, sculpture, literary realism, and the historically minded or positivist critic share a common drive toward the excavation of a truth prior to mere superficial appearance. 'Ce mouvement, qui pousse Sarrasine, l'artiste réaliste et le critique à tourner le modèle, la statue, la toile ou le texte pour s'assurer de son dessous, de son intérieur, conduit à un échec—à l'Échec—dont *Sarrasine* est en quelque sorte l'emblème.'[20] And he quotes another Balzacian example of this topos: Frenhofer, the artist of *Le Chef-d'œuvre inconnu*, wants to create a painting that will be *as real* as its model, but produces (apart from one perfectly formed image of a foot) only scribble—'le gribouillis de lignes, l'écriture abstraite, indéchiffrable'.[21] The aggression behind this drive is identified by Barthes as an act of *forage* or drilling—any realist drive to reach the essence of things is seen by him as sharing this *impulsion de percée*, which fails to realize that behind any artistic representation is less the real it purports to copy (the referent) than the act of Reference from one kind of writing to another: 'ce qu'il y a derrière le papier, ce n'est pas le réel, le référent, c'est la Référence, la "subtile immensité des écritures"'.[22] This is one way in which Barthes figures (without solving the problems of) the process of reference: instead of language referring to a world 'out there', the act of reference itself is a kind of pointing from one writing to another—there is thus no need for a leap from one category (the word) to another (the world) since both are subsumed under the category of writing. This is partly because he believes that perception cannot be separated from the language in which what is perceived is transcribed (so that we do not see mere sense-data which we then call 'a red patch', but see anything at all only because we have, in some sense, the words 'a red patch' available): this, especially in its political aspect, determines such

[19] *S/Z*, 131, 174. [20] Ibid. 129.
[21] Ibid. [22] Ibid.

statements as 'Le monde est toujours *déjà* écrit' in *Sollers écrivain*.[23]
So to write is less to represent that world than to continue it as 'un
tissu, un réseau d'écritures—et non un tableau que l'écrivain extrairait
de sa conscience ou de la réalité'.[24] And Barthes's belief that the
world is already written is partly a result of taking seriously Derrida's
idea of *archi-écriture*: in other words he thinks that all articulation is a
kind of writing, dividing up the world into its different aspects in the
very act of perception—or in the very act of action. As he puts it in
Sade, Fourier, Loyola, one can consider *l'écriture* as 'ni décorative ni
instrumentale, c'est-à-dire en somme seconde, mais première, anté-
cédente á l'homme, qu'elle traverse, fondatrice de ses actes comme
autant d'inscriptions'.[25]

Finally, in section lxxxviii of *S/Z*, entitled 'De la sculpture à la
peinture', Barthes shows how the move from *sculpture* (and hermeneutic drilling) to the realization that the underlying activity of all the arts
is a kind of *writing* is mediated by a swing towards *painting*. Having
discovered that Zambinella is symbolically empty, so that (as he
supposes) his statue of her is equally void of value, Sarrasine attempts
to destroy the statue—but the hammer he hurls at it misses. The
statue is saved by Zambinella's protector, Cardinal Cicognara, who
has it copied in marble: the de Lanty family finds it in the Albani
museum in 1791 and has it copied by the painter Vien. The sculpture
has become a painting. Sculpture raises various burning questions:
'what lies behind the surface of a sculpture (what is its model)?' and
'from what raw material has it been carved (what is its physical
origin)?' Barthes claims that painting tames the dangerous force of
such questions (though their corresponding obsession with the problematics of castration persists): we are, he claims, less inclined to
worry about the 'depth' of a painting than in the case of sculpture.
Barthes's point stands, but painting (that of Vien or Girodet, who
bases his own *Endymion* on the Vien copy) is still, in the early
nineteenth century, bound by the laws of perspective. Hence Frenhofer's attempt to collapse the distinction between two-dimensional
painting and three-dimensional sculpture—an attempt which prefigures attempts such as cubism to problematize the canvas surface as

---

[23] *SE*, 51.
[24] Ibid.
[25] *SFL*, 46. A more philosophically grounded approach to the problem of reference,
one that criticizes some of the assumptions behind Barthes's semiological treatment,
can be found in Christopher Prendergast, *The Order of Mimesis. Balzac, Stendhal, Nerval,
Flaubert* (Cambridge, 1986).

such. But in any case, for Barthes, painting is easier to assimilate to writing: both of them are *via di porre* rather than a *via di levare*—so that the Vien portrait, half representation, half copy (Vien's) of a copy (the marble statue) of Sarrasine's statue (and thus caught up in the 'citational' interplay that Barthes identifies with writing) can be absorbed into Balzac's own text, with its mixed status as partly representational (realist) and partly *scriptible*. 'Quant au dernier avatar, qui est le passage de la toile à la "représentation" écrite, il récupère toutes les copies précédentes, mais l'écriture exténue encore davantage le fantasme du *dedans*, car elle n'a plus d'autre substance que l'interstice'—the gaps between the codes that are starting to open up in Balzac's text.[26] In other words, from a solid, three-dimensional, and realist aesthetic which seems to invite an implicitly aggressive hermeneutic, a desire to get behind it all and penetrate the world of appearances to its core of truth, Barthes suggests that *Sarrasine* is allegorically staging a rather different drive to abandon, as futile and disastrous, such a vision in favour of a less violent aesthetic based on writing which is content to scribble, to write on in the absence of any locatable origin, definite meaning, or final truth.

Sarrasine, however, *is* dominated by a form of desire that takes the shape of a certain realism: but he is eventually forced to realize that behind his art is nothing. On the basis of his aesthetic, the truth of Zambinella's body is strictly unreadable for him, since it does not fit into any of his preconceived ideas about what is acceptable (*either* Zambinella is a woman, *or* he is a man: there is no third term). As text, the monster Zambinella is thus the equivalent of Nietzsche's *homo natura*: an unreadable oxymoron. Even the name 'castrato' is, as we have seen, elided in the text itself: for neither the text nor the characters it represents use the word (the Roman opera-goers who 'know' that Zambinella is a castrato do not name him as such to enlighten Sarrasine). It is this blank in his social text that leads Sarrasine to his death. He resembles the psychotic, in that there is one key signifier foreclosed to him.[27] He is blinded not only by the imaginary arts of music (Zambinella's 'seamless' voice, which provides him with total pleasure) and sculpture (to which he resorts in response to his desire for a total body, unbroached by castration): he cannot see

---

[26] *S/Z*, 214.
[27] For Jacques Lacan, the absence of the signifier of the Name of the Father is a central feature of psychosis. See 'D'une question préliminaire à tout traitement de la psychose', *Écrits*, (1966), 531–83 (558).

the symbolic (writing, which is woven from difference and castration—even when it attempts, in imaginary ways, to occlude that fact).[28]

Just as Nietzsche's attempt to reach the 'eternal basic text' stages, in its metaphors, a struggle between different arts (music, writing, painting: only writing is allowed, ultimately, to give us access to the *basic text*, the truth of *homo natura*—and even there that truth cannot be read as such), so *Sarrasine* shows us various artistic activities locked in combat. The two aspects of Sarrasine's art—as painter and scribbler on the one hand, as sculptor on the other—have a different role to play in the story (though they cannot be rigorously separated—drawing Zambinella is, as mentioned, a way of chiselling through to her innermost secrets). The former adds (so that Sarrasine's schoolboy scribbling over official culture is still, potentially, an augmentation of that culture's resources—it is, as Barthes notes, a romantic topos to depict the young artist as rebellious); the latter subtracts, but risks subtracting everything. (In any case, the text demonstrates that none of these arts succeed in mastering the force of a music which, as in a Hoffmann short story, seems to come, uncannily, from nowhere.)

What Sarrasine briefly glimpses, then, through a haze of denials and refusals, behind the multiple scribblings and daubs of culture and its lures, and behind the obstacles, blinds, feints, and tricks thrown in his path by Zambinella's colleagues and protectors, is the nothing of castration. The statue he has created is a mere surface constructed around this void—hence his attempt to smash it after realization has dawned on him. But the statue survives—so that the lack it embodies can cast its fateful radiance on the other main actors in Balzac's story, the narrator and the marchioness. For while art may not be true (there is nothing real behind it, it is pure surface, what Nietzsche called a 'beautiful appearance' (*schöner Schein*) floating over the void), it is certainly fertile: Balzac's horrified fascination with the way capitalism can apparently create something from nothing is ironically figured in the way castration motors the whole story he tells. The lack from which Zambinella's song emerges is reincarnated successively in Sarrasine's drawing, his sculpture, the copy of the sculpture made in marble on the orders of Cardinal Cicognara, Vien's painting of this copy (which inflames the marchioness with desire and leads to the

---

[28] Tom Conley, in 'Barthes's *Excès*: The Silent Apostrophe of *S/Z*' (*Visible Language*, 11: 4 (autumn 1977), 355–84 (364)), notes that *Sarrasine* tells the tale of 'the artist's failure to see the graphic nature of things'.

contract which is the source of the narrative), and the *Endymion* of Girodet based on Vien's painting. We can see a copy of the Girodet painting (itself in the Louvre) as the frontispiece of *S/Z*: so we can still see a version, however distant and culturally coded, of what Zambinella looked like at the age of 20. We should, perhaps, be aware of the risk involved in gazing at this painting.[29]

Barthes, as we have seen, views the way the statue is translated into painting and then into text as a way of muting the aggression associated with artistic realism and its corresponding hermeneutics. But it is not a way of defusing the dangers of art. The effect of the story on the marchioness and the narrator suggests otherwise: and *S/Z* itself is still trying to come to terms with castration, whether the fictional castration operated on the *ragazzo* from Naples probably in the 1740s, or the symbolic castration that, according to Lacan, is the condition of our entering language and being able to read Sarrasine's story in the first place. Barthes's treatment of Balzac's story is, after all, hardly devoid of its own aggression. And his pulverizing of the text in order to reveal the emptiness of any ideal of organic totality and to show that the text is not a total body—his naming and renaming of castration—is an attempt to master the void. In the very act of exploding the text, Barthes in pursuit of Balzac is like Sarrasine in pursuit of Zambinella. Who more than Balzac is more of a cultural totem figure, a survivor of the vicissitudes of critical taste in the France of the last two centuries? This 'monumental' Balzac is figured powerfully in Rodin's statue of him—at which, as it were, an irreverently affectionate Barthes takes a shot with his hammer, only to miss. Barthes's interest in this Prometheus of French literature, as André Maurois called him, while clearly based on profound knowledge of and admiration for Balzac's texts, is inseparable from his desire to find out what's behind it all. Literary historians will fob him off with facts and figures, or will try to work out who Balzac's models in real life may have been. But Barthes disregards *these* scribblers: he wants to see through to the text's most hidden secrets, the very mechanisms which enable it to work as a story. Hence his aggressive, sadistic, impulsive ripping apart

---

[29] Or in hearing the voice of a castrato. The end of *S/Z* fails to note that this is still possible: the last castrato was not, as Barthes, following the *code historique*, claims, Velluti, who died in London in 1861 (*S/Z* 220), but Alessandro Moreschi, 'l'angelo di Roma' (1858–1922), who died within Barthes's own lifetime. Barthes is no doubt repressing this fact as a means of defence. Prof. Moreschi's voice was, however, recorded, and can still be heard on disc. There is thus an emblematic sense in which we can not only see Zambinella, but hear his voice too.

of what at first reading seems a seamless garment: he tears it seme from seme. Is he a sculptor or a scribbler? Like Sarrasine, both: for ultimately, even Barthes's scribbling (the writing of *S/Z*) aims to reach some hidden secret (the bar of castration) which the text hides in its volume. His analysis, however polythematic, is as centred as it possibly could be, since at its heart is the text's monogram: the section entitled 'S/Z' has forty-six sections before it and forty-six after: Barthes's book is thus organized around the /. At its heart is a *trait*, a pure incision.[30] In this way, BartheS acts as the Sarrasine to BalZac's Zambinella, even if the aggressive sculpting after truth is ultimately diverted and baffled into the more complex figure of writing as scribbling.

The two attitudes (of sculpting and of scribbling) continue to coexist in other texts by Barthes, despite a general trend to move from images of sculpting and its correlates to images of painting and scribbling. Sarrasine in love is bound to experience the tension between the drive to discover the truth of his desire and the adoration of the imaginary wholeness of his love's object. The lover of *Fragments d'un discours amoureux* is also tempted by the prospect of reaching the truth of desire as it is incarnated and hidden in the depths of the loved one's body. This seems to presuppose that, in this aspect at least, the lover is symbolically masculine. But in any case, in succumbing to this drive (to interpret, to know the truth), the lover temporarily falls out of love and becomes a fetishistic maniac, saying 'je me mets à scruter longuement le corps aimé (tel le narrateur devant le sommeil d'Albertine). *Scruter* veut dire *fouiller*: je fouille le corps de l'autre, comme si je voulais voir ce qu'il y a dedans, comme si la cause mécanique de mon désir était dans le corps adverse.'[31] But this dismantling of the 'other' is different from the love that the *Fragments* depict as a state in which the 'other' is seen, not as a collection of part objects, but as an imaginary whole—as surface. In love, the lover is prepared to let the 'other' be (*non-vouloir-saisir*), not to tear the loved one's body apart, penetrate, or appropriate it.[32] From this we can deduce that in taming the desire for interpretation (for some inner truth), Barthes's lover is not merely showing a (rather Nietzschean) love of surfaces, but trying to live in a state of love that is neither superficial nor deep (both of which are fetishistic and ultimately narcissistic): a love that, as letting-be, recognizes the other as an other. Needless to say, this is not so

---

[30] *S/Z*, 113.   [31] *FDA*, 85.   [32] Ibid. 275–7.

much an overall rejection of the urge toward truth as such, rather a new image of truth as different from the desperate and narcissistic quest for a recognizable and objective finality.

Likewise, Barthes in his inaugural lecture at the Collège de France sets out the terms of the semiology he now wants to practise: it will be less interpretative and more creative. So the semiologist, he claims, is indeed an artist, but a painter, not a sculptor: 'la sémiologie (devrais-je préciser de nouveau: la sémiologie de celui qui parle ici) n'est pas une herméneutique: elle peint, plutôt qu'elle ne fouille, *via di porre* plutôt que *via di levare*'.[33] In his last decade, Barthes attempts to find forms of writing about art and literature that will not be a quest for the hidden truth, as *S/Z* in so many ways still is, but rather a continuation of the momentum inscribed within the works he discusses. It is worth noting that Barthes's essays on Philippe Sollers, collected in *Sollers écrivain*, do suggest that scrubbing (to reach some bedrock) is usually doomed to becoming another mode of painting, however caustic; its negativity will be converted into a new positivity. Discussing Sollers's experimental text *H*, in 'Par-dessus l'épaule', Barthes notes that it aims at scouring away some of the myths of the western world, but escapes from the usual aporia: 'pour décaper, il faut ordinairement un langage décapant, qui devient à son tour une nouvelle peinture'.[34] For Sollers's response is a 'solution plurielle: par les bris de langage, produire sur le mur (l'écran, la page) de la représentation, des taches multiples, des dessins bizarres, des écailles, des craquelures (l'écriture chinoise n'est-elle pas née, dit-on, des craquelures apparues sur des écailles de tortue chauffées à blanc?)'[35] The swarm of writing is still a volume that invites us to *fouiller*, but no longer in search of the truth, but of *'ce qui va me toucher'*.[36] I will be following the fortunes of Barthes's metaphor later: the cracks that appear in Sollers's text, and thus in the occidental mythologies Sollers is rewriting, are both a fine-lined scribble and an enigmatic ideography, like Chinese writing.

RÉQUICHOT: TOWARDS PURE WRITING

The combat between sculpting and scribbling is also charted in the work of the artist Bernard Réquichot. The various modes of Réqui-

---

[33] *L*, 39. [34] *SE*, 57.
[35] Ibid. [36] Ibid. 58.

chot's practice are subsumed under a variety of headings: Barthes at
one stage compares his artist to a cook, in that his paintings and
collages are either composed as displays of the viscosity and indeed
viscerality of their materials, or else because they use photos taken
from food magazines.[37] But these can be reduced to practices of
addition and subtraction, painting and sculpture. There is a practice
that exceeds either of these: as should by now be becoming clear, it is
that practice in which addition and subtraction are inextricably linked,
namely writing.

According to Barthes, Western letters are not written down on to a
surface so much as cut into it: 'la lettre n'est pas peinte (déposée),
mais grattée, creusée, emportée au poinçon': it is closer to sculpture.[38]
It is this, if we extrapolate from Barthes's argument, that makes the
letter always prey to meaning, for while an individual letter may be
meaningless, it tends towards a signification (to being linked with
other letters), and he continues to associate meaning with a hermeneutics of depth. Barthes's decision to identify the Western letter with *la
glyptique*, the art of carving or engraving, is meaningless unless we see
it as part of his complex of ideas associating Western regimes of
signification with a certain aggression (from which the Eastern
ideogram, as we shall see, may provide a certain release).

In describing Réquichot's attempt to overcome the separation of
the activities of adding (as in cooking, where raw ingredients are
added one by one, or drawing) and subtracting (as in the incision of
a letter), Barthes shows how Réquichot is really moving towards
writing. For while the letter tends to be read as part of language, and
pure drawing as part of the equally coded conventions of art, a
combination of the two is an unsettling signifier which, for Barthes,
is close to pure writing: neither meaning nor non-meaning, but a
temptation to read a meaning that is never disclosed (what Barthes
calls *signifiance*).[39] Réquichot in his last period draws more and more
frequently, with a pen, and the resulting scribbles (contorted spirals
lolling across the page) combine the discontinuity of the letter with
the cursivity of the graphic trace.[40] Such a drawing may tail off into a
line of writing. This *écriture illisible*—a form of semiography already

---

[37] *OO*, 196.
[38] Ibid. 198.
[39] Barthes refers to the fact that most drawings are perfectly coded as such in 'Le
message photographique', ibid. 9–24. (12 n. 2).
[40] Ibid. 199.

practised, notes Barthes, by Klee, Ernst, Michaux, and Picasso—is echoed by Réquichot's final texts, which are language, but of an indecipherable kind.

Two types of unreadability thus coexist in Réquichot's last work: the graphic trait tending to, but not attaining, the status of a letter; and the text tending to, but not attaining, pure figurality (it is still a text, not a drawing). We are always tempted to read meaning into Réquichot's work, just as the archaeologist Persson read the scratches and scribbles on a Mycenaean jar as if they were letters in some proto-Greek script (they are, Ventris later demonstrated, mere scrawls).[41] A good example of Réquichot's illegible writing is the 'letter of insults' reproduced in the Barthes catalogue *Le Texte et l'image*.[42]

This achievement, in Barthes's opinion, makes Réquichot an artist who has come close to outplaying (playing outside) all the codes. If what we see is, in a sense, Réquichot's body, outside any mediation, this is precisely because Réquichot's art was *not* expressive. Réquichot has managed to

accomplir l'impénétrable *définitif*, en un mot mettre toute l'écriture, tout l'art en palimpseste, et que ce palimpseste soit inépuisable, ce qui a été écrit revenant sans cesse dans ce qui l'écrit pour le rendre sur-lisible—c'est-á-dire illisible.[43]

This is clearly a new kind of palimpsest, one in which the writing already there is not scrubbed away but allowed to remain below the later surfaces, to return in them. And each time a new writing is added, we are forced to reread the underlying layers.

This is very different from another kind of modern art, namely pop art. Pop art plunges back to an *archē*, scouring the tradition of its meanings, giving us the things themselves ('le pop est un art de l'essence des choses' says Barthes in his essay 'Cette vieille chose, l'art . . .').[44] But Réquichot multiplies forms to the point where they make any origin unlocatable.[45]

There is an even more exasperated form of this unreadable writing in the work of Saul Steinberg, most of which consists of cartoon-like images. In his essay on Steinberg, *all except you* Barthes notes that scribbling (which much of Steinberg's work resembles) can never be pure, always tending towards meaning. But where we expect meaning

---

[41] *OO*, 201.   [42] *Le Texte et l'image* (1986), 66.
[43] *OO*, 201.   [44] Ibid. 187.
[45] Ibid. 212–13.

and identity, Steinberg debars it: even the *names* of some of his drawings are scribbled. 'Le tourment de l'écriture illisible atteint son comble lorsque Steinberg dessine une scène d'apparence fort complexe et feint d'en donner l'explication dans une légende écrite en caractères indéchiffrables. On est deux fois frustré.'[46] This writing is both *offerte* and *imprenable*: it hides nothing that we could excavate by attempting to *levare*, but it does not allow us to *porre* our own interpretation.

The avant-garde, says Eco, begins by destroying the past: it pushes backwards to origins, to primitivism, to raw materials: the avant-garde 'destroys the figure [that is, here, the representational image of figurative art], cancels it, arrives at the abstract, the informal, the white canvas, the slashed canvas, the charred canvas'. In literature this leads to 'destruction of the flow of discourse, the Burroughs-like collage, silence, the white page'.[47] But scribbling, in general, does not scrape away culture until it reaches the origin, does not attempt to start again from nothing: it deforms a prior text instead of liberating form from prior formlessness. If modernism often wants to make a clean start, it also (in its later, post-modernist mode) shows a willingness to preserve the tradition (and thus deny that any new start can be completely self-originating): but it preserves the tradition in a derisory, parodic, or disguised form. To generalize, sculpture is more modernist, scribble more post-modernist.

In 1919 Marcel Duchamp, ahead of his time as usual (for Dada is precisely the movement that, from within the period of high modernism, is already articulating the post-modern) exhibited a reproduction of the painting that everyone knows, the *Mona Lisa*, now embellished by a fine moustache. This Sarrasinean schoolboy scrawl can stand for the problematic relationship between post-modernism and the heritage over which it scribbles.

BATAILLE: SCRIBBLING AND TRANSGRESSION

Georges Bataille discusses scribbling, and reminisces on his own days as a schoolboy scribbler, in 'L'Art primitif', an essay for the review *Documents* in which Bataille links the prehistoric birth of representational wall-painting to a certain pleasure in destruction. What is

---

[46] *all except you*, 22. Scribble is thus a place in which names are undone.
[47] Eco, *Reflections*, 67.

destroyed is the material support of the painting—a wall in prehistoric times, a sheet of paper or a toy in our own century. For primitive peoples share with the child a need to deform the object given, in other words anything that can act as such a support. Bataille recalls a blissful lesson occupied in making similar *griffonnages* and daubing ink over his neighbour's jacket; the bliss lay not merely in the manual activity of daubing but in the fact that the young Bataille was enjoying his pastime as something *transgressive*. He mentions the idea put forward by G.-H. Luquet, that the daubs of prehistoric art should be classified, together with children's art, under the general heading of 'primitive art', but Bataille comments that the bliss he experienced in this activity was definitely transgressive—'du plus *mauvais* aloi'.[48]

This might seem a mere anecdote, but Bataille returns to his scribbling activities in 'Méthode de méditation', in a section whose principle preoccupation is the nature of sovereignty.[49] All his life, he says, he has worked, thereby submitting to the morality of the slave (in Hegel's dialectical model of the relationship between master and slave). Sovereignty, for Bataille, is a state of 'pure loss' in that it is not contained in the economic circuits of exchange and barter—it consists in giving (time, energy, property) for nothing, and thus demonstrating that there is something 'servile' in giving if one hopes for some reward. The sovereign (nothing to do with 'national sovereignty' or 'monarchy') is in this sense radically autonomous, which is why Bataille is sometimes led to identify certain kinds of art, equally autonomous (their exchange value is extremely doubtful), as sovereign—and Barthes follows him in this, sometimes using Bataille's own word *souverain*, sometimes the Freudian notion of 'perversion' (that activity which does not seem to generate anything outside itself and its own pleasures). Furthermore, in the act of sovereignty, one is released from the trammels of self-consciousness that Bataille saw as part of Hegel's model of the power relations between master and slave (each one of which is reduced to reading back an identity from the other). Bataille's generalization of the master–slave dialectic in Hegel's *Phenomenology of Spirit* is partly based on his reading of Nietzsche, who was also concerned to show how the modern, self-conscious sense of identity is inseparable from such power relationships.

What has given Bataille the power to write and to approach what he calls sovereignty is the same indocility that made it impossible for him,

---

[48] 'L'Art primitif', in *Œuvres complètes* (1970–87), i. 247–54 (252).
[49] 'Méthode de méditation', in *Œuvres complètes*, 191–234 (209–10).

as a schoolboy, to write under dictation. His stupidity, his refusal to hoard up the reserve of knowledge that the schoolmaster was, in that telling verb *dictating*, approached the transgressive movement of sovereignty:

En ce temps-là, je me rendis la vie difficile, *faute d'écrire sous la dictée*. Les premiers mots du professeur se formaient docilement sous ma plume. Je revois mon cahier d'enfant: je me bournais bien vite à griffonner (je devais me donner l'air d'écrire). Je ne pouvais le jour venu faire un devoir dont je n'avais pas écouté le texte: sous les punitions redoublées, je vécus longuement le martyre de l'indifférence.[50]

Another *cancre génial* like Sarrasine, then, prepared to scribble away the gifts of culture. But can they be squandered in this way? Sarrasine's scribbling was already an apprenticeship, already a way of adding to the stock of cultural goods—it led to, among other things, the statue of Zambinella, and that statue survived.

None the less, Bataille suggests the punishments his scribbling exposed him to: he is not merely doodling to pass the time: he is already a transgressor, and points out how compulsive this scribbling can be: it is part of the realm of the *heterogeneous*, everything which erupts into an officially sanctioned culture from outside. He cites as evidence the scribbles of Abyssinian children, who carry out their defacing activity uniquely on the walls and columns of churches, and are not to be put off by repeated beatings. Here it is a case of the sacred support of a culture (the church walls) being defaced by the *via di porre* of the children. In a similar way, the once empty courtyard of the Palais Royal in Paris now contains equally childish black-and-white striped columns, designed by someone (Buren) who clearly could not resist the temptation to scribble in this post-modernist fashion on to the open space of a consecrated architectural site. Bataille's own childhood scribbling, his refusal to copy the official text of culture, is more than a childish impatience with hard work: it is itself a moment of acculturation (and its products can always be recuperated, as the story of the avant-garde this century, with its passion for the 'primitive', suggests). It is libidinal and sadistic.[51] The young Bataille does not ignore his teacher's words, but starts to deform them. And in this process of deformation, representation itself comes into being. Bataille presents a micronarrative of his activity: his scribbling, initially undirected (no project, therefore, no rational

---

[50] *Œuvres complètes*, 210.   [51] 'L'Art primitif', 253.

direction), suddenly, by chance, begins to resemble something. (The representational moment of such art is therefore not primary: it results rather from a destructive attitude towards the given. Destruction and mimesis are inseparable, as we saw in the case of *Sarrasine* and the aggression of realism.) The new, transformed object, which 'looks like' something, is then submitted to new, random deformations, until it 'looks like' something else. Abstract figuration precedes representation. Cave drawings, originally pure pattern—albeit endowed with a significance we can only guess at—were discovered by their creators to represent something: this took place, claims Bataille, by chance.[52]

Representation is thus the result of an experimental process fuelled by sadistic and libidinal drives which lie outside the conscious control of the subject. In Bataille's case, this distortion takes the deformed form of the arabesques that he weaves around the forgotten dictation, consists in remaining deaf to the words of the 'dictator', in ignoring the signified and playing with the mute signifier. What the teacher's voice says is disregarded and converted into pure scribble.

Barthes, in *Barthes par lui-même*, writes out some fragments as if they were the kind of dictations he had to copy down at school. In this case, he is not scribbling, but he *is* mimicking and parodying *la rédaction scolaire* as one of the essential modes in which knowledge and a certain mastery of language is transmitted to children in the French educational system.[53] What Bataille and Barthes both suggest is the way culture (especially in traditional French education) relies to a massive degree on the subject's capacity to translate spoken into written language, to master the difference between them. All that is written, says this culture, can also be spoken, and speech follows the same linguistic rules as writing (so, as Barthes notes, traditional grammars are based on the sentence, even though in 'normal' conversational speech, sentence-structure may not be preserved—something I shall be examining later).[54]

BARTHES: 'ET MOI AUSSI JE SUIS PEINTRE'

Scribbles recur frequently in Barthes's work. There is one on the front cover of *Barthes par lui-même*: it is a picture entitled 'Souvenir

[52] *La Peinture préhistorique: Lascaux ou la naissance de l'art*, in *Œuvres complètes*, ix. 7–101 (37).
[53] *RB*, 49.
[54] See Ch. 5, below; *RB*, 49, *PlT*, 79–82.

de Juan-les-Pins'. Brightly coloured crayon traces mesh and meander erratically, and there is no sense of classical perspective. Is this kind of production a way of releasing somatic drives usually contained and controlled by more linear forms of composition? This is a claim Barthes frequently makes: scribble is the trace of a drive, it is the hand in a state of writing.[55] The fact that Barthes both shows and discusses his scribbles is a symptom of his need to examine the interface between writing as meaning and writing as something more enigmatic.[56]

Sometimes the scribble itself can take a writerly form: in *Barthes par lui-même* and elsewhere, Barthes presents texts in handwriting. The opening and closing remarks on the inside covers of *Barthes par lui-même* are a case in point, but the book deploys an insistent panoply of scriptural traces. We thus see the florid, self-assured, and perfectly legible copperplate signature of one of his ancestors, appended to a legal document.[57] In his study of Saul Steinberg, Barthes notes the imposing nature of these scribal flourishes, often mimicked in Steinberg's drawings and cartoons. The importance (and self-importance) of nineteenth-century bureaucrats 's'inscrit dans les volutes énormes et sophistiquées de la signature: lorsque le scribe dit "je", c'est la Loi qui parle'.[58]

The interweavings of handwriting and 'the law' are shown by the school essay scribbled over—magisterially this time—by Barthes's teacher.[59] I will be discussing this shortly. We are also shown a song set in score (which Barthes paradoxically gives as an example not of auditory but of graphic pleasure),[60] photographs of his handwritten index cards (used transgressively, claims Barthes, not for the scholarly reference, but for the sudden, impulsive notation of the fleeting idea: 'd'origine érudite, la fiche suit les tours divers de la pulsion'):[61] other

---

[55] Thus the overture to *RB* claims that once the parade of images and photos associated with his biography is over (up to p. 46), writing will be free to deploy its own, non-figurative signs: the only images that will be allowed to disturb the text will be 'celles de la main qui trace' (6), and these images are not figurative but figural.

[56] For Barthes's own productions as a visual artist, see Barthes, *Carte, segni* (Milan, 1981), and *Le Texte et l'image*. Barthes's writings on painting are discussed by Gilbert Lascault in 'Ébauche d'un dictionnaire de la peinture selon Roland Barthes', *Critique*, 423–4 (Aug.–Sept. 1982), 704–19.

[57] *RB*, 22.

[58] *all except you*, 64.

[59] *RB*, 36.

[60] Ibid. 61.

[61] Ibid. 79.

examples include the two *markers de couleur* compositions,[62] and a draft of the fragment on 'Le goût des algorithmes' (such algorithms themselves being 'diagrammatic', again involved in the tensions between the plan, drawing, or formalized equation and the meaning that it is supposed to convey as speech).[63] Here again, the rational aim of the text is subverted by a heterogeneous desire: corrections, claims Barthes, are made not in the interest of greater clarity or stylishness; rather, any such effect is merely the by-product of 'le plaisir d'étoiler le texte': as we saw with Bataille, the representational, or quasi-representational, function of the text is a moment of stasis, a by-product of a figural drive that subsumes it—as for Kristeva the pheno-text is a surface moment of the mobile, displaceable, and dynamic genotext that underlies it.[64] And, finally, there are two instances of an extremely pure form of scribbling, the first relatively abstract, the second skirting a resemblance to Arabic script. These last two examples have a subscript: 'La graphie pour rien . . . ou le signifiant sans le signifié.'[65]

Furthermore, the second of the two 'marker' compositions, transgressively couched on the official notepaper of the École pratique de Hautes Études, is subtitled 'Gaspillage': Barthes's hijacking of institutional channels for his own uses is reminiscent of the Abyssinian children scrawling on church walls and pillars. By attempting to *show* the pure loss of such scribble, Barthes of course compromises its purity—the 'wastage' of his tachiste composition on official notepaper is to a large extent recuperated by its inclusion here, in a book, a commercial object, and by the role it plays in the construction of that imaginary Barthes ('the Barthes who is enjoyably disrespectful of bureaucrats and institutions') that Barthes wants to put into circulation. He is deriving prestige from his wastage as do the Kwakiutl chiefs who spectacularly squander their wealth in a potlatch.[66] He is,

---

[62] *RB*, 91, 117.

[63] *RB*, 105.

[64] 'Within the signifying process, one might see the release and subsequent articulation of the drives as constrained by the social code yet not reducible to the language system as a *genotext* and the signifying system as it presents itself to phenomenological intuition as a *phenotext*; describable in terms of structure, or of competence/performance, or according to other models' (Kristeva, 'The System and the Speaking Subject', in *The Kristeva Reader*, ed. Toril Moi (Oxford, 1986), 24–33 (28)).

[65] *RB*, 187, 189.

[66] The equation of loss and wastage with sovereignty is a major theme in Bataille, and is partly based on his reading of Mauss, *Essai sur le don*. Bataille develops his theory of sovereignty most fully in *La Souveraineté*, in *Œuvres complètes*, viii, 243–456.

in other words, transgressive but not yet sovereign. But how could we *see* his subversion otherwise? We can only see transgression because it is made visible (allegorical) and thus, inevitably, recuperable: pure loss in any case cannot be shown, figural energies may always be interpreted by being seen *as* something, by becoming, if only for a fleeting instant, representational—like Rorschach blots.

This exemplifies a wider problem: where does scribble end and writing as communication, or drawing as representation, begin? When do we see the figure *as figure*? Is this even possible—does a figure seen as figure not always immediately become a representation or signification of a figure?[67] A scribble, for instance, may be writing as it tends to pure figurality, but as I will show in more detail below, Barthes's reliance on figures is not an escape from meaning, just a suspension of it, a distancing of the signified.

This opens out on to the less abstract problems caused by the figurality inseparable from language, the fact that writing can always be looked at as a figure (a pattern) and that apparently non-significant *traits* can be seen as a kind of writing. Saussure was a victim of a certain linguistic figurality when he became obsessed by the possibility that configurations of letters hidden in Vedic, Greek, and Latin verse in fact spelled out the name of some deity or hero.[68] Jean Sarobinski asks whether Saussure was right or wrong—and wonders what the criteria for such a judgement would be. Perhaps what Saussure deciphered as a name was ultimately a random linguistic figure closer to an ink blot than to anything semantically significant. 'Saussure s'est-il trompé? S'est-il laissé fasciner par un mirage? Les anagrammes ressemblent-ils à ces visages qu'on lit dans les taches d'encre?'[69] He adds an interesting comment: Saussure's plight was that of the critic trying to make the poet say what the critic has found.[70] I would make a slightly different point: that, apart from demonstrating that the boundary between an ingenious close reading and a delirious fantasy can, perhaps fortunately, never be secure, Saussure is in the frustrating and exalting position of the critic having to make the writer say something, when the writer has, first and foremost, written. Saussure is thus an exemplary figure of writing in that he demonstrates how the

---

[67] See Jean-François Lyotard, *Discours, Figure* (1971), 17, and, for an exposition and discussion, Geoffrey Bennington, *Lyotard: Writing the Event* (Manchester, 1988), 69.

[68] Jean Starobinski, *Les Mots sous les mots: les anagrammes de Ferdinand de Saussure* (1971).

[69] Ibid. 153.   [70] Ibid. 154.

problem of literary criticism is particularly prey to the interaction of figural and semantic trends within language, and thus to the tension between voiced meaning and a writing that, however clear and communicative it may be, always threatens to remain obtusely silent.

There is another aspect of Barthes's scribbles, in *Barthes par lui-même*: they seem to suggest that the invention of printing has become tied to an ideology of the alphabet, to meaning as discrete rather than continuous, digital rather than analog.[71] Such a reading might involve Barthes in a surreptitiously anti-technological ideology: in breaking away from logocentrism, and even grammatocentrism, he would be falling back on somatocentrism, privileging the body (especially 'la main qui trace') over the machine. But while there is certainly a trend in late Barthes which does exalt the body, he does not merely indulge in a nostalgic operation to salvage a threatened organic self-presence. For instance, he does not tell the story of artisanal modes of production (handwriting, calligraphy) being taken over by technology, but of the way they have become something which is neither techno-logical nor spontaneous. In other words, scribble is one of the places in which Barthes examines the interrelationship of meaning and figure, and also, as a partial extension of this, of machine and body. (There are other aspects to Barthes's critique of the mechanical modes of reproduction, of course, as in his refusal to see the gramophone record as anything but an *aplatissement* of musical performance: but I will not go into these problems here.)

What is especially noticeable in *Barthes par lui-même* is the extent to which different *technologies of writing* are deployed, and the way the book shows great attention to its disposition. Despite initial appear-ances, there is no sense in which Barthes finally privileges handwriting, for instance, over the printing press: what he does suggest is that the various written traces in the book *all* share a resistance to being spoken. *Barthes par lui-même*, fragmented, interwoven with photo-graphs and drawings, erratically indexed (as we saw in the last chapter), is difficult to paraphrase.[72] Barthes's careful choice of illustrations makes them more than instances of a general thesis that is clearly enunciated in the text and merely exemplified by the images.

---

[71] I take these terms from Anthony Wilden, *System and Structure: Essays in Com-munication and Exchange* (2nd edn., London, 1980). Wilden also suggests similarities between discrete digital elements and the symbolic order of Lacan, and between continuous analog patterns and the imaginary.

[72] The etymology of 'paraphrase' contains a reference to 'speech'—*phrazein* being to tell or declare.

There are, on the contrary, a number of major tensions between the readable and the visible aspects of the book, just as *L'Empire des signes* begins by warning us that 'texte et images, dans leur entrelacs, veulent assurer la circulation, l'échange de ces significants: le corps, le visage, l'écriture', so that it is as much the gap between text and image that is important, as any collusion between them.[73] This tension between the *lisible* and the *visible* aspects of a book is one to which Jean-François Lyotard has drawn attention, and I will be returning to his theory of the figure shortly.

Thus the reader is free to dwell on the three kinds of writing displayed on page 36 (the school exercise with teacher's comments): the young Barthes's clear handwriting, the more sophisticated and 'busy' scrawl of the teacher, and, above the reproduction, the present-day Barthes's commentary printed in italics: 'Toute loi qui opprime un discours est insuffisamment fondée.' But where is the voice of this oppressive law to be located? In the first instance, the law is announced by the teacher writing over and above the essay; in the second instance, this scribble is itself put in place, indeed overwritten, by the printed metalinguistic comment. This is paradoxical: for, in order to proclaim the law's impertinence, Barthes's critique has to adopt a generalizing ('*Toute* loi . . .'), authoritarian, and thoroughly legal tone itself. When writings meet and cross, it becomes difficult to discover which is the script of the law. And the effect of law can inhere in any discourse, whether it be the, after all, comparatively mild and unrepressive comments of the teacher, or Barthes's later denunciatory and dogmatic reply. We can *reculer le cran* at least one more degree: for Barthes's schoolboy essay itself is full of sententious propositions. It begins:

J'ai lu dans un livre qu'on nous apprend à vivre quand la vie est passée. La leçon fut cruelle pour moi, qui, après avoir passé la première partie de ma jeunesse dans l'illusion trompeuse d'être un homme invincible parce qu'instruit, me vois aujourd'hui, grâce aux hasards des mouvements politiques, réduit à un rôle secondaire et fort décevant.[74]

Barthes's narrator here obeys the law (of human nature) confidently pronounced in the opening sentence: life is copying *un livre*, as usual. And as the teacher pertinently remarks, who is this *on* who teaches us to live when it is too late?

---

[73] The same is true of *EpS*: 'Le texte ne "commente" pas les images. Les images "n'illustrent" pas le texte' (5).

[74] *RB*, 36.

It is in any case interesting that the actual criticism made by the teacher ('style un peu gauche par endroits') immediately shows the ideological jump that can be made from the gesture of handwriting (left-handedness is censured in the name of 'normality') to the style of what is written: we can call writing 'gauche' even if it is not written by someone left-handed, in other words even if we are not talking about their handwriting, but about their style. The effect of the law resides neither in handwriting nor in printing: scribal bureaucrats and scribbling teachers are put in their place by printed words that are elsewhere themselves seen as repressive, and scribbled over in their turn.

Already, it is clear that scribble is a paradoxical notion: it may be a way of wasting your time, but it can always be recuperated and made to work; it may seem purely figural, but slips over into representation (if only as the representation of its own figurality); it may appear to be transgressive, but it is scrawled across an institutional text or a firm support that is not erased but merely palimpsestically reinscribed. It attempts to show production, to demystify the authority of the book by demonstrating the doubts, hesitations, and equivocations behind the imperturbable lines of text, and by staging the way thoughts originate (as when Barthes shows us *fiches*, index cards, he has scribbled on in bed, in the train, or at his desk), but this demystification cannot work unless a certain temporary priority is wrested from the 'thought' as finished product and granted to the 'thinking' (the rough draft, the memorandum, the index card) as production.[75] We thus move closer to the origin—but we cannot reach it, since a rough draft is no more 'true' than the etymon of a word.

It is these latter scribbles that shed light on Barthes's inscribing of the body in the text. In bed, he thinks of *bêtise*, in the train he muses on the way he has more ideas than in an aeroplane, and at his work desk he reflects on homosexuality.[76] Rather than merely mystifying the body, posing it as a new, natural origin, Barthes does something rather different. He shows the body as being one link in a chain of production which has no clear beginning and no clear end.

A technical point will make this clearer. I would like to have quoted some of Barthes's scribbles, but such quotation is rendered difficult by the fact that a scribble, even one printed, is by definition something difficult to copy. A signature can always be copied, as Derrida has

[75] *RB*, 79.   [76] Ibid.

pointed out (we copy our own signatures every time we write a cheque: the iterability of the signature guarantees its uniqueness). We can even copy someone else's signature—so a signature is less inimitable an incarnation of our very individuality than we tend to think. But on the other hand, someone else's signature cannot always be copied well.[77] Forgery is an art: it has to be learnt—or else the technical mode of reproduction has to be changed. (It would have been difficult to copy Barthes's scribbles—his body—before the advent of certain types of printing technology, though now they are no doubt reproduced reasonably accurately in *Barthes par lui-même*.) Barthes indeed calls himself a forger in a *different* and more metaphorical sense: one of the figures of production that drive his texts is 'la *forgerie* (la forgerie est, dans le jargon des experts graphologues, une imitation d'écriture)', and forgery works by copying the conceptual manners of science without 'honouring' them. He copies ('forges') the opposition between denotation and connotation, for instance, but in his hands it is not an authentic coin, not something that he (or we) can exchange for real knowledge.[78] This is one way in which Barthes reacts against the commodification of the signified.

The point, however, is this: some signifiers are more easily transportable than others. If Barthes writes 'Tout ceci doit être considéré comme dit par un personnage de roman', I have no difficulty in quoting the words, but it would be more difficult to quote the handwriting. Even the photographic copy in *Barthes par lui-même* is still not Barthes's 'own' script. But is there such a thing?

Anton Ehrenzweig, in *The Psychoanalysis of Artistic Vision and Hearing*, develops an elaborate theory of the way an artistic signature is difficult to forge. By 'artistic signature' he does not mean the way a painter signs the canvas, but the inimitable brushwork of any painter's technique. Ehrenzweig's study of how the artistic process works, whether in creation or consumption of the artwork, is based on Freud's division of the psyche into conscious and unconscious functions, or what Ehrenzweig terms the 'surface' mind and the 'depth' mind. He suggests that a depth-psychological analysis of art needs to 'turn away from the consciously "composed" structure of painting and watch for the apparently accidental scribbles hidden in the inarticulate

<hr />

[77] On the signature as iterable, see Jacques Derrida, 'Signature événement contexte', in *Marges—de la philosophie* (1972), 365–93.

[78] *RB*, 95–6.

forms of artistic "handwriting".[79] What Ehrenzweig calls (even with reference to painting, not drawing) 'artistic handwriting' (which involves factors such as the pressure of the hand, or the nervous tremor of the brushstroke—'the minute, almost microscopic, scribbles which make up the technique of a great draughtsman or the brushwork of a great painter') cannot be copied.[80] It is unconsciously produced and the conscious eye will not necessarily be able to see it. Even if we do perceive the 'handwriting', our conscious attempt to imitate it will fail.[81]

Furthermore, Ehrenzweig gives a historical overview of the entire history of painting which depends on a dialectic between the surface mind, which composes *Gestalten* and sees art as representation, and the *Gestalt*-free, non-representational impulses of the deep mind, which tend to produce scribbles. All painting begins in scribble: this scribble is revised by the conscious mind, which reifies it (makes it represent real things in the external world).[82] The more 'civilized' an artist, in historical and cultural terms, the more that artist will tend to produce reified forms. This clearly parallels some of Bataille's intuitions on the emergence of representation from scribble. What has happened in modernism, says Ehrenzweig, is that, early in the twentieth century, 'the reification processes began to fail'—in the visual arts, in harmonic polyphony, and even in the sciences: 'surface perception gave way at last, in order to reveal the irrational layers of our own mind'.[83] Ehrenzweig notes how his historical account can explain such cultural quirks as the arrival of 'action painting'.[84]

---

[79] *The Psychoanalysis of Artistic Vision and Hearing: An Introduction to a Theory of Unconscious Perception* (3rd edn., London, 1975), 5. Ehrenzweig also contrasts the 'apparently accidental glissando and vibrato inflexions' in music to the articulate tone steps of melody. These inflexions are not exactly what Barthes refers to as *le grain*, which is always *de la voix*, requiring interference between the purely melodic and the spoken aspects of song: they are, however, important factors in what Barthes judges to be the materiality of music. See 'Le Grain de la voix' in *OO*, 236–45, where *grain* in singing is close to the way we hear e.g. Landowska's *corps interne* when she plays the harpsichord (244). According to Ehrenzweig—and this would be another difference between him and Barthes—the scribbles are perceived, but only unconsciously (*Psychoanalysis of Artistic Vision and Hearing*, 29). Barthes in general resists categorizing experience as conscious or unconscious: there is, in his work, no straight equating of e.g. body and unconscious.

[80] Ehrenzweig, *Psychoanalysis of Artistic Vision and Hearing*, 29.
[81] Ibid. 48.
[82] Ibid. 48 n. 1.
[83] Ibid. 174.
[84] Ibid., p. vii. A discussion of scribble should take note of Barthes's 'J'aime . . . Pollock' (*RB*, 120).

Ehrenzweig also notes that modern art withdraws not only background, but also foreground elements from conscious control: 'modern painting thus has background structure throughout'.[85] And he discusses one way of telling the story of the emergence of the avant-garde that has parallels in Barthes: 'Moholy-Nagy observes that allegedly "abstract" form elements in certain compositions by Kandinsky and the young Matisse could be conceived as enlargements ("close-ups") of small, inconspicuous form details in Cézanne's paintings.'[86] In *Le Plaisir du texte* one version of this emergence is presented thus: 'aujourd'hui sort d'hier, Robbe-Grillet est déjà dans Flaubert, Sollers dans Rabelais, tout Nicolas de Staël dans deux cm² de Cézanne'.[87] This emergence may, Barthes goes on to suggest, present too peacefully evolutionary a picture, but he none the less repeats these examples elsewhere, and their persuasive force is evident if one remembers the intractable difficulties that attend trying to imagine too great a discontinuity in the way the avant-garde comes into being, difficulties I discussed when dealing with drift.

Ehrenzweig's observations are clearly of great importance for my reading of Barthes, especially in so far as Barthes's own scribbles, to come back to my main point, are potentially a very pure form of writing: they are not painting in the sense of representing anything real in the external world (they are relatively *Gestalt*-free, whatever we might see them as; they do not observe the codes of drawing); nor are they writing in the sense of conveying articulate meaning. Furthermore, although I could reproduce them (photographically), I cannot easily set out to copy them manually, since, according to Ehrenzweig, their determinants are unconscious.

This in turn raises the question of whether the unconscious is, in psychoanalytic theories of art such as Ehrenzweig's, being used as a mode of individuation immune to copying. It may indeed be that scribble can be seen as a mark of uniqueness (as in the biological metaphor of the DNA 'signature'). But Barthes shifts attention from the unconscious determinants of such scribble partly because the unconscious is, for him, not private: he has learnt from Freud and, perhaps more directly, Lacan that (in the latter's words) 'l'inconscient, c'est le discours de l'Autre', so that the unconscious is not a dark secret within the individual psyche, but rather the psyche as a public

---

[85] *Psychoanalysis of Artistic Vision and Hearing*, 34.
[86] Ibid. 174.   [87] *PlT*, 35.

place open to language and society. Hence Barthes's increasing attention to the body, not the unconscious, as a 'proper', that which is most individual. For even if the body in turn is a *combinatoire* of analysable elements, not a mystic unity, it is still 'mine' in, to say the least, a vital sense. And this remains true even if Barthes continues to acknowledge that his body is already coded, his desires symbolically mediated, his drives the gears of a machine for technical and ideological reproduction: thus, any uniqueness that accrues to scribble is the uniqueness of a combination of preformed elements, not an organic totality. The body is continuous with the modes of reproduction that it also disrupts.[88]

But the question of technology raises other problems. What about different typefaces, of which there are a variety in *Barthes par lui-même*? It is difficult to quote the scrawls on page 187, but not the label that acts as a signified beneath them, *'La graphie pour rien . . .'*. But even here, I am not quoting the shape and size of those small italics as they appear on the page. For such details are usually considered to be insignificant. A text such as *Barthes par lui-même* does, however, lead us to ask at what level the typeface begins to signify.[89]

In the case of most books, the typography signifies hardly at all. But in the case of books which aim to show their status as writing in the most material sense of the word, and to point to the nature of the book as object, it is highly significant. Michel Butor is a major example. In his *Mobile: project pour une représentation des États-Unis*, on which Barthes writes an appreciative essay, Butor spreads his words across the page; mixes italics, roman, and capital letters; breaks up the sentence by distributing it across the page's space: 'toutes ces libertés concourent en somme à la destruction même du Livre: *le Livre-Objet se confond matériellement avec le Livre-Idée*, la technique d'impression avec l'institution littéraire, en sort qu'attenter à la régularité matérielle de l'œuvre, c'est viser l'idée même de littérature'.[90]

---

[88] Derrida suggests that a theory of traces—of generalized writing—would break down the opposition between human beings and machines, an opposition hitherto based largely on the fact that the former speak, whereas the latter do not—at least not 'properly' (*De la grammatologie* (1967), 19).

[89] In an excellent early review of *RB*, David Ellis insists on calling the book '*roland* BARTHES *par roland barthes*' all the way through, thereby scrupulously noting the typographical layout of the title on the book's front cover ('Barthes and Autobiography', *Cambridge Quarterly*, 7: 3 (1977), 252–66). Other books in the 'Écrivains de toujours' series do not have the same typographical eccentricity.

[90] 'Littérature et discontinu', in *EC*, 175–87 (176). Butor has written extensively about the book as an object: see the 5 vols. of essays and addresses collected as *Répertoire*, esp. 'Le Livre comme objet', in *Répertoire II* (1964) 104–23. On the book as

Derrida points out that the idea of the book presupposes the totality of the signifier, which in turn relies on some pre-existing totality of the signified. Once attention is paid to writing as such, in excess of any signified, the twilight of the age of the book is near. 'Si nous distinguons le texte du livre, nous dirons que la destruction du livre, telle qu'elle s'annonce aujourd'hui dans tous les domaines, dénude la surface du texte.'[91] In *Barthes par lui-même*, Barthes, without making such general claims, and without imitating the spectacular dispersal of *Mobile* (or Mallarmé's 'Un coup de dés', or Apollinaire's *Calligrammes*, to give two other examples he cites), is certainly questioning, more discreetly, the notion of book in general: hence his inclusion of scribble as well as typographical eccentricities.[92] One can—barely—imagine a civilization of the book in which quotation required a

---

a disposition of 2 objects, an 'objet de signification' that we understand ('nous l'*entendons*'), and an 'objet de signifiance, fait de signifiants graphiques *et plastiques* (blancs, variations typographiques, usage de la double page, distribution de signes sur cette surface)', see Lyotard, *Discours, Figure*, 71. Lyotard notes: 'Le premier objet fait comprendre le second, le second fait voir le premier.' The typography need not, of course, be eccentric for this to be the case.

[91] *De la grammatologie*, 31.

[92] It is Barthes's very discretion that is interesting—as so often, 'je suis plus classique que la théorie du texte que je défends' (*RB*, 77), and, as so often, this discretion itself, in its borderline nature, may be a defence against being read too quickly as 'experimental' and recuperated as such. Barthes's commentators may be more overtly experimental, in certain ways, than he is: this is true notably of the contributors to the special issue on Barthes of *Visible Language* (11: 4 (autumn 1977)), a journal devoted largely to questions of typography. Randolph Runyon's 'Fragments of An Amorous Discourse: Canon in U^bis' (387–427) imitates, visually, the lay-out of a canon, running over the page to such an extent that it becomes difficult to read. It may be, however, that the figural drive in Barthes's writing has yet to be properly appreciated, although the *Visible Language* issue on Barthes is a good start. Annette Lavers notes the strangeness of Barthes's late texts and asks whether they are 'really read', rather than being 'immediately transcribed into a predictable orthodoxy' (*Roland Barthes: Structuralism and After* (London, 1982), 213): a figural approach may help to reach the subtleties of Barthes's texts. Randolph Runyon's numerological speculations lead to his highly imaginative treatment of Barthes and other writers in *Fowles, Irving, Barthes: canonical variations on an apocalyptic theme* (Columbus, Ohio, 1981), which takes wing from such considerations as the fact that the cover of *FDA* depicts a scene from the story of Tobias and the angel. An intriguing study by Ralph Sarkonak, 'Roland Barthes and the Spectre of Photography' (*L'Esprit créateur*, 22: 1 (spring 1982), 48–68) detects a high degree of organized figurality in the lay-out of *CC*, whose 48 chs. were written in the 48 days 'between' (non-inclusively, Sarkonak has to say) 15 Apr. and 3 June 1979: there are 24 elements in the bibliography, 25 reproductions (24 in monochrome and 1 preliminary one in colour), 12 albums and reviews cited, and 48 reversed gives us 84, apparently the age of Barthes's mother when she died. While there are shades of Saussure's anagrams here, that is all to the good: and it does seem that the 48 chs. of Barthes's last book are a homage to another great contrapuntal figure, J. S. Bach.

reproduction of the exact shape and size of each letter being quoted: anything else would be considered not a quotation, but a mere paraphrase, or a piece of literary criticism. From this end of the chain (my quotations of Barthes, here) we can likewise imagine a chain of bodies (including technological bodies) that stretches back to the body that, desk-bound, train-borne, or insomniac, produced the kind of scribbles (scribble: to write in a hasty manner) that we are shown in *Barthes par lui-même*.

Furthermore, it is precisely one idea of the person whose dissolution Barthes attempts allegorically to show in *Barthes par lui-même*—not in the text (which follows alphabetical, not chronological order), but in the scribbles that begin and end the book. For if at the beginning we have Léon Barthes's fine copperplate script, approved by Berthe Barthes and signed in flowing curlicues, the last pages present us with an *encre* and a *graphie* that are illegible.[93] Léon Barthes's writing thus represents legibility and legality: his grandson's scrawls represent the indecipherably figural. Writing begins as a form of memory: a signature is the sign that a debt will be honoured. But in the decay of bourgeois modes of experience charted in *Barthes par lui-même*, these old debts are about to be reneged on, this bureaucratic accrediting rejected. Beneath the promissory note on page 22, Barthes writes:

L'écriture n'a-t-elle pas été pendant des siècles la reconnaissance d'une dette, la garantie d'un échange, le seing d'une représentation? Mais aujourd'hui, l'écriture s'en va doucement vers l'abandon des dettes bourgeoises, vers la perversion, l'extrémité du sens, le texte . . .

Barthes is thus, in common with much of modernism, reversing the process of constant reification which, according to Ehrenzweig, has been the fate of scribble throughout centuries of representational art. He is also attempting, at least in the limited area of his own work, to release writing from its bureaucratic origins, its source—historically— as a mechanism of the State's authority. Barthes is often fascinated by the farcical or menacing aspects of bureaucracy: the official rubber stamp, as a kind of inimitable, chronologically and geographically defined writing tied to its origin, is for him a potent stamp of power. In *all except you* he notes how Steinberg attempts to exorcize this power by mimicking, over and over again, such stamps.[94]

So his obsession with scribble should not lead us to condemn Barthes for falling prey to a spontaneity that his work so insistently

---

[93] *RB*, 187, 189.   [94] *all except you*, 65.

criticizes.[95] There is no immediate escape from the artificialities and alienations of technological culture. Even children's scribble is too applied, too careful, tends to be an attempt to grow up, to copy the firm and legible writing of adults.[96] By putting 'le signifiant sans signifié' at the end, Barthes is suggesting that scribble is not the beginning of writing, but its Utopia. The consequences of this are potentially very great, especially in any discussion of what is Barthes's most difficult keyword, the body. It would be impossible for the body to be seen as a centre or origin: the body would no longer be merely something Barthes falls back on when the treadwheel of theory becomes too public and tedious: the body too would become a Utopia, something to be learnt.[97] This might help in any re-examination of the politics of Barthes's last works. For where it is easy to see his praise of scribble as a relapse into expressionism (the body expressing itself directly in handwriting, scribbling, drawing, painting), his highly complex meditations on, and usages of, scribble, makes such a simplification impossible.

Thus what may seem to be individual, precious, or trivial concerns in Barthes take on a more general theoretical importance when the fine detail (the formal disposition of *Barthes par lui-même*, for instance) is examined. In any case, the question of writing, in all its problematic materiality, is far from marginal: it can help to demonstrate (or disrupt) underlying ideological or theoretical options.

Two parallels will make this clear. First, Hegel, in the *Phenomenology of Spirit*, gives a clear formulation of the place handwriting and other bodily productions occupy in his scheme: they are expressions of the individual body, and stand between it and the even more external

---

[95] See his criticism of the surrealists in a 1975 interview with *Le Quotidien de Paris:* the practice of automatic writing does not liberate anything spontaneous, but in fact something highly coded—a series of stereotypes. Surrealist scribble therefore fails to be a suitable model. 'L'idée d'écriture automatique implique une vue idéaliste de l'homme, divisé en sujet profond et sujet parlant' ('Les Surréalistes ont manqué le corps', in *GV*, 230–2 (231)).

[96] The child 'travaille dur pour rejoindre le code des adultes' ('Sagesse de l'art', in *OO*, 163–78 (173)).

[97] Burnier and Rambaud have Barthes replying fatuously to all objections with the serene response that 'Doubtless, my body is not the same as yours' (*Le Roland-Barthes sans peine*, 41). It is quite true that Barthes says similar things ('*J'aime, je n'aime pas . . . tout cela veut dire: mon corps n'est pas le même que le vôtre*' (*RB*, 121)), but as this ex. shows, the difference of bodies is not a mere restatement of *de gustibus non est disputandum*, but a rather alarmed questioning of what, now, constitutes 'the individual'. The body is not a last word and Barthes frequently analyses the historical determinants inscribed in it: 'ce corps de jouissance est aussi *mon sujet historique*' (*PlT* 99).

attributes of action. The chain leads from body to voice to writing to action: each of these may be seen as an expression of the one before.

Thus the simple lines of the hand, the timbre and compass of the voice as the individual characteristics of speech—this too again as expressed in writing [*Schrift*], where the hand gives it a more durable existence than the voice does, especially in the particular style of handwriting [*Handschrift*]—all this is an expression of the inner, so that, as a *simple externality*, the expression again stands over against the *manifold externality* of action and fate, stands in relation to them as an *inner*.[98]

It is this equation of handwriting, or the timbre of the voice (comparable to what Barthes calls the grain), with an expression of the body, that Barthes questions: he does not like the idea that what is inner comes first and is then expressed as an outer. (Hegel himself does, of course, suggest the dialectical complexity of the interface between the different media in the expressive chain.)

Secondly, Adorno, in his *Aesthetic Theory*, notes that artworks arise from an interplay of spirit, materiality, and sensuality: curiously, he sees spirit's transformative power on materiality as creating a 'handwriting' (*Schrift*): it is this handwriting that safeguards the artwork from being reduced to mere spiritual content. While it would be too simplistic to identify Adorno's 'spirit' with Barthes's 'signified', it is worthy of note that Adorno uses the word 'handwriting' in a way close to what I mean by scribble, seeing it not as the expression of a lost origin (the body), but as an enigmatic supplement.

The spirit [*Geist*] of works of art transcends their materiality [*ihr Dinghaftes*, their status as thing] as well as their sensuality [*das sinnliche Phänomen*], and yet spirit exists only to the extent to which these two are its moments. In a negative sense, this means that in works of art nothing is to be taken literally [*buchstäblich*], least of all their words. Spirit is their ether; it speaks through them; or more strictly, perhaps, it transforms them into a handwriting [*Schrift*].[99]

Adorno, despite his Hegelian philosophical background, and his allegiance to artistic expressionism, hesitates to see either handwriting or spirit as mere expression, and privileges the metaphor of handwriting over that of voice—as does Barthes.

I will now turn to other ways in which Barthes investigates this problem. For, having used scribble to complicate the division between

[98] *The Phenomenology of Spirit*, trans. A. V. Miller (Oxford, 1977), 189.
[99] *Aesthetic Theory*, trans. C. Lenhardt, ed. Gretel Adorno and Rolf Tiedemann (London, 1984), 129.

inner and outer, between body and technology, I want briefly to exploit
its potential to destabilize the opposition between discourse and figure.

DISCOURSE, FIGURE

I take these terms from Lyotard, whose *Discours, figure* is a sustained
and complex assault on a certain form of semiotic imperialism—one
which insists on reading all phenomena in linguistic terms. The world,
he protests, is not legible: it gives us something to see as well as
something to read.[100] The linguistic space of invariant elements is
ultimately inseparable from another spatial dimension, that of the
figure. In disrupting both linguistic space and even visual space, the
figure is an event, an unpredictable transgression or crossing-over. (I
will be examining the notion of event in Barthes's work in Chapter 6.)
This deformation can be seen: 'Un coup de dés' is meant to be visible
as well as legible.[101] Lyotard's analysis of figural energies suggests that
a pure figure as such cannot be the object of knowledge and would, in
fact, be invisible.[102]

While Lyotard's discussion of the different categories of figurality
is highly complex, I am adopting his terms because they are a useful
way of describing a tension in Barthes's work between the semiotic
imperialism which, as Lyotard suggests of much contemporary work
inspired by structural linguistics, leads to an attempt to read everything
(including cinema stills, photos, meals, and music), and, on the other
hand, an attempt to categorize in more cautious terms what might
resist such a treatment. Above all, in Barthes's case, discourse is
predominantly that which can be spoken, while the figure is something
that resists being translated into this speech: the figure may be pointed
out, its effects detected; it may point elsewhere, while itself remaining
obstinately silent.[103] I will return to some of these themes in Chapter 6.

EMPIRE OF WRITING

Barthes finds a space in which the spoken word becomes irrelevant
and writing is deployed in all its forms in the 'Japan' of *L'Empire des*

---

[100] *Discours, Figure*, 9.   [101] Ibid. 61–2.
[102] Ibid. 17: for a discussion, see Bennington, *Lyotard: Writing the Event*, 69.
[103] Here again we encounter the difference between 'saying' and 'showing'. I return
to these themes in Ch. 6, below.

signes. (Although Barthes claims that his Japan is very different from the real Japan, being a Utopian extrapolation of everything he finds most valuable in Japanese culture and a rejection of the rest (Americanization, technocracy), I will from now on follow his own practice in omitting scare quotes from Japan.) A twelfth-century example of Japanese calligraphy represents a stream of calligraphic characters on a background of colours and leaves—or rather, background and foreground, script and figure, run into each other, showing the plastic quality of the gesture that lies behind both of them. Barthes's commentary reads: 'Pluie, Semence, Dissémination, Trame, Tissu, Texte, Écriture'.[104] A similar example is the ink composition 'La cueillette des champignons': 'Où commence l'écriture? Où commence la peinture?'[105] Barthes's comments here presuppose his ignorance of the semantic charge of the Japanese script: a native would see a signified where Barthes sees only a signifier, but it is largely the *imaginaire* of a deliberate foreigner that Barthes is depicting, and this does not affect his presentation of Japan as a country in which painting and writing cannot be separated.

The front cover shows a woman about to write a letter. This image is reproduced in the book.[106] And in the 'Table des Illustrations' Barthes details it as follows:

Verso d'une carte postale qui m'a été adressée par un ami japonais. Le recto en est illisible: je ne sais qui est cette femme, si elle est peinte ou grimée, ce qu'elle veut écrire: perte de l'origine en quoi je reconnais l'écriture même, dont cette image est à mes yeux l'emblème somptueux et retenu.[107]

This image is an emblem of pure writing in so far as its signified has been lost. The image of this woman, an exemplary figure of writing, occurs in the middle of a section of *L'Empire des signes* devoted to the 'Papeterie', where 'la main rencontre l'instrument et la matière du trait'.[108] Japanese writing seems to us to come from painting, but Barthes, aware of the *archi-écriture* presupposed by all articulation, spoken or written, likewise operates a reversal of value: in Japan, ideography founds painting: 'il est important que l'art ait une origine scripturale, et non point expressive'.[109] It is even more important that, in *L'Empire des signes*, writing—oriental writing—for Barthes is start-

---

[104] *EpS*, 14–15. [105] Ibid. 31.
[106] Ibid. 114–15. [107] Ibid. 149.
[108] Ibid. 113. [109] Ibid. 116.

ing to be less a *via di levare* (an incision) than a *via di porre*, less analysis and meaning than superimposition, the laying down of a trace. (We have already seen this distinction between the Western letter, an act of carving, and the Eastern ideogram as painting, in the Réquichot essay.)[110]

Japanese writing, for instance, is in theory uncorrectable, since 'le caractère est tracé *alla prima*':[111] There is thus no need for an eraser, used in the West to correct the signified or the imaginary image one wants to present. Since Japan has always already erased the signified, the problem does not arise; and as for the imaginary, the order of one's self-images, in Japan 'le miroir est vide'. Furthermore, Japanese writing is both *incision* and *glissement* but, given the grainy texture of the paper, more the latter. Exercise books have

les pages ... pliées en double, comme celles d'un livre qui n'a pas été coupé de façon que l'écriture se meut à travers un luxe de surfaces et ignore la déteinte, l'imprégnation métonymique de l'envers et de l'endroit (elle se trace au-dessus d'un vide): le palimpseste, la trace effacée qui devient par là un secret, est impossible.[112]

This pure addition, in other words, abolishes (without repressing) the memory of what has gone before, becoming, allegorically, a pure present in the act of inscription. Saussure compared meaning to the cutting out of a piece of paper: on one side, the signifier; on the other, the signified.[113] In Japan, it seems, paper has only one side (that of the signifier, which, deprived of its verso, can of course hardly be named as a signifier any more). Indeed, Japanese paper is even more one-sided than the Möbius strip which Lacan uses to figure his new topology of the subject. (The 'impossible' palimpsest, the sort Barthes rejects, is that in which the writing already there is erased but haunts what is superinscribed: as we have seen, he is quite fond of the paradoxical palimpsest in which every layer is preserved in complete— and increasingly illegible—detail.)[114]

Furthermore, while our writing used to be done with quill pens which could only 'gratter le papier toujours dans le même sens', the Japanese brush does not scratch, but glides. Japanese characters rely on a whole volume of movements: 'le pinceau, lui, peut glisser, se tordre, s'enlever, la trace s'accomplissant pour ainsi dire dans le

---

[110] *OO*, 198.
[111] *EpS*, 116.
[112] Ibid. 116–17.
[113] *Course in General Linguistics*, trans. Wade Baskin (London, 1974), 113.
[114] Saussure's anagrams as palimpsest: *OO*, 111.

volume de l'air, il a la flexibilité charnelle, lubrifiée, de la main'.[115] The felt-tipped pen—as opposed to the scratchy biro—is, typically, Japanese.[116]

An interview collected in *Le Grain de la voix* and entitled 'Un rapport presque maniaque avec les instruments graphiques' gave considerable material for sarcasm to Burnier and Rambaud, cited at the head of this chapter: we learn from this interview all about Barthes's problems in finding the right kind of pen.[117] The futility of these remarks is inseparable from their insertion into the larger thematic I am dealing with here, but they do come across as vaguely comic. An example: the wonderful sentence 'Il y a d'abord le moment où le désir s'investit dans la pulsion graphique, aboutissant à un objet calligraphique' which, being *unfairly* translated, means 'J'aime écrire à la main'.[118] It is true that the references to psychoanalysis and calligraphy are important, but Barthes's insistence on the signifier should not blind us to his merits as a comic writer. 'Il aurait voulu produire, non une comédie de l'Intellect, mais son romanesque' he claims.[119] But the comedy of intellect is never far away, from the rather self-defensive neologisms of *Mythologies* (*la bouvard-et-pécuchéité*) to the idea that by being turned into a ready-to-consume media image he has become *une frite*.[120] Since both Chaplin and, especially, the Marx Brothers, are important influences, we should take him seriously when he acknowledges the power of the *saugrenu*, the absurd or preposterous detail that lightens the demonstrative assertiveness of theoretical writing (such as that of Fourier, as well as his own): he suggests, for instance, that the logical future of metaphor, taken over the top, beyond *bienséance*, is the gag.[121]

In any case, the kind of pen one writes with is precisely the kind of question that future historians may find highly significant, as historians of everyday life are already concentrating on the material appurtenances of private life in the Byzantine period or the nineteenth century. And, returning to Japan, it raises the more general question of technology. Whereas the Western typewriter is already designed to promote the signified, says Barthes, the Japanese typewriter, with its immense panoply of characters arranged on drums, has a profoundly figural aspect: it calls out for 'le dessin, la marqueterie idéographique dispersée à travers la feuille, en un mot l'espace'—the sign is 'jeté en

[115] *EpS*, 117. [116] Ibid. [117] *GV*, 170–4.
[118] Ibid. 171. [119] *RB*, 123. [120] *BL*, 394.
[121] *RB*, 84.

écharpe, à toute volée, dans toutes les directions de la page'. All writing thus becomes similar to what Zen, referring to the *alla prima* nature of calligraphy, calls a controlled accident.[122] And the *espace* that is implicated in such writing is profoundly important: empty space is a major element in Barthes's celebration of Japan. Even in Western writing, *espacement*, spacing, is, as Derrida sees it, a direct challenge to the self-presence that phonocentric ideologies always promise. Visibility and spatiality make holes in that self-presence: since they are an undeniable feature of writing, they are one of the reasons for which writing has been seen as secondary to speech in much of the Western tradition.[123]

Walter Ong uses the term 'chirography' to describe writing cultures, as opposed to oral cultures.[124] Since Barthes is a foreigner in Japan, and cannot speak the language, he is forced, not to regress to body-language (as a repertoire of gestures meant to replace speech), but to advance to a new chirography, in which it is not only the hand which writes, but the whole body. A native jots down an improvised street map, and the absence of verbal communication opens the city of Tokyo (itself identified as an ideogram) to an exploration that is not, as usual, dominated by the mere search for an address—in other words by the attempt to make the cityscape coincide with the plan, guide, or telephone directory.[125]

The body, claims Barthes, communicates something over and above the explicit message. Barthes squanders the time he should be using in order to reach his destination, savouring the gestures of the citydweller sketching out his street-map, which is a map scribbled, so to speak, on top of the official one: 'visiter un lieu pour la première fois, c'est de la sorte commencer à l'écrire: l'adresse n'étant pas écrite, il faut bien qu'elle fonde elle-même sa propre écriture'.[126] Barthes is here alluding to the fact that in Tokyo, streets are

[122] *EpS*, 118. D. T. Suzuki discusses the black-and-white sketches produced on very delicate paper in the art of Sumiye: no deliberation is allowed, and no retouching (*Essays in Zen Buddhism: Third Series* (London, 1953), 350).

[123] Spacing is an essential aspect of *différance*: but *espacement* is not reducible to *espace*, i.e. to the fact that there are spaces between letters. This does not prevent Barthes from seeing the empty spaces of Japanese culture as offering a mode of dispersal, allowing self-presence to be rarefied to the maximum degree.

[124] *Orality and Literacy: The Technologizing of the Word* (London, 1982).

[125] *EpS*, 44. See also 'Sans adresse', ibid. 47–51. The Library of Congress Catalogue perspicaciously gives, as subject-heading for *EpS*, 'nonverbal communication', as well as the more obvious (but more controversial) 'Japan'.

[126] Ibid. 51.

frequently unnamed: this means that the body has to mediate between writing in the limited, pragmatic sense of noting addresses and directions, and the generalized writing that cannot be separated from other activities.

And when Barthes does extol the ideogram, it is precisely in so far as it is not alphabetical. His praise of ideographic writing is never philosophically founded, and does not, for example, distinguish between the different levels of the Japanese language (between the syllabic *kana* and the *kanji*: only the latter are properly speaking ideogrammatic: they are characters that have been borrowed from Chinese). But what he likes about the idea of Japanese characters that he constructs in *L'Empire des signes* is their unvoiced quality. Japanese characters always write more than they say: they are language visible: the Japanese language is, for Barthes, *un vide de parole*, 'devoid of the spoken word'.[127] Barthes thus, in his way, continues the long story of fascinated incomprehension shown by Western alphabetic cultures for their non-alphabetic counterparts—a story examined in detail by Derrida, who focuses on the way a philosopher such as Hegel attempts to accommodate the challenge posed to his own system by oriental writing. Hegel's low estimation of Chinese characters is expressed clearly in paragraph 459 of the *Philosophy of Mind*: Hegel condemns such characters as being divorced from the spoken language, which he privileges—'phonocentrically', in Derrida's terminology. 'Alphabetic writing is on all accounts the more intelligent' says Hegel.[128] And a hieroglyphic system, in which a character can be analysed in a variety of ways, has the disadvantage that 'the relation of concrete mental ideas to one another must necessarily be tangled and perplexed'.[129]

Derrida discusses Hegel's complex but generally negative attitude towards hieroglyphics in 'Le Puits et la pyramide: introduction à la sémiologie de Hegel'.[130] Such oriental scripts bypass the privilege accorded, in the West, to the *phonē*, the voice as the place of self-presence and truth. Derrida extends his critique of Hegel to conclude that all writing—even alphabetic writing—always contains a surplus of graphic material (diacritical marks, punctuation, spacing) that resist phoneticization. He traces the repression of this surplus of writing

---

[127] *EpS*, 10.
[128] *The Philosophy of Mind: Part Three of the Encyclopedia of the Philosophical Sciences (1830)*, trans. William Wallace (Oxford, 1971), 216.
[129] Ibid. 217.
[130] *Marges—de la philosophie*, 79–127.

back at least as far as the *Phaedrus* of Plato in which, as he summarizes the position, the fear of writing as such and the longing for the presence of speech means that writing itself is split into two kinds, one closer to speech, and the other closer to 'pure' writing in all its dangerous uncontrollability: the first, says Derrida (in 'La Pharmacie de Platon') is 'une bonne écriture (naturelle, vivante, savante, intelligible, intérieure, parlante)', the second is 'une mauvaise écriture (artificieuse, moribonde, ignorante, sensible, extérieure, muette)'.[131]

This casts light on our earlier appraisal of the place of names in Barthes's work, for in a discussion of Hegel in *De la grammatologie*, Derrida had noted that non-phonetic writing destroys *le nom*—both the name as proper and the noun.[132] Barthes's praise of non-phonetic scripts can thus be seen as motivated partly by his fear of the name, and of the reification it and the noun impose, as units of breathing and the signified, both in turn identified with *la parole*, the spoken word. And what is, for Plato, 'bad' writing, exterior and mute, is for Barthes 'good'—though such an evaluative reversal is only part of the story: Barthes is well aware that the empire of Japanese signs is partly the construct of a Western mind, and our very image of non-phonetic writing needs to be expressed—to be voiced—in alphabetic language, so that Japanese characters and roman letters cannot be rigorously separated. His re-evaluation does, however, invade his own style: we may thus consider, for example, Barthes's 'matt' writing as an attempt to imitate, in a phonetic language (French) some of the muteness of the Japanese character. According to Jay Caplan, Barthes's position is that modern writing 'must become mute (be pronounced with a temporary stoppage of breath—that is, of the soul)'.[133] To make writing 'matt' is to shift the emphasis from the signified to the signifier. Thus of his *anamnèses*, short fragments of memory gathered in the middle of *Barthes par lui-même*, Barthes says: 'Ces quelques anamnèses sont plus ou moins *mates* (insignifiantes: exemptées de sens). Mieux on parvient à les rendre mates, et mieux elles échappent à l'imaginaire.'[134]

---

[131] *La Dissémination* (1972), 96–198 (172).

[132] 'L'écriture non-phonétique brise le nom. Elle décrit des relations et non des appellations. Le nom et le mot, ces unités du souffle et du concept, s'effacent dans l'écriture pure' (*De la grammatologie*, 41).

[133] Jay Caplan, 'Nothing But Language: On Barthes's *Empire of Signs*', in *Visible Language*, 11: 4 (autumn 1977), 341–62 (344).

[134] *RB*, 114.

Thus Japan is 'le pays de l'écriture'.[135] In it, Barthes can enjoy 'une langue inconnue' 'sans paroles'.[136] Even cooks and flower-arrangers write, the chopsticks act as pens (but are less aggressive than their Western equivalents).[137] And the voice is kept in its (minor) place in, for instance, Bunraku puppet theatre, which thus avoids the hysteria Barthes associates with the Western actor's voice.[138] That Barthes sees Japan as the land of writing rather than of the voice is symptomatic of his desire to see the latter give way to the former, and I will be examining this in more detail in Chapter 5.

MASSIN/MASSON

This figurality, identified originally with the Japanese character, is read back into the way Barthes considers the Western alphabet. Two essays in *L'Obvie et l'obtus* are significant in this respect: one is a review of Massin's *La Lettre et l'image* called 'L'Esprit de la lettre'.[139] The other is devoted to an André Masson exhibition and is called 'Sémiographie d'André Masson'.[140] I will not dwell on either in much detail. The Massin essay recalls how letters in the West have been metaphorized (seen as figures—as looking like things) as well as being the mere atoms of words, and Barthes glances eastwards again to suggest a different way of seeing the problem. 'En Orient, dans cette civilisation idéographique, c'est ce qui est *entre* l'écriture et la peinture qui est tracé, sans que l'on puisse référer l'un à l'autre.'[141] In the West we have to separate *les graphistes* from *les peintres* and *les romanciers* from *les poètes* (and, indeed, the former pair from the latter: a novelist like Butor has shown considerable interest in overcoming this separation, both in a 'book' like *Mobile* and in his essay *Les Mots en peinture*). Barthes insists: 'l'écriture est *une*: le discontinu qui la fonde partout fait de tout ce que nous écrivons, peignons, traçons, un seul texte'.[142]

And the Masson piece suggests in turn how this liberation from the alphabet has been accomplished in Masson's painting, which has anticipated avant-garde theory by postulating *le Texte*. Masson's Asiatic period of painting is indeed thoroughly intertextual—his scribbles

---

[135] *EpS*, back cover.
[137] Ibid. 38, and 58–9 respectively.
[139] *OO*, 95–8.
[141] Ibid. 98.

[136] Ibid. 11–18.
[138] Ibid. 66, 77.
[140] Ibid. 142–4.
[142] Ibid.

allude to Chinese ideograms.[143] In other words, one might say, a kind of drawing mimics and deforms what is a cross between a kind of drawing and a kind of writing. The result is neither drawing nor writing, but a kind of illegible writing. (An example of this, Masson's 'Message de mai', is reproduced in *Le Texte et l'image*.)[144] Barthes deduces: *'pour que l'écriture soit manifestée dans sa vérité* (et non dans son instrumentalité), *il faut qu'elle soit illisible'*.[145] To read a signified is to miss the signifier, and to see the signifier requires us to keep the signified at a distance—hence the emphasis on illegibility.

We have already seen Réquichot producing illegible writing, and I will shortly be discussing Twombly, in whom writing and painting become one: first, the alphabetese of Erté.

HERBÉ/ERTÉ

One of Barthes's longest meditations on the figure is his essay on Erté, called 'Erté *ou* A la lettre'.[146] By composing his alphabet as a series of women, Erté gives us a double series (of women and letters) whose teasing attraction resides in the oscillation that enables us to shift from letter to woman and back again merely by changing the way our eyes accommodate the image. Letter and woman exchange attributes in a ceaseless chiasmus: the woman ceases to be figural and turns into the letter of some unknown script: and the letter is never merely a letter but becomes figurative. This effect is corrosive: it disturbs the way we habitually look at letters (even if they are not 'meant' to look like women they may suddenly acquire a strange opacity and body—just as, in illuminated manuscripts, decorated letters constantly look like dragons or angels even if they do not represent any such creatures). It also disturbs the way we tend to look at bodies (again the question of 'body-language': what does the body mean? can its gestures be deciphered?):

---

[143] *OO*, 142.
[144] *Le Texte et l'image*, 60.
[145] *OO*, 144.
[146] Ibid. 99–121. This essay is discussed by Steven Ungar in 'From Writing to the Letter: Barthes and Alphabetese', *Visible Language*, 11: 4 (autumn 1977), (391–428), and in the ch. 'Alphabetese' of id., *Roland Barthes: The Professor of Desire* (Lincoln, Nebr., 1983).

nous voyons se profiler derrière toute femme de Erté (figurine de Mode, maquette de théâtre) une sorte d'Esprit de la lettre ... Ces peintures sont, comme on dit, non figuratives, et c'est en cela qu'elles sont vouées à l'alphabet (fût-il inconnu), car la lettre est le lieu où convergent toutes les abstractions graphiques.[147]

As far as Erté himself is concerned, Barthes suggests that there is nothing idyllic or innocent about this release of figural energy: as for Bataille, it is still largely destructive and sadistic. In this case, it explicitly relies on the deformation of women's bodies, or more precisely expropriates something of their very bodiliness in order to give it to the letter (à la lettre, as the subtitle to Barthes's essay puts it): 'en *figurant* la lettre, Erté *infigure* la femme (si l'on permet ce barbarisme, nécessaire puisque Erté ôte à la femme sa figure—ou du moins l'évapore—sans la défigurer'.[148] This masculine sadism is troubling, and Barthes does not always note the ambiguities it creates, just as when discussing Erté's letter M he decides that it owes nothing to the image of woman: in fact, as the reproduction in *L'Obvie et l'obtus* shows unclearly[149] and that in *Le Texte et l'image* more clearly,[150] Erté's M has two women kneeling within the two triangles of flame it figures. So Erté reduces woman to a silhouette, deprived of a body and of sexuality, turned into a sign.[151] It is this which Barthes finds vaguely erotic: woman as letter, letter as woman. His main concern, in other words, is less the gendered nature of these images than the fact that Erté is managing to subvert the alphabet by showing it as figural: M, 'amour' and 'Mort'.

In the course of his essay, Barthes refers to the psychoanalytic theme of the letter: an example would be the way Freud's 'Wolf-Man' becomes obsessed with the letter V, which he associates with the shape made by legs raised in coitus, with the wings of a wasp (in German *eine Wespe*), and (in inverted form) with the ears of the wolves of which he dreams.

This leads to another theme linked with that of scribble: the *lapsus*. Barthes's initial resistance to the typewriter (at least, its Western version) is clearly expressed in, for instance, 'Un rapport presque maniaque avec les instruments graphiques'.[152] A 'brief personal digression' in 'Erté' shows how, even at the typewriter, Barthes cannot help but be a scribbler—someone who undoes the system of *langue*— in his repeated mistakes. He notes an annoying failing: he frequently

---

[147] *OO*, 107.   [148] Ibid.   [149] Ibid. 121.
[150] *Le Texte et l'image*, 72.   [151] *OO*, 102.   [152] *GV*, 171–2.

commits an involuntary metathesis or transposition of letters. He also interprets this failing (as a *lapsus*—not a *lapsus linguae* or even *calami*, but, so to speak, *machinae*):

> combien de fois (animé sans doute d'une irritation inconsciente contre des mots qui m'étaient familiers et dont par conséquent je me sentais prisonnier) n'ai-je pas écrit *sturcture* (au lieu de *structure*), *susbtituer* (pour *substituer*) ou *trasncription* (pour *transcription*)?[153]

It is what Barthes interprets as a protest on the part of the body at the structures of language forced on it that makes Barthes not so much a structuralist or even post-structuralist as a sturcturalist.

This spelling mistake is at least audible: other 'respellings' one might want to indicate have the virtue of making no difference to phoneticization: Derrida's *différance*, for instance. And *S/Z*, after all, owes its existence to another spelling mistake, this time a silent protest of Bataille's body against the spelling 'Sarrasine' where the rules of French onomastics would usually prescribe 'Sarrazine'. *S/Z* is the hieroglyph of this *lapsus*. Balzac, according to Barthes, sees Z as a bad letter ('la lettre de la déviance' says Barthes, referring to the story 'Z. Marcas'). Barthes looks at the shape of the letter Z: it reminds him of cutting and thus of castration: and the initial Z in the name of the castrato Zambinella supports his case. In Sarrasine's name, the Z which should have been in the place of the middle S has been repressed, as if Sarrasine were already afraid of castration: the story tells how this repressed returns (as the inevitability of castration) when Sarrasine finally confronts Zambinella.[154] The fragment 'Fautes de frappe' in *Barthes par lui-même* makes a similar point, noting that Barthes also types z for s in plurals (another return of the repressed?) and in handwriting makes only one mistake: 'dans l'écriture à la main, je ne fais jamais qu'une faute, fréquente: j'écris "n" pour "m", je m'ampute d'un jambage, je veux des lettres à deux jambes, non à trois'.[155] Scribble, in both these cases, seems to be linked to a castration complex. Barthes gently notes: 'il est vrai qu'une bonne dactylo ne se trompe pas: elle n'a pas d'inconscient!' in case we take these figures of castration too seriously. (But it does seem a little hard on the humble secretary to deprive her of an unconscious and thus turn her into a pure machine.)

---

[153] *OO*, 113.
[154] *S/Z*, p. 271 n. 1 and discussion on p. 113.
[155] *RB*, 101.

In 'Écrivains, intellectuels, professeurs', Barthes contrasts two kinds of typing error: in the first, the new word produced is nonsense (not in the dictionary—as when one types *offivier* for *officier*); in the second, the new word is a proper word too (*ride* instead of *rude*). The first kind of mistake is emblematic of the radical freedom of association claimed by an extremist form of criticism, for which there is no limit to the associations a text may open up; the second is prepared to accept meaning, the signified as well as the *grésillements* of the signifier that accompany it.[156] The first, we might say, is close to the automatic writing of the surrealists (which Barthes found lacking in interest).[157] The second would seem to be much closer to the art of the anagram and to all the controlled experiments (lipograms, palindromes, metatheses, and so on) of Oulipo, though it has to be said that Barthes's own preference seems to be for new meanings being produced in less deliberate ways. He is thus charmed by the spellings of Darmès, who attempted to kill Louis-Philippe and expressed his contempt for the ruling class, as Victor Hugo tells us, in the spelling *haristaukrassie*.[158] Barthes's hostility to the practice of judging people by their spelling and discriminating against poor spellers would probably not have endeared him as an educationalist to our own Conservative politicians.[159]

One further point: Barthes, especially in *Barthes par lui-même*, sometimes writes his name thus: 'R. B.', a fashion begun by Sollers. Initials are a figure of writing too: that we can vocalize them (as 'Herbé') is the result of naming the letters individually rather than trying to pronounce the word 'rb', and this naming is mediated by the code of the alphabet.[160] Just as the initials of Romain de Tirtoff become R. T. and thus Erté, the new name is based on a passage through 'infigured' writing.[161] When Barthes refers (for reasons that remain enigmatic) to the artist Cy Twombly as 'TW', the result is more difficult to vocalize, with the result that 'TW' becomes almost a

---

[156] *BL*, 360–2.
[157] *GV*, 230–2, esp. 231.
[158] Cited in *PlT*, 103.
[159] *BL*, 57–8.
[160] See the pleasantries exchanged on this subject in C 146.
[161] Jane Gallop submits Barthes's various texts and the letters of which they are composed to a flurry of infigurations in 'BS', *Visible Language*, 11: 4 (autumn 1977), 364–87. She notes e.g. the way Sade's initials D. A. F. (Donatien-Alphonse-François) haunt the title of *Fragments d'un Discours Amoureux*. Her pulverizing anagrammatization of Barthes's work, like the other contributions to this issue of *Visible Language*, is accompanied by a variety of ingenious allegorical interpretations.

character in a non-phonetic script, not even subvocalized as we read Barthes's essay. Is this because Twombly is an even purer figure of writing than Erté? Does he overcome the last vestiges of *aggression* that we still find in Erté?

R.B./TW

Le tableau est fini quand il a effacé l'idée.

Matisse

Barthes's two beautiful essays on Cy Twombly are his last major writings on a painter.[162] Twombly is one of the greatest of scribblers because the last vestiges of sculpture (of inscription as cutting) seem to have been eradicated from his work. His canvases are frequently daubs, brief blotches of colour, trails and traces of paint that dash evanescently across the slightly soiled whiteness of the background. They frequently contain scrawls and scribbles that hesitate between writing and drawing.

'Qui c'est, Cy Twombly (ici dénommé TW)? Qu'est-ce qu'il fait? Comment nommer ce qu'il fait? Des mots surgissent spontanément ("dessin", "graphisme", "griffonnage", "gauche", "enfantin").'[163] The fascination of this art lies in its resistance to being named—Barthes is forced to try out a variety of different words in his attempt to find the one which best 'fits' Twombly's work. He adds one name to another but still cannot find the proper one. Scribble, which consists of an endless oscillation between discourse and figure, is particularly apt at suspending this naming activity, a suspension to which, as I showed in my last chapter, Barthes aspires. Twombly's canvases are not writing so much as a constant allusion to writing. Having produced a semblance of writing—a proper name scrawled across the painting, a shape familiar to a letter—he then abandons the allusion: and, noting this, Barthes suggests that Twombly's distance from any 'cultivated' or deliberately 'artistic' calligraphy is a way of showing that writing itself is not what we thought it to be.

---

[162] See 'Cy Twombly ou *Non multa sed multum*', in *OO*, 145–62, and 'Sagesse de l'art', ibid. 163–78.
[163] Ibid. 145.

TW dit à sa manière que l'essence de l'écriture, ce n'est ni une forme ni un usage, mais seulement un geste, le geste qui la produit *en la laissant traîner*: un brouillis, presque une salissure, une négligence.[164]

Barthes's article constantly resorts to the vocabulary of Bataille, in his claim that the essence of any object lies in its excess, namely everything that is not subsumed under the general heading of 'use value' (or indeed of 'exchange value', for such excess is so radical as to question any notion of value whatsoever: it is excess as the moment of sovereignty). But Barthes sees excess in moments of 'negligence' more than in the strident exploration of limits negotiated by Bataille.

What is the essence of a pair of trousers? Not, according to Barthes, the fact that they can be found neatly folded and ready to wear, but rather in their avatar as a heap left by an adolescent undressing. (Barthes eroticizes the negligence of such acts in the terms of his own sexuality, although the Eros in question is here, precisely, a hazy and diffuse one, perhaps closer to what he elsewhere calls 'sensuality' than to sexuality.) If writing is often imagined as a heroic act (the struggle with recalcitrant material, the battle against the aphasia of the empty page), Barthes sees Twombly's scribble not as *archi-écriture* but as a kind of *après-écriture* in which the will-to-power has been temporarily suspended.

L'essence d'un objet a quelque rapport avec son déchet: non pas forcément ce qui reste après qu'on en a usé, mais ce qui est *jeté* hors de l'usage. Ainsi des écritures de TW. Ce sont les bribes d'une paresse, donc d'une élégance extrême; comme si, de l'écriture, acte érotique fort, il restait la fatigue amoureuse: ce vêtement tombé dans un coin de la feuille.[165]

From Bataille's perspective, in which the project is seen as essentially servile, a certain sovereignty can be found in abdication—in the evacuation of any project, in the curlicues, daubs, and smudges that are the final trace left by writing as it evaporates, and that remain to haunt the official text of reason and purpose.

Indeed, scribble is the essence of writing—Barthes reverses the usual evaluation following which all scribble (that of the child or of the primitive) is a debased form of writing. Just as for Bataille, the essence of the human lies in excess (an excess that exceeds essence itself), so scribble can be seen as the purest of gifts—useless, excrementitious, thrown away, for nothing, maybe for nobody. Writing

[164] *OO*, 146.   [165] Ibid.

as scribble, residing more in the luxury of a gesture than the communicative end-product, is an absolute superfluity. 'N'est-ce pas à cette limite extrême que commence vraiment "l'art", le "texte", tout le "pour rien" de l'homme, sa perversion, sa dépense?'[166]

Twombly's art is one of perpetual posing and disposing: he makes a free sketch, sees a vague resemblance between it and a real object, and then, rather than continuing to capitalize on that resemblance, gives it away, for nothing, scrawling off in a new direction:

la main a tracé quelque chose comme une fleur et puis s'est mise à traîner sur cette trace; la fleur a été écrite, puis désécrite; mais les deux mouvements restent vaguement surimprimées; c'est un palimpseste pervers; trois textes (si l'on y ajoute la sorte de signature, de légende ou de citation: *Sesostris*) sont là, l'un tendant à effacer l'autre, mais à seule fin, dirait-on, de donner à lire cet effacement: véritable philosophie du temps.[167]

Scribble oscillates between defacement and representation, as in Bataille's examples, or between *Gestalt*-free and *Gestalt*-bound forms, as Ehrenzweig puts it. But is this scribble still masculine and sadistic? Barthes identifies the gesture of giving and then withdrawing with the 'game' of *Fort-Da* whose rhythm, according to Freud, marks the perpetual fluctuation of the death-drive.[168] In Twombly, the production of the scribbled trace is both seminal (Eros) and excremental (Thanatos): the latter aspect recalls the sadistic element Bataille detected in the graffiti of the Abyssinian children. On one reading, Freud sees the child's game as an attempt to bind the psychic excitation (or tension) produced by the repeated absences of the mother: in throwing away the toy which represents the mother, the child in repetition masters the pain of loss. What binds and masters is the ego, so that the *Fort*—on this reading—exists only for the sake of the *Da* (the child can bring back the toy—and by symbolic implication the mother). What Freud's analysis skirts over is the fact that the game consists principally in a throwing-away, which is not necessarily performed with the ultimate aim of bringing back.[169]

Barthes is careful in his discussion of Twombly *not* to privilege Eros over the death-drive or vice versa. He thus remains faithful to Freud's remarks at the end of 'Beyond the Pleasure Principle' that the

---

[166] *OO*, 148.

[167] Ibid. 152.

[168] See 'Beyond the Pleasure Principle', in *Pelican Freud Library*, xi. 269–338.

[169] This is one emphasis brought out by Derrida in 'Spéculer—sur "Freud"', *La Carte postale de Socrate à Freud et au-dela* (1980), 275–437.

distinction between Eros and Thanatos remains enigmatic.[170] Twombly's repeated letter 'a's for instance are indeterminately Eros and Thanatos, the joy of procreation and the uncontrollable, stereotypical repetition associated with the death-drive: 'elles ont à charge, dirait-on, de lier dans un seul état ce qui apparaît et disparaît', life and death being bound together so as to become indistinguishable: this is art as Utopia, *Vie-Mort*.[171] It is also scribble as a pure rhythm, but one which is less incisive than the 'rhythmic' marks Barthes suggests elsewhere were at the origin of the earliest scratches made on cave walls.[172]

Lyotard locates the most profound of his *figures*, the *figure-matrice*, in a tension between Eros and Thanatos. Eros, as a binding of psychic energy, is engaged in a struggle with Thanatos the death-drive, a movement towards total energetic discharge.[173] The relation between the figural and discourse is similar to that between Thanatos and Eros. Geoffrey Bennington summarizes Lyotard's position thus:

The figural is not simply the death of discourse, but discourse never quite successfully binds the figural either: desire is never quite literalised, the death-drive is what is never quite brought back to presence, the force that repeats the *fort* in the fort/da game.[174]

The unconscious (as a mode of the figural) can be recognized only by being bound (made discursive), and thus necessarily separated from itself: 'it is the death-drive which is to be found as the principle of figurality'.[175]

Barthes intuitively recognizes a similar problematic in Twombly's repetition of the letter 'a'. He does not work it out in discursive terms with the complexity of Lyotard: he does, however, emblematically, figure it. He wishes, that is, to imitate the relative lack of binding he appreciates in Twombly—and he is correct in noting that while Twombly's canvases do include violent elements, scratches, scribbles, scrawls, and scrubbings out, the final impression they leave is of tension discharged, of profound peacefulness (the fact that many of them allude to Mediterranean seascapes—as in the *Bay of Naples*,

---

[170] 'Beyond the Pleasure Principle', 336–8.

[171] *OO*, 152.

[172] See 'Écoute', ibid. 217–30 (220).

[173] This struggle between Eros and Thanatos is, very schematically, the theory put forward in Freud's 'Beyond the Pleasure Principle', whose own internal tensions and drives are discussed both by Lyotard in *Discours, Figure*, and Derrida in 'Spéculer—sur "Freud"'.

[174] *Lyotard: Writing the Event*, 99.

[175] Ibid.

reproduced on the cover of *L'Obvie et l'obtus*—also helps to create this impression). Again, Lyotard suggests that the work of art fulfils its critical function not by attempting to present the unconscious—for, presented, the unconscious is Prometheus bound in the chains of secondary revision—but by resisting absorption 'into the secondary from within the secondary', as Bennington puts it.[176] I will be suggesting that Barthes sees *écriture*, writing at its most radically other, as resisting *parole*, the spoken word, from within *parole*, in Chapter 5. As for Twombly, he resists secondary revision by constantly skirting it—including within his canvases names and words that seem to explain them, but in fact need, themselves, to be explained. They have no metalinguistic distance (they are part of the painting as well as outside it as a name).

Thus Twombly is in many ways the supreme writer in that he has largely suspended the aggression of writing as inscription or scraping (and thus as sculpture, *via di levare*) and has reinscribed it as painting (*via di porre*). His art is superimposed on something prewritten, but in such a way as not to cover that support, but to let it appear through the superimpositions (we become aware of the grain of the canvas). This creates a space whose aggression has largely been disarmed. By scrawling, once relatively legibly, and then above that in a distorted, almost unrecognizable form, the name 'Virgil', Twombly is both citing classical culture and deforming it at the same time.[177] The appropriation of classical culture is parodic and reverential, inseparably.

Twombly paints and draws on to paper which is already 'sali, altéré, d'une luminosité inclassable'.[178] He is thus different from the writer, who is faced with the anguish of the immaculately white empty page that seems to resist being soiled by writing. (The writer is of course more terrified of the idea of whiteness, as the concept of blankness and sterility, than of the materiality of the paper.) Furthermore, some of Twombly's canvases resemble graffiti, and despite the etymology of the word (*graffiare* in Italian means 'to scratch'), Barthes does not see it as subtractive, aggressive, or incisive but as additive (closer to painting), since it is prepared to use anything at all as a support.[179] Barthes, that is, shifts his attention to a new opposition: that between the writer as painter and the writer as philosopher. The painter is prepared to work on the prewritten (the artefactual), whereas for the philosopher, the material support of writing is ideally absent: the

---

[176] *Lyotard: Writing the Event.* 100.   [177] *OO*, 147.
[178] Ibid. 153.   [179] Ibid. 153–4.

philosopher's writing is thus, again ideally, an absolute beginning: hence the problematic of beginnings, the terror of the supreme philosophical question of knowing what to put first.[180] This aspiration to making a clean break with the philosophical heritage is one that philosophy shares with a certain modernism, and the strains engendered in both are extremely important. If Twombly is exemplary as far as Barthes is concerned, it is in so far as he accepts the apparently secondary nature of his art. Twombly's art is always soiled by the trace (the spoor) of the other: it accepts this condition:

On sait bien que ce qui fait le graffiti, ce n'est à vrai dire ni l'inscription, ni son message, c'est le mur, le fond, la table; c'est parce que le fond existe pleinement, comme un objet qui a déjà vécu, que l'écriture lui vient toujours comme un supplément énigmatique: ce qui est *de trop*, en surnombre, hors sa place, voilà qui trouble l'ordre; ou encore, c'est dans la mesure où le fond *n'est pas propre*, qu'il est impropre à la pensée (au contraire de la feuille blanche du philosophe), et donc très propre à tout ce qui reste (l'art, la paresse, la pulsion, la sensualité, l'ironie, le goût: tout ce que l'intellect peut ressentir comme autant de catastrophes esthétiques).[181]

Philosophy itself, of course, raises questions about its own *feuille blanche*. The recognition that even philosophical writing cannot make an absolutely new beginning informs Derrida's introduction to the French edition of William Warburton's *Essai sur les hiéroglyphes des Égyptiens*. That introduction is called 'Scribble'. In it, Derrida refers to the text as a palimpsest and the illusion that we can scrape away the layers of historically accumulated material in order to reach the original text:

Il y a toujours de la surcharge d'écriture et on ne peut l'analyser (en dissoudre telle ou telle force) qu'on en rajoutant. C'est ce que veut dire archi-écriture: non pas une écriture préalable faisant l'objet d'une archéologie mais toujours une écriture déjà, à même le sol des écritures.[182]

Since there is no original text, it becomes paradoxical to speak of a palimpsest, says Derrida.[183] All writing is scribble: impure and entangled, non-original, incapable of freeing itself from earlier writing. The end of the book may take the form of generalized scribble like that

---

[180] This is clearly linked to my earlier discussion of Husserl and the *tabula rasa*: on the more general problem of where the philosopher is to begin, see Derrida, 'Hors livre', in *La Dissémination*, 7–67.
[181] *OO*, 154.
[182] 'Scribble: pouvoir/écrire', in William Warburton, *Essai sur les hiéroglyphes des Égyptiens*, trans. Leonard des Malpeines (1977), 7–43 (13).
[183] Ibid. 42.

with which Barthes, in handwriting, 'ends' *Barthes par lui-même*: 'Quoi écrire, maintenant? Pourrez-vous encore écrire quelque chose?—On écrit avec son désir, et je n'en finis pas de désirer.'

In any case, it is interesting to note that for Barthes on Twombly, the aesthetic is yet again a catastrophe in that its 'impurity' is not tolerated by a philosophy (or a science) conceived as conceptually pure. We saw this catastrophe at work in drift. And here too, in Twombly, it is a catastrophe of gentleness, not of violence: it is a self-deposition, a turning down, the most gentle of additions: 'l'instrument traceur (pinceau ou crayon) descend sur la feuille, il atterrit—ou alunit—sur elle, c'est tout: il n'y a même pas l'ombre d'une morsure, simplement un *posé*'. This is movement at its most extenuated and oriental: 'il ne saisit rien, il dépose, et tout est dit'.[184] But this scribble is not, as I have shown, an easy option: even the peace of Twombly's canvases has to be won over the constant return of aggression and interpretation, just as the controlled accident of Zen can only be attained after disciplined practice. I will be returning to the ways in which the seductiveness of scribble can wound the subject into attempting to mimic it in Chapter 6. Here I will merely note that Barthes does attempt to write in such a way that aggression is defused as much as it is in Twombly's canvases. For Barthes, what will survive is paradoxically what is most delicate and vulnerable.

We have already seen Adorno using the figure of handwriting as an emblem of art's defence against evaporating into pure spirit (philosophy). In another section of the *Aesthetic Theory* entitled 'Enigma, Scrawl, Interpretation', Adorno notes the ascendancy of the concept of *écriture* in the visual arts, 'inspired perhaps by certain drawings by Klee that seem to shade over into a human scrawl [*die einer gekritzelten Schrift sich nähern*]', and he suggests that *all* art resembles a handwriting (*Schrift*), and artworks 'hieroglyphs for which the code has been lost'.[185] It is only because they are handwriting or enigmatic hieroglyphs that they are works of art: the loss of the code is 'constitutive of their essence as art works', and they demand interpretation because this code is lost: 'Only *qua* handwriting do they have a language, do they speak.'[186] But their 'writerliness' is what means that interpretation is never completed: 'The riddle lives on,

---

[184] *OO*, 158.

[185] *Aesthetic Theory*, 182.

[186] Adorno's German is characteristically terse: 'Sprache sind Kunstwerke nur als Schrift': I follow the standard English trans. in reading *Schrift* as 'handwriting', although *Schrift* (writing as script) is less specific.

though, even after the work has been interpreted.' The work of art for Adorno speaks only in so far as it is silent (written): neither aesthetic nor philosophical understanding can exhaust the script. The full complexity of Adorno's discussion debars me from comparing him directly with Barthes, but he casts an indirect light on the Barthesian themes that this chapter sets out: scribble, handwriting, hieroglyph, interpretation.[187]

Barthes's discourse too aspires to the status of figure, but could reach it only at the cost of abandoning the quest. For a pure figure is as impossible as a pure discourse: and even without taking the terms to their most radical degree of abstraction, the mere figure is as legible (the coded drawing) as is ordinary writing. Barthes's work attempts, in some of its most experimental moments, to be the mixed mode between them. In this way he writes ideas: he uses terms taken from systems of thought in an emblematic way, practising 'une sorte d'idéographie philosophique'.[188] Roland Champagne, noting the way Barthes's interest in ideograms is partly based on the fact that they can inscribe various elements, including the presence of the writer's body, all in a single graphic figure, suggests that 'writing is an attempt by a writer to make his or her body perpetual in time'.[189] But the form of writing chosen is important: it must be a 'script', at the border between the visible and the legible, just as the grain of the singing voice is neither pure *melos* (pure music) nor pure *logos* (the words being sung as the 'signified'). Barthes presents scribble as the grain of writing, where articulate meaning, determined by the code of *langue*, meets an inarticulate, *Gestalt*-free, figural energy embodied in the graphic trace. This scribble is the figure of the end of interpretation as a *via di levare*, being itself a pure *via di porre*. It is the written trace in so far as it refuses the abreaction of the speaking voice: in so far, that is, as it refuses psychoanalytic interpretation as a 'talking cure'. For what subtends Barthes's fascination with scribble, his love of the ideogram, and his hostility to phonetic alphabets, is a constant distancing of the power and violence that he sees as inherent in the voice, and I wish to devote the next chapter to excursus on this mistrust of the act of speech, a mistrust that determines so many of Barthes's theoretical and ideological options.

---

[187] See also the Borges story, 'The God's Script', in *Labyrinths* (Harmondsworth, 1970).

[188] *RB*, 78.

[189] *Literary History in the Wake of Roland Barthes*: Re-Defining the Myths of Reading (Birmingham, Ala., 1984), 97. See also *Alors la Chine?* (1975), 10.

5

EXCURSUS
CONTRA VOCEM

Qui veut se donner à la peinture, doit commencer par se faire
couper la langue.

                                                              Braque

The opposition between 'speech' and 'writing' has been a theme
running throughout my discussion. Barthes shares this interest with
Derrida. But whereas the latter examines it from a predominantly
philosophical point of view, Barthes invests it with a certain existential
passion of his own. For he actively dislikes *the voice*—dislikes it in so
far as it *says* something. Where his theories touch on the voice, he will
almost always attempt to free the voice from what it says in order to
turn it into yet another organ of writing.

Why should this be so? There are two main reasons. First of all,
Barthes sees the voice as the locus of social division: we demonstrate
our class provenance by the way we speak (accent, lexicon, syntax).
Secondly, for him, the voice is always potentially arrogant: to speak
is to exercise power. It is as if the voice is always that which is giving
orders. Thirdly, his constant drive to see the world as an activity of
writing leads him to try to suspend the last residues of voice in
writing—residues that he frequently identifies with the signified
(writing in so far as it *says* something): this involves an attempt to
produce what he imagines as a *silent writing*. In the first two cases
(voice as social division, voice as power), Barthes's values are very
much in the enlightenment tradition: social division and power are
both to be questioned, in the name of emancipation. But to fall back
on writing, rather than, for instance, dialogue, is *not* part of that
tradition. And to suspend the signified (what a person or a text may
actually be saying) and to extol silent writing as a pure formalism (the
formalism of the trace or the *trait* he sees as the essence of *écriture*) is
to move away from that enlightenment tradition. I will examine these
three 'moments' in Barthes's critique of the voice.

First of all, Barthes is particularly sensitive to the ways in which the
divisions of society are inscribed into speech. Three important essays

collected in *Le Bruissement de la langue* raise this question: 'La Paix culturelle', 'La Division des langages' and 'La Guerre des langages'[1]

In 'La Paix culturelle', Barthes suggests that culture appears so all-embracing that there is nothing outside it or opposing it—so that a *Pax culturalis* seems to reign. But the *languages* of that culture are in fact at war. Barthes takes his own case: as a French intellectual the only thing he shares with a *vendeur des Nouvelles Galeries* is the French language as a basic medium of communication: but communication (the transmission of information) is a tiny part of what a language does, and Barthes is divided from his less intellectual fellow-citizens by all the connotations, allusions, and indirections that he prizes in language. He is not snobbishly saying that the *vendeur des Nouvelles Galeries* is not interested in these subtleties—on the contrary. But the latter's set of connotations are different from those of Barthes. The resulting linguistic division between them is *un deuil permanent*. And this division does not merely pass between subjects; it passes through each individual subject too: 'en moi, chaque jour, s'accumulent, sans communiquer, plusieurs langages isolés: je suis fractionné, coupé, éparpillé (ce qui, ailleurs, passerait pour la définition même de la folie'.[2] In this essay, however, Barthes tends to imagine culture as too massified, and 'low' culture as merely a degraded version, formed under the pressure of the mass media, of 'high' culture.

This permanent blind spot in Barthes's thinking about culture has been well analysed by Michael Moriarty, and I will not develop it here.[3] But there is another problem too. This essay first appeared in English (*The Times Literary Supplement*) in 1971, and Barthes does not seem to have changed his mind about the immobility of culture and the social alienation reflected in its conflicting languages right up to the time of his death. Here, the dissociation of languages within one single individual is seen as close to that analysed by psychoanalysis (as a schizoid mentality). But in *Le Plaisir du texte*, published two years later, despite an epigraph from Hobbes ('La seule passion de ma vie a été la peur') that would suggest, on the face of it, that social division as a linguistic war of all against all is going to be a major source of discomfort for the subject, what we find is such dissociation being celebrated. What is the difference between 'La Paix culturelle' and *Le Plaisir du texte*?

---

[1] *BL*, 107–12, 113–26, 127–31, respectively.
[2] *BL*, 107–12.
[3] See *Roland Barthes* (Cambridge, 1991).

There are really two such differences. In 'La Paix culturelle', Barthes oversimplifies the nature of the division of languages as it cuts through the individual: it is not certain that this division should be described as a dissociation—in other words, it is not true that the different languages in any one subject exist *sans communiquer*.[4] Rather, if there is indeed to be a state of war between them, they must communicate—as enemies locked in conflict. Barthes's model is psychotic where it should be neurotic. But the models of linguistic division proposed in *Le Plaisir du texte* are almost without exception psychotic. The fragment 'Babel', for instance, imagines the reader of the text as someone who can abolish all barriers between languages. As Barthes imagines it, however, the result is not a homogenized language, but the coexistence of radically different and non-synthesizable languages within the one subject, the reader—'qui mélangerait tous les langages, fussent-ils réputés incompatibles'.[5] Barthes's point is that the reader can combine such languages (from the text being read and from 'real life') with a sovereign disregard for the fact that they should not, in strict logic, be able to coexist. In fact they do thus coexist, but in a state of peaceful dissociation rather than being (neurotically) at war. Barthes's model is lateral rather than vertical (despite his leading metaphor, the tower of Babel): languages exist together on the same plane (no dominance and no subjection), and this model is very different from one in which subjugated (or, in more psychoanalytical terms, repressed) languages would struggle to wrest power from the languages above them. 'Alors le vieux mythe biblique se retourne, la confusion des langues n'est plus une punition, le sujet accède à la jouissance par la cohabitation des langages, *qui travaillent côte à côte*: le texte de plaisir, c'est Babel heureuse.'[6]

In other words, where in 'La Paix culturelle' Barthes saw linguistic division as a *deuil permanent*, here it becomes a source of pleasure: what was a rather neurotic image of the alienations of language here becomes a psychotic (or schizoid) but thoroughly pleasurable image of the polyphonic text. *Le Plaisir du texte*, indeed, emphasizes that the neurosis of the writer is only the first stage towards the creation of textual pleasure: it must be completed by the schizoid dissociation within the reader. For the writer cannot actually be psychotic without risking complete silence, so that the tensions of neurosis are unavoid-

[4] *BL*, 109.   [5] *PIT*, 9.   [6] Ibid. 10.

able. Barthes is here being revisionist: much of the activity of *Tel Quel* concentrated on 'psychotic' writers such as Artaud. But Barthes's point is that such writers cease to be completely schizoid in so far as they write, in other words in so far as they are still out to seduce the 'other'—the reader.[7]

The fragment 'Babel', celebrating psychosis (languages working side by side), is followed by the fragment 'Babil', in which a text that is making too noisy demands on its reader is condemned. 'On me présente un texte. Ce texte m'ennuie. On dirait qu'il *babille*'—and this 'babble' is the result of a mere need (*un simple besoin d'écriture*), of that demand for love which for Barthes almost always seems to pass through speech. 'On peut dire que finalement ce texte, vous l'avez écrit hors de toute jouissance; et ce texte-babil est en somme un texte frigide, comme l'est toute demande avant que ne s'y forme le désir, la névrose.'[8] Barthes's terms are here taken from Lacan, for whom the infant progresses from mere physiological need, via the demand for love (the demand to have its needs recognized and attended to), to the desire which insertion into the order of language, with its infinite surplus of signifiers over signifieds and its slippages and overlaps, inevitably creates. This desire is perverse in that the demand for love both turns in on its own medium (becomes, as it were, self-reflexive), as when an infant starts to play with language in its less communicational aspects (not just signalling 'feed me!'), and at the same time turns out towards the 'other', now seen as a subject to be seduced (by the teasing and active forces of language—those in which, says Lacan, not just need but desire is made manifest). So the text must exceed the babble of demand, must be prepared to desire the other.

And this other in turn—the reader—is cloven, sometimes experiencing the euphoria that comes from feeling at home in a text, sometimes experiencing the loss of such ego-centred identity and coherence, as when encountering radically challenging texts (as in avant-garde productions) or moments of indeterminate fascination (the result of the intense intersubjective involvement coupled with semantic undecidability sometimes experienced in the reading of an otherwise classical text). Since the latter experience (*jouissance*) is itself one of dissociation, and there is a cleavage between the former experience (ego-coherent *plaisir*) and the latter (ego-dissociative *jouissance*) in any one reader, Barthes concludes that such a

[7] *PlT*, 13.   [8] Ibid. 12.

reader is 'deux fois clivé, deux fois pervers'.[9] Conflict (which is neurotic) should be replaced by difference (which is closer to the *schize* of schizoid mechanisms).[10] But what is even more important is that, taking his cue from Lacan, and the Lacanian psychoanalyst Serge Leclaire, Barthes founds his opposition between *plaisir* and *jouissance* on the fact that the former can be said and the latter cannot. While a *texte de plaisir* can be endlessly commented on, a *texte de jouissance* seems to resist being incorporated into, or discussed from the position of, any metalanguage. There is thus an immediate difference between the garrulity of the former and the speechlessness of the latter.

So when Barthes returns to the theme of the war of languages, he tends to identify this war as a war between types of speech, and thus one that can be temporarily halted in the written text. The section 'Guerre' makes it clear that ideological systems are spoken: they are relatively consistent fictions produced by different factions of society and put into competitive circulation. 'Chaque fiction est soutenue par un *parler* social, un sociolecte, auquel elle s'identifie'; each such fictionally consistent language is the responsibility of a *classe sacerdotale* which is there 'pour le *parler* communément et le diffuser'; 'chaque *parler* (chaque fiction) combat pour l'hégémonie'; the *doxa*—the language of ideology—disguises its origin as just another language because it is in power and so can pretend to be perfectly natural: 'c'est le *parler* prétendûment apolitique des hommes politiques, des agents de l'État, c'est celui de la presse, de la radio, de la télévision, c'est celui de la conversation; mais même hors du pouvoir, contre lui, la rivalité renaît, les *parlers* se fractionnent, luttent entre eux'.[11] *Le parler* as speech, way of talking, is clearly the locus of the warlike aggressivity Barthes detects in social languages. The idea that 'le langage vient toujours de quelque lieu, il est *topos* guerrier' adds the further twist that what is aggressive is too present and tied to its origin. In the text, on the other hand, the force of the origin has been suspended. It is not a *parler*: it is a truce in the midst of the war of languages. Barthes nicely reminds us of a moment in *Mother Courage* when Courage's sons stretch out in the sunlight, enjoying a mug of beer despite the ravages of the Thirty Years War, and he adds: 'Entre deux assauts de *paroles* [*my emphasis*], entre deux prestances de systèmes, le plaisir du

---

[9] *PlT*, 26.
[10] Ibid. 27.
[11] All quotations, ibid. 46–7, all emphases mine.

texte est toujours possible, non comme un délassement, mais comme le passage incongru—*dissocié*—d'un autre langage, comme l'exercice d'une physiologie différente.'[12]

In other words, the dissociation of the text is allowed, whereas the dissociations of speech (closer to neurosis than to *schize*) are disallowed. This is one aspect of Barthes's elevation of writing above speech that runs through *Le Plaisir du texte*, in which alienation is identified firmly with speech, with the voice. Behind the ideal text, he states, there is no voice.[13] And when, in the last section, he praises the art of reading aloud, he is clearly not extolling the voice which speaks (the voice of conversation) but the voice in so far as can it act as an instrument (in the musical sense) of writing: *cette écriture vocale* is not at all the same thing as *la parole*.[14]

Barthes's comments on linguistic alienation are, in his own view, somewhat vulnerable, as he admits in *Barthes par lui-même* where he notes that, probably because of his habit of fetishizing language, he experiences real social divisions in their linguistic form alone, as a problem of interlocution.[15] Presumably his point is that a fully fledged socio-linguistics (of the kind he sketches out in the two other essays I mentioned, 'La Division des langages' and 'La Guerre des langages') needs to examine other aspects of the division of labour and power in society than those that can be brought under the heading of language. But this does not lessen the acuteness of his analyses of the discomforts of speaking in an alienated society. Other anecdotes in *Barthes par lui-même* focus on the difficulties of maintaining a conversation with someone from a different linguistic caste: the *boulangère* in his village in south-west France does not respond to his remarks about the beautiful summer light, whence he pessimistically concludes that even to pass the time of day with one's neighbours is a linguistically demanding enterprise: 'rien de plus idéologique que le temps qu'il fait'.[16] It is typical of Barthes to concentrate on the division of speech and to show almost complete indifference to the question of whether the *boulangère* could read with enjoyment any of his *writings*. Indeed, the exordium to *Barthes par lui-même* goes so far as to suggest that the text he is writing is a way of escaping from his own limited subjectivity towards a generalized language that he identifies, curiously, with that of 'the people':

---

[12] *P/T*, 49.   [13] Ibid. 51.   [14] Ibid. 104.
[15] *RB*, 170.   [16] Ibid. 178.

Le Texte ... emporte mon corps ailleurs, loin de ma personne imaginaire, vers une sorte de langue sans mémoire, qui est déjà celle du Peuple, de la masse insubjective (ou du sujet généralisé), même si j'en suis encore séparé par ma façon d'écrire.[17]

There is a reminiscence of Michelet here, whose attempts to adopt the language of the people, the class his historical writings celebrated, failed—a theme of some pathos to which Barthes continually returns, since he sees Michelet's quandary as typical of the modernist writer.[18]

There is another echo of Barthes's desire for the Text to take him towards the *langue du Peuple* in Kafka, equally obsessed (as has been observed by many writers, including Deleuze and Guattari) with a writing that would register some of the force and flavour of 'the popular' (especially of minorities outside power, notably the Yiddish-speaking population of the late Austro-Hungarian Empire), and equally concerned to overcome the alienation of the artist from the community.[19] This is expressed in his last short story, 'Josephine the Singer, or the Mouse Folk': after a lifetime of singing songs that gave the community a sense of identity, Josephine dies: but perhaps her song was not as essential as it seemed, being merely another expression of the silence that was already enough to keep the community together:

So perhaps we shall not miss so very much after all, while Josephine, redeemed from the earthly sorrows which to her thinking lay in wait for all chosen spirits, will happily lose herself in the numberless throng of the heroes of our people, and soon, since we are no historians, will rise to the heights of redemption and be forgotten like all her brothers.[20]

It is doubtful whether Barthes hopes for such a redemption as this, although his last works suggest a weariness with the consistently intellectual (cerebral) language that he identified as the major symptom of his own alienation from the popular, and look forward to his dissolution back into the forgetfulness of what in *Barthes par lui-même* he calls the *langue sans mémoire* of the People. Thus his final interview ends with the statement that the writer produces writing as a kind of

---

[17] *RB*, 6.
[18] *Mi*, 19.
[19] See Deleuze and Guattari, *Kafka: pour une littérature mineure*, (1976).
[20] *The Collected Short Stories of Franz Kafka*, (1983), ed. Nahun N. Glatzer, 360–76 (376).

seed that may fructify even after the individual's death: 'on peut estimer qu'on dispense une sorte de semence et que, par conséquent, on est remis dans la circulation générale des semences'.[21]

To return from these metaphysical considerations to the more socio-linguistic terms of 'La Guerre des langages', Barthes suggests that the 'speech' in speech can be, as it were, written out: since intellectuals have to participate in the alienated languages around them (have to show some commitment), but at the same time cannot abandon the Utopian quest for a *langage désitué, désaliéné*, he advises them to keep both reins (of *engagement* and of *jouissance*) in their hands. This will result, ideally, in the practice he calls *texte*, and it is writing rather than speech in the following ways. First, only writing can 'assumer le caractère *fictional* des parlers les plus sérieux, voire les plus violents, les replacer dans leur distance *théâtrale*'[22] Again, the equation of speech with violence and presence: a violence that the distance (the inbuilt irony) of writing can mute. (Barthes's example is the *parler* of psychoanalysis, which he claims he can borrow while in fact using it surreptitiously as a *langage romanesque*.) Secondly, only writing can '*mélanger* les parlers', mingling psychoanalysis, Marxism, and structuralism—as his own works do. Writing can thus achieve the full syncretism denied to speech—or the '*hétérologie* du savoir' as he prefers to call it, giving it the dignity associated with heterology in Bataille and Bakhtin. Finally, only writing can 'se déployer *sans lieu d'origine*', escape from the laws of rhetoric and genre, and the power-effects they encode.[23] The transition from speech to writing thus involves the muting of the violence of speech, a distancing of its presence, an interruption of its coherence, an ironization of its contents (the information it communicates), and a mixing of its different modes.

It is curious that an example which Barthes uses twice here is psychoanalysis. For psychoanalysis is precisely a science of speech rather than writing: Freud analysed not the writings of his patients, but the discourse they produced when lying on his couch. Lacan in turn emphasized the need for attention to the *parole* of the patient and the intersubjective nature of the psychoanalytic encounter. But Lacan was especially concerned to use the babble of the patient (the *parole vide* of a desire that cannot recognize itself) in order to lead to a *parole pleine*, a language that would have transcended the empty verbosity of

---

[21] *GV*, 339.   [22] *BL*, 131.   [23] Ibid.

neurosis. Barthes draws on this psychoanalytic theme in two main ways.

First, his awareness of the psychoanalytic exploration of the linguistics of neurosis led him to mistrust spoken language as a *leurre*, a smoke-screen in which the subject can hide. Hence his sensitivity to the falsity of any speech, the fact that speech tends to bathe in the immediacy of the imaginary (the realm of one's images of self and other): to speak is to deploy these unmediated images, to be trapped in the dialectic of recognition (which is always, for Lacan, the recognition of falsely imprisoning identities centred on the ego and alienated from the real subject of desire). But whereas for Lacan this alienation can be at least partly overcome in the spoken encounter of psychoanalysis (the patient learns to speak into the silence of the analyst and therefore learns not to expect any ratification of self-images, which are thereby slowly dissolved), Barthes seems far less convinced of the efficaciousness of the spoken word. For him, the *logos* that may overcome imaginary alienation is not spoken, but written. (While accepting the neurosis that drives the writer, he none the less believes that it can lead to the dispersal of such images in the disseminating ambiguities, the emancipating polysemia, the 'carnivalesque' polyphony of writing as a symbolic activity.) The intertextuality of writing is more effective than the intersubjectivity of the psychoanalytic encounter, with its dialectic of speech and silence. For Barthes, intertextuality, the fact that to write is to open oneself to a cultural space of unlimited contextual possibilities, already mediates the writer's subjectivity into the general symbolic realm of language and culture on a far deeper level than anything available in speech, which for him almost always seems to be a *parole vide*.

Secondly and inseparably from this, Barthes exploits the psychoanalyst's sensitivity to the fact that the spoken word is the presentation of a self-image, in order to detect in every *parole* an exercise in *parade*. The spoken word imposes on its listener: this is the Barthesian leitmotif running through the works of his last decade. Writing is terrorist (you cannot reply to it or question it) and at the same time curiously deprived of power: in the last resort, on Barthes's theory of writing as internal distance and difference, there is no subject in writing to ensure that its message is received in the right way (or received at all). Speech on the other hand is liberal (you can question a speaker) but at the same time repressive: the subject of speech is there, parading knowledge and acquiring identity as a result. The power of the spoken word is, of course, vulnerable, since it can be contested. But it can be contested only by another spoken word, which can be contested in turn, and so on. For Barthes, who rejects the value of dialogue whether Socratic or psychoanalytical, this is merely for power to oscillate from one speaker to the other without ever coming to rest—something very different from the exemption of power he expects from writing.

Thus Barthes uses psychoanalytical insights into the alienation of *parole* but rejects the corollary that such alienation can be overcome only by fully accepting the purgatorial necessity of speaking in order to dissolve, painfully, the very self-images that subtend one's speech. He would rather abandon *parole* altogether. He thus shows little interest (unlike, for instance, Jürgen Habermas) in harnessing the discoveries of psychoanalysis to explain, and correct, the ways in which communication is distorted in an alienated society.

Something of the complexity of Barthes's view of speech, the way it mixes idiosyncratic emotional investments with more objectively theoretical concerns, can be gauged from one of his most important essays on the opposition between speech and writing as social phenomena: 'Écrivains, intellectuels, professeurs'. In the course of this essay, first published in *Tel Quel* in 1971 (the same year as 'La Paix culturelle') and now in *Le Bruissement de la langue*, Barthes tackles the problem in a digressive rather than systematic way, but makes several suggestive points. His ideas spring from the notion that teaching and the spoken word (*la parole*) are essentially linked: from this uncontroversial notion he draws far-reaching consequences.

The teacher is on the side of *parole*; the writer is on the side of *écriture*; and the intellectual is half-way between them, a teacher turning into a writer, producing a *parole* which is then published. For Barthes, the writer has an entirely different status from the other two: 'l'écriture commence là où la parole devient *impossible*'.[24]

What is the nature of *parole*? It is irreversible: one can correct it only by adding more spoken words.[25] Psychoanalysis capitalizes on this (the Freudian slip and the subject's attempts to explain it), whereas Barthes views it almost entirely negatively. He further sees *parole* as being constrained by its need for clarity, and, from the fact that ambiguity is foreclosed to it, deduces that '*toute parole est du côté de la Loi*'.[26]

---

[24] *BL*, 345.   [25] Ibid. 345–6.   [26] Ibid. 346.

Parole is also limited by two natural features: breath, and sentence structure. The speaker has to pause for breath (and cannot speak too fast or too slowly). This unremarkable fact acquires extra significance if we remember that, for Barthes, breathing is associated with that 'stupid' organ, the lungs. This is clear from his discussions of the art of singing. 'Le Grain de la voix' contrasts the singing of Dietrich Fischer-Dieskau with that of Barthes's own singing-master, Charles Panzéra: the former is condemned (as was Gérard Souzay in 'L'Art vocal bourgeois', one of the *Mythologies*) for singing in too *espressivo*, a way, dwelling on consonants (Souzay sang of a 'tristesse affffreuse', says Barthes) and wringing the maximum emotion from the meaning of every word (the signified).[27] But above all, Fischer-Dieskau's style involves, as it were, too much heavy breathing: 'la diction est dramatique, les césures, les oppressions et les libérations du souffle interviennent comme des séismes de passion'.[28] Musical training concentrates far too much, in Barthes's view, on *le mythe du souffle*.

En avons-nous entendu, des professeurs de chant, prophétiser que l'art du chant était dans la maîtrise, la bonne conduite du souffle! Le souffle, c'est le *pneuma*, c'est l'âme qui se gonfle ou se brise, et tout art exclusif du souffle a chance d'être un art secrètement mystique (d'un mysticisme aplati à la mesure du microsillon de masse). Le poumon, organe stupide (le mou des chats!), se gonfle mais il ne bande pas: c'est dans le gosier, lieu où le métal phonique se durcit et se découpe, c'est dans le masque que la signifiance éclate, fait surgir, non l'âme, mais la jouissance.[29]

Barthes identifies the breath with the soul and, because of his deep-rooted hostility to what he perceives as the idealism of the latter notion, rejects both it and the mass-media mysticism of Fischer-Dieskau's numerous recordings. His own images suggest a far more phallic image: the singing voice begins, not in the lungs, but in the tensed larynx. For Barthes, indeed, Panzéra (the singer one could never hear breathing) is a better artist because he allows the words of the song to be clear without being sentimentally expressive: he is content to let *signifiance*, the effect of meaning in which the signified is held at a distance rather than being foregrounded, arise from the friction between the phonetic raw material of language on the one hand, and music on the other. 'Il faut que le chant parle, ou mieux encore, *écrive*.' Where Fischer-Dieskau's caterwauling runs the risk of

---

[27] *My*, 169.   [28] *OO*, 239.   [29] Ibid. 239–40.

saying something (being too expressive and meaningful) and thus reinforcing the stereotypes of an aesthetic which recognizes only 'ce qui, dans la musique, *peut être dit*',[30] Barthes praises the discretion of Panzéra for not imposing his music, just as he values the death of Mélisande, in Debussy's *Pelléas et Mélisande*, because 'Mélisande meurt *sans bruit*'.[31] Singing should be not speech, but writing.

This brings us back to the quandaries of *parole* in 'Écrivains, intellectuels, professeurs'. *Parole* is still too much determined by breath (and thus by soul) to be writing. It is also constrained by sentence structure. Barthes's attitude to the sentence is complex. In 'La Guerre des langages' he suggests that there is a direct link between the sentence and power: a sentence is a closed structure whose very closure makes it a potential instrument of power: 'il y a une maîtrise de la phrase qui est très proche d'un pouvoir: être fort, c'est *d'abord* finir ses phrases'.[32] Or, as he states in 'Écrivains, intellectuels, professeurs': 'la phrase nette est bien une sentence, *sententia*, une parole pénale'.[33] *Le Plaisir du texte* has a section called 'Phrase' which cites Julia Kristeva to this effect: 'Toute activité idéologique se présente sous la forme d'énoncés compositionnellement achevés', and then adds Barthes's own vice versa, suggesting that any closed *énoncé* runs the risk of being ideological. Teachers and politicans strive to finish their sentences, the latter because to stumble, hesitate, or trail off during an interview is perceived as a signifier of dishonesty or incompetence.[34]

None the less, that is not the only thing Barthes says about the sentence. For we need to remember his own thousands and thousands of sentences, all, whatever their degree of ellipsis and parataxis, 'compositionally complete' and closed. Furthermore, in 'Phrase' it rapidly becomes clear that Barthes is applying double standards. The sentence is a boundary between speech and writing, and his evaluations of the sentence veer according to whether he identifies it as a mode of speech, or a mode of writing. Thus he is suspicious of the spoken sentence partly because he thinks that to speak in sentences is to transfer, without thinking, the norms of the written language to the realm of the spoken. And the spoken as such is *not* dominated by the need to finish one's sentences. Dozing in a bar, he becomes aware of the 'flux' of language around him, in which he can detect no sentence:

---

[30] *OO*, 241. [31] Ibid. 243. [32] *BL*, 130.
[33] Ibid. 346. [34] *PlT*, 81.

this flux—and the only loosely sentential nature of spoken language, which, he suggests, ought to have its own grammar—is something in which he rejoices.[35] He also enjoys sentences because their construction can be treated as a game—but here he is already starting to think of the sentence as something written rather than spoken.[36] And he decides that the writer is a *Pense-Phrase*, citing the example of Valéry, who claimed that we think not in words but in sentences. (It should be remembered, at this juncture of speech and writing, that both Valéry and Barthes were extremely interested in rhetoric, which is a codification of *parole* but one dominated by the laws of written grammar.)[37] A *Pense-Phrase*, says Barthes, is 'pas tout à fait un penseur, et pas tout à fait un phraseur'. The writer is thus once again lodged in the interstices between the philosopher (who deals in concepts) and the *phraseur*, the empty-headed phrase-monger of beautiful but vacuous sentences. In short, because Barthes thinks that writing is already, potentially at least, ludic and ironic in ways denied to speech, he comes out with a basically four-tiered evaluation of the sentence.

1. The avant-garde work can experiment on the borders of speech and writing: like Céline or Queneau or, more recently, Sollers, it can mimic the unfinished, non-sentential nature of speech, the capacities of speech for verbal and phonetic inventiveness, especially when this leaves a trace on the written language into which it is transcribed (Queneau's 'phonetic' spellings mark the trace of the spoken in the written); it can also mimic the flux of speech, always being broken off and begun in a different place. Barthes welcomes these experiments in letting the forces of speech disrupt the sentences of writing.

2. The writer in general can take pleasure in constructing sentences, as Barthes himself does. But this more classical approach runs the risk of sounding sententious and authoritarian. (Barthes notes this is so in his own case, analysing the *clausules*, the polemically very effective final sentences that conclude some of the *Mythologies*[38] and deciding on the basis of other stylistic evidence taken from his own work that—in tones of mock horror—'je suis

[35] *PlT*, 79.
[36] Ibid. 81–2.
[37] On rhetoric, see 'L'Ancienne Rhétorique', in *AS* 85–164: the art of the *disputatio* as an explicit codification of the potentially neurotic aggression of public debate is described on 112–14: see also Patrick O'Donovan, 'The Place of Rhetoric', *Paragraph*, 11 (1988), 227–48.
[38] *RB*, 60.

du côté de la structure, de la phrase, du texte phrasé ... *j'écris classique*.[39] Barthes therefore realizes that there is necessarily something assertive about such writing and that ultimately, whatever stylistic ploys he may resort to, nothing within its structures can destabilize this assertiveness. He therefore decides that he will have to rely on the reader to ironize the text, reading it on as many different levels as possible. The Barthesian sentence is therefore a *don d'amour* to the reader, but one that is meant as discretely as possible: the reader is required to keep it at a distance if it is to lose its potentially magisterial authority.

3. The speaker can produce sentences provided that their sentential nature is codified. Barthes himself (as teacher, lecturer, and interviewee) speaks like a writer: other speakers can resort to rhetoric, but only on condition that this rhetoric constantly signals itself as a constructed code, not as something natural. This is dangerous territory and the risks of ideological imposture are far greater than in writing: the distinction between a *Pense-Phrase* holding forth at a conference and a politician being interviewed, both of them remorselessly finishing their sentences, is not always very evident. (Barthes knows that in these situations, clarity is at a premium, but he insists on that clarity being almost caricatural—anything rather than the pretence that to speak in sentences is natural.)

4. The speaker generally does not speak in sentences, and Barthes thinks that this non-sentential speech has its own merits, though again, he assumes that not to finish sentences is automatically to avoid the risk of power. The menacing 'Quos ego ...' (roughly: 'Why, I'm going to ...') of Neptune in the *Aeneid* (cited by Flaubert in the opening pages of *Madame Bovary* and, frequently, by Barthes as in the preface to *Fragments d'un discours amoureux*),[40] is a counter-example: a very powerful no-sentence. At an even lower level, Barthes enjoys 'le bruissement de la langue', that rustle of language he detects in the criss-cross of conversation in a bar, where sentences are unfinished and aggression is defused. There is a kind of spontaneous naturalness about speech of this kind, though Barthes listening to it (rather than partaking in it) does not apply the word, for when he says 'nature' he really means 'culture that is no longer perceived as cultural'. So he hears the meshing of languages in the bar as a 'parole à la fois très culturelle et très sauvage'.[41]

---

[39] *RB*, 96.   [40] *FDA*, 10.   [41] *PlT*, 79.

As on many occasions, Barthes has to exaggerate in order to shake off the weight of the *doxa*.[42] And in any case, what emerges is a constant prejudice in favour of writing (in which sentences are allowed, albeit with qualifications) over speech (in which they are problematic, although again there are borderline cases of acceptability). This prejudice is not really a prejudice at all, but a refusal to accept that speech and writing can ever be translated into each other without remainder.

It is case number 3 above that poses the most problems because of the context in which speech is being forced to operate: the teacher, the politician, are both attempting to say something: their speech should carry authority. And this authority has as much to do with the context as with what they are saying. So even a teacher who does not finish sentences, but demotically hesitates, in order to signify a certain distance from the pedagogue's role, is still seen as just a more 'liberal' authority. Barthes's conclusion, to return to 'Écrivains, intellectuels, professeurs', is grim: 'Rien à faire: le langage, c'est toujours de la puissance; parler, c'est exercer une volonté de pouvoir: dans l'espace de la parole, aucune innocence, aucune sécurité.'[43] Barthes's sensitivity to these effects of power is so great that it debars him from asking whether or not there might be legitimate forms of authority that could find a vehicle in speech, but this theoretical *parti pris*, assimilating all authority to power, is one that affects most of his French contemporaries too (especially Foucault).

None the less, Barthes's honesty about the discomforts of teaching (when his values are all those of a writer) is acutely registered. He compares himself to the analysand talking into the silence of the analyst (his audience): but the result is far from therapeutic. And again, this is because of his hostility to speech. For when writing flows away, he is relieved of his imaginary, but when speech flows away he is still trapped in that imaginary (his words constitute an image of him in the audience's mind, an image which he reads back in a distorted form): in the latter case, the imaginary is merely more insecure—full of holes, says Barthes: 'il suffit que je parle, il suffit que ma parole coule, pour qu'elle s'écoule'.[44] The section 'Une odeur de parole' of

---

[42] 'In psycho-analysis nothing is true except the exaggerations', Theodor Adorno, *Minima Moralia: Reflections from Damaged Life*, trans. E. F. N. Jephcott (London, 1974), 49.
[43] *BL*, 347.
[44] Ibid. 349.

'Écrivains, intellectuels, professeurs' sets out the problem in vivid terms.

> Une fois qu'on a fini de parler, commence le vertige de l'image: on exalte ou on regrette ce qu'on a dit, la façon dont on l'a dit, on *s'imagine* (on se retourne en image); la parole est sujette à rémanence, elle *sent*.
>
> L'écriture ne sent pas: produite (ayant accompli son procès de production), elle *tombe*, non à la façon d'un soufflé qui s'affaisse, mais d'une météorite qui disparaît; elle va *voyager* loin de mon corps et pourtant elle n'en est pas un morceau détaché retenu narcissiquement, comme l'est la parole; sa disparition n'est pas déceptive; elle passe, elle traverse, c'est tout.[45]

These remarks are characteristic of the way Barthes negotiates the speech/writing opposition. First, in a synaesthetic move that governs many of his writings, he sees 'speech' as instantly convertible into 'image'—and, in this case, one that 'smells'. Writing, far more nobly, is silent, visible only as a flash in the sky (a meteorite), and odourless. A key image is that of speech as a *soufflé* collapsing once it has been uttered: a *soufflé*, or that into which too much *souffle* (too much soul) has been pumped. Speech is a fetish in that Barthes invests his identity in it, wants to hold it close to himself: writing (and any identity it may imaginarily shelter) can be let go. So great is Barthes's dislike of speech that he detects its smell even in the passage in which he is discussing it: not even writing can altogether liquidate the speech to which it is forced to refer, and Barthes concludes that 'dans cette écriture-ci, *il y a encore du référent*, et c'est lui qui *sent* à mes propres narines'.[46] By occupying the position of the referent in *this* passage, speech comes to be identified with *all* referents: this legerdemain is again characteristically Barthesian, in that he wishes to release writing from its obligation to refer to anything real.

Parole is thus inseparable from a psychoanalytic transference relationship in that it automatically sets up currents of power (although the analysand, the one who speaks, is in fact the traditional figure of authority, the teacher, which complicates matters); but it is a transference relationship that leads to no cure. None the less, Barthes ends his essay by suggesting ways in which the power of the spoken word can be muted: *la parole paisible*—a teaching relationship without polemics or aggression—is his recommendation, and it should pro-

---

[45] *BL*, 358.   [46] Ibid. 359.

duce 'une certaine dépropriation de la parole (proche dès lors de l'écriture) . . . ou encore *une certaine généralisation du sujet*'.[47]

A later paper, 'Au séminaire', takes up this theme: what is curious is that this seminar (Barthes's seminar at the École pratique de Hautes Études) seems curiously silent. (It is significant that when Barthes dedicates *S/Z* to the participants in his seminar, he calls it a 'texte qui s'est écrit selon leur écoute'—no mention of any discussions.) He himself acts as *un régisseur*, setting out the rules of the game rather than the laws of any scientific discourse, and what he says is less important than the way it enables a horizontal transference (between students, rather than between each individual student and the teacher) to be established: all this is closer to the *texte* than to any *parole*.[48] Rather than any traditional *enseignement*, the transmission of know-ledge from teacher to pupil (a practice which Barthes seems to imagine as the worst Gradgrindery), he sees the seminar as a place for *apprentissage* and *maternage*. In apprenticeship, the teacher becomes a practitioner and the pupil watches in order to learn how to do the same thing. This is both theatrical and silent:

le 'maître' . . . ne parle pas, ou du moins il ne tient pas de discours; son propos est purement déictique: 'Ici, dit-il, je fais *ceci* pour éviter *cela* . . .' Une compétence se transmet silencieusement, un spectacle se monte (celui d'un faire), dans lequel l'apprenti, passant la rampe, s'introduit peu à peu.[49]

'To point in silence' is one of Barthes's most insistent metaphors for the text. And in 'mothering', Barthes picks up—perhaps from the psychoanalyst Winnicott, a frequent reference in his late works—the idea that the mother (again a non-discursive and non-authoritarian figure) calls to the child who learns to work by responding to her call. It must be remembered that Barthes is referring to a very special kind of seminar: his own, in which there is no knowledge to transmit, since the object of enquiry is actually a practice (the *texte*) which comes into being in the seminar itself.

Barthes's attempts to revise our usual images of the teaching relationship are suggestive. For one thing, they do not merely collapse distinctions: there is still a need for the role of the teacher: Barthes was suspicious of the formless anarchy that was sometimes the product of experiments in teaching in the post-1968 years. His one extended discussion of 1968, 'L'Écriture de l'événement', detects fragments of

---

[47] *BL*, 367.   [48] Ibid. 369–71.   [49] Ibid. 374.

écriture in some of the practices (new modes of distribution of ideas—
inventive graffiti, parodic pamphlets) of the student movement, but is
suspicious of the primacy given to *parole* as supposedly spontaneous
and natural (an ideological option best summed up in the slogan 'sous
les pavés, la plage'): what the students should have been questioning
was not *écriture* so much as the *parole imprimée* of the bourgeoisie.[50] So
when, in 'Au séminaire', Barthes refers to *le maître* he says that such a
model is oriental, that of the Zen master, for instance, whose replies
to the pupil's questions are frequently absurd or oblique, and whose
own discourse is meant as a way of initiation that will lead beyond
itself—this time very much *like* Wittgenstein's ladder. (In *Sade,
Fourier, Loyola* Barthes makes a very different point: in Sade's world,
it is the masters who speak and the victims who are forced to be
speechless—or to scream.[51] But Barthes is not particularly interested
in exploiting this fact so as to denounce Sade as the author of a
'repressive' (or 'sadistic') work: rather, he ultimately decides that when
Sade's characters interact, they do so in near silence, like a well-oiled
machine.[52] In other words, by dismissing the real power relations as
merely a question of who has access to *parole*, Barthes can depict
Sade's world as one of writing, and his model of the seminar mimics
this feature.)

The image of the imperturbable and ironic oriental master is also,
despite Barthes's hatred of Socrates as the one who always had to
have the last word, Socratic, if we accept Socrates's discourse as
in intention maieutic. Socrates was, it is true, no mother, only a
midwife's son. But, despite never committing his ideas to the imperfect
medium of the written word, he may indeed have been a Barthesian
writer.

This raises another question: in Barthes, the already unstable
speech/writing opposition cuts across another, that of gender (mas-
culine/feminine). Since Barthes suggest *maternage* (silent or at least
non-discursive mothering) as a crucial role for the teacher, does he
see *parole* as masculine? The answer is complex. On the one hand,
there is an immediate equation: *parole* is linked with power and the
signified, and these in turn with 'the paternal'. For instance, Barthes
cites with approval one of the research students contributing to the
1972 special issue of *Communications* devoted to the work of *Jeunes
chercheurs*: 'Peut-être notre travail ne consiste-t-il qu'à repérer des

---

[50] *BL*, 180.   [51] *SFL*, 36, 147.   [52] Ibid. 169–70.

lambeaux d'*écriture* pris dans une *parole* dont le Père reste le garant.'[53] And in 'Au séminaire' he identifies the Father as the one who says things (usually, perhaps, if we remember Lacan, what the Father says is 'non!'): 'le Père, c'est le Parleur: celui qui tient des discours hors du faire, coupés de toute production; le Père, c'est l'Homme aux énoncés', and to deprive the Father of this authority, we have to see him as the subject of *énonciation* (of language still springing from a source deeper than the speech/writing opposition).[54] But this vision is complicated by a fact of Barthes's biography on which he insists: it was his grandmothers (not his taciturn grandfathers) who spoke. 'Dans ces deux grand-familles, le discours était aux femmes.'[55] Furthermore, his father was killed at sea while he was only 11 months old. 'Par le relais maternel, sa mémoire, jamais oppressive, ne faisait qu'effleurer l'enfance, d'une gratification *presque silencieuse*.'[56] In the fragment 'Au tableau noir' he remembers how one of his teachers at Louis-le-Grand would write up Barthes's father's name on the blackboard—as 'one of the fallen'—only to wipe it off: so much for the *Nom du Père*.[57] Barthes therefore associates *his* father (and grandfathers) with silence. And his mother and grandmothers? With the gentle gossip, the discursive matriarchy, of the French provinces. But here the binary opposition starts to fall apart: although Barthes does, in *La Chambre claire*, praise his mother for her discretion ('elle ne me fit jamais, de toute notre vie commune, une seule "observation"'),[58] he does not show any hostility to the feminine language (what he calls, in an important fragment of *Barthes par lui-même*, *la langue maternelle* (*la langue des femmes* that surrounded him as a child)).[59] So while *parole* = *Père* (the symbolic Father of culture and power), it is not true that Barthes sees his own father in this light: on the symbolic level, the father speaks incessantly; on a biographical level, the father is silent. Furthermore, although on a biographical level the matriarchate is talkative, so that *parole* is feminine, this is not allowed to extend into the symbolic, where *parole* is, as we have seen, masculine. And in any case, apart from *Sur Racine* and *S/Z* where Barthes constantly shows that the biologically female characters tend to be in positions of symbolic power, and are thus symbolically masculine, he does not seem to be particularly interested in gender as such (that is, in the real

---

[53] *BL*, 101, my emphasis.
[54] Ibid. 377.
[55] *RB*, 14–16.
[56] Ibid. 19, my emphasis.
[57] Ibid. 49.
[58] *CC*, 109.
[59] *RB*, 119.

divisions of power and labour in his society—despite a generally
'progessive' attitude demonstrated most clearly in *Mythologies*). Or,
more precisely, he is interested in revising stereotypes of gender, but
his way of doing that is to avoid, in general, the binary opposition
masculine/feminine in favour of the opposition father/mother. And
since his own mother of practical necessity played both roles for him,
this opposition fails to work on a personal level: it only works when
aufgehoben—cancelled, raised, and preserved—into the symbolic,
where the paternal tends to be bad and the maternal good. His very
last essay, on Stendhal's *La Chartreuse de Parme*, repeats this opposition, albeit as one between *le Père* (especially the father of the hero,
Fabrice del Dongo, but all the other symbolic fathers too, such as the
repressive Austrian regime) and *les Femmes* (as objects of male desire
but also as maternal figures, if we remember the duchesse de
Sanseverina).[60] Even here, it is complicated by another element in
Barthes's own thematic obsessions: his habit of picturing the liberated
text as a *dissémination*, the dispersal of seeds. This can be done very
delicately: relying on images taken from the materialist authors he
admires, he frequently sees writing as a process of fission: the resultant
atoms enter 'la circulation générale des semences'.[61] Likewise, the
biographical details (*biographèmes*) of his own life might one day
'voyager hors de tout destin et venir toucher, à la façon des atomes
épicuriens, quelque corps futur, promis à la même dispersion'.[62] But
it is striking that in these last images, seeds seem merely to meet other
seeds of the same kind: there is no image of fertilization or gestation—
Barthes countering another *doxa*, perhaps.

Even this needs to be qualified, for Barthes frequently sees hearing
(the hearing of the 'parole') as both receptively passive and as
subversively active (hearing what was *not* said—'c'est dans l'écoute
qu'est la faille de la Loi').[63] Masculine *parole* must not fall on stony
ground but into receptive ears, where its authority may be dissolved.
All of which suggests that Barthes's images of gender do not add up
to any one paradigm, and that when they encounter the speech/
writing opposition, no term remains stable for very long.

Barthes's revision of the images we associate with writers, intellectuals, and teachers is thus performed under the constant pressure of
his distancing of the powers of the spoken word in favour of writing.
At crucial moments, he uses this question to make an evaluative

---

[60] *BL*, 342.   [61] *GV*, 339.
[62] *SFL*, 14.   [63] *BL*, 373.

manœuvre, as when he saves the speech of the teaching relationship by deciding that it is really a form of writing, or condemns certain types of intellectual writing as being still too full of speech. In this re-evaluation, the binary opposition speech/writing is drifted out of: there can be speech in writing (if that writing is too fixated on the signified, not self-reflexive enough, or too implicated in the mechanisms of power) just as certain kinds of speech can be turned into a form of writing. Science—especially 'bourgeois science'—speaks where it should write.[64] The common enlightenment model for authentic communication—the dialogue—is dismissed as unworkable since it cannot overcome the distorting effects of desire and power (the transference): one needs rather 'une descente profonde, patiente et souvent détournée, dans le labyrinthe du sens'.[65] Indeed, no act of speech, not even saying 'Je t'aime', is free from these effects: it means imposing yourself on the 'other': it is an implicit *demande d'amour*, and Barthes suggests that the only remedy would be for two people to utter this phrase to each other *simultaneously* thus producing a *discours jubilatoire* that seems to consist in the abolition of the nefarious effects of *parole*.[66] Otherwise, dialogue risks degenerating into *potin* (gossip) or into a *scène*. Barthes's animadversions against these forms of *parole* are many and varied, notably in *Fragments d'un discours amoureux* in which gossip is seen as particularly baleful in its reduction to the third person (the absent *il/elle*) of a person who should ideally—thinks the lover—be only ever an address (a *tu*) and not a referent. 'Le troisième pronom est un pronom méchant: c'est le pronom de la non-personne, il absente, il annule . . . Pour moi, l'autre ne saurait être un *référent*: tu n'es jamais que toi, je ne veux pas que l'Autre parle de toi.'[67] Here *l'Autre* is the symbolic Other, the cultural demand that breaks in on the love relationship and constantly threatens to evict it from its imaginary paradise (the two subjects glued to each other—to their images of each other): it is the Other, for instance, that reduces every relationship in its uniqueness to a mere example of the banal generalities of love, and is eager for 'love stories'—narratives of seduction and loss—because it cannot face the intensities associated with the anarchic intensities of love, with its randomly fluctuating emotions of exaltation and anguish. It is Barthes's own homage to the status of the loved one that while he is prepared to represent the

[64] *BL*, 15, 198.   [65] Ibid. 27.
[66] *RB*, 116.   [67] *FDA*, 219.

speech of the lover (albeit an inner and fragmented speech), the loved one is perfect because silent (again, no 'dialogue'—or rather, any dialogues that can be represented in this book tend to be low points in the love relationship—quarrels brewing, petty jealousies being expressed). Barthes's portrait of the lover from within shows us 'une place de parole: la place de quelqu'un qui parle en lui-meme, amoureusement, face à l'autre (l'objet aimé), qui ne parle pas'.[68] It is clear that, however much Barthes may at times vent his sarcasm on what he detects as a potent myth (that of silence as being above speech—'la grande intelligence silencieuse, lourde d'expérience et de mutisme',[69] he wants the loved one at least to be speechless, the object of a certain contemplation (of a *theoria*, not a theory—Barthes's last works increasingly, and very beautifully, incorporate a number of motifs from Plato and Neoplatonic mysticism). The text, too, when it is not being figured as a praxis offered for collaborative re-creation by the reader, is something to be loved, in reading—an object of contemplation. Barthes finds that there are certain texts that he loves so much that he cannot talk about them: he refuses to analyse them, to break apart the imaginary wholeness and perfection they have for him—thus he extols *War and Peace*, but only to say that he would like to rewrite it, word for word. There are shades here of Bouvard and Pécuchet devotedly copying the scripts of culture, and also of Pierre Menard rewriting *Don Quixote*. But Barthes's point is that metalanguage (the language of theory and criticism) misses something if it is always in the mode of 'gossip' (positioning the text as a referent—an *il/elle*—to be discussed behind the text's back). The reader is to be distinguished, according to *Critique et vérité*, from the critic who is ultimately condemned to speech, even when writing, having to adopt 'un certain "ton"': 'seule la lecture aime l'œuvre, entretient avec elle un rapport de désir. Lire, c'est désirer l'œuvre, c'est vouloir être l'œuvre, c'est refuser de doubler l'œuvre en dehors de toute autre parole que la parole même de l'œuvre.'[70] The reader is thus like the lover, 'qui parle en lui-même, amoureusement, face à l'autre (l'objet aimé), qui ne parle pas'. And this presumably implies that the act of reading is a 'dis-cursus', an interior monologue consisting of *bouffées de langage* that it is difficult to synthesize or theorize (or even understand).[71] Barthes's intuitions here are supported by reader-

[68] *FDA*, 7.   [69] *BL*, 347.
[70] *CV*, 78–9.   [71] *FDA*, 9.

response theories whose attempts to formalize what happens in reading become so complex that order and chaos are difficult to tell apart—and such theories find it difficult to cope with the sheer contingency of reading, the fact that it is interrupted and resumed in accordance with constraints that are largely independent of what is being read. Barthes's own honesty about this aleatory quality of reading is registered in many ways, as when he admits to skipping passages in Proust—but never the same ones twice.[72] (Italo Calvino has written a novel, *If on a Winter's Night a Traveller*, which consists in all the ways the reading of a book—even a 'loved' book—can be interrupted.)

Although the *Fragments* are in many ways a catalogue of the servitudes of speech in a relationship which ought to be liberated from them, writing is, for once, not offered as any solution. Even writing is too general to capture the singularity of the other: when offered as a *don d'amour* (as when a writer dedicates a book to a loved person), writing smothers the other in its indifference to any addressee, or rather in the potential plurality of its address.[73] Writing is thus not the positive opposite to the negative of speech as far as the love relationship goes, since Barthes concludes again that to write is in a sense to exclude such love: 'ces choses que je vais écrire ne me feront jamais aimer de qui j'aime.'[74] This distance is the essence of writing, as he had already noted in the last of the *Essais critiques*.[75]

So the *Fragments* stage a problem that frequently affects Barthes's later texts. In the presence of something supremely valuable, he refuses to resort to metalanguage. And yet he equally refuses (or is not yet capable) of writing what he loves in any non-metalinguistic way (such as the Fiction he postulates in one of his 1978 lectures, 'Longtemps, je me suis couché de bonne heure').[76] He is thus condemned to discussing what he loves (what he values as supremely real) *from within speech but against speech*. The result of this is a *parole* on the edge of audibility, but one that cannot quite cross over into the eloquent silence of writing. (Here we have another version of the speaker stranded on Mount Pisgah, looking out over the Promised Land of writing.)

This theoretical *parole* is indeed frequently summed up as a single word. For instance, deciding that the loved one cannot be described

---

(so no adjectives), cannot be deciphered or understood (so no hermeneutic), Barthes resorts to the word *tel*—the loved one 'just is', a collection of perfections that can be pointed to (as the child—the *infans*, without speech—points to something it wants) but not named. 'Et ce qui ressemblerait le mieux à l'être aimé *tel qu'il est*, ce serait le Texte, sur lequel je ne puis apposer aucun adjectif: dont je jouis sans avoir à le déchiffrer.'[77] So Barthes can also point to the *sens obtus*, the enigmatic point of subjective meaning in an Eisenstein still, or its near correlative, the *punctum* of the photograph, and talk *around* these points while never being able to 'speak them' as such, since they resist—he allows them to resist—metalinguistic expansion. (I will be returning to this theme in Chapter 6.) It is worth emphasizing that Barthes's later writing is prepared to entertain a range of references that are surprising given his basically 'enlightened' stance—to Kierkegaard, to the mystics (Angelus Silesius, Ruysbroek, Meister Eckhart), and to Zen Buddhism. In every case, what is important about these reference points is that they offer the promise of an immediate sense of reality (that is, one that is not mediated by the generalities of language as speech). But Barthes is well aware of the dangers of this promise: to operate on the very edge of discourse is to be close to madness—like the mad son in Dreyer's film *Ordet*, whose prophetic speech is a strained rejection of the human discourse around him (but is still on behalf of that humanity—only *he* says the word that raises the dead woman), or like Kierkegaard's Abraham, an increasingly important figure, cited for instance in Barthes's preface to Chateaubriand's *Vie de Rancé*.[78] In this relatively early preface (1965) Barthes admires Abraham who represents the absolutely individual and so is 'condamné à ne pas parler', but notes that the writer cannot sabotage discourse in this way, since to write is to attempt to mediate an irreducible existence in the general categories of language.[79] (It is in this essay that Barthes's views on anacoluthon as a figure of ellipsis— of *silently* leaping from one *énoncé* to the next—are developed, though some of his examples are less of anacoluthon as a failure of grammatical co-ordination than of a more general parataxis.) But the need to safeguard that irreducibility becomes much more acute in Barthes's last decade, hence his strategy of speaking against speech, and on behalf of writing, but from within speech (since writing would already have its own silence and would not need defending).

[77] *FDA*, 261–3.   [78] *NEC*, 106–20, and *BL*, 402.
[79] *NEC*, 119.

Sometimes this increasing 'voicelessness' in Barthes is explicit. His own way of speaking is evoked with affection and admiration by Edgar Morin in his foreword to *Le Texte et l'image*, a catalogue of visual images and Barthes's writings on them: Morin notes how 'il était, en parole, l'écrivain'.[80] But a different preface (that by Marshall Blonsky to his collection of semiotic essays, *On Signs*) gives a very different picture of Barthes's spoken discourse as being, for all the eloquence of his material (the paper 'Proust and Me'), on the edge of aphasia, strewn with sighs and frequently punctuated with a *moriendo* 'n'est-ce pas?' Even at the Colloque de Cerisy, Barthes's voice was the object of comment—too low, complained Robbe-Grillet.[81] This same colloquium sees Barthes reflecting on the status of writing *vis-à-vis* speech: writing is almost impossible to define (metalinguistically—in speech): 'L'écriture ne dit pas rien, elle ne dit pas quelque chose et elle ne dit pas tout'.[82] And he continues:

On est là dans une région qu'on peut qualifier provisoirement d'impossible; je dirais volontiers que l'écriture, c'est de l'ordre du dire 'presque quelque chose', et que si c'est de l'ordre du 'presque quelque chose', ça entraîne vers une épistémologie tout à fait nouvelle, qui se cherche peut-être, à partir de régions plutôt nietzschéennes: une sémiologie ou une textologie, si on peut dire, des intensités et non pas des messages, le 'presque' renvoyant à un différentiel d'intensités et non pas à un différentiel de messages.[83]

And he continues to develop this idea of the *dire 'presque quelque chose'* quite seriously, especially when he claims that his own semiology has taken insufficient notice of the differential of intensities that he locates in the *presque*, the writing just avoiding relapsing into speech, the signifier just floating above the signified.[84]

One other way in which Barthes figures writing from within his own speech (his own discursive theoretical analyses) is as a pointing in silence. The *numen* of Napoleon crossing another frontier (the Alps, in David's painting), the silent authority with which he points towards Italy, is one emblem of this figure that seems to have fascinated Barthes. He also writes of *numen* as the *geste suspendu* with which God silently creates meaning, as in 'Les Planches de l'*Encyclopédie*'.[85] Zeus nods (Greek *nueien*, to nod) and all Olympus trembles, though since Barthes often sees *numen* as a kind of pointing, his evocations of it are

---

[80] *Le Texte et l'image* (1988), 8.   [81] *C*, 262.
[82] Ibid. 21.   [83] Ibid. 21–2.
[84] Ibid. 30.   [85] *NEC*, 103.

also evocative of the movement with which Michelangelo's creator points to, and infuses life into, Adam. Another such emblem is taken from the Resnais film, *L'Année dernière à Marienbad*, scripted by Robbe-Grillet. Barthes decides that the statue of Charles III and his wife can stand as an allegory of Robbe-Grillet's entire work:

admirable symbole d'ailleurs, non seulement parce que la statue elle-même est inductrice de sens divers, incertains, et cependant nommés (*c'est vous, c'est moi, ce sont des dieux antiques, Hélène, Agamemnon*, etc.), mais encore parce que le prince et son épouse y désignent du doigt d'une façon certaine un objet incertain (situé dans la fable? dans le jardin? dans la salle?): ceci, disent-ils. Mais quoi, *ceci?* Toute la littérature est peut-être dans cet anaphorique léger qui tout à la fois désigne et se tait.[86]

In a similar way, Barthes in his last years wanted to write, showing and pointing, rather than to speak. He continued, however, to speak about this future writing—since he never produced the Fiction he promised, his last writings are produced by a speech turning against itself, but not quite falling silent. In my final chapter, I want to examine some of the ways this final trend is also the logical conclusion to a fascination with everything that, within theory, seems to resist theory, as its trauma.

[86] *EC*, 205.

6

THE TRAUMA

'Je m'intéresse au langage parce qu'il me blesse ou me séduit.[1] Barthes goes on to ask what historical determinants there may be behind this obsessive relation to language as a source of intensities either seductive or wounding. He suggests that while pleasure depends on the ego feeling at home in culture, *jouissance* radically challenges our images of ego and culture: so that while pleasure can perhaps be explained in historical and sociological terms, *jouissance*, as something 'asocial', seems to lie beyond such mediations.[2] At the same time, Barthes is reluctant to concede that even *jouissance* is entirely immediate in this way, and a later section insists that since the body and its affirmations or refusals is ultimately a fully historical entity, the *jouissance* of the body is also historical: 'ce corps de jouissance est aussi *mon sujet historique*'.[3]

Jouissance is thus something of a stumbling-block—Barthes attempts to talk about it in a variety of ways in *Le Plaisir du texte* and elsewhere, but it does not stay conceptually or even metaphorically still. It is an ambiguous phenomenon—sometimes an experience of intense subjective pleasure, sometimes closer to fear; at times immediate and almost mystical, at others quite susceptible to historical and causal analysis. This ambiguity places *jouissance* in a strange space— beyond pleasure and pain. And Barthes's hesitations (or subtleties) in seeing it as historical or (more often) transhistorical, suggests that there may be a link between its wounding and seductive force and a reality that is both historical (timebound) and ecstatic (cutting through time). As Barthes's texts return again and again to this question of the seductive wound. I have subsumed this theme under the general rubric of what is, for psychoanalysis, the seductive wound *par excellence*: the trauma. My discussion therefore requires a short presentation of some of the main features of this theory of the trauma.

[1] *PlT*, 62.
[2] Ibid. 62–3.
[3] Ibid. 98–9.

THE THEORY OF THE TRAUMA: FREUD AND LACAN

In September 1897 Freud announced to Fliess that he no longer believed in his 'neurotica', his first major theory of the origins of the psychoneuroses.[4] This theory had attempted to explain the cases of hysteria he had been treating by reference to real or attempted sexual seduction in early childhood. This original 'primal scene' was supposed to have unleashed a trauma in the patient's mind. Freud took the term 'trauma' (originally the Greek word for 'wound') from physiology, where it referred in general to a violent irruption into the body from outside. To this meaning, he added an essential economic (or quantitative) sense: a trauma is an event experienced with such intensity that the mind cannot defuse it. It disturbs what Freud called 'the principle of constancy', by which the mind attempts to maintain an equilibrium by disseminating energy input through its associative channels.

I shall not here rehearse the sequence of events which led Freud to jettison his earliest theory of the aetiology of hysteria and to replace it with a more refined one, in which, however, trauma still played a crucial role.[5] I do, however, want to pick out certain features of the trauma, as theorized by Freud and Lacan, which I shall use to cast light on a complex of ideas and problems running through Barthes's work.

One important element in Freud's theorization of the trauma lies in his indefatigable attempts to make of it a *real* basis for his increasingly complex models of the mind. The hysterics he treated, were, as he soon realized, remarkably unreliable in the comments, associations, and memories they offered him. What truth lay behind their apparent deception? He devoted much of his analytic acuity to disinterring from the hysteric's mind the memory of an original, datable event that could be seen as the cause of the illness. The hysteric would seem to oblige, coming up with memory after memory of past insults and humiliations. But the more the analysis progressed, the less could any of these events be taken as a bedrock. Each one seemed to be screening

---

[4] Letter 69 (21 Sept. 1897), in *The Origins of Psychoanalysis; Letters of Wilhelm Fliess, Drafts and Notes, 1887–1902*, ed. Marie Bonaparte, Anna Freud, and Ernst Kris, trans. Eris Mosbacher and James Strachey (London, 1954), 216.

[5] This story can be followed in Freud's letters and papers collected in *Origins of Psychoanalysis*.

something that lay even further back in the patient's life. The trauma receded into the past.

These two factors—time and fantasy—came to dominate the theory of the trauma as Freud elaborated it at the turn of the century. Put schematically, the way traumatic illnesses arise is this. Early in the patient's life, an event takes place to which Freud gives the name 'primal scene' or 'scene of seduction': the patient, as a child, either witnesses or is subjected to an act that is sexual in nature. But this event is as yet meaningless: the child, not yet having crossed into puberty, does not experience any sexual fear or desire. The memory of this first event is preserved—Freud's theory does not make it entirely clear where: neither in the conscious nor the unconscious mind, but in a preconscious state, isolated from the rest of the mind like a 'foreign body'.[6] Much later, after puberty has begun, a second event occurs which may well be completely innocuous, but which none-the-less recalls, often on the basis of the merest similarity, the first. The difference is that this time, the first event is suddenly flooded with meaning, since the pubertal child can now experience sexual feelings. The memory of the first event thus retroactively becomes traumatic. Since this process takes the subject by surprise, there is no way of warding off the influx of affect by turning away the attention. The only defence to which the mind can now resort is a pathological one: the memory of the first event is thus repressed.

It is the element of retroactivity (what Freud calls *Nachträglichkeit* and his French commentators the *après-coup* effect) that makes this early Freudian model of psychic development so complex. Lacan was the first to draw attention to the importance and complexity of Freud's notion of *Nachträglichkeit*, and Derrida has demonstrated in detail how it undermines images of psychic self-presence.[7]

---

[6] See Freud and Breuer, 'Preliminary Communication', in *Studies of Hysteria*; *The Pelican Freud Library* ed. Angela Richards (Harmondsworth, 1973–86), iii. 57.

[7] Freud: 'we invariably find that a memory is repressed which has only become a trauma *after the event*. The reason for this state of affairs is the retardation of puberty as compared with the remainder of the individual's development' ('Project for a Scientific Psychology', in *Origins of Psychoanalysis*, 347–445 (413). For an analysis, see Derrida, 'Freud et la scène de l'écriture', in *L'écriture et la différence* (1967), 293–340: the whole essay is of great importance for an understanding of the *après-coup* effect, which, as Derrida suggests, forces us to rethink the whole issue of time and memory in terms of writing. 'Le post-scriptum qui constitue le présent passé comme tel ne se contente pas, comme l'ont peut-être pensé Platon, Hegel et Proust, de le réveiller ou de le révéler dans sa vérité. Il le produit' (317). Jean Laplanche notes that the trauma poses a challenge to any attempt to tell the life story of a subject: 'we never manage to fix the traumatic event historically', so that a Heisenberg-like principle of indeterminacy now

The problems that finding one original trauma posed for Freud led
to an eventual recasting of his entire theory and, concurrently with his
own self-analysis, to the birth of psychoanalysis. The child, he
decided, is already, long before puberty, a sexual creature in thrall to
desire. In the letter to Fliess cited above, Freud notes that 'there is no
"indication of reality" in the unconscious, so that it is impossible to
distinguish between truth and emotionally-charged fiction'.[8]

Thus the psyche follows its own timetable and its own laws, which
are not those of empirical, observable reality. And the trauma straddles
binary oppositions which are fundamental to the way we unreflectingly
tend to categorize experience. It is not one event, but always, at least,
two: it splits time (being neither a 'then' nor a 'now') and meaning
(being neither significant nor nonsensical): it is neither pure fact nor
pure fantasy, it comes both from within the subject (the endogenous
fantasy) and from without (the original scene of seduction, and the
second, possibly quite banal event that recalls it).[9] The trauma disrupts
all forms of self-presence, even when its disastrous effects on the
patient's life set the analyst off in pursuit of origins, events, dates, the
'real'. This disruption and the desire for origins are, as we have seen
in our discussion of scribbling, inseparable from writing, whose
longing for an original empty page or *tabula rasa* actually obstructs it
from ever reaching them. The trauma is, like scribble, a figure of
writing. But what is the nature of this real that seems so important a
feature of the theory of the trauma?

It is Lacan who makes the 'real' a part of his tripartite mapping of
existence, together with the symbolic (the order of language and all
symbolic systems) and the imaginary (the order of images of identity
in self and other). The place of the real is, in this scheme, difficult to
locate, and this is a deliberate ploy on Lacan's part. The real, above
all, is that which disturbs any neat binary oppositions from being
maintained. It is refractory and resistant: as Alan Sheridan puts it, in

---

comes into play: 'in situating the trauma, one cannot appreciate its traumatic impact,
and *vice versa*' (*Life and Death in Psychoanalysis*, trans, Jeffrey Mehlmen (Baltimore,
1976), 41). This principle, as I shall be showing, affects Barthes's attitude to the analysis
of cultural phenomena: their often erratic 'force', the unthought of structuralism,
increasingly becomes the object of his theoretical attentions.

[8] Letter 69, in *Origins of Psychoanalysis*, 216.

[9] Human sexuality is essentially anachronistic, notes Laplanche (*Life and Death in
Psychoanalysis*, 105), and the repressed memory of an apparently external event becomes
an 'internal alien activity' that attacks the subject from within—from 'an isolated and
encysted interior' (43).

his English translation of Lacan's *Séminaire XI*, the imaginary falters before the real, and the symbolic stumbles over it.[10] It must necessarily remain as elusive as what it names. None the less, Lacan continually associates it with the trauma. The real is the 'objet d'angoisse par excellence'.[11] The trauma, as a *frappe* or *Prägung* (a stamping, minting, or embossing—as of a coin or medal), resists integration into the symbolic: 'le réel, ou ce qui est perçu comme tel, est ce qui résiste absolument à la symbolisation'.[12] It acts as a 'fixation imaginaire inassimilable'.[13] As something which cannot cross from the imaginary into the symbolic, it behaves, *vis-à-vis* the symbolic, as a real element, but one difficult to tie down, 'un réel qui se dérobe'.[14] Lacan rewrites the Freudian theory of traumatic events as a story in which the subject always meets the real unexpectedly: the real is a *tuchè* (the Greek word for chance or accident—that which 'befalls' someone); so the real is an encounter, and the trauma is a missed rendezvous in so far as the subject always encounters the object of desire too early or too late.[15] The real as *tuchè* is what lies *behind* the 'automaton', the network of signifiers which works by itself.[16] It lurks in wait for an always unprepared subject: 'La réalité est là en souffrance, là qui attend.'[17]

In primal repression, which Lacan associates with the traumatic constitution of sexuality, a 'primal signifier' forms a traumatic kernel, often constituted as a complex of phonemes, or as a *figure* (what Leclaire calls a 'letter').[18] This repressed signifier not only evades symbolization (it is meaningless by virtue of its isolation: no link can be made between it and another signifier): it also acts as the very kernel of the unconscious, a *noyau primitif* on a deeper level than the

---

[10] See Sheridan's notes on key Lacanian terms in his trans. of Lacan, *The Four Fundamental Concepts of Psychoanalysis* (Harmondsworth, 1979), 280.

[11] *Le Séminaire*, ii. *Le Moi dans la théorie de Freud et dans la technique de la psychanalyse* (1978), 196.

[12] Id., *Le Séminaire*, i. *Les Écrits techniques de Freud* (1975), 80.

[13] Ibid. 312.

[14] Id., *Le Séminaire*, xi. *Les Quatre Concepts fondamentaux de la psychanalyse* (1973), 53.

[15] Ibid. 54–5, 67.

[16] Ibid. 51.

[17] Ibid. 55

[18] *Le Séminaire*, i. 30–1: see also Serge Leclaire, *Psychanalyser: un essai sur l'ordre de l'inconscient et la pratique de la lettre* (1968), where the key element in the unconscious of the subject is a traumatic figural pattern that may be an alphabetical letter (V, W, or M for Freud's 'Wolf Man') or an equally figural (non-lexical) word ('Poordjeli' is the signifier at the root of the desire of Leclaire's patient, Philippe) (124). This latter case is discussed in detail in Jacques Laplanche and Serge Leclaire, 'L'Inconscient: une étude psychanalytique', *Temps Modernes*, 183 (July 1961), 81–129.

later products of repression, those *avatars du refoulement* which, by a process of psychic gravity, it drags down to it.[19] It is a knot of resistance, a central lack of meaning around which the subject's mental life orbits. Questioning the article by his disciples Leclaire and Laplanche on primal repression, Lacan rejects the idea that in analysis all interpretations are possible, and protests: 'Ce n'est pas parce que j'ai dit que l'effet de l'interprétation est d'isoler dans le sujet un cœur, un *kern*, pour s'exprimer comme Freud, de *non-sens*, que l'interprétation est elle-même un non-sens.'[20] Interpretation is a crucial and responsible analytic task: but ultimately it is not the content of that interpretation which counts, but that the limits of any interpretation should be shown: 'ce n'est pas cette signification qui est, pour l'avènement du sujet, essentielle. Ce qui est essentielle, c'est qu'il voie, au-delà de cette signification, à quel signifiant—non-sens, irréductible, traumatique—il est, comme sujet, assujetti.'[21] The trauma is thus real in so far as it is outside meaning. This attempt to centre the mind around an empty sign (ultimately assimilable, as in Lacan's discussion of the 'Wolf-Man' case, to castration) makes Lacan vulnerable to approaches that are suspicious of any attempt to locate in the mind something original, real, and outside meaning.[22] None the less, since I think elements of this Lacanian theory of the real as something that is always a trauma for totalizing philosophical or ideological systems subtend many of Barthes's images and preoccupations, I will pursue it. For after all, the idea that the real cannot be exhausted by interpretation or assimilation, that it is not altogether commensurable with any subject, that it cannot be mastered by mind or language, is a powerful one. Where some kinds of idealism, for instance, notably those derived from Hegel, work (albeit prospectively) within the horizon of a final reconciliation of the real and its meaning, of object and subject, of world and language, a traumatic theory concentrates on all that impedes progress toward this goal. Furthermore, trauma underlies the aesthetics of shock that are an essential

---

[19] Lacan, *Séminaire*, i. 55.

[20] *Séminaire*, xi. 226.

[21] Ibid. 226. It is clear that Lacanian theory has a tendency to identify this kernel signifier with the singularity of the subject.

[22] What the 'Wolf Man' saw, was the appearance/disappearance of his father's penis (ibid. 67). Again, this illustrates the strong drive in Lacanian theory to centre the subject on a trace which thereby becomes reified: hence the criticism of Lacan expressed by Derrida in 'Le Facteur de la vérité' (*La Carte postale de Socrate à Freud et au-delà* (1980), 439–524) and by Philippe Lacoue-Labarthe and Jean-Luc Nancy in *Le Titre de la lettre* (1972).

part of twentieth-century artistic activity: Dada, for instance, is clearly meant to *traumatize* the perceiving subject, whom it bombards with signifiers torn from any context of cultural meaning: these disorganizing intensities are meant to lead to a breakdown of psychic (and ultimately even political) economy. The shock experience is central, albeit in different ways, for Benjamin and Adorno. What is interesting in this connection is that both of them, especially the former, show more interest in Freud's reworking of the theory of trauma in 'Beyond the Pleasure Principle'. Basing his development of the notion of trauma on his treatment of soldiers shell-shocked in the trenches of the First World War. Freud decided that certain massive excitations were so intense as to put the pleasure principle (which he had hitherto thought governed the economy of the psyche) out of operation. The irruptive breakthrough of energy has to be bound by other means, since repression is no longer sufficient. The protective role of repression is taken over by a 'repetition compulsion', which attempts to master the event. To his clinical experience with such cases, Freud added his own observations of a child playing a rather complex game (interpreted, imaginatively, by Freud as what he calls a *Fort-Da* game): in this, a child attempts to master its feelings of being abandoned by its mother by throwing a reel out of its cot to mime her disappearance (the child says *Fort!* = 'gone') and pulling it back to represent her return (*Da!* = 'there!', in other words—says Freud—'back again!'). On the basis of considerations such as these, Freud developed his theory of the death-drive, the notion that the tensions of living are such that the psyche has an immanent desire to escape from them by returning to the inorganic state. And Adorno and Benjamin relied on this theory to develop their own very different insights into artistic shock-tactics.[23] While Barthes in general does not establish any pure aesthetics of the shock effect, the wounding, seductive energies he locates, in language as in life, are, in their various ways, just as traumatic.

For trauma, as theorized by Freud and Lacan and their followers, covers a complex of ideas that recur in various guises throughout Barthes's work. The trauma as a hidden, unconscious origin dictates Barthes's analysis of style. The trauma as a problematic, split event posed problems for Freud that are paralleled by Barthes's own

---

[23] See Walter Benjamin, 'On some Motifs in Baudelaire', in *Illuminations*, trans. Harry Zohn (London, 1973), 157–202, and the refs to shock in Theodor Adorno's *Aesthetic Theory*, trans. C. Lenhardt, ed. Gretel Adorno and Rolf Tiedemann (London, 1984).

investigations into the problem of writing the event, and into the nature of time and narrative. The trauma is a limit to meaning, and a challenge to theory: Freud, especially when he is forced to speculate that Eros is not the only psychic force, but is locked in battle with Thanatos, the death-drive, never manages to master the trauma, to bind the energies that as infantile seduction or exploding shells it releases into his own work.[24] This casts light on Barthes's own attempts to isolate certain elements in the literary text and locate certain limits to commentary. The trauma as a figure (an elementary signifier) resists incorporation into the symbolic and abreaction into speech just as, according to Barthes, certain textual configurations cannot be translated into the speech of theory. This figurality of the trauma is one way in which, like the figures of my last chapter, it resists translation into certain types of theory.[25] The trauma as 'real' illuminates the nature of denotation and reference in language—which, like the unconscious, seems to be deprived of any certain 'indication of reality': this has consequences for our habitual ways of discussing literary realism. The trauma as something past, already there, no longer to be mastered because we missed the rendezvous the first time round, haunts Barthes's examination of other, non-literary crafts, notably the photograph. Finally, since the trauma condemns the subject to repeat a piece of symptomatic behaviour, in what way does Barthes repeat the trauma or attempt to theorize repetition? All these questions tend to interact in Barthes's texts, where they are inseparable from the problematics of writing that he is developing: it is for this reason that I consider them all to be figures of trauma, and the trauma in turn to be a figure of writing.

STYLE: THE BODY'S SECRET

In *Le Degré zéro de l'écriture*, Barthes is already fascinated by the carnal reality that underlies style. It is the isolation of the writer's body that shelters style as an *individual* phenomenon. There are two modes of sociability according to which writing operates: *langue*, the natural language into which the writer is born, and within whose horizon any act of linguistic communication has to take place; and *écriture*, which

---

[24] Samuel Weber, *The Legend of Freud* (Minneapolis, 1982), discusses in detail Freud's repetitive attempts to bind and master the trauma in his own theory.

[25] For Freud, repression is a failure of translation from one layer of the mind into another. See letter 52, in *Origins of Psychoanalysis*.

is the particular form that the writer consciously chooses in order to signal a commitment to ethical, social, or political values. Style, however, lies outside these sociable and communicative modes of writing. Where Lacan saw style as an intersubjective phenomenon, suggesting that 'le style c'est l'homme ... à qui l'on s'addresse', Barthes in his first major text sees style as something which addresses itself to nobody.[26] Neither learnt nor chosen, it grows from the writer's closed memory: it is an axis of intensity whose roots lie deep in the subject's apprehension of the world of mere matter, in the psychic depths where in some primordial encounter 'le premier couple des mots et des choses' is formed.[27] Style is thus original in two senses: it is the marker of the writer's individuality, not of any ethical or political sociability; and it springs from the original encounter of mind with matter. Style is, in other words, a symptom whose origin lies in the writer's past.

Barthes's highly florid, metaphorical, incantatory evocation of style continues in the same vein. He notes that style is a way of preserving in writing the distant memory of the very foundation of the desire to write. It is a linguistic phenomenon, but one rising from non-linguistic depths: 'ce qui se tient droit et profound sous le style, rassemblé durement ou tendrement dans ses figures, ce sont les fragments d'une réalité absolument étrangère au langage'.[28] Here, then, we meet for the first time in Barthes the hypothesis that there is indeed a reality that resists language. Barthes rarely couches the question in such abstract and schematic terms, but it seems to be a (necessarily hypothetical) presupposition for some of the things he says. Style thus becomes the repetitive symptom (it is always an *insistent* set of writing techniques) of a trauma that cannot be linguistically apprehended in any non-figural form. For Barthes's reference, in the above quotation, to *figures* is telling: style not only deploys figures (those classified by centuries of rhetoric): it is itself a figure—more precisely, a metaphor of a reality that cannot be discursively apprehended. As the index of a secret locked in the unconscious, style invites interpretation but resists integration into the verbalization of *la parole*: outside the pact which binds the writer to society (the *écriture* every writer is forced to choose in order to signal complicity or revolt), style is a disrupting factor. Since the 'pact' is a central feature of the symbolic order as theorized

[26] See Jacques Lacan, *Écrits* (1966), 9.
[27] *DZ*, 12.
[28] Ibid. 13.

by Lacan, we can extrapolate Barthes's comments and suggest that style stands outside that order as the trauma stands outside the symbolic. That is why style is natural, not historical, fateful rather than responsible, and devoid of the social meanings (the commitment to certain public values) signalled by *écriture*. Style is 'la "chose" de l'écrivain, sa splendeur et sa prison, il est sa solitude'.[29] It should be remembered that this view of writing as a way of expressing social and historical values is very different from the later images of writing developed by Barthes: in *Le Degré zéro de l'écriture*, he thinks there is a finite number of *écritures* available in any one society and any one period: the writer has to choose the *écriture* best fitted to signal ethical and political choices. This kind of *écriture*, as an act of communication, is relatively clear and thus is actually closer to the sociability (albeit, as Barthes eventually decides, the alienated sociability) of *parole* as I characterized it in Chapter 50. Later on, as well as emphasizing the 'figurality' of writing, Barthes suggests (as in the preface to *Sade, Fourier, Loyola*) that writing is an *excess* that transcends any such ethical or political intelligibility, and he makes a different set of distinctions, most of which turn on the speech/writing opposition.

The isolated, silent, unconscious drive that creates style turns the writer into 'une Fraîcheur au-dessus de l'Histoire'.[30] The writer's private chronology is here seen by Barthes as independent of the public chronology of historical determination. This is a somewhat simple model, but follows from Barthes's decision to locate the historical dialectic between writer and society in *écriture* alone, not in style, which has its own time-scale. And there is a parallel here with Freud's trauma, for Freud had seen the isolation of the traumatic memory as the source of its 'freshness and affective strength': this intensity survives because abreaction is denied, and in this way the trauma (especially when it is seen as inseparable from primary repression) means that the unconscious will never be entirely drained of its energies.[31]

Style is thus based on repression: it is written and figural rather than being spoken and communicative: it is traumatic. It can be found at its purest, says Barthes, in the paradoxical silence of modern poetry. He quotes few examples and names only René Char, but it is clear that for him the silence of such poetry is the effect of its abrogation of

[29] *DZ*, 12.
[30] Ibid. 13.
[31] See Freud and Breuer, 'Preliminary Communication', 62.

pact or *parole*. Modern poetry is vertical like style (*parole* and *écriture* are horizontal): it is 'un pilier qui plonge dans un total de sens, de réflexions et de rémanences: il est un signe debout'.[32] Saturated with so many potential meanings that the reader cannot choose between them, the poetic sign accomplishes a quantum leap: the overload on the associative network is so great that the poetic sign becomes, not information, but pure energy: the signs of poetry fuse into one traumatic word: 'le consommateur de poésie, privé du guide des rapports sélectifs, débouche sur le Mot, frontalement, et le reçoit comme une quantité absolue, accompagné de tous ses possibles'.[33] Barthes's comments on style and modern poetry are extremely vulnerable, especially in so far as they position the body's deep and secret encounter with matter entirely outside social mediations. This runs close to creating a mystique of the body ('le style . . . s'élève à partir des profondeurs mythiques de l'écrivain, et s'éploie hors de sa responsabilité).[34] It is in any case corrected by Barthes in later accounts of style (such as *Élements de sémiologie*, in which he notes that style might be subsumed under the rubric of idiolect, 'encore que le style soit toujours imprégné de certains modèles verbaux issus de la tradition, c'est-à-dire de la collectivité').[35] None the less, the notion of style as being something deeply rooted, resistant, and unmediated by social structures persists throughout Barthes's earlier work.

Barthes's interest in style as symptom links him with the thematic analysis founded by Bachelard as *psychanalyse substantielle* and practised by J.-P. Richard.[36] A thematic interpretation groups constellations of figures that can be treated in various ways: always as indicators of the writer's bodily attractions and repulsions; sometimes, more psychoanalytically, as a key to particular psychological complexes in the writer's life. In his book on Michelet, Barthes's stylistic analyses are of this thematic type: he concentrates on what sets Michelet apart—his body, and thus his style. (This suggests, in contradistinction to *Le Degré zéro de l'écriture*, that there is an ethic apart from that of conscious commitment: Michelet's values—his ethical and political values—emerge more surely in his style than they do in

---

[32] *DZ*, 37.
[33] Ibid. 38. The trauma can be seen, schematically, as an excess of energy over information, in the terms used by Anthony Wilden in *System and Structure: Essays in Communication and Exchange* (2nd edn., London, 1980).
[34] *DZ*, 12
[35] 'Éléments de sémiologie', in *AS*, 17–84 (I. 7, 16).
[36] See the works by Bachelard in the Biblio.; and Jean-Pierre Richard, *Littérature et sensation* (1954), and *Poésie et profondeur* (1955).

his ideology, which is summarily, and comically, dismissed in fourteen lines.)[37]

And what is the secret which dominates Michelet's stylistic obsessions? Blood, images of which flow through Michelet's historical works, but which he seems to have associated, thanks to his own voyeuristic complex, with the sight of a woman menstruating. This original scene, claims Barthes, was 'un véritable traumatisme—physique ou existentiel—dont il tire, comme toujours, une nouvelle organisation de l'univers'.[38] Barthes speculates that Michelet's diary (unpublished when Barthes wrote his study) had menstruation as a constant theme—as was later confirmed. Barthes does not seem to ask whether Michelet's obsession was the result of a displaced castration complex, in other words one of the sources of that anxiety about sexual division that runs through Michelet's work: one of the ways Michelet attempts to palliate this is by his intellectual androgyny: Barthes takes as the epigraph to his study Michelet's words 'je suis un homme complet, ayant les deux sexes de l'esprit'. But in any case, Michelet's style is seen by him as the florid symptom of a trauma.[39]

There are other forms of literary analysis which treat form in a causal and psychological way. Sartrean analysis, notes Barthes in 'Le Mythe, aujourd'hui', treats literature as the signifier of 'la crise originelle du sujet (la séparation loin de le mère chez Baudelaire, la nomination du vol chez Genet)': the work of literature, as the union of literary signifiers with this signified crisis, operates in a way similar to Freud's parapraxis, dream, or neurosis, in Barthes's analogy.[40] In Sartre's analysis, priority is still given to the signified, which is an original, traumatic event, which the writer's words circle around ever afterwards.[41]

In *Michelet par lui-même*, Barthes's use of psychoanalysis is of the 'substantial' or thematic kind, looking at the substances that underpin, in more or less explicit ways, Michelet's universe. Later, Barthes's

---

[37] *Mi*, 12.

[38] Ibid. 129.

[39] 'Symptoms are metaphors. They symbolize, at the level of an organ or a function, an unconscious signifier', Anika Lemaire, *Jacques Lacan*, trans. David Macey (London, 1977), 188. While Lemaire is here ignoring the possibility that symptom-formation may occur by metonymy, it is certainly true that thematic analysis of the Bachelard–Richard type tends to operate in terms of metaphor, and is thus particularly prone to see style as symptomatic. Barthes sees thematic analysis as closer to the metaphorical than the metonymic pole in 'Éléments de sémiologie', III. i. 1., in *AS*, 55.

[40] *My*, 196–9.

[41] See *Baudelaire* (1954), and *Saint Genet, comédien et martyr* (1952).

psychoanalysis becomes more structural: *Sur Racine* maps Racine's tragedies as variants on a basic structural kernel (A has all power over B; A loves B who does not love A) complicated by the Freudian model of the primal horde.[42] But this affects the structure of Racine's plays, not their style (it is in any case paradoxical to talk of style in such coded works): nor does Barthes extend his analysis to Racine's biography. (I shall be returning to some of the traumatic elements in Racine's plays in a moment.) In 'Éléments de sémiologie', Barthes notes that it is not substance or contents that are unconscious, but forms (in other words, signifiers).[43] There is thus, as Barthes moves into structuralist modes of analysis, a shift away from the idea that interpretation can be centred around some original trauma in the writer's life. (Given the mutation in the idea of the author signalled by 'La Mort de l'auteur', Barthes's later work in any case finds little systematic place for biographical interpretation as offering any causal explanation for elements of form or meaning in the text, though he becomes increasingly interested in the habits and rituals surrounding the act of writing.) He also distances himself from thematic analysis, though this recurs, in disseminated forms, for the rest of his career: what in *Michelet par lui-même* is taken as the ultimate object of thematic analysis (Michelet's body as incarnated in his style) is made part of the increasingly important category of the *body*. However, the passage through structuralism temporarily increases Barthes's hostility to determinism (and thus to his loss of interest in the notion that style is the direct product of some trauma), analogy (as if the blood irrigating French history flowed directly from Michelet's wives and mistresses), and the symbolist nature of modern poetry (which seems to speak without social mediation). In this sense, style is replaced by figure, in two senses: the first is the one I examined in Chapter 4 (scribble as a figure of the body in writing); the second is closer to what might be called isolatable elements in a cultural text, often cut away from context and framed as a tableau, in ways I discussed in connection with Barthes's general tactic of framing in Chapter 3. But what is framed here is an event that has been, for the purposes of Barthes's analysis, frozen.[44] For Barthes, the event as such becomes a theoretical site in which a variety of traumatic effects can be located.

---

[42] *SR*, 14, 29.

[43] 'Eléments de sémiologie', I. ii. 1, in *AS*, 29.

[44] The trauma is another frame situation, a scene that excludes the subject and constitutes its subjectivity by so doing.

WRITING THE EVENT

While moving away from a fascination for the trauma as a secret in the writer's body, Barthes shows an increasing interest in the nature of the event. The status of the traumatic event had posed severe problems for Freud: did it really take place? If so, when? Barthes's reading of Racine is based largely on a version of structuralist narratology, and heavily influenced by psychoanalysis. Structuralism has always, says Derrida, found the category of the event difficult to theorize, has always suspected it and wished to reduce it.[45] In Racine's plays, according to Barthes, there are few events. The heroes and heroines are trapped in language: an event (usually death) comes as a deliverance. Racine's tragedy is one of language, not action: events are devolved on to the servants and confidants who, as it were, do the protagonists' living for them.[46] Indeed, the only events to which Barthes gives any importance are particularly traumatic ones, not just in the sense that tragedy is the story of things suffered, but in the more specific sense, that, firstly, the trauma condemns the subject to repetition, and secondly, the trauma is a problematic event composed of what happens and what is fantasized (or turned into a fantasmatic image that haunts the subject's memory). This is especially true of those encounters in which one character sees, and falls irrevocably in love with, another: 'l'Éros racinien (du moins l'Éros immédiat dont il s'agira désormais ici) n'est jamais sublimé; sorti tout armé, tout *fini*, d'une pure vision, il s'immobilise dans la fascination perpétuelle du corps adverse, il reproduit indéfiniment la scène originelle qui l'a formé'.[47] The subject is captured by an image (by something that thus is already, partly, outside language)—as when in *Britannicus*, Nero first catches sight of Junie: 'l'image ainsi constituée a un pouvoir de traumatisme: extérieure au héros à titre de souvenir, elle lui représente le conflit où il est engagé comme un objet'.[48] The scene is turned into an image of photographic clarity which the hero can summon up at will (Barthes talks—and this is significant given his later examinations of photography—of *photogénie*).[49] The protagonist does everything

---

[45] 'La Structure, le signe et le jeu dans le discours des sciences humaines', in *L'écriture et la différence*, (1967), 409–28 (409).
[46] *SR*, 13.
[47] Ibid. 18.
[48] Ibid. 27.
[49] Ibid. 27.

possible to re-experience the original scene, including whatever went wrong in it—to re-encounter the real that presented itself at that time in all its seductive and traumatic intensity: the tragic protagonist is fixated on the past, source of pleasure as well as pain.[50] The original scene is punctual in that it happens outside any dialectical or historical process of maturation. Barthes considers events in Racine to be mathematically abstract: they frequently take the form of the past historic—Barthes cites '*il lui plut*', '*je la vis*', '*je l'aimai*'.[51] The event outside time (as a point) organizes time around itself, as repetition. The meaninglessness of the original scene cannot be transcended, hence the fascinated and obsessive repetition to which it is subjected.

Is Barthes too a *Homo racinianus*, caught in the prison-house of language?[52] There is a sense in which the Racinian protagonist's tragedy lies in a fundamental isolation from 'la cuisine triviale du faire'[53] which is the domain of the plebeian underclass. *Sur Racine* is based on a model in which language—especially as organized around tyrannical binary oppositions—is contrasted with a real that is outside, tempting and menacing the protagonist simultaneously. The irruption of the real is the end of the meanings the protagonist has lived by. The event, in other words, stands in an oblique relation to the narrative: for, while a narrative depends on events (things happening), it also depends on the symbolic (the meanings with which we invest happenings). The trauma has stood in a similarly insecure and problematic relation to the narrative (the case history) of the analysand on Freud's couch. For the trauma is the reason why there is any story at all (there is a sense in which it founds the psyche in all its singularity). But the trauma is also that which obstinately refuses to be integrated into the story (the primal signifier to which, in Lacan's words, the subject is subjected is outside any assimilation into symbolic, narrative forms).

There is, however, a sense in which any event, as such, may be considered as challenging any narrative which may subsequently absorb it. If we define what counts as an event as something new, singular, and unexpected, the event will also challenge the meanings which are an integral part of the way narratives function. Geoffrey

[50] *SR*, 28.
[51] Ibid. 97.
[52] Comparisons have been drawn between Barthes's and Racine's characters, most eloquently by Mary Bittner Wiseman, *The Ecstasies of Roland Barthes* (London, 1989), 78–82.
[53] *SR*, 13.

Bennington suggests that the work of Jean-François Lyotard can be considered as a sustained attempt to think, and write, the event in all its singularity, and that this endeavour has much in common with other areas in post-structuralism.[54] As a singularity, the event will necessarily pose a problem for languages, for 'insofar as language is the domain of generality, then it cannot deliver its objects as concepts without betraying them'.[55] *Discours, figure*, which I have already referred to in connection with the problem of scribble, is thus also preoccupied with the category of the event, linked by Lyotard with both violence and truth.[56] Truth, not knowledge—this seems a distinction relevant to the life of the subject according to psychoanalysis (where knowledge—for instance of psychoanalytic theory—may well hinder the emergence of the truth of the subject's desire, a truth frequently experienced as traumatic in its intensity when it is not actually the revelation of some primal event or signifier). It is relevant, too, to Barthes, for whom truth is increasingly associated with an individual event (an event which happens to an individual—even if that event is the realization of some universal: this is true, for instance, of *La Chambre claire*, where the subjective point of the photo is ultimately raised into the heuristic key to the essence of photography, as I shall be showing below). Truth need not be negotiable, without remainder, in the symbolic order (of meaning and narrative): in those terms, the truth may well be 'meaningless'.

To return to Bennington's discussion of Lyotard, however, means noting that the event cannot stand outside language: its relationship is disruptive and oblique rather than oppositional.[57] According to Lyotard, the statement 'je te musique' is an event because it could not have been predicted by a generative grammar.[58] One of his essays takes the narrativization of an event as its main theme: that event is the death of Pierre Overney during a demonstration outside Renault's Billancourt factory in 1972. Lyotard analyses the way Renault in their

---

[54] *Lyotard: Writing the Event*, (Manchester, 1988), 9.

[55] This formulation suggests at least a parallel with Kierkegaard, and this would not be surprising given that one of Lyotard's targets is Hegel. But this does not seem to be a path that Lyotard is interested in following, though, as I suggested in Ch. 5, above, Barthes does resort to Kierkegaardian language when evoking language as generality.

[56] Note, however, Barthes's dislike of this element of violence.

[57] *Lyotard: Writing the Event*. 75.

[58] Ibid. 28. This problem affects theory, the language of generality *par excellence*, and thus particularly prone to recuperate the singular (46). Barthes's later work insistently sees language's generality as posing a problem in certain specific cases—all of which can be subsumed under the heading 'trauma'.

press statement narrativized this event.[59] What is the status of this event? Is there, indeed, an event there, prior to any interpretation, any apportionment of responsiblity? Lyotard's response is complex and involved, but it allows us to cast retrospective light on one of the major problems faced by Freud and Lacan, and prospective light on a major topic in Barthes. According to Bennington, Lyotard 'is not for a moment contesting that in this case the event is the death of Pierre Overney. But in this analysis we can no longer simply accept the traditional view that the event "comes first" in an unquestionably "real" world, nor, in the simple reversal-model, that it is purely "produced" by the narrating agency.'[60]

What this suggests is that many of the difficulties of the trauma theorized by psychoanalysis are inseparable from more general questions, such as the relationship between an event and its meaning, and thus between what happens and the way it is narrated. The stories psychoanalysis tells could be susceptible to the kind of structural analysis of narrative practised by Genette and utilized by Lyotard in his discussion of the Overney case.[61] Freud's constant reversion to the real datability of the traumatic event, Lacan's attempts to locate a primal signifier, however vulnerable to the charge that they involve a naïve separation of the real from meaning, could also be seen as rearguard actions fought to defend the singularity of the event, which is thus not just a modality of language, but something that stands obliquely against it. Bennington says that the event is 'not to be found simply on the side of referentiality, in the "real", but in the disruption, still thought of here in terms of tension and energy, of a restrictive narrative temporality'.[62] In other words, the event is real not so much in so far as it happens 'out there', but in so far as it is senseless, refusing to be 'absorbed into the *order* of a classical narrative'.[63] There is thus a more than a (quite justifiably) emotive sense in which Overney's death is traumatic, for, says Lyotard, while the factory may, like Hegel's *Geist*, absorb all that is exterior and create a memory for it, Overney's death will neither be forgotten, nor can it be recalled and assuaged (or, so to speak, abreacted). What can neither be

---

[59] 'Petite économie libidinale d'un dispositif narratif: la régie Renault raconte le meurtre de Pierre Overney', in *Des dispositifs pulsionnels* (1980), 171–213.

[60] *Lyotard: Writing the Event*, 107.

[61] Lyotard's essay concentrates on the narrative structures examined by Genette in 'Discours du récit', in *Figures III* (1972), 67–273.

[62] *Lyotard: Writing the Event*, 108. See also Lyotard, 'Petite économie libidinale', 184–5.

[63] Bennington, *Lyotard: Writing the Event*, 109.

forgotten nor recalled is what Lyotard sometimes calls the 'immemorial': another commentator on Lyotard, Bill Readings, gives a brief definition of the 'immemorial' in his glossary to leitmotifs in Lyotard's work, and I will quote his definition here, since it will be clear how this theme in Lyotard parallels some Barthesian topics I have been discussing—the figure, the singularity, and even the question of voice versus silence (as in Barthes's attempt to make possible a 'silent writing'). Under the entry 'immemorial', Readings writes:

That which can neither be remembered (represented to consciousness) nor forgotten (consigned to oblivion). It is that which returns, uncannily. As such, the immemorial acts as a kind of *figure* for consciousness and its attempts at representing itself historically. The prime example is Auschwitz, which obliges us to speak so that this event remains an event, so that its *singularity* is not lost in historical representation, so that it does not become something that happened, among other things. The task of not forgetting, of anamnesis, is the task of the avant-garde, which struggles to keep events from sinking into the oblivion of either representation (voice) or silence.[64]

What is curious in this account is the way one of history's supremely traumatic moments is almost turned into the paradigm of all events, and in his glossary entry on 'event' Readings notes how, in Lyotard's terms, it is impossible to tell whether events happen all the time (like unexpectedly meeting someone in the street, perhaps) or hardly ever (like Auschwitz—one hopes). The important thing is the 'it happens' rather than the identity or name we give to this (the 'what is happening'): the event 'disrupts any pre-existing referential frame within which it might be represented or understood'—it 'leaves us without criteria' (and this, in turn, is reminiscent of the Lyotardian aspects of Barthes's drift as discussed in Chapter 1).[65] So the event is indeed a trauma, and narratives, as they recount events, are attempts to control and master them, to bind and neutralize their 'quantitative charge', as Bennington puts it, referring to Freud's 'principle of constancy'.[66]

Lyotard's discussion of the event (Overney's death) as recounted by

---

[64] *Introducing Lyotard: Art and Politics*, (London, 1991), p. xxxii.
[65] Ibid. p. xxxi.
[66] *Lyotard: Writing the Event*, 110. See also 160, referring to Lyotard, *Le Différend*, 219, on narrative as that which hides the event, since it is arranged teleologically, its last sentence putatively giving meaning to all the sentences that have gone before: a case of retroactive or *après-coup* causality. This in turn raises the question: do psychoanalytical narratives *hide* the trauma in so far as they force the analysand to integrate events into a life story?

Renault is paralleled by his long-standing attempt to see the event as close to the Freudian *lapsus* or the limit-experience of *jouissance*: all of them involve radical difference, the juxtaposition of heterogeneous states.[67]

If this puts the psychoanalytic preoccupation with events and meanings into a wider context, it also acts as a framework for my discussion of one aspect of Barthes's entertainment of traumatic themes. I have noted the importance of events in so far as they refuse to happen as anything other than catastrophic irruptions in Racine's dramas as read by Barthes. What of events—especially in their relation to narrative—as they occur in Barthes's later investigation of the alienations of love, *Fragments d'un discours amoureux*?

The main way in which the *Fragments* attempt to respect singularity is by refusing to fit into any narrative mode. They are fragments of the lover's internal monologue—a private and obsessive mulling over the 'figures' of love's discourse, which is discourse only in the most fragmented and unstructured sense.[68] Each figure resists incorporation into any larger-scale structure. In this sense, already, each fragment fulfils the role of a kernel fantasy, that returns repetitively and obsessively to plague the subject. Furthermore, the world that is disclosed through the *Fragments* overall—for the basic ethos of the writing is a mode of realism ('Une figure est fondée si au moins quelqu'un peut dire: *'Comme c'est vrai, ça! Je reconnais cette scène de langage'*)[69]—is traumatic in a variety of ways. Most simply, because the subject experiences reality as disconnected random events asserting their power and force, breaking into the love relationship from a violent and mysterious outside. (Even an event in love itself is a disruption of the amorous state, which for Barthes is close to hypnotic fascination.)

Furthermore, separation from the loved one is assimilated to the trauma of separation experienced by Freud's grandson, Ernst, and the way the lover manipulates that absence is compared to Ernst's game of *Fort-Da*: the lover attempts to bind the excessive intensities

---

[67] *Discours, Figure* (1971), 137. We have already seen how Lyotard's *figure* casts light on, without being assimilable to, a similar preoccupation in Barthes. The figure may indeed be traumatic in so far as it is a disruption of discourse and thus 'difficult to talk about': it is this which makes it easier to see the figure as event, linked to truth rather than knowledge, for knowledge 'presupposes precisely the neat separation of its own discourse from its object of knowledge' that the figure disturbs (Bennington, *Lyotard: Writing the Event*, 69).

[68] See 'Comment est fait ce livre', in *FDA*, 7–12.

[69] Ibid. 8. See also *'c'est cela!'* (*PlT*, 73).

unleashed by the experience of loss (but never gets as far as that form which Barthes poses as the supreme non-theoretical mechanism for binding the excitations produced by random, meaningless events: the novel, which in the *Fragments* is seen as the only generality the lover can be positioned against, in the absence of theory).[70] In Lyotard's terms, Barthes attempts to depict the experience of love as one in which there is neither any grand narrative nor any last sentence (no final figure says Barthes, no teleology, no linear time-scale, no development, no history, no progress):

En termes linguistiques, on dirait que les figures sont distributionnelles, mais qu'elles ne sont pas intégratives; elles restent toujours au même niveau: l'amoureux parle par paquets de phrases, mais il n'intègre pas ces phrases à un niveau supérieur, à une œuvre; c'est un discours horizontal: aucune transcendence, aucun salut, aucun roman (mais beaucoup de romanesque).[71]

Since love is an experience of the imaginary at its most paroxystic, the lover is one debarred from the symbolic order in its guise, not as division and difference (or of the gender oppositions of castration), but as that realm of the general in which those wounds can be bound. For Lacan, the same configurations of experience can be treated as now imaginary, now symbolic, now real: the trauma is an experience of the real as other: it is also the entry of the subject into self-division (the move from the imaginary into the symbolic) as well as, consequent to that, the constitution of an alienated ego whose new, bitterly defended imaginary identity isolates the subject in the larger symbolic realm of social, historical community. In leaving one imaginary (fusion with the mother), the subject enters another (imaginary ego-identity): viewed both ways, the trauma is a moment of alienation whose effects the subject will continue to negotiate in more or less successful ways.

Of course, since Barthes is concerned to valorize the intensity of the experience of love over its comprehensibility ('Je veux comprendre (ce qui m'arrive)!' thinks the lover, knowing at the same time that understanding would lower the value of being in love), he shows love as a trauma that would, precisely, disappear if it were abreacted.[72] The singularity of love lies, for Barthes, in its refusal of abreaction: events stay as events, banal, random but all the more powerful. The

---

[70] See esp. the figures 'Absence', 'Attente', and 'Drame': in the latter, we read 'Seul l'Autre pourrait écrire mon roman' (*FDA*, 109).

[71] Ibid. 10–11.

[72] For 'Comprendre', see ibid. 71.

fragment entitled 'Événements, traverses, contrariétés' has a rubric or
argument, as Barthes calls it, which reads:

CONTINGENCES. Menus événements, incidents, traverses, vétilles, mesqui-
neries, futilités, plis de l'existence amoureuse; tout noyau factuel d'un
retentissement qui vient traverser la visée de bonheur du sujet amoureux,
comme si le hasard intriguait contre lui.[73]

The event is a kernel of nonsense that refuses to be interpreted,
although it tempts the subject into thinking that it is not a pure event
(a pure contingence), but a sign. 'L'incident est pour moi un signe,
non un indice: l'élément d'un système, non l'efflorescence d'une
causalité';[74] there must be a meaning (presumably a menacing one)
behind the whisperings of X and Y[75] and that meaning is part of the
entire symbolic order from which I am excluded. The trauma shows—
and this applies to its theorization in psychoanalysis too—that meaning
is intersubjective. (To return briefly to the original theory of trauma
in psychoanalysis, the ultimately traumatic events lack meaning for the
child who cannot understand a sexual meaning located in the Other.)
What is traumatic is precisely this interface between the lover,
constituted by exclusion as a painfully consistent, situated, imaginary
identity, and the Other, as the locus of desire ('le désir de l'homme,
c'est le désir de l'Autre', says Lacan) and of the symbolic order (which
founds desire). The lover's kernel fantasy, fragmented across the
contingencies of everyday life, could be expressed as: 'they can tell the
story of my life which is foreclosed to me: they understand what I
cannot'. For the subject in the imaginary, the symbolic is itself
endowed with the wholeness of the imaginary: it is both desired as a
place of self-division in which the dice can again be thrown and
identity renegotiated, and feared as a monstrous and asphyxiating
system in which the subject's singularity will be crushed (and in which
the loved one will end up as the object of gossip).

Hence the low status of narrative in the *Fragments*, shunned
precisely because it would end the lover's existence as isolated,
alienated, separated lover. The lover in society is like a trauma in the
mind, a foreign body charged with wayward energies, refused any
language except that of generality. The lover in the *Fragments* is thus
a reactionary and counter-enlightenment figure who refuses dialogue:
the lover is also one of the foreign bodies who resist integration,
absorption, and recuperation into any social totality—foreign bodies

---

[73] *FDA*, 83.   [74] Ibid. 84.   [75] Ibid. 83.

who are celebrated in various modes of modernism. Barthes even claims that such minorities are less excluded than the lover in so far as they have elaborated their own codes of subversion and languages of resistance: Bataille, Deleuze and Guattari, and Foucault suggest a similar valorization of heterogeneous forces that prevent society from settling into homogeneous and thus oppressive self-identity: workers, blacks, homosexuals and lesbians, delinquents, drug-addicts, the insane. *Fragments d'un discours amoureux* does not occupy such problematic ground, but it does attempt to mimic the discourse of one of these excluded figures from the inside. It is as much about alienation as about love: together with Barthes's late diary fragments ('Soirées de Paris', in *Incidents*) it depicts various forms of class-bound, socially determined, and historically situated dereliction ('De l'autre côté de la vitre, sur une affiche murale, Coluche grimace et fait le con');[76] it is a portrayal of an attempt to overcome fear and misery in the Fifth Republic. When Barthes sacrilegiously (and he knows it) compares the lover to one of the victims of Dachau it is because the lover is in a state of near psychosis, and experiencing a limit situation that seems bound to be totally destructive.[77] But another factor that may be partly responsible for such blasphemy is the basic and far-reaching instability in the status of *any* event, from the Shoah to what Barthes calls 'un incident futile, enfantin, sophistiqué, obscur, advenu à un sujet confortable, qui est seulement la proie de son Imaginaire' once it has been so questionably decided that the event is going to be *anything* which disturbs meaning and narrative.[78]

The lover may live in a world of events whose intensity is never defused by metalinguistic or narrative manipulation, and that repeat themselves randomly and obstinately, as figures. But the lover still does not 'write the event'. Since, as I have shown, Barthes is operating with a scheme whose basic, if implicit, premiss separates an event from the meaning it may be given in metalinguistic (interpretative) or narrative terms, it is not surprising that he should be drawn to modes of writing that seem to refuse the imposition of such meaning. Sometimes this will involve writing the event (the haiku, the *anamnèse*, the *incident*): sometimes, it will lead Barthes, as interpreter of the phantasmagoria of culture, to try and locate at their heart a kernel element that challenges the very meanings that such phantasmagoric images seem to be generating. In both cases, Barthes shows a

---

[76] Ibid. 103.   [77] Ibid. 60.   [78] Ibid.

characteristic interest in kinds of text that resist the very modes of reading (especially those variants of semiological analysis) that he himself had been so successful in developing.

What kind of text is best equipped to defend itself against such interpretation? For one of the key shifts in Barthes's work can be located in two images of the 'ideal' text that we find in two works published in the same year: *S/Z* and *L'Empire des signes*. The first proposes the image of the writable text, which refuses to be interpreted, cannot be spoken, resists (so far) recuperation and, far from being realistic, is itself the real. In what way? 'Le texte scriptible, c'est *nous en train d'écrire.*'[79] This is often read as a demand for the reader to participate in the making of the text, and this is at least part of Barthes's argument. But all texts, whether classical or avant-garde, require such participative re-creation, and the category of the *scriptible* or radically avant-garde text can be seen in a stronger sense in which writing is no longer separable from other forms of praxis, so that the writable text is not an object but an act, a real—an event. The fact that such a praxis may not be presentable as such is clearly one element in Barthes's general abandonment of the notion of *le texte scriptible* after *S/Z*: its place is taken by, for instance, the *texte de jouissance* of *Le Plaisir du texte*, in which the codes are not blown apart in some galactic explosion, but, rather, played off against each other. Where the *texte scriptible* is a praxis, the *texte de jouissance* can be presented because what is important is the effect it has, an effect which is often produced as the interstice between the codes, and thus between the levels of the text that each, individually, makes perfect sense but when mixed together create considerable and salutary unease—as when Sade describes unbelievable sexual atrocities in the purest French, turned with courtly politeness, elegantly subjunctival: the *jouissance* of such a text resides in the gap between the poise and control of the language, and the radical nature of the sexual loss that it is attempting to represent.[80]

Barthes still imagines what an ideally radical text might look like, however. One such form is evidently traumatic. In *Barthes par lui-même*, he notes that beyond the writable texts of the avant-garde that always outstrip current conventions of reading, there exists a form of text even less easy for the commentator to process, what he calls not the *scriptible*, but the *recevable*—'l'illisible qui accroche, le texte brûlant', to which the only response can be 'je ne puis lire ni écrire ce que vous produisez, mais je le *reçois*, comme un feu, une drogue, une désorganisation énigmatique'.[81] An enigmatic dis-organization: a trauma.

THE HAIKU AND THE KOAN

While presenting a *texte scriptible* will always be simplistic, there is thus a sense in which the ideal text might, if we follow the criteria set out at the beginning of *S/Z*, look like this:

c'est pas l'pied clouéc' te passion néon an 2000 après quoi un peu de satyricon vomi bains culeurs sans freins entassés d'éphèbes lors vautrés bidoche merdée rouge à lèvres déclamant comme un vol de gerfauts hors du charnier natal se pâmant sous l'ardeur de l'astre occidental palpant l'maniaque à coup d'gong bouffé borborygme slip[82]

However, to come to the other image of the radically challenging text that Barthes proposes in 1970, an equally ideal text looks like this:

> La vielle mare:
> Une grenouille saute dedans:
> Oh! le bruit de l'eau.

This haiku of Bashō, translated and presented in *L'Empire des signes*,[83] is an example of the ways in which Barthes's encounter with and subsequent fictional (but non-narrative) reworking of Japan will cast light on the complex of ideas I call trauma.

In Japan, as we have seen, Barthes is a foreigner abroad. He is thus exposed to a variety of adventures, rituals, and encounters all of which operate a sudden loss of sense: they thus come to have the status of events, outside time and outside meaning. Since Barthes cannot speak the language, he is, literally, an *in-fant*, bombarded with the signs of the Other's desire that are both unintelligible and seductive.

Barthes fastens on the haiku as exemplary in the way it refused to allow a Westerner to read it in accordance with western interpretative practices. The haiku is perfectly readable: its signifiers do not explode in apparent hysterical proliferation as in the text of Sollers quoted above: yet its enigma is all the greater. Where modernist poetry in the

---

[81] *RB*, 122.
[82] Sollers, *Paradis*, in *Tel Quel*, 57 (spring 1974), 7.
[83] *EpS*, 93.

West is too rich in symbolic meaning (such was the claim of *Le Degré zéro de l'écriture*), the haiku seems exaggeratedly litotic—no wordplay, punning, baroque exuberance, or struggle with the magma of language here.

The haiku, then, is clear but means nothing.[84] What does the Westerner make of it? Barthes is here in the position of a critic before whom is placed a text for commentary. But the associations dry up. The haiku can be read neither as symbol (poetry) nor as syllogism (logic): it blocks metalinguistic description. The only commentary one can give is tautologous (or, as Barthes does here, one can discuss at some length *why* commentary is so difficult).

It is like the koan, the Zen riddle that is too hard a nut for even the keenest intellect, because it is explicitly designed to throw the mind's verbalizing and discursive machinery out of gear. D. T. Suzuki has emphasized the crucial importance of the koan in Zen. The pupil is given a koan (usually a question-and-answer exchange between master and pupil that has achieved canonical status) and has to concentrate on it until the koan's very impenetrability leads to a illumination, a sudden and never-predictable satori, that cannot be summarized in discursive terms. Suzuki quotes a number of such koans, all characterized by the fact that a direct, serious question is answered by an often spectacularly irrelevant phrase or action. 'A monk asked, "All things are said to be reducible to the One, but where is the One to be reduced?" Chao-chou answered, "When I was in the district of Ch'ing I had a robe made that weighed seven *chin*." '[85]

For satori to occur, continues Suzuki, the mind must first be baffled, arrested in a logical impasse.[86] The koan has no crack, nothing for a pupil's 'intellectual teeth' to prise apart[87]—an idea Barthes echoes in his reference to the haiku, which has the same resistance to commentary.[88] The pupil who attempts to comment, in an intellectual and thus intellectualist fashion, on the koan, risks being derided, or physically struck, by the master. For to offer such commentary is necessarily to have missed the point. And when a commentator attempts to say something about a haiku of Bashō, the product is a mere summary. (Barthes chooses to ignore the fact that Bashō's haiku

---

[84] *EpS*, 89.
[85] *Essays in Zen Buddhism: Second Series* (London, 1953), 94. Barthes quotes a version of the same koan in the 'Vérité' section of *FDA* noting: 'La vérité: ce qui est *à côté*', 273.
[86] *Essays in Zen Buddhism: Second Series*, 95.
[87] Ibid. 96.
[88] *EpS*, 94.

have in fact given rise to a continuous flood of commentaries, but he is correct in suggesting that these commentaries are often tautologous.) The Zen pupil chews over the koan but can never digest it, wear it down, assimilate it. Such a pupil is a 'remâcheur d'absurde'.[89] The haiku effaces 'le règne des Codes'.[90] In it, 'c'est le symbole comme opération sémantique qui est attaqué'.[91]

There is another sense in which the haiku and the koan resemble the trauma: all three depend on an event, and one, furthermore, that cannot be precisely located. Satori, indeed, is *the* event, according to Zen—for every satori may be the one incident which will change a life, hence the Zen masters' attention to every apparently trivial happening, of the sort catalogued in the repertoire of haiku.[92] The kind of events notated in haiku form, and seen as possible triggers of an unpredictable satori or shaking-apart of one's fixed mental set, are curiously like a variety of events that Barthes was aware of from his reading in western literature. On one occasion, for instance, a monk came to realization while stumbling in a courtyard.[93] Zen is particularly sensitive to such moments as these and the 'smell of burning leaves on a morning of autumn haze, a flight of sunlit pigeons against a thundercloud, the sound of an unseen waterfall at dusk, or the single cry of some unidentified bird in the depths of a forest'.[94]

These erratic singularities, which it is the aim of the haiku to transcribe, are similar to the enigmatic moments of intensity that Lacanian analysis attributes to certain configurations in everyday life, which assume the status of key signifiers. 'The smell of a woman's neck on the way back from a walk; the acidulated edge of something sweet; the modulation of a voice; a beauty spot or mole; the fullness

---

[89] *EpS*, 94.

[90] Ibid. 97.

[91] Ibid. 98.

[92] On satori, see D. T. Suzuki, *Essays in Zen Buddhism: First Series* (London, 1950), 237. Generally speaking, the classical Japanese haiku consists of 17 syllables (5–7–5), contains some reference to the natural world, 'refers to a particular event' (rather than being a generalization) and 'presents that event as happening *now*—not in the past': these guidelines are taken from Harold G. Henderson, *Haiku in English* (Rutland, Vt., 1967), 14. A more detailed history and analysis of the haiku can be found in Kenneth Yasuda, *The Japanese Haiku: Its Essential Nature, History and Possibilities in English with Selected Examples* (Rutland, Vt., 1957).

[93] Suzuki, *Essays in Zen Buddhism: Second Series*, 200. Proust's Narrator also, of course, stumbles in a courtyard on his way to the Hôtel des Guermantes in *Le Temps retrouvé*: from the insight to which this gives birth springs the series of revelations that lead to the decision to write the *Recherche*.

[94] These ex. are taken from Alan Watts, *The Way of Zen* (Harmondsworth, 1962), 200. Barthes knew the work of both Suzuki and Watts.

of the hand as the ball is caught'—these are all, according to Serge Leclaire, elements of pure singularity.[95] But in psychoanalysis, and to a certain extent in the case of the Proustian *mémoire involontaire*, the singularity is ultimately integrated: the Narrator's stumbling in the Paris courtyard, in *Le Temps retrouvé*, recalls, after a micronarrative of suspense and doubt, the earlier stumbling in the baptistry of San Marco, and the elementary signifiers of psychoanalysis are significant because of the way they are linked to configurations of signifiers (frequently traumatic, having to do with, for instance, separation from the mother) in the subject's unconscious: they are where desire insists. Zen does not see its events as significant in this way: if anything, they disclose, in a punctual and timeless way, the being-there of the world: even more radically, in the case of satori, the only response to the happening may be, not an ordering of it in the subject's memory (which, integrative or otherwise, plays little part in Zen), but an exclamation: 'Ah, this!'[96] In other words, satori throws out of gear the 'monkey chatter' of the mind and reveals the world in a non-discursive way. This may seem a somewhat different model from psychoanalysis, in which the patient's 'monkey-chatter' or babble is a necessary purgatorial stage to be traversed in order to achieve insight: but the same is in fact true of Zen, which requires a deep acquaintance with the very logic whose straitjacketing constraints it aims eventually to throw off. Like silent writing, the haiku and the koan point beyond themselves in so far as they cannot be contained by speech, whether the speech of paraphrase or commentary or even psychoanalysis. (Collections of koans, notoriously, do *not* lead to enlightenment: just read off the page, they merely sound like some of the nonsense jokes that gave Freud so much theoretical trouble.)[97]

So the haiku leads to an interruption of the usual codes, narrative and perceptual, by which we process the passing of time. The haiku is not descriptive in any realist sense of the word: it does not posit any 'real' which exists prior to the act of writing: rather, it becomes an event itself—a language-event in which what it names briefly appears: 'moment à la lettre "intenable", où la chose, bien que n'étant déjà que langage, va devenir parole, va passer d'un langage à un autre et se

---

[95] These exx., taken from Leclaire's article 'La Réalité du désir', in *Sur la sexualité humaine* (Centre d'Études Laennec), are cited in Anika Lemaire, *Jacques Lacan*, trans. David Macey (London, 1977), 163.

[96] Suzuki, *Essays in Zen Buddhism: Second Series*, 103.

[97] See *Jokes and their Relation to the Unconscious*, in *Pelican Freud Library*, vi. 189–90.

constitue comme le souvenir de ce futur, par là même antérieur'.[98] Both trauma and haiku straddle the binary opposites event and memory, reality and fantasy, happening and language: both of them are a present that can only be reconstructed as past because of the logic of deferral and retroaction (Freud's *Nachträglichkeit*): as the hysteric reconstructs a primal scene or scene of seduction, so the haiku is a false anamnesis: 'Ainsi le haïku nous fait souvenir de ce qui ne nous est jamais arrivé; en lui nois *reconnaissons* une répétition sans origine, un événement sans cause, une mémoire sans personne, une parole sans amarres.'[99]

The haiku thus blocks the operations of a binary opposition on which Western commentary tends to be based; we cannot manipulate it. Even in our (Western) language, it seems to demand and at the same time resist translation (into the metalanguage of commentary): precisely because it seems not to mean anything, it gains the status of an event, and correspondingly, of the real. Since it arrests interpretation, what can the commentator do with it?

One answer is: repeat it—not any one particular haiku (for this would be to deprive it of its singularity, and even the echo-like repetition to which the haiku is subjected in recitals is meant to keep it outside codes of interpretation), but the haiku as form.[100] Barthes's attempts to imitate the haiku leads to *Incidents*, as well as the 'Anamnèses' section of *Barthes par lui-même*, which gives a list of events from Barthes's childhood: their value is that these *anamnèses* are (like the 'immemorial' anamnesis of Lyotard) neither entirely forgotten (they are, after all, memories) nor entirely remembered (in that they do not fit into the symbolic unfolding of a narrative—of Barthes's 'life-story'). Here, as examples, are two such *anamnèses*:

L'appartment meublé, loué par correspondence, était occupé. Ils se sont retrouvés un matin de novembre parisien, dans la rue de la Glacière avec malles et bagages. La crémière d'à-côte les a recueillis, elle leur a offert du chocolat chaud et des croissants.

Vers 1932, au studio 28, un jeudi après-midi de mai, seul, je vis *le Chien andalou*: en sortant, à cinq heures, la rue Tholozé sentait le café au lait que

---

[98] *EpS*, 100.

[99] Ibid. 104.

[100] Barthes suggests that the haiku is recited twice to underline its nullity (ibid. 99): in 'Brecht et le discours: contribution à l'étude de la discursivité', in *BL*, 243–53, his emphasis is rather different, and he suggests that the haiku is said three times, in order to release its resonances (246–7). The essential thing is that the repetition is not a means of approaching the haiku's 'meaning'.

les blanchisseuses prenaient entre deux repassages. Souvenir indicible de décentrement par excès de fadeur.[101]

(I have deliberately selected two which seem to me closer to haiku than some of the others, in that they deal with *one* event: the majority of the *anamnèses* are in fact in the imperfect, in other words deal with the 'memory' of *habitual* actions in the past.)

Are these fragments traumatic? Barthes leaves them without commentary; one form of symbolic sociability (that metalinguistic form known as theory) is deliberately foreclosed. They are events—they both refer to events, and behave as events *vis-à-vis* any totalizing interpretative or theoretical discussion which might try to incorporate them (as examples of a general trend in Barthes, or symptoms of his ideological fixations). That the event is both the language used and its referent is an idea developed by Lyotard. With regard to Barthes we might ask: what counts as an event for theory? The answer would involve a list of all the places in which Barthes presents us with cultural phenomena that he claims resists theoretical binding and thus threaten the theoretical ego, with its demands for homogeneity, coherence, and totality. Haiku, *anamnèses*, and *incidents* would be included in any such enumeration.

Whatever their tense, the 'past' of the *anamnèses* in *Barthes par lui-même* is a peculiarly present one: they are acts (writing acts rather than speech acts), and in so far as they are as dispersed as the universe of all possible haiku that Barthes imagines in *L'Empire des signes*, they mirror the dispersal (and not the integration, psychoanalytical or otherwise) of the subject that writes them. 'J'appelle *anamnèse* l'action—mélange de jouissance et d'effort—que mène le sujet pour retrouver, *sans l'agrandir ni le faire vibrer*, une ténuité du souvenir: c'est le haïku lui-même.'[102]

Also included in this category would be those places in which Barthes attempts to isolate a key element in a cultural product: for when this happens, the element identified as central is immediately endowed with the characteristics I associate with the trauma: such an element will be meaningless, isolated, non-associable, in some sense more real than its context, figural rather than discursive, and, in many cases, will involve a disturbance in linear time, being linked, frequently, to a past that constantly erupts into the present, and will not be narrativized once and for all.

---

[101] *RB*, 112–13.   [102] Ibid. 113.

I will look first at a number of occasions on which Barthes fastens on one key element in the literary text.

THE EFFECT OF THE REAL

Barthes's fascination for the haiku is a result both of its demure exoticism and of its tantalizing brevity. The haiku resists the kind of interpretation Barthes gives of *Sarrasine* because the haiku cannot be analysed, that is, broken down into constituent elements: the cultural coding to which it is subject in Japanese (Bashō's frog is in fact a common and recognizable symbol in Bashō's own culture) no longer obtains when read in translation: it becomes round and smooth, and meaning cannot force its way in. Western hermeneutic endeavour concentrates the attempt to '*percer* le sens, c'est-à-dire à le faire entrer par effraction'.[103] Balzac's text can be broken and entered, its meanings scattered: nor the haiku. This brevity, as I have said, situates the haiku as close to being a language-event—almost a performative. Furthermore, like the koan, the haiku has something atomistic about it, precisely because it cannot be divided.

The psyche has an atom too: the traumatic original signifier from which the subject is, in Lacan's term, suspended.[104] Do the signifiers of the literary text rotate around a similar kernel? Is there, in the text, something beyond which analysis cannot go?

Barthes constantly raises this question. Many early essays pay special attention to the status of the *object* in the literary text: Barthes praises Robbe-Grillet for having cleansed objects of the anthropomorphic, metaphorical, and symbolic meanings that realism has traditionally foisted onto them. Robbe-Grillet's objects (the notorious tomato in *Les Gommes* being emblematic) resist any poetic reading, in so far as his novel, unlike those of romantic writers such as Balzac or Michelet, are difficult to analyse thematically, in terms of the attraction or repulsion with which the writer experiences matter. But Robbe-Grillet's novels are traumatic in another way: they interrupt any recuperative reading, arrest the flow of narrative time, and estrange the reader from any world the fiction would otherwise seem to be disclosing. Robbe-Grillet's objects are indeed, according to 'Littérature objective', objective. And Barthes repeats Robbe-Grillet's assertions

[103] *EpS*, 94. [104] *Séminaire*, xi. 226.

that his novels are attempts to present the mere being-there of things—that they cleanse our perceptions of the outside world, erasing meaning.

In a later essay, however, Barthes rejects this account of Robbe-Grillet's practice.[105] Things are *not* merely there: nature is always already endowed with meaning, and it may require artistry to make it de-signify. Robbe-Grillet's objects do not, therefore, survive as unanalysable atoms in the text: they do not denote: rather, they connote their own meaninglessness, and this connotation, as artifice, can be analysed. As in many of his investigations into the nature of the literary text, Barthes sees connotation, however 'guilty' it may be in acting as the bearer of latent ideological attitudes, as language's fundamental sociability. It is what swings any supposed denotation (which implicitly supposes the primacy of a pure deictic function in language, as if language could merely indicate, outside of all ideological attitudes or context-bound markers of *énonciation*, the being-there of the world) back into the social and symbolic structures of discourse.

This provides us with a clue as to the potentially traumatic nature that, across his analyses of certain types of literary language (and, as we shall see, other cultural phenomena too), Barthes comes to see as inherent in denotation. For, despite stating very early on that connotation is inevitable, the fascination he shows for denotation means that he cannot lay the problem to rest. It is as if something in him resisted the universal triumph of connotation. He repetitively attempts to master a denotation that itself seems to resist being integrated entirely into any systematic theoretical approach. Denotation becomes a central concern in two senses: it challenges theory; and, concurrently with this, it seems to form a potential kernel of unanalysable opacity at the heart of various forms of representation.

The struggle between connotation and denotation dominates, for instance, Barthes's celebrated essay 'L'Effet de réel'.[106] This begins with examples of 'useless details'—in the writing of history (details of the door on which Charlotte Corday heard someone knock while waiting for the arrival of her executioner, in Michelet's account) and of fiction (the barometer gracing Mme Aubain's piano in Flaubert's 'Un cœur simple'). It is especially the barometer that attracts Barthes's attention: whereas everything else in the text can be seen as functional and thus integrated into structuralist analysis, the barometer resists. It

[105] 'Le Point sur Robbe-Grillet?', in *EC*, 198–205.
[106] *BL*, 167–74.

may perch, rather unsteadily, on a pyramidal pile of boxes on top of Mme Aubain's piano: but what is more intriguing is the way Barthes sees it, initially, as standing outside the story's structure. As he says, structuralist analysis is predicated on exhaustivity and cannot allow erratic details to go uncoded: everything signifies, and anything that would resist the total meaningfulness of the story would be a scandal.[107] Barthes notes that apparently useless details can usually be made to work for a structuralist analysis by being classified as catalyses ('fillers' which do not advance the action but have an indirect function as indices of character or atmosphere).[108] Surely the barometer is an index of 'atmosphere' if ever there was one? (We are, after all, in rainy Normandy.) But Barthes refuses to allow this, and turns the banal object into a particularly unsettling feature of Flaubert's story.

He finally decides that the meaningless detail does mean: it signifies *le réel concret*.[109] It does not merely denote: it connotes its denotativity. It is not 'just there': it is not, after Barthes has for the length of the essay toyed with the idea, an atom:[110] instead of being outside the structures of narrative realism, it actually founds them. Its very meaninglessness is thus recuperated, *in extremis*, as meaningful. The barometer does, as most readers will easily agree, connote: an erratic and obstinate detail is finally integrated, at the end of the essay, into the great symbolic matrix of Western narrative meaning.[111]

What Barthes focuses on here, it must be noted, is not an event so much as an object, and, as with Robbe-Grillet, the object attracts some of the interest Barthes elsewhere shows for the event in so far as the two seem, for different reasons, to challenge the kind of structural analysis of texts that Barthes had helped to found. There is thus a sense in which the object, especially its problematic status for analysis, *is* an event for the structural analyst. There is always something unpredictable about the event-object. Barthes as the novelist of the intellect imitates its *écart* from expectations by filling his theoretical writing with objects that are unusual and excessive (in that they seem to transcend the mere functions of demonstration): he

---

[107] 'Ces notations sont scandaleuses (du point de vue de la structure)', *BL*, 168.

[108] These are discussed in 'Introduction à l'analyse structurale du récit', in *AS*, 167–206 (178–83).

[109] *BL*, 172.

[110] Ibid. 168.

[111] For a discussion of this essay, a suggestion of the connotations that can be read into the barometer, and some of the problems Barthes's analysis fails to solve, see Christopher Prendergast, *The Order of Mimesis: Balzac, Stendhal, Nerval, Flaubert* (Cambridge, 1986), 64–74.

discusses this practice in a fragment called 'Passage des objets dans le discours' in *Barthes par lui-même*, which ends by noting that certain types of haiku accomplish this double feat, being both events and objects at once: 'Ainsi, parfois, dans les haïkus du Japon, la ligne des mots écrits s'ouvre brusquement et c'est le dessin méme du mont Fuji ou d'une sardine qui vient gentiment occuper le lieu du mot congédié.'[112] This reminds us that 'scribble'—the figure—can be an event too, something that erupts into speech or discourse in the same way that the sardine leaps into the haiku. Even early essays by Barthes show a longing to gain access to some world of pure objects uncontaminated by discourse. His preface to Chateaubriand's *Vie de Rancé* betrays a considerable fascination with the *chat jaune* of the abbé Séguin, Chateaubriand's confessor. This cat plays something of the same role for Barthes here as did Madame Aubain's barometer. For *chat jaune* is both more and less than its meaning (the connotation of *chat jaune* is that the abbé Séguin is poor but kind-hearted—kind enough to look after 'un chat disgracié, perdu': but Chateaubriand does not *say* these connotations). It both enables meanings (connotations) to be generated but is not absorbed by those meanings—the yellow cat is 'just' a yellow cat as well as being a signifier of poverty and goodness. 'Peut-être ce chat jaune est-il toute la littérature.'[113] Barthes is fascinated by the way Chateaubriand's writing seems to leap from one object to another in ways that tend to disturb the ideological, symbolic, and narrative patterns of biography he is writing. Words like *gant* and *algue* appear surprising in their contexts: 'à travers cet écart cultivé, c'est toujours une substance surprenante (*algue, gant*) qui fait irruption dans le discours'—like the sardine emerging into its haiku. And from these considerations he derives his own, albeit fragmentary, Cratylean dream.

La parole littéraire (puisque c'est d'elle qui'il s'agit) apparaît comme un immense et somptueux débris, le reste fragmentaire d'une Atlantide où les mots, surnourris de couleur, de saveur, de forme, bref de *qualités* et non d'idées, brilleraient comme les éclats d'un monde *direct*, impensé, que ne viendrait ternir, ennuyer aucune logique: que les mots pendent comme de beaux fruits à l'arbre indifférent du récit, tel est au fond le rêve de l'écrivain.[114]

---

[112] *RB*, 139. Réda Bensmaïa, in *Barthes à l'Essai: introduction au texte réfléchissant* (Études littéraires françaises, 37: Tübingen, 1986), sees the irruption of objects into discourse as a heterogeneity essential to Barthes's constitution of a new form of the essay-genre.

[113] *NEC*, 116.

[114] Ibid. 113.

Logic and narratives are both down-graded—to the status, as it were, of catalysers, which get us from one succulent word-object to the next. Barthes does not say that logic and narrative are dispensable, but it is curious how what he says about Chateaubriand (an author who persisted, whatever Barthes says, in telling long stories, however elliptical) comes close to the values he will later express in his praise of the haiku. *Le Plaisir du texte* likewise notes how in apparently innocuous descriptions, this time in a writer almost the stylistic opposite of Chateaubriand, Stendhal, is generated a minor satori of astonishment. In one of his anecdotes, Stendhal mentions food, and Barthes decides that his pleasure in reading about this food is not one of representation (since he does not like the food being detailed): rather, what he is reacting to is the *intraitable* of the description, and on this basis he makes a distinction (drawn from Lacan) between a realism that concentrates on *le réel* (the real as symbolized and intelligible) and *la réalité* (the real as contingency).[115] The novel can mix these two kinds of realism: in 1791, as today, restaurants served 'une salade d'oranges au rhum'. Barthes sees this anecdote as typically novelistic: it represents a first stage towards historical understanding (it is the kind of detail that historians of everyday life have become increasingly interested in), but also, more simply, 'l'entêtement de la chose (l'orange, le rhum) à *être là*'.[116] Despite Barthes's denial, food is a good example of this 'obtuse' realism, partly because food is on the edges of need (we need to eat) and desire (we do not need, but may desire, to eat oranges in rum). Whether these words are fruits hanging on a tree or reposing on a restaurant table, they become an emblem of the kind of text that Barthes likes—that which, while not 'eating its words', allows us to do so.

Returning to 'L'Effet de réel', Barthes's criteria for what would constitute denotation seems to involve the direct presentation, to the reader, of an object, as if the barometer were suddenly to burst out of the page and appear before our eyes. Once Barthes has decided that everything in the text connotes, denotation could only occur as a psychotic aberration (the collusion of referent and signifier, without the mediation of the signified). The attempt to settle the running boundary dispute between denotation and connotation shifts, however, to another medium: photography.

---

[115] *P/T*, 73–4.   [116] Ibid. 74.

PHOTOGRAPHY, FACT AND FICTION

Photography had already been a source of imagery for Freud's models of psychic functioning. He suggests that almost every process exists first at the unconscious level, only thereafter becoming conscious 'just as a photographic picture begins as a negative and only becomes a picture after being turned into a positive'.[117] Not every negative is developed—and not every unconscious process reaches consciousness.

A more interesting 'development' of this metaphorical 'flash' of inspiration can be found in *Moses and Monotheism*, where Freud explains in simple terms what he understands by *Nachträglichkeit*. Everybody knows that the first five years of life are decisive for one's character and destiny, but Freud underlines the strength of impressions which impinge on the child at an age before its mental apparatus is completely receptive. By going on to introduce the metaphor of the mind as a camera, the film as *tabula rasa*, Freud is of course ignoring the problem of infantile sexuality. That the subject is determined by events for which the psyche is not yet prepared requires, says Freud, an explanation: 'we may make it more comprehensible by comparing it with a photographic exposure which can be developed after any interval of time and transformed into a picture'.[118] Not a very sophisticated image, but one which reminds us of what had happened in 1897. Freud had thought his patients were remembering a real event (infantile seduction), whereas it transpired that what they were reporting was a fiction (a fantasy) constructed by infantile sexual impulses. Freud had, so to speak, wished that the hysteric's mind had been a camera capable of presenting him with a snapshot of the primal scene. For this would have been a scientific guarantee of that event's reality: we again come up against the relation of the trauma and the real.

Barthes asks whether the photo, which seems to re-present the real before our very eyes, will give us access to the reality that language (in which, as in the unconscious, there is no indication of reality) withholds. As early as *Mythologies*, he is persuasively demolishing the idea that the photo gives us a pure referent unmediated by ideological

---

[117] *Introductory Lectures on Psychoanalysis, Pelican Freud Library*, i. 336. Freud's use of photographic metaphors is noted in Derrida, 'Freud et la scène de l'écriture', in *L'Écriture et la différence*, 293–340 (320 n. 1).

[118] *Moses and Monotheism*, in *Pelican Freud Library*, iii. 237–386 (374).

attitudes. The photographs of actors, of elaborate magazine-recipe meals, of aspiring politicians, are all scrutinized for their socio-political connotations, as are two photographic exhibitions, one of which ('La Grande Famille des hommes') abusively suggests an essential human identity underlying what it tacitly ignores as the mere contingencies of class, race, or sexual difference, and another of which ('Photo-chocs') fails to deliver the advertised *frisson* for the simple reason that the shock is one intended by the photographer: what is really shocking, as Barthes points out, is something which shocks in the absence of any signifying intention—something which is not coded as shocking, which does not connive with cultural expectations of what may be outside culture: 'réduite à l'état de pur langage, la photographie ne nous *désorganise* pas'.[119] Photos are always 'framed' in both senses of the word: selective in their subject-matter, and careful to keep off frame the process of their own production. They also claim an objectivity (the alibi that 'because it is photographed it must be real') which masks the way in which they deliberately communicate attitudes towards the objects that they display.

A later essay, 'Le Message photographique', attempts to estabish a more scientific basis for a semiotics of the photograph.[120] But Barthes's question is formulated differently. Can this most analogical and imitative of techniques pin down the real, or is that real always linguistic? Tempted as usual to take the semiotic model as far as it will go, he doubts whether there can be such a thing as an insignificant, neutral photograph, one that shows a real before it can be formulated in language—hence his preference for talking or 'reading' a photograph rather than 'seeing' or 'perceiving' it. (It is precisely this semiotic imperialism against which Lyotard protests in *Discours, Figure*.)

Barthes cites in evidence the hypothesis of Bruner and Piaget according to which the photograph is verbalized at the same time as it is perceived. But he also refers to Cohn-Séat, who does admit the possibility of a time-lapse between perception and verbalization: if the process of understanding is delayed, 'il y a désordre de la perception, interrogation, angoisse du sujet, traumatisme'.[121]

---

[119] *My*, 106, my emphasis.
[120] *OO*, 9–24. Much has been written on Barthes's treatment of photographs, esp. in *CC*. See Jean Delord, *Roland Barthes et la photographie* (1981), and numerous articles including Jacques Derrida, 'Les Morts de Roland Barthes', in *Psyché: inventions de l'autre* (1987), 273–30; Éric Marty, 'L'Assomption du phénomène', *Communications*, 423–4 Aug.–Sept. (1982), 744–52; Claude Reichler, 'L'Ombre', *Critique*, 423–4 (Aug.–Sept. 1982), 767–774.
[121] *OO*, 21.

Barthes's further question is this: can there be such a thing as photographic denotation? His first answer is negative: there is no infralinguistic level of perception: the photograph, and thus what it presents as the real, is always already connoted by language. But the question is not entirely resolved there, and returns later in the essay: it is true that the effects of connotation extend very far but there may be a space beyond for them. For if pure denotation exists, says Barthes, it is (perhaps) not at the level of the insignificant or neutral photo, but rather 'au niveau des images proprement traumatiques: le trauma, c'est précisément ce qui suspend le langage et bloque la signification'.[122] These photographs are traumatic in so far as they represent an event (usually violent) in which a trauma has been suffered. Properly traumatic photos are rare, because there is usually some rhetorical mediation—a cultural code across which they are filtered. It is true that, as for the earlier Freud, the trauma is intimately linked to the reality of the scene: 'en photographie, le trauma est entièrement tributaire de la certitude que la scène a réellement eu lieu'.[123] The certainty would seem to be an index of unfakable reality: because the photographer was there to record the event, it really did happen. Connotation menaces the purity of denotation even here, though, because this certainty itself is verbalized as the mythical definition of denotation, namely *il fallait que le photographe fût là*—which is itself already a connotation.

Barthes's grounds for discussing denotations are already shifting, because it is clear that if you let language in on the process of perceptual interpretation too early, you will quite simply debar any possibility of the pure kind of denotation he is relentlessly pursuing. It is here that his analysis merges into his general preoccupation with the limits of the kind of investigation he is trying to undertake. For he suggests that there could indeed be a traumatic photo, but it would be that of which there is nothing to be said.[124] The trauma itself in this way changes position: it is not what is denoted (not an event which is reported or re-presented), but is itself, as a cultural construct which stands obliquely to any theoretical manipulation, an event. And this curious formulation, *rien à dire*, which Barthes increasingly employs as a gambit to ward off the potential totality, and thus closure, of theory, shows the nature of the limit being proposed. Like the haiku which refuses commentary, like the traumatic kernel which resists associative

[122] *OO*, 23   [123] Ibid.   [124] Ibid.

abreaction or symbolic integration, the traumatic photo arrests language.

But in what sense? To say that something arrests language is to attract two immediate rejoinders. Firstly, it does not arrest language at all: you are still in a sense talking about it even as you discuss its ineffability. Secondly, once any one person has claimed to identify a certain blind spot, moment of meaninglessness, or element of pure denotation in a cultural product, someone else, if only by virtue of that very fact, will be able to see round the blind-spot, flood the meaningless with significance, and read connotations into the denotation—if only the very connotation of 'denotativity'. However, the point is that this theme of *rien à dire* which runs through much of his later work is, as we have already seen, itself a resistance to theory as speech, and to the abreaction of local intensities and ephemeral events. In his micronarrative of how research happens, in which he is prepared to register his hesitation, false trails, and backtrackings, Barthes is following the spirit of Freud. For while, outside the case histories, Freud rarely presents us with anything like a narrative of how exactly he came to reach his theoretical conclusions, psychoanalysis is in many respects rooted in the investigator's own sense of vulnerability, and inability to speak a magisterial metalanguage. There is a far from trivial sense in which psychoanalysis springs from the death of Freud's father, and Freud's attempt to overcome his sense of loss by attempting to theorize his feelings. Psychoanalysis is thus based on one man's trauma.[125]

In his last piece of research, *La Chambre claire*, Barthes without himself drawing any parallel between his own endeavour and that of Freud, similarly decides to found a theory of photography on his own, private trauma, the loss, in his case, of his mother. (I shall be returning to this shortly.) What is clear even in the earlier essays on photography I am discussing here is that Barthes's concentration on denotation is not only an objective, scientific interest: he is using it to draw the subjective limits of theory: his account of theory is thus both historical and subjective, in that it demonstrates how apparently theoretical problems (the 'effect of the real' or the existence of pure denotation) simultaneously position the subject attempting to master them as a subject—one who may have 'nothing to say' about the cultural phenomenon being investigated, not just because of stupidity, but

[125] Freud's father died in 1896, the same year that Freud introduced the term 'psychoanalysis': Freud's self-analysis began the following year.

because, either in the text or in that subject, something resists. By Barthes's own criteria, what resists is most real. The trauma (that of which there is nothing to be said) is the locus of the real, not for everyone, but for the subject that is struck by theoretical dumbness at precisely that point. Barthes (following Lacan) frequently equates intense emotion with *bêtise*. Both *bêtise* and the trauma resist metalanguage, and both cannot be analysed away be mere self-reflexivity: they are obstinate, silent, individual, and Barthes uses of them such words as *insécable, primitif, noyau, intraitable*.

Furthermore, Barthes's interest in the photo is partly a consequence of his hostility to connotation. In his early analyses, connotation is the way a particular culture manages to slip across its own ideological attitudes without ever coming clean about this process. Connotation is thus a symptom of the falsity of prevailing social relations. And Barthes's hostility constantly tends to broaden, in more or less surreptitious ways, to a belief that anything intelligible risks being corrupted by that falsity, that all opinion (everything that can be said) is *doxa*.[126] What most interests him in film and photography, both arts which come into existence in periods of rapid industrialization, as technological means for diffusing cultural products, is, paradoxically, something private, something wounding: the real for him, even if he believes that the categories he has laid bare can be recognized by others too, albeit located in different places.

This explains why Barthes's later essays on photography attempt to preserve it from collapsing into language, by defining it as a procedure with its own specificity. This is true, for instance, of 'Rhétorique de l'image'.[127] According to this essay, the photo can transmit a message without a code. It is true that pure denotation is a utopian horizon, but it is also true that he wants to affirm this difference of photography, since only then can photography be seen as an epistemological, and not merely a technical, rupture, inaugurating what he calls a type of consciousness without precedent. Only then, in other words, can the invention of photography count, not as a mere linear development already inscribed within society's cultural grammar, but as, itself, an event.

But if the photo introduces into history a consciousness without precedence, it is also one without presence. This brings us back to the

---

[126] In 'Le discours prévisible', a fragment in *RB*, Barthes overhears a conversation in which every comment is flat and foreseeable: this 'voix qui ne choisit personne' is for him the voice of 'la Doxa inexorable' (*RB*, 152).

[127] *OO*, 25–42

haiku, and the trauma. In the case of photography, the factor of exclusion (the spectator's present is fascinated by a photographic past that is bizarrely present) is crucial. The new way of seeing is also a breakdown of seeing, a chronological split which shatters previous forms of perception. Like Freud, what fascinates Barthes about the photograph is, despite the medium's visibility, less space than time: the fact that here we have a combination of referential certainty (the photographer really was there) and the time-lapse mechanism to which it owes its existence. The photographic print is always the record of what has been—it shows not a here and now, and thus not the *être-là* of the referent, but its *avoir-été-là*, what Barthes calls a 'real unreality'. This is a major revision, for where Barthes in general, and with the reservations mentioned above ('entêtement de la chose (l'orange, le rhum) à être là'),[128] refuses to allow literature to give us any 'being-there', he does permit photography to give us a 'being-there'—but one that is irrevocably past. Its apparent unreality is not that of fantasy, but that which is instituted by a split in time. This sense of exclusion, allied to a high degree of subjective involvement, is also noted at the beginning of *Barthes par lui-même*, where he is faced with photos of 'his' childhood in which he cannot recognize 'himself'. According to 'Le Message photographique', the more traumatic a photo is, the more it keeps fantasy at bay—you cannot dream about it. Nor can you use it as a point of departure for projective imagination (it limits creative speculation—and thus, claims Barthes, the photograph is not used in psychological association tests, unlike drawings). The traumatic photo excludes the spectator: 'le *cela a été* bat en brèche le *c'est moi*': this is what the subject of the trauma could say about the traumatic event which arouses memories of the primal scene: it really happened, and this fact defeats the 'it's me', the ego's sense of its own imaginary identity. Photography is thus a traumatic event in history, representing a new and absolute quality, a 'mutation capitale des économies d'information',[129] or what Walter Benjamin, who with rather different emphases sees photography as a traumatic loss of identity in a world given over now to endless reproduction, calls the 'tremendous shattering of tradition which is the obverse of the contemporary crisis and renewal of mankind'.[130] Benjamin shows that this is because the photograph, being implicated in a new technology

[128] *PlT*, 74.
[129] *OO*, 36.
[130] 'The Work of Art in the Age of Mechanical Reproduction', in *Illuminations*, trans. Harry Zohn (London, 1973), 219–53 (223).

of reproduction, 'substitutes a plurality of copies for a unique existence' (an aspect which Barthes plays down), destroys the context-
bound nature of artistic perception, and—this is the crucial point for
out parallel with Barthes—'detaches the reproduced object from the
domain of tradition'. While Barthes sees the photographic referent as
past, Benjamin sees it as detached from tradition. Both writers are
suggesting that tradition is a way of actualizing the past here and now,
that this depends on models of narrative continuity, and that photographs interrupt such continuity. The photograph, in other words, is
in itself a challenge to the narrative forms in which tradition tends to
be embodied.[131] (Can there be a 'history of photography'?)

Extending his analysis of photography to the film still, Barthes goes
beyond classical semiotics to identify an obstinate kind of detail which
behaves like a floating signifier within the image, locatable without
being easy to integrate into the analysis. In this essay ('Le Troisième
Sens'), Barthes's stills are taken from various Eisenstein films.[132] He
describes, to begin with, two levels of meaning. The first is informa-
tional and communicative: as a category, it seems to subsume what in
the more narratological analysis of S/Z had been divided into the
proairetic code (sequences of actions), and the cultural and hermeneutic codes: this level of analysis of the still (the photogram) deals with
decor, characters, costumes, anecdotes (diegesis), and so on. The
second level of meaning is the symbolic: this evidently includes
symbolic and semic codes (in the terms of S/Z), but Barthes redistrib-
utes the categories of the analysis he carried out on Balzac, so that 'Le
Troisième Sens' talks of a diegetic symbolism. This second level is
called signification.

Both first and second levels have remained within a semiotics of the
sign, but the third level which Barthes finds relies on an incomplete
sign, a signifier without, as yet, a signified, which provokes an effect
of *signifiance*, of a meaning not yet fully emerged into signification.
Certain details, areas, or aspects of the photogram (that is, the film
still) hold Barthes's attention in a peculiarly forceful way, and do not
fit into the analysis of the first two levels, which are thus not
exhaustive: for, he says, once I have dealt with the levels of information
and signification,

---

[131] A full comparison between Barthes and Benjamin on photography would need to
take into account major differences of outlook: Barthes, e.g., devalues reproducibility
where Benjamin sees its potentially liberating aspects. See also Peter Collier, 'Roland
Barthes: the Critical Subject (An Idea for Research)', *Paragraph*, 11 (1988), 175–80.

[132] *OO*, 43–61.

je ne peux encore me détacher de l'image. Je lis, je reçois, (probablement, même, en premier), évident, erratique et têtu, un troisième sens. Je ne sais quel est son signifié, du moins je n'arrive pas à le nommer, mais je vois bien les traits, les accidents signifiants dont ce signe, dès lors, est composé ... Je ne sais pas si la lecture de ce troisième sens est fondée—si on peut la généraliser—, mais il me semble déjà que son signifiant (les traits que je viens de tenter de dire, sinon de décrire) possède une individualité théorique.[133]

This signifier is irreducible to the mere *être-là* of the body, and disturbs reading, deferring understanding: Barthes calls the reading that it provokes 'poetic', which needs to be seen in the light of *Le Degré zéro de l'écriture* and the *Mythologies* postface 'Le Mythe, aujourd'hui', where a poetic reading is one in which critical intelligibility comes up against its limit—the limit formed by the resistance of some enigmatic materiality. Here, the third meaning cannot be absorbed by the intellect: if the second level (*signification*) is *obvie*, the third level (*signifiance*) is *obtus*, and constitutes the essence of the filmic in that it cannot be described or represented but only located.

This third level is valorized by Barthes not only because it holds his attention, but also because it provides a theoretical basis for the attraction of mixed genres—those precisely which rely on an interweaving of image and language: Barthes cites as examples the photo-novel and the comic-strip. The photo-novel is affecting in its very vulgarity, the way in which it is outside high culture, as the shadow, parody, or carnival of that culture. The *sens obtus* is indeed obtuse in the sense of being stupid, and its very obtuseness is something of a trauma for the theoretician: earlier in the essay, Barthes had suggested that the obtuse meaning, if it could be described, would take the form of a haiku: 'geste anaphorique sans contenu significatif, sorte de balafre dont est rayé le sens (l'envie de sens)',[134] and now he explicitly equates significance with the trauma in that in both cases meaning is held in suspense, referred back indeterminately to a distant past or deferred to a future, replicating the time-scale of *Nachträglichkeit*, destroying the possibility of self-presence:

j'éprouve pour ma part ce léger trauma de la signifiance devant certains photo-romans: *'leur bêtise me touche'* (telle pourrait être une certaine définition du sens obtus); il y aurait donc une vérité d'avenir (ou d'un très ancien passé)

---

[133] *OO*, 44   [134] Ibid. 56.

dans ces formes dérisoires, vulgaires, sottes, dialogiques, de la sous-culture de consommation.[135]

It is worth remembering the fragment from *Le Plaisir du texte* I quoted in my discussion of drift, for at the end of that fragment Barthes sketches a rapid equation between *dérive*, *l'Intraitable*, and *la Bêtise*.[136] The intractable stupidity of drift (which is also seen as 'anachronistic')[137] lies in its disturbing of such oppositions as old/new, outdated/modern, past/present, high culture/low culture, meaningful/meaningless. This is stupid because, outside such oppositions, it is difficult to *say* anything. We are reminded of Barthes listening with stupefied delight to a language (Japanese) that he will never understand—and that he does not want to understand (at least on the level of *signification*) in *L'Empire des signes*.

In *La Chambre claire*, finally, Barthes distinguishes between two qualities of attention: the *studium*, a general, cultural interest without any particular intensity, and the *punctum*, which disturbs this floating attention and constitutes a sudden irruption of peculiarly intense affect in which the control of the theoretical ego is breached. 'Cette fois, ce n'est pas moi qui vais le chercher (comme j'investis de ma conscience souveraine le champ du *studium*)', c'est lui qui part de la scène, comme une flèche, et vient me percer.'[138] The effect of the *punctum*, as its name suggests, is to pierce, to wound: Barthes talks of it as a *piqûre* and a *blessure*: it is both *douleur* and *jouissance*[139] and therefore, like the trauma, suspends the operation of the pleasure principle (that sense of theoretical comfort and security which accompanies the perception and analysis of the photographic *studium*): '*punctum*, c'est aussi: piqûre, petit trou, petite tache, petite coupure—et aussi coup de dés. Le *punctum* d'une photo, c'est ce hasard qui, en elle, *me point* (mais aussi me meurtrit, me poigne)'.[140]

In each photograph that enables Barthes to locate a *punctum* that he cannot name,[141] the isolated element is the real—for him (and, almost as a logical corollary, *not* for us: Barthes again refuses to see the real in terms of generality, or even in dialectical terms).[142] And in the second part of *La Chambre claire*, Barthes takes up the insight of earlier theoretical writing on the photograph to suggest that the photographic trauma lies precisely in the way the photo gives us access

---

[135] *OO*, 59–60 n. 1.   [136] *PlT*, 33.   [137] Ibid. 99.
[138] *CC*, 49.   [139] Ibid. 51.   [140] Ibid. 49.   [141] Ibid. 84.
[142] 'Toujours ce refus français de l'hégélianisme', as he puts it in 'Une philosophie simpliste' (*RB*, 170).

to a reality that is always past, an essence of the photo which he baptizes *ça-a-été*. This final revelation of the essence of photography is mediated by, in the ordinary sense of the word, a personal 'trauma', the death of Barthes's mother, what, more than anything, counts as a real event which cannot easily be talked about. By refusing the abreactions of theory in the first part of his book, Barthes can develop a new theory better able to respect the singularity of the event (his mother's death) and at the same time to universalize it into the noema of photography in general—a universality that is not predicated on any grand narrative, but on the recognition of the recurrent (and uncannily present) pastness of the past, its immobile and moving obtuseness. *La Chambre claire*, which is already tending towards the Utopian mode of fiction (its past historic tense, its proleptic announcement of writing as henceforth the aim of Barthes's life), is also moving towards an awakening from the cultural codes. Photography is thus the vehicle of a satori—'l'éveil de l'intraitable réalité'[143]—but this is not the conclusion of a defeated semiologist no longer able to engage with the world of conflict and contradiction: it is the acknowledgement of a new subjective certainty (the bedrock of the *ça-a-été* and the realization that this certainty can be the beginning of writing and action, not its end. The *rien à dire* of the theorist becomes the *tout à écrire* of the novelist-to-be.

The *punctum* thus joins the list of those many Barthesian sites where language's representational capacities seems to reach a limit, which Barthes himself allegorically suggests by the exclamatory reduction to which such experiences force language: *c'est ça!*', *tel!*, *ça-a-été!* What these exclamations point to cannot be named properly, cannot be an object of knowledge as such, if knowledge (*savoir*) involves metalinguistic distance, as it does for Barthes. These mystical (mute) deictics point the way (of initiation) to something which can only be apprehended.[144] That which is most intense Barthes wants to keep outside of any classical semiotic analysis and outside representation. These exclamations are a restatement of a constant theme running through his work: that of the literary text as a figure that points in silence to something outside itself, but to which our only access is the text itself.

What is pointed to may be unsayable in more radical senses than

[143] *CC*, 185.
[144] Weber makes a similar point about the traumatic real that, for Freud, has to remain a 'capital X' (*Legend of Freud*, 59).

those I will deal with here.[145] While Barthes does not in general attempt to 'position' such absolute historical traumas, he does give us images of historical suffering, such as the traces inscribed in the face of the woman at Vakoulintchouk's funeral (*Battleship Potemkin*, discussed in 'Le Troisième Sens'). We must not forget that here we have an actress mimicking a real event, not 'the real itself' that Barthes seeks in *La Chambre claire*: none the less, Barthes's description of her stricken features, and of the 'third meaning' it typifies, brings together all the aspects of the trauma, as well as many other Barthesian themes: he is certain of the force of the immobilized photogrammatic image for him, but not of how to theorize it; from it there comes 'un trait pénétrant'; it occasions 'une sorte de scandale, de supplément ou de dérive'; it is like a mask, uncanny and pitiful; it disturbs time (although as a still it should be absorbed into the narrative of the film, it refuses such reintegration, is a left-over from the story); it is deictic (it can be pointed to if not easily described); it is 'ce qui, dans l'image, est purement image' and thus it is outside speech (but, as inscription, it is close to the figurality of pure writing); it sterilizes metalanguage; if it could be described it would have the form of a haiku, as an attempt to respect singularity while not condemning it to muteness.[146]

AH!

I suggested at the beginning of this chapter that the trauma is a figure of repetition. The infant, in Freud's theory, is seduced into sexuality (into the repetition of desire) by a failure to understand. We can take this as another example of the myth of the origin of writing, most concisely suggested in Barthes's discussion of Cy Twombly, whom we have met before. This new myth will complement the story I told earlier, in my discussion of anaclitic drift. Here I want briefly to consider the challenge to Barthes as critic posed by Twombly's work. As images, his canvases call up the symbol: as writing, however scribbled, they invite meaning. Like a great deal of minimalist art,

---

[145] I have already mentioned Auschwitz. In *RB* Barthes follows Brecht in suggesting that realism is no longer capable of representing the sheerly surprising nature of the world today, esp. such 'stupefying' events as Auschwitz ('La littérature comme mathésis', *RB*, 122–3). Lyotard, who faces the problem of how to locate such events more directly, notes that for Adorno, Auschwitz is the wound which *Geist* can never heal (*Le Différend*, 2).

[146] *OO*, 48–58.

Twombly's works seem to be exhausted at a glance. But what is more interesting is the way this threat of critical aphasia is turned into an affirmation of artistic practice. As in 'Le Troisième Sens', Barthes's analysis, in 'Sagesse de l'art', includes considerations not usually encountered in semiotics.[147] He divides the spectator of a Twombly painting into five subjects: the cultural subject, who recognizes the mythical allusions (to Virgil, to Sesostris, etc.) in the picture; the art-specialist subject, who slots Twombly into historical place (both these subjects can talk 'about' the picture); the subject of pleasure, which cannot be expressed directly (this subject is condemned to appreciative interjections or silent contemplation—Barthes sees the limits to a purely hedonistic approach to criticism, as he does at the end of the first part of *La Chambre claire*); and, fourth and fifth, the subjects of memory and production. The subject of memory is subject to memory's *Nachträglichkeit*, in the simplest, most narratival sense of the word—a commonplace remark, except for the fact that Barthes does not leave it in isolation but links it, precisely, to the fifth subject. What is remembered is a detail, a trace:

Sur une toile de Twombly, telle tache m'apparaît d'abord hâtive, mal formée, inconséquente: je ne la comprends pas; mais cette tache travaille en moi, à mon insu; la toile abandonnée, elle revient, se fait souvenir et souvenir tenace: tout a changé, la toile me rend rétroactivement heureux.[148]

The object has to be lost, the effect of the trace being experienced only in the absence of the original painting, and this turning away from the origin which cannot be spoken opens the door to the fifth subject, that of production. Barthes cannot verbalize his emotions 'about' Twombly: his critical metalanguage is paralysed: there is nothing to be said except '*ça me plaît*'. He has been seduced into muteness. But just as the *texte scriptible* is not so much to be commented on as that which arouses the desire to write *tout court*, Barthes now experiences the desire to 'faire la même chose'. The birth of sexuality is traumatic and the trauma—the failure to under-stand the desire of the other—is seductive. That whereof one can-not speak, one must repeat. In trying to imitate Twombly, Barthes will always fail, just as his attempts to write a haiku always seem to lead to products that are too coarse, not attenuated enough. But both Twombly and the haiku arouse the desire to write by being placed, at a certain moment, outside writing: by being untranslatable into the

---

[147] *OO*, 163–78.   [148] Ibid. 176–7.

critic's own metalanguage. The chain of desire thus depends on repression. The secret within the work is not one that can be interpreted, but it is one that can be learnt, in *practice*. The idea (expressed in *Le Degré zéro de l'écriture*) that only *langue* and socially coded *écriture* (rather than *style*) are modes of sociability is thus finally demonstrated to be fallacious, as is the belief that only theory or self-reflexivity—which aim at liquidating guilty secrets and demystifying the opaque resistance of language (its distance, what Benjamin called its aura)—can be responsible modes of writing.[149]

What do we do with a phenomenon that cannot be absorbed, understood, defused, explained, judged, or even spoken? One answer, at least in the case of a literary phenomenon, is: repeat it—and when Barthes refers to a repetition, he occasionally means it quite literally, as we have already seen (Barthes threatening to express his admiration for *War and Peace* by rewriting it, word for word).[150] That rewriting is, however, partly what reading always performs, in silence. This suggests that there is a sense in which, for Barthes, the 1,500 pages of *War and Peace* constitute a gigantic haiku—or a koan, a riddle with no answer. Barthes's desire to rewrite *War and Peace* suggests that in his last years literature itself is, for him, something always already there, complete in itself, cut off from historical determinants, beyond analysis. No longer prepared to speak of it, Barthes prepares to repeat it, to write a novel, a story with characters. He loses the social prosthesis of speech (of theory), he falls silent, withdrawing into his tradition, now identified as history and symbolically as his mother's body, the place where he has always been before. This is partly the result of the failure of theoretical defence when faced with certain limit situations. Benjamin, who, as I said earlier, shows great interest in Freud's later theory of shock, suggests that Baudelaire's reflection, his heightened awareness, his theoretical intelligence, is closely linked to the shock experience.

Without reflection there would be nothing but the sudden start, usually the sensation of fright which, according to Freud, confirms the failure of the shock defence. Baudelaire has portrayed this condition in a harsh image. He

---

[149] Aura, says Benjamin, is 'the unique phenomenon of a distance, however close it may be' ('The Work of Art in the Age of Mechanical Reproduction', in *Illuminations*, 224).

[150] 'Je suis si heureux en lisant ce roman qu'il n'est pas possible que je n'aie pas tout simplement envie de le refaire, tout bêtement, tout littéralement' (C, 367).

speaks of a duel in which the artist, just before being beaten, screams in fright. This duel is the creative process itself.[151]

This can be paralleled by an anecdote from Japanese culture. The poet Bashō, in his nomadic journeys across Japan, translates events, sights, and places into the tenuous language of the haiku. His mastery of this is well attested: he becomes a celebrity. He can turn into seventeen syllables the sound of a frog jumping into a pond, the sighting of a violet on a mountain path, or the beauty of a moon at four in the morning. He visits the pine islands of Matsushima: their beauty paralyses his capacity to make a haiku on them: he is struck by aphasia and escapes only by repetition. The master of haiku cannot master his emotions. What eventually emerges to mark this fiasco when faced with a nature that is obstinately there?

> Matsushima ya
> ah!
> Matsushima ya
> Matsushima ya.[152]

ET APRÈS?

Ah!—like *tel!*, *c'est ça!*, *ça-a-été!*—would seem to be the last of my figures of writing, in so far as they mark the stigmatic trace of a real that can, as Bashō's experience suggests, only be indicated, as if this were the only way of naming it, properly but expletively: writing attempts to point off frame, hence Barthes's fascination for figures of writing that are pure indices, figures that cannot be translated out of figurality into speech, and that seem to promise—as phenomenology, one of Barthes's last new philosophical interests suggests—a new beginning, an obstinate 'being there' that is both subjective and

---

[151] Benjamin, 'Some Motifs in Baudelaire', in *Charles Baudelaire*, 117.

[152] Aitken, in *A Zen Wave: Bashō's Haiku and Zen* (New York, 1978), discusses this 'failed' haiku—which is only apocryphally attributed to Bashō—as in fact part of a conventionally exclamative trend in Japanese haiku writing, thus suggesting that the codes accompany Barthes even as they point 'beyond'. In 'On échoue toujours à parler de ce qu'on aime' (*BL*, 333–42), Barthes notes how Stendhal's immediate notations of pleasure in things Italian remains equally conventional: to transfer his passion to the reader, Stendhal has to adopt the mediations of another and more highly-formalized and social convention, that of the large-scale symbolic narrative structure. It is some form of narrative that Barthes finally aspires to in order to disprove the title of this (last) essay: you cannot necessarily speak about what you love, but you can write it, via the mediation of the Other, in a fiction.

historical. As events, these discoveries punctuate Barthes's final texts, which often treat of exclusion, alienation and a wounding if seductive singularity. But even as language shrinks to a vanishing point, its tensions remain. For *La Chambre claire* may attempt to found a *mathesis singularis*, but it finally turns away from the merely exclamatory identification of the real as punctual and subjective, even when its new certainties are based on those moments: it looks to a new sociability: it accepts the mode offered by a tradition (that of the novel in the past historic) that it positions in the historic past, and that it, none the less, prepares to repeat. All our figures of writing have seemed to point to somewhere outside themselves, hence the momentum they impart to a body of work that never relapses into stasis: and Barthes's projected novel is also a pointer, from theory to a real that would paradoxically be written as fiction. But, for Barthes, the novel is yet to come and this emergence is interminable: the novel becomes the Utopia of theory.

BIBLIOGRAPHY

I. WORKS BY BARTHES

These are listed in chronological order of publication. Details of first edition are given in square brackets if this differs from the edition I use.

Le Degré zéro de l'écriture [Seuil, 'Pierres vives', 1953] (Seuil, 'Points', 1972). (The 1972 reprint includes *Nouveaux essais critiques*.)

'Pouvoirs de la tragédie antique', *Théatre populaire*, 2 (Sept. 1953), 12–22.

Michelet par lui-même (Seuil, 'Écrivains de toujours', 1954).

Mythologies [Seuil, 'Pierres vives', 1957] (Seuil, 'Points', 1970). (The 1970 reprint includes a new preface.)

Sur Racine [Seuil, 'Pierres vives', 1963] (Seuil, 'Points', 1979).

Essais critiques [Seuil, 'Tel Quel', 1964] (Seuil, 'Points', 1981).

La Tour Eiffel, with André Martin (Delpire, 1964).

Critique et vérité (Seuil, 'Tel Quel', 1966).

Système de la mode [Seuil, 1967] (Seuil, 'Points', 1983).

'Un cas de critique culturelle', *Communications*, 14 (Nov. 1969), 97–9.

S/Z [Seuil, 'Tel Quel', 1970] (Seuil, 'Points', 1976).

L'Empire des signes [Skira, 'Les Sentiers de la création', Geneva, 1970] (Flammarion, 'Champs', 1980).

Sade, Fourier, Loyola [Seuil, 'Tel Quel', 1971] (Seuil, 'Points', 1980).

Nouveaux essais critiques (Seuil, 'Points', 1972).

Le Plaisir du texte [Seuil, 'Tel Quel', 1973] (Seuil, 'Points', 1982).

Alors la Chine? (Christian Bourgois, 1975).

Barthes par lui-même (Seuil, 'Écrivains de toujours', 1975).

'Barthes puissance trois', *Quinzaine littéraire* (1–15 Mar. 1975), 3–5.

Fragments d'un discours amoureux (Seuil, 'Tel Quel', 1977).

Image-Music-Text [Fontana, London, 1977] (Fontana, 1984): a collection of Barthes's essays selected and transl. by Stephen Heath.

Leçon inaugurale de la chaire de sémiologie littéraire du Collège de France, prononcée le 7 janvier 1977 (Seuil, 1978).

Sollers écrivain (Seuil, 'Tel Quel', 1979).

La Chambre claire: note sur la photographie (Gallimard, 'Les Cahiers du cinéma', 1980).

'Cher Antonioni', *Les Cahiers du cinéma*, 311 (May 1980), 9–11.

Sur la littérature, with Maurice Nadeau (Presses de l'Université de Grenoble, Grenoble, 1980): text of a dialogue broadcast on French radio.

Le Grain de la voix: entretiens 1962–1980 (Seuil, 1981).

'Une leçon de sincérité', *Poétique*, 47 (Sept. 1981), 259–67.

Carte, segni (Electa, Milan, 1981): catalogue of an exhibition of Barthes's paintings and drawings at the Casino dell'Aurora, Rome (Feb.–Mar. 1981).

A Barthes Reader [Hill & Wang, New York, 1982] (Cape, London, 1982): a selection, by Susan Sontag, of Barthes's works in English trans.

L'Obvie et l'obtus (Seuil, 'Tel Quel', 1982).

all except you ('Repères', Galerie Maeght, 1983).

Le Bruissement de la langue (Seuil, 1984).

L'Aventure sémiologique (Seuil, 1985).

Le Texte et l'image (Pavillon des Arts, 1986): catalogue of an exhibition based on Barthes's writings on the visual arts, May–Aug. 1986.

Incidents (Seuil, 1987).

II. WORKS ON BARTHES

Books and Articles

BENSMAÏA, RÉDA, *Barthes à l'essai: introduction au texte réfléchissant* (Études littéraires françaises, 37; Tübingen, 1986).

BURNIER, MICHEL-ANTOINE, and RAMBAUD, PATRICK, *Le Roland-Barthes sans peine* (1978).

BUTOR, MICHEL, 'La Fascinatrice', in *Répertoire IV* (1974), 371–97.

CALVET, LOUIS-JEAN, *Roland Barthes: un regard politique sur le signe* (1973).

—— *Roland Barthes* (1990).

CAPLAN, JAY, 'Nothing but Language: On Barthes's *Empire of Signs*', *Visible Language*, 11: 4 (autumn 1977), 341–62.

CHAMPAGNE, ROLAND, *Literary History in the Wake of Roland Barthes: Re-Defining the Myths of Reading* (Birmingham, Ala., 1984).

COLLIER, PETER, 'Roland Barthes: the Critical Subject (An Idea for Research)', *Paragraph*, 11, (1988), 175–80.

COMPAGNON, ANTOINE (ed.), *Prétexte: Roland Barthes*, Actes du Colloque de Cerisy, 22–9 June 1977 (1978).

CONLEY, TOM, 'Barthes's *Excès*: The Silent Apostrophe of *S/Z*', *Visible Language*, 11: 4 (autumn 1977), 355–84.

CULLER, JONATHAN, *Barthes* (Fontana Modern Masters, London, 1982).

DELORD, JEAN, *Roland Barthes et la photographie* (1981).

DERRIDA, JACQUES, 'Les Morts de Roland Barthes', in *Psyché*, 273–304.

ECO, UMBERTO, and PEZZINI, ISABELLA, 'La Sémiologie des *Mythologies*', *Communications*, 36 (Oct. 1982), 19–42.

ELLIS, DAVID, 'Barthes and Autobiography', *Cambridge Quarterly*, 7: 3 (1977), 252–66.

FAGES, J.–B., *Comprendre Roland Barthes* (Toulouse, 1979).

GAILLARD, FRANÇOISE, 'Barthes juge de Roland', *Communications*, 36 (Oct. 1982), 75–83.

GALLOP, JANE, 'BS', *Visible Language*, 11: 4 (autumn 1977), 364–87.

HEATH, STEPHEN, *Vertige du déplacement: lecture de Barthes* (1974).

JOHNSON, BARBARA, 'The Critical Difference: Balzac's *Sarrasine* and Barthes's *S/Z*', in YOUNG (ed.), *Untying the Text*, 162–74.

JOUVE, VINCENT, *La Littérature selon Barthes* (1986).

KRISTEVA, JULIA, 'Comment parler à la littérature', in ead., *Polylogue*, 23–54.

LASCAULT, GILBERT, 'Ébauche d'un dictionnaire de la peinture selon Roland Barthes', *Critique*, 423–4 (Aug.–Sept. 1982), 704–19.

LAVERS, ANNETTE, *Roland Barthes: Structuralism and After* (London, 1982).

LUND, STEFFEN NORDAHL, *L'Aventure du signifiant: une lecture de Barthes* (1981).

MCLEOD, IAN, 'Powers Plural: Barthes's "Lecture"', *Oxford Literary Review*, 4: 1 (autumn 1979), 29–30.

MALLAC, GUY DE, and EBERBACH, MARGARET, *Barthes* (1971).

MARTY, ÉRIC, 'L'Assomption du phénomène', *Critique*, 423–4 (Aug.–Sept. 1982), 744–52.

MORIARTY, MICHAEL, *Roland Barthes* (Cambridge, 1991).

O'DONOVAN, PATRICK, 'The Place of Rhetoric', *Paragraph*, 11 (1988), 227–48.

PATRIZI, GIORGIO, *Roland Barthes o le peripezie della semiologia* (Rome, 1977).

POMMIER, RENÉ, *Roland Barthes ras le bol!* (Vincennes, 1987).

REICHLER, CLAUDE, 'L'Ombre', *Critique*, 423–4 (Aug.–Sept. 1982), 762–74.

ROGER, PHILIPPE, *Roland Barthes, roman* (1986).

RUBINO, GIANFRANCO, *L'intellettuale e i segni: saggi su Sartre e Barthes* (Letture di pensiero e d'arte, 69; Rome, 1984).

RUNYON, RANDOLPH, 'Fragments of an Amorous Discourse: Canon in Ubis', *Visible Language*, 11: 4 (autumn 1977), 387–427.

SARKONAK, RALPH, 'Roland Barthes and the Spectre of Photography', *L'Esprit créateur*, 22: 1 (spring 1982), 48–68.

THODY, PHILIP, *Roland Barthes: A Conservative Estimate* (London, 1977).

ULMER, GREGORY L., 'Fetishism in Roland Barthes's Nietzschean Phase', *Papers on Language and Literature*, 14: 3 (summer 1978), 334–55.

UNGAR, STEVEN, 'From Writing to the Letter: Barthes and Alphabetese', *Visible Language*, 11: 4 (autumn 1977), 391–428.

—— *Roland Barthes: The Professor of Desire* (Lincoln, Nebr., 1983).

WASSERMAN, GEORGE, R., *Roland Barthes* (Twayne's World Authors Series; Boston, 1981).

WISEMAN, MARY BITTNER, *The Ecstasies of Roland Barthes* (Routledge, 'Critics of the Twentieth Century': London, 1989).

Special Numbers of Reviews and Periodicals devoted to Barthes

Tel Quel, 47 (autumn 1971).

Critique, 302 (July 1972).

L'Arc, 56 (1974).

Le Magazine littéraire, 97 (Feb. 1975).
Visible Language, 11: 4 (autumn 1977).
Journal of Practical Structuralism, 1 (July 1979).
Lectures, 6 (Dec. 1980).
Studies in Twentieth Century Literature, 5: 2 (spring 1981).
Poétique, 47 (Sept. 1981).
L'Esprit créateur, 22; 1 (spring 1982).
Critique, 423–4 (Aug.–Sept. 1982).
Communications, 36 (Oct. 1982).
Textuel, 15 (Oct. 1984).
Paragraph, 11; 2 (July 1988).

Bibliographies on Barthes

The most complete bibliography based on Barthes's own list of his writings is the 'Bibliographie générale (textes et voix)' drawn up by Thierry Leguay, in the special Barthes issue of *Communications*, 36 (Oct. 1982), 133–73. There is also a full, but not exhaustive, English-language bibliography: Sanford Freedman and Carole Anne Taylor, *Roland Barthes: A Bibliographical Reader's Guide* (New York, 1983). There are useful selective bibliographies in the works by Heath, Lavers, Ungar, and Moriarty, listed above, as well as in the special Barthes issues of *Tel Quel* and *L'Arc*, also listed above.

III. OTHER WORKS CITED

ADORNO, THEODOR, *Minima Moralia: Reflections from Damaged Life*, trans. E. F. N. Jephcott (London, 1974).
—— 'On the Fetish Character in Music and the Regression of Listening', in Andrew Arato and Eike Gebhardt (eds.), *The Essential Frankfurt School Reader* (New York, 1977), 270–99.
——*Aesthetic Theory*, trans. C. Lenhardt, ed. Gretel Adorno and Rolf Tiedemann (London, 1984).
Aesthetics and Politics: Debates between Bloch, Lukács, Brecht, Benjamin, Adorno (London, 1977).
AITKEN, ROBERT, *A Zen Wave: Bashō's Haiku and Zen* (New York, 1978).
ALEXANDRIAN, SARANE, *Surrealist Art* (London, 1970).
ALTHUSSER, LOUIS, *Lenin and Philosophy and Other Essays*, trans. Ben Brewster (London, 1971).
—— *Positions* (1976).
ATTRIDGE, DEREK, BENNINGTON, GEOFF, and YOUNG, ROBERT (eds.), *Post-Structuralism and the Question of History* (Cambridge, 1987).

Austin, J. L. *How to Do Things with Words*, ed. J. O. Urmson and Marina Sbisà (2nd edn. Oxford, 1975).

Bachelard, Gaston, *L'Eau et les rêves: essai sur l'imagination de la matière* (1942).

—— *L'Air et les songes: essai sur l'imagination du mouvement* (1943).

—— *La Terre et les rêveries de la volonté: essai sur l'imagination des forces* (1948).

—— *La Terre et les rêveries du repos: essai sur les images de l'intimité* (1948).

Bacon, Francis, *The Essays*, ed. John Pitcher (Harmondsworth, 1985).

Bataille, Georges, *Œuvres complètes*, 10 vols. (1970–87).

Beckett, Samuel, *Watt* (London, 1976).

Benjamin, Walter, *Illuminations*, trans. Harry Zohn (London, 1973).

—— *Charles Baudelaire: A Lyric Poet in the Era of High Capitalism*, trans. Harry Zohn (London, 1973).

—— *Understanding Brecht*, trans. Anna Bostock (London, 1973).

—— *One Way Street and Other Writings*, trans. Edmund Jephcott and Kingsley Shorter (London, 1979).

Bennington, Geoffrey, *Lyotard: Writing the Event* (Manchester, 1988).

Bettelheim, Bruno, *Freud and Man's Soul* (London, 1983).

Blanchot, Maurice, *Le Livre à venir* (1959).

Bloch, Ernst, *The Principle of Hope*, trans. Neville Plaice, Stephen Plaice, and Paul Knight (Oxford, 1986).

Borges, Jorge Luis *Labyrinths: Selected Stories and Other Writings*, ed. Donald A. Yates and James E. Irby (Harmondsworth, 1970).

Bourdieu, Pierre, *Choses dites* (1987).

Bowie, Malcolm, *Freud, Proust and Lacan: Theory as Fiction* (Cambridge, 1987).

Butor, Michel, 'Le Livre comme objet', in *Répertoire II* (1964), 104–23.

Compagnon, Antoine, *La Seconde Main, ou, Le Travail de la citation* (1979).

Deleuze, Gilles, *Proust et les signes*, (4th edn., 1976).

—— and Guattari, Félix, *Capitalisme et schizophrénie, i. L'Anti-Œdipe* (1972).

—— and Guattari, Félix, *Kafka: pour une littérature mineure* (1976).

—— and Guattari, Félix, *Capitalisme et schizophrénie, ii. Mille plateaux* (1980).

de Man, Paul, *Blindness and Insight: Essays in the Rhetoric of Contemporary Criticism* (2nd edn., London, 1983).

Derrida, Jacques, *La Voix et la Phénomène. Introduction au problème du signe dans la phénoménologie de Husserl* (1967).

—— *De la grammatologie* (1967).

—— *L'Écriture et la différence* (1967).

—— *La Dissémination* (1972).

—— *Positions* (1972).

—— *Marges—de la philosophie* (1972).

—— *Speech and Phenomena, and Other Essays on Husserl's Theory of Signs*, trans. and introd. David B. Allison (Evanston, Ill. 1973).

—— *Limited Inc abc . . .* , *Glyph*, 2 (suppl.) (Baltimore, 1977).

—— 'Scribble: pouvoir/écrire', pref. to Warburton, *Essai sur les hiéroglyphes des Égyptiens*, 7–43.

—— *La Vérité en peinture* (1978).

—— *La Carte postale de Socrate à Freud et au-delà* (1980).

—— *Glas* (1981).

—— *Otobiographies: l'enseignement de Nietzsche et la politique du nom propre* (1984)

—— *Psyché: inventions de l'autre* (1987).

DESCOMBES, VINCENT, 'An Essay in Philosophical Observation', trans. Lorna Scott Fox, in Alan Montefiore (ed.), *Philosophy in France Today* (Cambridge, 1983), 67–81.

ECO, UMBERTO, *The Name of the Rose*, trans. William Weaver (London, 1984).

—— *Reflections on 'The Name of the Rose'*, trans. William Weaver (London, 1985).

EHRENZWEIG, ANTON, *The Psychoanalysis of Artistic Vision and Hearing: An Introduction to a Theory of Unconscious Perception* (3rd edn. London, 1975).

FOUCAULT, MICHEL, *Ceci n'est pas une pipe* (Montpellier, 1973).

—— *Surveiller et punir: naissance de la prison* (1975).

—— 'What Is an Author?', in Harari (ed.), *Textual Strategies*, 141–60.

FREUD, SIGMUND, *The Pelican Freud Library*, ed. Angela Richards, 15 vols. (Harmondsworth, 1973–86), based on *The Standard Edition of the Complete Psychological Works of Sigmund Freud*, trans. from the German under the general editorship of James Strachey in collaboration with Anna Freud, assisted by Alix Strachey and Alan Tyson, 24 vols. (London, 1953–74).

—— *The Origins of Psychoanalysis; Letters to Wilhelm Fleiss, Drafts and Notes, 1887–1902*, ed. Marie Bonaparte, Anna Freud, and Ernst Kris, trans. Eris Mosbacher and James Strachey (London, 1954).

GENETTE, GÉRARD, *Figures I* (1966).

—— *Figures III* (1972).

—— *Mimologiques: voyage en Cratylie* (1976).

—— *Palimpsestes: la littérature au second degré* (1982).

HARARI, JOSUÉ V. (ed.) *Textual Strategies: Perspectives in Post-Structuralist Criticism* (London, 1980).

HAWKES, TERENCE, *Structuralism and Semiotics* (London, 1977).

HEGEL, G. W. F., *The Phenomenology of Spirit*, trans. A. V. Miller (Oxford, 1977).

—— *The Philosophy of Mind: Part Three of the Encyclopedia of the Philosophical Sciences (1830)*, trans. William Wallace, with *Zusätze*, trans. by A. V. Miller (Oxford, 1971).

HENDERSON, HAROLD G., *Haiku in English* (Rutland, Vt., 1967).

HOLLIER, DENIS, *La Prise de la Concorde: essais sur Georges Bataille* (1974).

HOLUB, ROBERT C., *Reception Theory: A Critical Introduction* (London, 1984).

JONES, ALFRED ERNEST, *Sigmund Freud: Life and Work*, 3 vols. (London, 1953–7).

JOYCE, JAMES, *A Portrait of the Artist as a Young Man*, in *The Essential James Joyce*, ed. Harry Levin (Harmondsworth, 1963).

JOYCE, JAMES, *Ulysses*, repr. with corrections (Harmondsworth, 1971).

KAFKA, FRANZ, *The Collected Short Stories of Franz Kafka*, ed. Nahum N. Glatzer (Harmondsworth, 1983).

KANT, IMMANUEL, *The Critique of Judgement*, trans. James Creed Meredith (Oxford, 1952).

KERMODE, FRANK, *Essays on Fiction 1971–1982* (London, 1983).

KRISTEVA, JULIA, *Polylogue* (1977).

—— *The Kristeva Reader*, ed. Toril Moi (Oxford, 1986).

LACAN, JACQUES, *Écrits* (1966).

—— *Le Séminaire*, i. *Les Écrits techniques de Freud* (1975).

—— *Le Séminaire*, ii. *Le Moi dans la théorie de Freud et dans la technique de la psychanalyse* (1978).

—— *Le Séminaire*, xi., *Les Quatre Concepts fondamentaux de la psychanalyse* (1973).

—— *The Four Fundamental Concepts of Psychoanalysis*, trans. Alan Sheridan (Harmondsworth, 1979).

—— *Le Séminaire*, xx. *Encore* (1975).

LACOUE-LABARTHE, PHILIPPE, and NANCY, JEAN-LUC, *Le Titre de la lettre* (1972).

LAPLANCHE, JEAN, *Life and Death in Psychoanalysis*, trans. Jeffrey Mehlman (Baltimore, 1976).

—— and LECLAIRE, SERGE, 'L'Inconscient: une étude psychanalytique', *Les Temps Modernes*, 183 (July 1961), 81–129.

LARRAIN, JORGE, *The Concept of Ideology* (London, 1979).

LECLAIRE, SERGE, *Psychanalyser: un essai sur l'ordre de l'inconscient et la pratique de la lettre* (1968).

LEMAIRE, ANIKA, *Jacques Lacan*, trans. David Macey (London, 1977).

LENIN, *The State and Revolution: The Marxist Theory of the State and the Tasks of the Proletariat in the Revolution* (revised edn. Moscow, 1965).

LUNN, EUGENE, *Marxism and Modernism: An Historical Study of Lukács, Brecht, Benjamin, and Adorno* (London, 1985).

LYOTARD, JEAN-FRANÇOIS, *Discours, Figure* (1971).

—— *Dérive à partir de Marx et Freud* (1973).

—— *La Condition postmoderne*, (1979).

—— *Des dispositifs pulsionnels* (1980).

—— *Le Différend* (1983).

—— *Tombeau de l'intellectuel et autres papiers* (1984).

MACHEREY, PIERRE, *Pour une théorie de la production littéraire* (1966).

MALLARMÉ, STÉPHANE, *Poésies* (1945).

—— *Igitur, Divagations, Un coup de dés* (1976).

MONTEFIORE, ALAN (ed.), *Philosophy in France Today* (Cambridge, 1983).

MOUNIN, GEORGES, *Introduction à la sémiologie* (1971).

NABOKOV, VLADIMIR, *Pale Fire* (Harmondsworth, 1973).

NIETZSCHE, FRIEDRICH, *Werke*, ed. Karl Schlechta, 5 vols. (6th edn., Frank-furt-on-Maine, 1969).

—— *On the Genealogy of Morals*, trans. Walter Kaufmann and R. J. Hollingdale (New York, 1967).

—— *Thus Spake Zarathustra*, trans. R. J. Hollingdale (Harmondsworth, 1969).

—— *Beyond Good and Evil*, trans. R. J. Hollingdale (Harmondsworth, 1973).

—— *The Gay Science*, trans. Walter Kaufmann (New York, 1974).

NORRIS, CHRISTOPHER, *Derrida* (London, 1987).

ONG, WALTER J., *Orality and Literacy: The Technologizing of the Word* (London, 1982).

PLATO, *Cratylus, Parmenides, Greater Hippias, Lesser Hippias*, ed. and trans. H. N. Fowler (Cambridge, Mass., 1963).

—— *Protagoras and Meno*, trans. W. K. C. Guthrie (Harmondsworth, 1956).

PRENDERGAST, CHRISTOPHER, *The Order of Mimesis: Balzac, Stendhal, Nerval, Flaubert* (Cambridge, 1986).

—— (ed.), *Nineteenth-century French Poetry: Introductions to Close Reading* (Cambridge, 1990).

PROUST, MARCEL, *Du côté de chez Swann*, ed. Bernard Brun (1987).

PYNCHON, THOMAS, *V* (London, 1975).

READ, HERBERT, *A Concise History of Modern Painting* (new edn. London, 1974).

READINGS, BILL, *Introducing Lyotard: Art and Politics* (London, 1991).

RICHARD, JEAN-PIERRE, *Littérature et sensation* (1954).

—— *Poésie et profondeur* (1955).

ROBBE-GRILLET, ALAIN, *Le Miroir qui revient* (1984).

ROUSSEL, RAYMOND, *Nouvelles Impressions d'Afrique* (1963).

RUNYON, RANDOLPH, *Fowles, Irving, Barthes: canonical variations on an apocry-phal theme* (Columbus, Ohio, 1981).

SAID, EDWARD W., *Orientalism* (London, 1978).

SARTRE, JEAN-PAUL, *Baudelaire* (1954).

—— *Saint Genet, comédien et martyr* (1952).

SAUSSURE, FERDINAND DE, *Course in General Linguistics*, trans. Wade Baskin (London, 1974).

SCHOLEM, GERSHOM, *On the Kabalah and Its Symbolism*, trans. Ralph Manheim (New York, 1965).

SOLLERS, PHILIPPE, *Paradis*, in *Tel Quel*, 57 (spring 1974), 3–15.

STAROBINSKI, JEAN, *Les Mots sous les mots: les anagrammes de Ferdinand de Saussure* (1971).

STENDHAL, *Correspondance*, ed. H. Martineau and V. del Litto, 3 vols. (1962–8).

SUZUKI, D. T., *Essays in Zen Buddhism: First Series* (London, 1950).

—— *Essays in Zen Buddhism: Second Series* (London, 1953).

—— *Essays in Zen Buddhism: Third Series* (London, 1953).

WARBURTON, WILLIAM, *Essai sur les hiéroglyphes des Égyptiens*, trans. Leonard des Malpeines (1977).

WATTS, ALAN, *The Way of Zen* (Harmondsworth, 1962).

WEBER, SAMUEL, *The Legend of Freud* (Minneapolis, 1982).

WILDEN, ANTHONY, *System and Structure: Essays in Communication and Exchange* (2nd edn. London, 1980).

WILLIAMS, RAYMOND, *Marxism and Literature* (Oxford, 1977).

WITTGENSTEIN, LUDWIG, *Tractatus Logico-Philosophicus*, trans. D. F. Pears and B. F. McGuinness (London, 1961).

WOODCOCK, ALEXANDER, and DAVIS, MONTE, *Catastrophe Theory* (Harmondsworth, 1980).

YASUDA, KENNETH, *The Japanese Haiku: Its Essential Nature, History, and Possibilities in English, with Selected Examples* (Rutland, Vt., 1957).

YOUNG, ROBERT, 'Post-structuralism: The End of Theory', *Oxford Literary Review*, 5: 1 and 2, 'Papers from the OLR/Southampton Conference' (1982), 3–20.

—— (ed.), *Untying the Text: A Post-Structuralist Reader* (Boston, 1981).

INDEX